THE DYNAMICS OF DATA BASE

THE DYNAMICS OF DATA BASE

W. H. Inmon
Coopers & Lybrand

Thomas J. Bird, Jr.
Innovative Designs

PRENTICE-HALL

Englewood Cliffs, New Jersey 07632

Library of Congress Cataloging-in-Publication Data

INMON, WILLIAM H.
   The dynamics of data base.

   Bibliography: p.
   Includes index.
   1. Data base management.   I. Bird, Thomas J.
II. Title.
QA76.9.D3I5393   1986   005.74   85-19436
ISBN   0-13-221474-1

Editorial/production supervision and
   interior design: Reynold Rieger
Cover design: 20/20 Services Inc.
Manufacturing buyer: Gordon Osbourne

Printed in the United States of America.

10 9 8 7 6 5 4 3 2 1

ISBN   0-13-221474-1   025

PRENTICE-HALL INTERNATIONAL (UK) LIMITED, *London*
PRENTICE-HALL OF AUSTRALIA PTY. LIMITED, *Sydney*
PRENTICE-HALL OF CANADA INC., *Toronto*
PRENTICE-HALL HISPANOAMERICANA, S.A., *Mexico*
PRENTICE-HALL OF INDIA PRIVATE LIMITED, *New Delhi*
PRENTICE-HALL OF JAPAN, INC., *Tokyo*
PRENTICE-HALL OF SOUTHEAST ASIA PTE. LTD., *Singapore*
EDITORA PRENTICE-HALL DO BRASIL, LTDA., *Rio de Janeiro*
WHITEHALL BOOKS LIMITED, *Wellington, New Zealand*

For my mother and father,
Stella and Tom Bird, Sr.;

who have
inspired me to strive
for excellence throughout
my life.

Contents

Chapter 2

BASIC CONCEPTS AND BASIC OPERATIONS

23

Chapter 3

DATA MANAGEMENT

45

Chapter 4

DATA STRUCTURING

72

Chapter 5

PROGRAM EXECUTION 96

Chapter 6

UTILITIES 136

Chapter 7

MISCELLANEOUS TOPICS

148

Chapter 8

DATA BASE DESIGN

164

SECTION II
Specific DBMS Examples

Contents   xi

SECTION III
Data Base Tutorial

Preface

Effective use of data base begins with an in-depth understanding of the environment—its components, how they interact, and the results achieved by the components. To use and control the data base environment effectively requires much more than a superficial syntactic understanding of data base. Success in the data base environment requires an understanding of data base syntax *and* the underlying activities at the system level. An attitude of keeping the system activities ''under the covers'' is not acceptable to the developer and user who must come to grips with making data base work.

This book addresses two types of data base environments, the operational environment and the decision support environment, from three levels, the physical level, the system level, and the user level. The operational environment is typified by IMS. The decision support environment is typified by FOCUS, and by SQL, as implemented under DB2. Model 204 is discussed as a DBMS sharing some of the better characteristics of both operational and decision support environments, in both the mainframe and micro environments. Ashton-Tate's dBASE II is discussed in the micro environment.

Prior to discussing the DBMS in specifics, the reader is led through basic data management concepts that all data base management systems share in one form or another, such as indexing, randomization, variable length data, variable field data, and physical blocking. The physical media on which data base exists is discussed, including optical disk storage. Once data management techniques are established, the execution of a program in the batch, online, and interactive modes is outlined in detail so that the reader understands the dynamics of the computer/data/program relationship. At this point some of the specific differences in the operational environment and the decision support environment are addressed. Of particular interest is the focus on I/O—what it is, how it occurs, and why it is of such importance.

A chapter is devoted to the utilities that typically accompany a DBMS. The utilities of data base initialization, reorganization, recovery, and monitoring are discussed. A separate chapter addresses data base machines based on the Britton-Lee machine. The reader is exposed to what data base machines are, the role they play, how they are implemented, and their special capabilities.

A chapter is written on physical data base design for both batch and online systems. Of particular interest are the design practices for online performance and availability. The standard work unit, management of multiple occurrences of data, and the implementation of control data bases are some of the concepts discussed. Prefacing the material on physical data base design is a section on conceptual data base design. This material parallels previously published material on the subject (Inmon, *Information Systems Architecture*, Prentice-Hall, 1986) in condensed form, with an emphasis on data design.

The last chapter in the first section addresses the distribution of data bases.

The second section of the book is directed toward an in-depth review of the syntax, the physical implementation, the usage, and the economics of IMS, Model 204, SQL, FOCUS, and dBASE II. The reader is able to use this part of the book for specific in-depth knowledge of these systems.

The final section is a tutorial in some of the data base management systems discussed that directs the reader through the creation, update, access, and other usage of the data base systems. Upon completion of the tutorial the reader will be conversant, on a practical basis, with the DBMS.

In addition, selected chapters have inserts that feature such topics as content addressable memory, non-vendor-supplied utilities, design review, "deadly embraces," and so forth. The questions at the end of the chapter are designed to allow the student to master the topics discussed in the chapter. The tutorial is designed to lead the student through "hands on" experience with the DBMS.

This book is for serious students of data processing, practitioners in the industry, and anyone with a need for an in-depth, complete understanding of data base. The book is written in a "step-by-step" fashion, so that the reading of the book in order of the chapter does not present difficulties to the reader. It is assumed in Chapter 1 that the reader has little or no knowledge of data base. The technical concepts built upon in one chapter are previously introduced in an earlier chapter so that the reader is not overwhelmed by technical concepts or jargon.

The questions and exercises that appear at the end of the chapters are designed to lead the reader to a greater in-depth understanding of the issues. As such the questions and exercises extend the reader beyond the material covered in the chapter in many cases. Some of the questions can be answered by reading the material in the book, and some questions require the reader to go beyond the scope of this book.

Upon reading the book, completing the exercises, and doing the tutorial the reader will be able to use and control data base effectively in a day-to-day environment. The book ensures that the reader is armed with more than a superficial understanding of the syntax of a DBMS language in confronting the very real application of data base.

ACKNOWLEDGMENTS

Many thanks to Kathy Allan for her review of the earliest version of this book. Her remarks and insights, both at the technical and the conceptual level, are found throughout the text. A special thanks to Delilah Perkinson who brought a down-to-earth perspective to her review of the book.

The insights of L. Montfort (Lance) Myers were instrumental in the writing of Chapter 10, on Distributed Data Bases. Lance is truly one of the few experts in the field of distributed data base architecture. He has brought a distinctive blend of academic and practical understanding to a field that is short on theoretical underpinnings and even weaker on practical application.

Rod Erdmann was responsible for providing information on the Britton-Lee data base machine, one of the first such machines in the marketplace. Rod also provided several other perspectives on new technology that are found throughout the text.

Fred Wright and Judy Grote have reviewed the book and have provided useful advice and suggestions. Fred will not admit to being one of the pathfinders in data base systems but his historic perspectives and experiences in the field lead to other conclusions. Judy's experience with IMS and data base performance helped during the review of those parts of the book.

Dale Irvine, while working on his MBA at Pepperdine College, reviewed and critiqued the text. His business acumen provided valuable understandings of the application of data base systems.

Wayne and Susan Chan made many worthwhile comments concerning the readability, clarity, and incisiveness of the entire book. Given the target audience of the book, this input was indeed valuable.

Jan Bird and Melba Inmon gave support that merits special mention. Jan suffered through six drafts of distributed data bases, data base machines, and other assorted material in Tom Bird's first major publishing effort. Melba suffered through several drafts of the remaining parts of the book in Bill Inmon's seventh major publishing effort. Only a "football wife" suffers in same measure the long hours and inattention that an author's wife suffers. Jan and Melba's forbearance is greatly appreciated and not unnoticed.

W. H. INMON
THOMAS J. BIRD, JR.

SECTION I

BASIC CONCEPTS

"I think there is a world market for about five computers."
Thomas J. Watson,
International Business Machines (IBM) (1958)

CHAPTER 1

The Data Base Environment

The importance of data base is best understood in the context of the world as it existed prior to data base. Prior to data base the world of data processing was dominated by sequential media, on which data was stored. The sequential media consisted of mostly tapes (magnetic and punched paper) and 80-column punched cards. There was limited usage of direct access storage devices (DASD, or disk), and for the most part DASD was used as a replacement for magnetic tape and little else.

While there is nothing inherently wrong with the sequential (primarily tape) environment, there are certain limitations. One limitation is that to get to any occurrence of data, it is necessary to access all data that physically occurs before the desired data. Typically a magnetic tape accesses 100% of the tape to get at the 5% that is actually desired. But there are other limitations to the sequential environment.

In the sequential environment the systems designer must always be conscious of the number of tape drives that any given program uses. This awareness is necessary for several reasons: There are never enough tape drives to go around, magnetic tapes do not tend to wear well over time, and a tape being read by one program cannot concurrently be read by another program.

These limitations of sequential systems have a twofold effect: the creation of many redundant master files and the creation of large, multifunction batch programs. When a designer builds a sequential system, one of the first steps of design is to decide what data the system is to use. Typically the designer creates a **master file,** which contains the data that is most relevant to the requirements of the system. It is common for the master file also to contain data from other master files. The

2

data from other master files arrives at the system being developed by means of a **strip program,** where data is periodically read off of one master file and loaded onto another. The purpose of duplicating data in sequential systems is to prevent many master files from other systems from having to be read and synchronized at once in order to run the system at hand. Duplicating data minimizes the number of tape drives used for any given program. The resultant master file containing the duplicated data concentrates data so that the operation of the system is clean.

An attribute of a sequential master file is that it contains all or most of the data necessary for the satisfaction of immediate processing requirements—i.e., it contains data from many diverse environments. Combining much diverse data on a single master file cuts down on the number of tape drives needed for execution at any moment in time for a single system but, of course, greatly multiplies the total amount of processing being done by all systems. The program that processes the master file is typically a "do-everything" program. Once the data from the master file is in hand, it is desirable to accomplish all functions that ever need to be done to the data, thereby minimizing the number of times the tape must be run. Such large, multifunction programs do data updates, creations, deletions, strips, calculations, and a myriad of other functions, all in the same batch program.

While systems designers historically have done a nice job of creating sound sequential systems, from a larger, shopwide perspective there are many problems that are created by the general approach to sequential design. As long as there are not too many sequential systems, as long as the sequential systems are not highly interrelated, and as long as the sequential systems do not involve processing massive amounts of data, the sequential environment serves quite adequately (as it continues to do in many shops today). But when a shop grows in size or complexity (as nearly all shops do), the sequential environment begins to become unmanageable. The duplication of data, the synchronization of duplicated data that has been updated, the redevelopment of entire systems (in whole or in part), and the maintenance of duplicated programs begin to be an ever-increasing burden, so much so that a whole new approach to processing data is necessary. In the face of growth, the sequential environment is soon fraught with inadequacies.

The answer to many (but not all!) of the problems of the sequential environment is data base, where data can be accessed directly rather than sequentially. Data base is controlled by software known as a **data base management system (DBMS).** DBMS allows data to be accessed easily and directly. In addition, data bases can be accessed concurrently by more than one program, which opens the door for online processing (which, for all practical purposes, is not possible in the sequential environment).

DBMS entails an entirely new approach to the accessing and usage of data that addresses many problems of the sequential environment at a profound and effective level. Historically, the first DBMS addressed the problems of direct access of data and concurrent access of data, but soon facilities for online access followed. Data base gives the users the tools to solve many of the problems of the sequential environment. In many cases data base is used effectively. But in many other cases designers use data base as if it were a simple replacement for sequential access of data and, in doing so, repeat many of the problems of the sequential environment.

When data base is used merely as a replacement access method, DBMS turns into nothing more than a fancy file access system. Ironically, the difference in success attained in the data base environment has more to do with the users and designers of data base systems than it does with the quality of the DBMS software. It is common to find many successful *and* unsuccessful users of the same software package.

Using data base software successfully implies an underlying understanding of the software. To be successful it is not enough to understand data base at a superficial level if there is to be long-term success. Data base must be understood at at least three levels: the syntax level (or the how-to-do-it level), the physical storage level (or the underneath-the-covers level), and the system level, where the architectural differences between the different DBMS surface. All three levels must be understood if data base is to be used as more than a sophisticated access method. When a programmer executes a call, the programmer must understand not only the results of the call but also what the system had to do to satisfy the call. The designer must understand not only how to shape the data but what the implications of the shaping are. This level of understanding mandates that data base be understood at the storage, syntax, and system levels. The order of the chapters is designed to take the reader through the different steps required in understanding the three levels. The storage level—the basic data management level that is common in one form or another to all DBMS—is presented first. Then the syntax level is presented, along with other relevant topics. Finally, different DBMS are discussed at the system level.

The chapters at the system level are not designed to be substituted for reference manuals. The amount of detail that accompanies any DBMS is well beyond the scope of this book. Instead, the chapters on different DBMS are designed to tie the storage, syntax, and system levels together, something that many DBMS reference manuals do not do.

DATA BASE MEDIA

A **data base** is a physical collection of data organized to reflect a user's requirements. As such, it can exist on a variety of physical media (Fig. 1.1). For example a data base could exist on

— A stack of papers (such as canceled checks, bills, or receipts)
— Card files, punched 80-column cards
— Magnetic tapes
— DASD
— Main storage of a computer (memory)

Each of these physical media has its own set of advantages and disadvantages and its own peculiar properties. The physical medium on which a data base exists *greatly* influences the capabilities and uses of the data base. For example, a data base made up of assorted scraps of paper is very slow to research, as each page must be scanned by hand to find information. It is bulky to store and is awkward

Basic Concepts   Section I

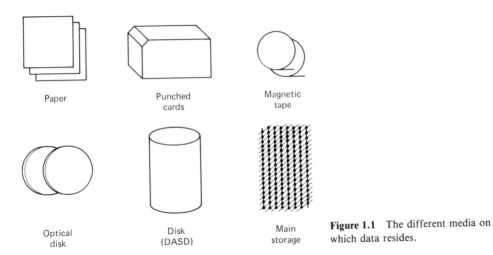

Paper

Punched
cards

Magnetic
tape

Optical
disk

Disk
(DASD)

Main
storage

Figure 1.1 The different media on
which data resides.

to update. But it is very cheap to create, since the paper that makes up the data base comes as a byproduct of a business or personal transaction of one kind or another.

The table in Fig. 1.2 depicts some of the differences in the physical media. For example, the table illustrates that a data base in the main storage of a computer is very fast to access and is very compact but is expensive.

As an example of the influence of the media on the use and capabilities of a data base, consider a data base that represents each of the accounts in the Social Security system of the United States. Such a data base will certainly be very bulky because there are many social security numbers, each of which has much data related to it. If the data base were stored on paper or punched cards, the data base would be very large (in terms of the space it occupies) and would be very difficult to update, as each update would require manual location and manipulation of cards

	Speed	Space	Cost per Unit of Data	Update
Paper	Very slow	Very bulky	Very cheap	Very difficult
Punched cards	Slow	Bulky	Cheap	Difficult
Magnetic tape	Moderate	Compact	Moderate	Moderate
Optical storage	Fast	Compact	Cheap	Not optimal
DASD	Fast	Compact	Expensive	Easy
Main storage	Very fast	Very compact	Most expensive	Very easy

Figure 1.2. Different media on which data is stored—some considerations.

Chap. 1   The Data Base Equipment

or paper. For these reasons the lower end of the table (Fig. 1.2) is not appropriate for the Social Security data base. By the same token, main storage is not appropriate because of the expense of main storage. Main storage is very quick to get to, but there is no need for excessively quick access of massive amounts of social security data, most of which is historical and accessed infrequently. Thus magnetic tapes or DASD are appropriate for the social security data base. Furthermore, a microprocessor is not appropriate to process the social security data base, whereas a mainframe would be appropriate due to the differences in processing power.

Now consider another type of data base. A bank controls its daily business by means of a tables data base. The data base contains tables from which many banking cycles are controlled, such as when to generate checking statements, when to accrue savings interest, when to bill credit cards, and so forth. Throughout the day the tables are read by many programs so that the checking, savings, or other processing activity is done in a consistent fashion. The tables data base is small but is constantly being referenced throughout the day. Storing the data base on paper is nonsensical because of the volume of people needing to see the data base, the frequency with which they need to see the data, and the difficulty in circulating the data base to them. By the same token, storing the tables data base on tape would require that the tape be read over and over throughout the day. Because the tables data base is small and regularly accessed, it makes sense to place the data base on a DASD or in main storage, where it can be quickly and easily accessed.

Consider yet another type of data base, a tax data base for an individual keeping track of medical payments. The most convenient form of this data base is paper or documents (assuming that the individual has a moderate or small amount of medical activity). If the individual has a personal computer, it may make sense to keep records on the computer, but in any case a full-fledged mainframe data base application (on tape, DASD, etc.) is simply not warranted, even if the individual has access to such facilities. The cost of constructing a data base application under a full-fledged DBMS and operating it in a data base environment on a mainframe processor precludes any other justification for building a personalized medical file system for a single individual.

DASD, TAPES, AND MAIN STORAGE

A full function DBMS is one that can handle large amounts of data, a large amount of simultaneous on-line activity, and maintain a high degree of data integrity. In the full-function data base environment, there are three primary media on which data is stored, DASD (or disk), magnetic tape, and main storage. Each medium has its own characteristics. Far and away the most common media is DASD. DASD exists external to the computer. Data is transported to and from DASD and the computer by a channel that is dedicated to the specific purpose of computer/DASD communications. In the microprocessor environment DASD may be on a hard or a floppy disk.

DASD is made of several physical plates (or disks). The disk is a physical device that sits and spins, much like a record on a turntable. Data is written onto the disk by means of magnetic pulse that causes patterns of bits (1s and 0s) to be stored on the surface of the plate. A disk can be written and read many times. The same physical location can be written over many times; each time the previous contents of the location are destroyed. In the mainframe environment, multiple disks or plates are typically on a **spindle.** The plates store data on both the top and the bottom surfaces. The plate is written on and read by means of a read/write head that is located on an arm (Fig. 1.3). The arm locates the location on disk to which it is directed and transfers data to or from the location. In some cases the arm is fixed; in other cases it moves mechanically from one location to the next. Because data is referenced by an address, data is able to be randomly accessed. To arrive at the nth record on a disk does not require an access to the 1st, 2nd, 3rd . . . $(n - 1)$st record.

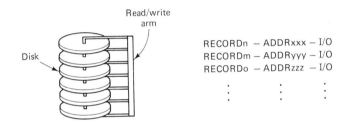

Read/write arm

Disk

```
RECORDn — ADDRxxx — I/O
RECORDm — ADDRyyy — I/O
RECORDo — ADDRzzz — I/O
```

Figure 1.3

The act of retrieving or writing a record is known as an **input/output operation (I/O).** In a conventional mainframe environment, an I/O will take from 30 to 50 milliseconds to execute, depending on many factors, such as the hardware, the disk device, and the software supporting the system. DASD is commonly used for a very wide variety of data base applications. A far less common medium for data base is magnetic tape. A magnetic tape is a rolled ribbon on which images of bit patterns (1s and 0s) are densely stored (Fig. 1.4). The tape is written and read by a device known as a **tape unit.**

The bit patterns on the tape are packed in varying physical densities, 1600 bpi (bits per inch) being a common density. Data on a tape must be accessed sequentially, i.e., to get to record n, records 1, 2, 3 . . . $n - 1$ must first be accessed. Tapes can be written over more than once, but each rewrite destroys the previous contents. Tapes typically hold large amounts of data and do so quite compactly. One difficulty with tapes is that they do not age particularly well because of scratching or cracking. Over time tapes tend to become unreadable. Tapes are connected to the computer by a channel dedicated to the transfer of data to and from the tape unit and the computer. Tapes are most commonly used for storage of massive

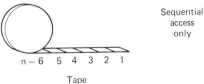

Sequential access only

n − 6   5   4   3   2   1

Tape

Figure 1.4

amounts of data and certain other specialized applications where only sequential storage of data is required.

The third medium on which data bases are commonly stored is main storage of the computer (i.e., in memory) (Fig. 1.5). In this case data is stored in bit patterns (as it is in DASD and on tape) and can be accessed randomly or sequentially. Data is accessed in main storage in much the same way as it is accessed on DASD. There is one major difference between DASD accesses and main-storage accesses, however. No I/O is required to access data in main storage, as is required for disk or tape access, thus making main-storage data bases very quick to access. In general, main-storage data bases can be accessed in terms of nanoseconds (1×10^{-9} seconds), whereas data on DASD or tape is accessed in terms of milliseconds (1×10^{-6} seconds). However, because of the cost of main storage and the need to use it for other purposes, available space inside the computer (mainframe or micro) is almost always limited. Typical data bases that are put in main storage are tables data bases, control data bases, security data bases, and so forth. In general, small data bases that require very quick access and that are used often and by many users are candidates for main-storage data bases.

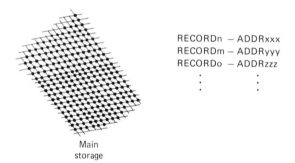

RECORDn — ADDRxxx
RECORDm — ADDRyyy
RECORDo — ADDRzzz

Main
storage

Figure 1.5

OPTICAL DISK

Strictly speaking, optical disk storage is a form of DASD. However, because of the common widespread usage of magnetic disk storage and its standard nomenclature—DASD—optical disk is often not referred to as DASD. To use an analogy, because of standard nomenclature many copying machines are called Xerox machines when they are not made by the Xerox company. Because of standard nomenclature, optical storage in fact is DASD, but it is not referred to as such in many cases.

Optical disk shares some of the characteristics of tape and some of DASD. Optical disk is written by lasers. It is a write-only medium in that once it is written, it cannot be written over. Optical disk is economically effective because of its low cost (it is very cheap compared to other media) and because of its high reliability. For types of data (e.g., historical records) that are seldom, if ever, changed, optical disk is very cost effective. Typically, an optical disk can hold many times the amount of data that can be stored on tape.

Because optical storage is so inexpensive and because so much data can be put onto a single volume, a form of update is possible even when the data cannot be written over. When data on optical disk must be changed, the original data is destroyed and a new updated copy of the data is written elsewhere in available space. A pointer is placed on optical disk showing the location of the new copy of the data. In such a manner, an update can be done on a write-only medium.

DATA BASE ENVIRONMENTS

Data base environments can be classified into two types: the **operational** (or production) **environment** and the **decision support**—the **dss**—(or planning and trend-analysis) **environment.** The work done in the operational environment runs the enterprise. The day-to-day detailed decisions of running the business are made by operational systems. Typical operational environments are an airline reservation system, a bank teller system, a manufacturing assembly routing and control system, and an insurance claims processing system. When there are problems with operational systems, the operations of the company are immediately stopped or at least seriously impaired. The other type of data base environment—the decision support (or "dss")—is used to manage the company. Typical decision support activities compare this quarter's accounts receivable versus those of the past four or five quarters or analyze the demography of a potential customer base. Financial projections and modeling are other uses for decision support systems. Decision support systems typically have access to archival data bases (i.e., data that reflects past activities).

As an example of the differences between operational and decision support environments, consider the case of Ms. Jones' bank account. One morning Ms. Jones deposits a large sum in her checking account. Later that morning she writes a large check, which is verified by a bank teller. The system that accepts Ms. Jones' deposit and verifies her account is an operational system. The operational system must keep track of the up-to-the-minute details of many accounts. If Ms. Jones is denied check-cashing privileges when she has money in her account, she is going to be rightfully upset. Her concerns (like all account holders) are about the accuracy and timeliness of her account.

Now consider Ms. Jones' account from another perspective—that of the bank vice-president in charge of account planning. On a periodic basis the vice-president analyzes whether account balances are rising or falling and compares the figures with previously derived figures (last month's figures, last year's figures, and so forth). The vice-president uses a decision support system for this type of analysis. The vice-president could care less whether or when Ms. Jones has made a deposit (as far as the report and the analysis are concerned) on any particular morning. The variations in Ms. Jones' account are quickly averaged out in light of the bank's many other account activities. The activity and accuracy of Ms. Jones' account hardly affect the vice-president's analysis. The timeliness and the accuracy of a single account are of little concern in the decision-support environment where trends are being analyzed.

THE OPERATIONAL ENVIRONMENT

The operational environment can be broken into four rough classifications:

— Online environment
— Batch environment
— Mixed (online/batch) environment
— Time-sharing (interactive) environment

Each of these environments has its own traits and particular advantages.

OPERATIONAL ONLINE

By far the most technically complex and potentially most powerful environment is the online environment. The great usefulness of the online environment is that it maximizes the time of the user of the system, and it does so in a detailed, responsive manner. In other words, in the online data base environment, the computer system (the hardware, software, etc.) is designed to optimize the time of the user of the system, not the efficiency of the processing. The online mode unlocks the greatest potential of the computer. A typical online environment is depicted by Fig. 1.6.

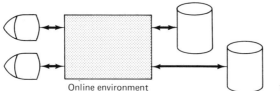

Online environment   **Figure 1.6**

The mainframe computer is connected to data bases and terminals (or CRT, cathode ray tubes) by a network and/or channels. The CRT allows a user to enter a request for data (to retrieve it, to change it, etc.). The request is then sent to the computer by means of the network. Once inside the computer, the request interacts against the data bases. The business is transacted and a reply acknowledging the fulfillment of the request is sent to the user. All the activity, from the time the user enters the transaction until the reply is received by the user, takes place in a few seconds. If the activity takes longer than that, the time of the user at the terminal is wasted, as there is nothing the user can do in waiting for online activity to be transacted. The flow of activity through the system is shown by Fig. 1.7.

One characteristic of online systems is that once changes are made to data, then those changes are reflected throughout the system (otherwise known as **data integrity**). For example, if terminal A accesses data whose value is 50 and then changes the value to 66, when terminal B at a later moment in time accesses the data, the value 66 will be retrieved. This facility allows for a central control of data, which is at the heart of the usefulness of the online systems.

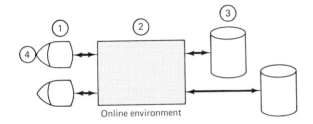

Online environment

1. Message is entered.
2. Message is received by processor and goes into execution.
3. Data bases are accessed. ,
4. Response is sent to terminal.

Figure 1.7

Transactions that are run in the online environment are typified by a series of short, limited accesses. A typical sequence of online transactions might look as follows.

```
computer>>enter customer name, account #
user >Ms. J. Jones, 459-70-1872
computer>>enter request-balance, update,
     stops, admin, activity?
user >balance
computer>>current balance=$500.36 next
user >activity
computer>>last 5 checks
830301-$26.32
830227-$247.64
830226-$17.99
830221-$395.66
830220-$181.21
More Activity?
user >yes
computer>>
830217-$16.00
830216-$195.44
830119-$1042.36
830118-$59.62
More Activity?
user >no
computer>>Another request?
user >no
    .
    .
    .
    .
```

Every activity from one double arrowhead (>>) to the next double arrowhead represents a single online transaction. In all, six online transactions, or activities, are performed in the example shown. Each activity resulted in a limited amount of processing. In all, several activities were accomplished, but they were accomplished in a limited amount at a time. This breaking up of activities into small units is typical of the online environment. In other environments (i.e., the batch or time-sharing environments) where much function is accomplished at once, the same request would have looked as follows.

```
computer>>enter customer name, give acct no.,
     current balance, last 10 items of activity
user >ms. J. Jones
computer>>ms. J. Jones, 459-70-1872
current balance-$500.36
last ten checks-
830301m-$26.32
830227-$247.64
830226-$17.99
830221-$395.66
830220-$181.21
830217-$16.00
830216-$195.44
830119-$1042.36
830118-$59.62
```

In the online environment there are very few limitations to the activities that can be accomplished. But the activities that are accomplished are done a small amount at a time.

Typical software environments for the online environment are IBM's IMS/DC and IMS/CICS and Cullinet's IDMS/DC (which are all appropriate to the mainframe environment).

The primary issues in the operational online environment are performance (or *response time*) and availability (or *system up time*). Performance refers to the amount of time a given transaction takes to execute, from the time the transaction is entered into the terminal and shipped down the line into the computer, through execution, until it returns to the receiving terminal (Fig. 1.8). On the average, an operational online response time in excess of 10 seconds or more greatly hinders the capability of the user to work effectively in the online environment. If airline reservation clerks

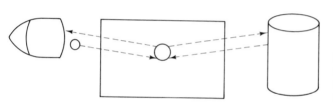

Figure 1.8 Performance is the amount of time that elapses from when the online transaction is entered until the reply is returned.

or bank tellers are forced to wait long periods of time (i.e., in excess of 10 seconds) for information, the ability of those people to do their jobs is seriously impaired.

The other vital issue to the online environment is availability. Availability refers to the amount of time the user's system is up and available. High availability is a product of reliability of many different components: the terminal, the network, the mainframe processor, basic system software, application software, data, etc. (Fig. 1.9). If *any* of these components breaks (i.e., becomes disfunctional), the system is down and is unavailable for use. The end user does not care *what* is wrong (whether it is the network or the processor at fault, for example). The end user knows only that the system is unavailable.

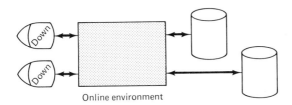

Online environment

Figure 1.9 Availability. Terminals, lines, processor hardware and software, and data bases must all be up.

There is no priority between the issues of availability and performance. If a system is down, performance is a moot point. If a system is up but is performing poorly, availability is a moot point. *Both* availability and performance are essential to success in the environment.

OPERATIONAL ENVIRONMENT—BATCH

An environment that is simpler technically than the online environment is the batch environment. The batch environment is dominated by sequential processing, usually of tapes and disks but sometimes of punched cards. The physical configurations that are typical of the batch environment are depicted by Fig. 1.10. In this figure a computer is shown attached to a tape-drive unit and a card reader. Disks can be accessed and in some cases are used in a direct fashion (i.e., data is accessed randomly), but for the most part disks are accessed sequentially, as if they were tapes.

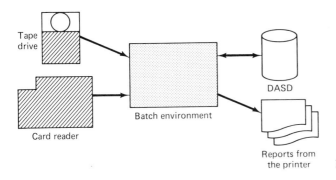

Tape drive

Card reader

Batch environment

DASD

Reports from the printer   **Figure 1.10**

The output of sequential processing is usually reports and/or updated tapes (i.e., master files), as shown in Fig. 1.11. When a tape is updated, the entire tape must be physically replaced because writing over an existing tape destroys the original contents. Update occurs as follows: A tape is read (the *old master*), the data is manipulated inside the computer and is written out to a separate tape (the *new master*). Thus tapes have different generations as they are updated (the old tape is the "father," and the new tape is the "son"). During update, records can be added, deleted, or altered. The data structures found on tapes are universally **flat**—i.e., one record laid end on end with another record. Typically, an update to a master file will involve at most 10% of the data on the file, even though 100% of the data must be accessed (since to get to record n, the record to be altered, records 1, 2, 3 ... $n - 1$ must be accessed).

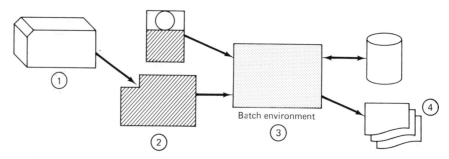

1. Throughout the day, input is collected and batched together.
2. At night the input is entered into the system.
3. The input is run against existing files and data bases.
4. Reports, new files, and updated data bases are produced.

Figure 1.11

In the batch data base environment there is an almost universal use of disks for storage, and unlike disk usage in the non–data base batch environment, direct access of data (as well as sequential accessing of disks) is frequently done. The batch data base environment is not limited to flat data structures but has many forms, such as hierarchical or network, which will be discussed in later chapters. Programs are used to manipulate data in the batch environment (typically COBOL or PL-1). An example of a program (using pseudocode) that reads a data base and then transacts activity against it might look like this:

```
open tx file
do while file open
read tx file, at end close
get account record using txkey
update account
insert activity in acct activity
return
end program
```

The transactions have been collected throughout the day on a file (the **transaction file**) and are ready for processing. In this simple program the transaction file, or tx file, is read sequentially. A key from the transaction activity is used to locate a record in the account data base. Once the account data base record is located, it is transacted against (i.e., transaction values are used to modify existing values in the data base). Once transacted against, the account activity is inserted with other previously transacted account activity into an activity account data base.

Such a simple program might be written for nightly updates of credit-card activity, where the charge amount changes the balance owed on the credit card (in the account record) and the activity is stored for future reference. In this case a tape or disk that holds the transactions that have been batched is read sequentially, and a data base is accessed randomly to locate the account daily. [Examples of data base software that run in the batch data base mode are IBM's IMS (batch) and Cullinet's IDMS (batch). These software packages run on mainframes.]

The primary issues in the batch environment are system throughput and programmer productivity. **Throughput** refers to the total amount of work (the amount of data and programs) that can be run through a machine. Programmer productivity is a large issue especially relevant to the batch environment because of the nature of sequential processing. Because data must be read sequentially and because the programmer wants to minimize the amount of time a tape drive or disk is monopolized, batch programs tend to do as many activities as possible. In an effort to do as many activities as possible once the data is at hand, batch designers conglomerate different data types onto a few files to optimize the use of tape or disk drives. The result is much data and process redundancy across different systems, accompanied by complex interconnections between systems. The resulting redundancy that is typical of the sequential environment implies that similar functions are rebuilt many times, each one requiring a new development and maintenance effort. The increased development and maintenance effort in turn require an emphasis on programmer productivity. Even where batch data bases are used and hence are not subject to the physical limitations of sequential processing, there is a strong tendency to build unintegrated data base applications, where each user has his or her own data base, regardless of what kind or how much data is shared with other users. This tendency is a result of the user's attitude toward data and system ownership. It does not have a technical foundation. Because of the unintegrated nature of the batch data base environment, systems and programs tend to become very complex from an application standpoint. The differences in the way batch and the online environments accomplish function are illustrated by Fig. 1.12. In this figure the online environment accomplishes function a limited amount at a time, while the batch environment accomplishes a great deal of function at once.

In the batch environment work is done in a way that optimizes the processing of the computer at the expense of the user. There is little the user can do after he or she submits batched activity until the activity is transacted, which is often overnight. But batching activity ensures that the maximum throughput of the machine can be achieved. So the batch environment optimizes machine processing at the expense of the user, whereas the online environment optimizes the user's time at the expense of the machine.

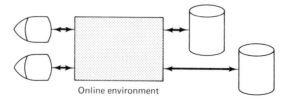

Online environment

— "What is the balance in Mrs. Jones' account right now?"
— Limited amounts of very quick processing.

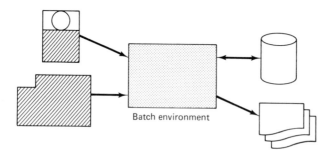

Batch environment

— List and summarize all monthly account activity by
  branch, teller, and time of day.
— Large amounts of processing (usually sequential) done
  in a lengthy timeframe.

Figure 1.12

OPERATIONAL ENVIRONMENT—MIXED ONLINE/BATCH

Despite the basic differences between the online environment and the batch environment, it is often desirable to have a mixture of the two. Most operational environments require some amount of both batch and online processing. Mixing the batch and the online environments is a very delicate task. To a large extent, the performance that is achieved in the online environment is a function of the workload being run in the environment, i.e., online performance directly relates to the amount of the workload and basic format of the workload. The online environment operates well where the work being performed is broken into small units of processing. The batch environment is characterized by a workload that is conglomerated into very large units. Thus when batch and online environments are mixed (if in fact they can be mixed), they must be mixed so that large, long-running batch jobs do not interfere with short, quick-running online jobs. The mixing is usually managed at the system or DBMS level or occasionally at the application level. The insulation of batch processing from online processing is done by other than the applications designer. The applications-design implications of building batch processes online may be as simple as periodically releasing commonly shared resources that may be used in conjunction with the online environment. Such a release is usually accomplished by a special command that the batch programmer includes in the application code.

Because of the essential processing differences between the batch and online environments, it is common to dedicate the processor at different times of day to each environment. For example, for a bank the hours of 9 A.M. to 4:30 P.M. are usually the busiest (in terms of customers' online activities). Those hours are then dedicated to running online transactions. But the online-customer workload drops off dramatically at the end of the workday (when the doors of the bank close). Then the processor becomes free for batch processing. A typical batch window is from 7 P.M. to 5:30 or 6 A.M. By the judicious use of processing windows, batch and online environments can be mixed. An example of a mixed environment (for mainframe) is IMS/DC, where both batch and online programs are run.

OPERATIONAL ENVIRONMENTS—TIME SHARING

Another environment that shows some of the characteristics of both batch and online environments is the time-sharing (or interactive) environment. In the time-sharing environment, a user interacts directly with the computer by means of a CRT and, in some cases, interacts with the system in a very rapid response mode.

Another user's interaction in the time-sharing environment is the initiation of a batch job. The batch job is run in the background, and the output may be directed back to the user's terminal, to a printer, or elsewhere. Normally the user does not sit and wait for a response when the computer is processing in the background mode because responses may be from 10 minutes to several hours.

An example of a time-sharing system is IBM's TSO or VM/CMS. Interestingly, whereas VM/CMS runs as a mainframe operating system, for all intentional purposes the mainframe is divided (logically, not physically) into a number of micros, where each user has his or her own micro.

DECISION SUPPORT ENVIRONMENT

The nonoperational data base environment—the decision support environment—can be roughly divided into three types of processing: the **query mode,** the **relational mode,** and the **inverted list mode.** *In general the distinctions between the decision support modes of processing are not nearly as clear as are the different modes of operational processing.* For example, the inverted list mode displays many relational-like characteristics, the relational mode can be used in purely a query mode, and so forth. Nor is the physical machine environment as clear. Operationally, the mainframe environment is used exclusively. But dss systems run often interchangeably in the mainframe and the microprocessor environments.

In the decision support mode, data update is usually not as nearly as important as in the production mode because the decision support environment usually operates on data that has been **downloaded,** or extracted from the operational environment. There is a single system of record that normally resides in the operational environment. A download is illustrated by Fig. 1.13. In addition to operating on

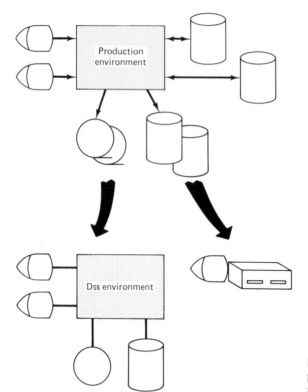

Figure 1.13 A download from a production mode to a decision support system.

downloaded data, the decision support environment often operates on data that is summarized or data that has been screened (i.e., edited, merged, recalculated, etc.). The primary value of the decision support environment is that the end user is easily able to alter the way data is viewed, much more easily than in the operational environment. Whereas the operational environment is oriented towards online performance and data integrity at the expense of flexibility, the decision support environment is oriented toward flexibility and ease of use at the expense of online performance and data integrity. In the operational environment, when there is a change in user requirements, the implementation of the change may require major worker involvement and machine resources as well as disruptions in the operation of existing systems. But in the decision support environment, a change in user requirements has relatively minor implications and can be done easily. By the same token, the operational environment (when properly designed) can be expected to handle large amounts of data and large amounts of transactions, maintain a high degree of integrity, and still yield adequate response time. Under the same conditions—large amounts of data, large numbers of transactions, and a high degree of update integrity—decision support systems typically yield spotty response time at best. Because of this fundamental difference in characteristics, most large data processing shops find that a single DBMS is inadequate for their needs. Most shops employ one type of DBMS for operational systems and another type (or types) of DBMS for decision support systems.

DECISION SUPPORT ENVIRONMENT—QUERY

Query-type processing is divided into two classifications: queries to a single unit of data and queries to massive amounts of data (otherwise known as **single record** queries and **set** queries, i.e., queries for a set of records). As an example of a query to a limited amount of data, consider the request, "What was the amount of the deposit that Ms. Jones made on February 15?" In this case, a single unit of data is accessed (assuming that Ms. Jones in fact made a deposit on the 15th of February). As an example of a massive query of data, consider the request, "What were the highest, lowest, and average deposits made by all customers on February 15?" Depending on the way the data was organized, the request would search each account first for deposits, then deposits made on February 15, and then the highest, lowest, and average deposits (average would be calculated). Many deposits (and much data) would have to be searched to answer the query. Note that no update is being done to the data by the query. The processing is done against data that has been previously created. As an example of selectivity, the user might ask, "For all commercial accounts, what are the highest, lowest, and average amounts deposited on February 15?" or "For all accounts owned by someone named Smith, what was the average amount deposited on February 15?" An example of user-friendly query languages are QBE and NOMAD2. (*Note:* the distinction between types of decision support environments is not nearly as clear as the distinction between the different types of production environments.)

DECISION SUPPORT ENVIRONMENT—RELATIONAL

The relational environment is one of unstructured usage and easy access to data. Data is initially defined to the relational environment in a simple, tabular file form. Once the user sits down and begins to use the data, then the user can dynamically select how the data is to be connected (or interrelated, i.e., joined). The relational environment is highly flexible in that an absolute minimum of effort is required to recreate and change data relationships. Relational processing encompasses query processing because both limited and massive queries, as well as updates, can be done. The primary difference between the query and relational environment lies in the ability of the relational environment to define relationships dynamically. Strictly speaking, in a query language environment, the definition of the data is made at the moment the data is created and is seldom changed. The query language then operates on data in its prescribed form. Relational systems, in addition to being able to process like query languages, are free to alter the basic form of data. However, the flexibility of relational systems does not come free. In general, in the relational environment, when activity is run on large amounts of data or a large number of activities are entered in the same time frame, the resulting performance is poor because of the volume of work to be done. As is discussed in Chapter 13, the very power of relational software requires massive machine resources, which in turn, hampers performance. An example of relational software is IBM's DB2.

DECISION SUPPORT ENVIRONMENT—INVERTED LIST

Another form of decision support system is the inverted list. The term **inverted list** refers to the basic structuring of the data (as is discussed in later chapters). Inverted lists often share some of the capabilities of relational systems and some of the capabilities of the operational environment. For example, inverted list processing often operates well against large amounts of data and still is able to be used in a relatively unstructured manner, thus combining two desirable characteristics from the different environments. As long as inverted processing is done within the normal definition and usage of data (which is described in detail in Chapter 12), processing is efficient and operates nicely on large amounts of data. The drawback to inverted list processing comes when there is a desire to use the system beyond the normal boundaries. When this type of activity occurs, inverted lists may perform slowly and require large amounts of processing resources. An example of an inverted list processing system is CCA's Model 204.

OPERATIONAL TO DSS DOWNLOAD

The processing differences between operational and decision support systems are such that the environments are usually not mixed. However, data from operational environments can be shared with the decision support environment by means of a download. A download occurs when data is stripped or extracted from the operational environment and shipped off to the decision support environment. To illustrate the effect of a download, consider the following example.

At 2 P.M. Ms. Jones makes a deposit of $1000 in her banking account. At 2:10 P.M. she cashes a check for $100 at another branch. Because the system operates in the operational environment, when Ms. Jones makes a deposit at 2 P.M., it is known throughout the system very quickly (a matter of seconds). At 4:30 P.M. a sequential program is run, stripping off all account balances. Ms. Jones' account is shown to have $900 as the strip is run. The stripped data is sent to the decision support environment, and for as long as the data is used there, Ms. Jones' account will show $900. At 6:30 P.M. Ms. Jones withdraws $150 from her automated teller machine (ATM), reducing her balance to $750. But that night, decision support analysis is done, showing Ms. Jones with $900.

Is this discrepancy serious? Not really, because decision support analysis normally does not rely upon up-to-the-minute balances, as does the operational environment. Ms. Jones' account balance will be calculated with many other accounts, thus negating the importance of detailed accuracy. Of course, if Ms. Jones has no account activity the next day and another download is done, her account balance will be $750 and will be correct in both the operational and decision support environments.

QUESTIONS

Data Base Media

1.1. Describe the different media on which data bases are stored.
1.2. List the advantages and disadvantages of each medium.
1.3. What costs are associated with each medium? the limitations of each medium?
1.4. In order of magnitude, how much more expensive is main storage than DASD?
1.5. How much faster is main storage than a DASD?

Media Criteria

2.1. What factors make DASD the most popular choice for data base storage?
2.2. What are the limitations of tape?
2.3. Why is sequential access of data such a limitation?
2.4. Describe the environments where optical storage can be used efficiently and effectively.
2.5. Describe environments where optical storage is inappropriate.

Punched Cards

3.1. Why aren't punched cards used commonly as a medium on which data bases are stored?
3.2. How well do punched cards age?
3.3. Can punched cards be reused?
3.4. Where is the most efficient place to store punched cards?

Economies of Scale

4.1. What economies of scale are there in building a data base?
4.2. Does it ever make sense to build a data base for a single individual?
4.3. When does it become cost effective to build a data base?

General Data Base Considerations

5.1. Is there ever too much data to go into a data base?
5.2. When is a collection of data merely a collection of data and when is it a data base?
5.3. What are the advantages of direct access of data?
5.4. What implications are there for direct access of data to the programs that must be built? For the hardware that runs the system?

Data Base Environments

6.1. What is meant by the operational data base environment? What happens to the business of the company when operational systems fail?
6.2. What is meant by the decision support data base environment? What happens to the business when decision support systems fail?

6.3. Why is there a difference between the operational and the decision support environments?

6.4. Are the differences between these two environments always clear-cut?

6.5. What are the characteristics of the online environment?

6.6. What are the characteristics of the batch environment?

6.7. Why must the two environments be mixed carefully?

6.8. Is the time-sharing environment online or batch?

Redundancy

7.1. What is a download?

7.2. Is downloading a sign of data redundancy?

7.3. Is data redundancy necessarily an undesirable characteristic?

7.4. Is data redundancy ever beneficial?

7.5. What kinds of data redundancy are there?

EXERCISES

1. Write a COBOL or PL-1 program that opens a tape file, reads it, and writes out a program. Now write a corresponding COBOL or PL-1 program that reads a data base and produces an equivalent report. Add a new type of occurrence of data to the tape-file data structure and to the data base. What modifications to the COBOL or PL-1 program are necessary?

2. Determine the packing density for tape in your shop. Determine the transfer rate for tape. How much data will a tape hold? How much data will a disk hold? Determine the transfer rate for DASD in your shop. How much data will main memory hold? At what speeds can each of these media be accessed? How many of these media do you have in your shop? What is the unit cost per byte of each of these media? What is the unit cost of optical disk?

CHAPTER 2

Basic Concepts
and Basic Operations

The basic components of the data base environment are

— The processor
— Main storage (or memory)
— External storage (direct access storage device, or DASD)
— The communication channel
— The data base management system (DBMS)

The relationship among the different components is shown by Fig. 2.1. The computer is the hardware that is at the center of the system (in the vernacular of data processing, the computer is referred to as *iron*). The computer may be a mainframe, a minicomputer, or a microprocessor. Programs are executed inside the computer. The programs control applications, lines and terminals, other programs, and the

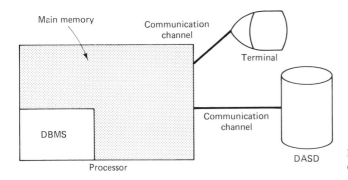

Figure 2.1 Basic components of the data base environment.

management of data. The computer is the engine of the computer system. Inside the computer is main storage, or memory. Main storage holds data or programs that are being executed. One of the programs that main storage contains is the DBMS. The DBMS manages the movement and usage of data within the processor and on external storage. The movement of data into and out of the computer is by means of a channel. The channel connects the computer and DASD. Data is located on DASD by means of an address, which marks the physical location of data on DASD. The transfer of data (either going into the computer or out of it) is referred to as an I/O, or input/output, operation. An I/O is one of the most (if not *the* most) important aspects of the data base environment because the throughput of most data base environments is directly dependent upon the amount of I/O that can be done. The more I/O that can be done, the more throughput the environment will sustain. The importance of I/O stems from the fact that a computer runs at electronic speeds (nanoseconds), but data is accessed at mechanical speeds (milliseconds).

The difference between the two speeds is not trivial. An analogy will illustrate the difference. Suppose a trip (a curious trip at that!) is planned between San Francisco and New York. The first leg of the trip is by jet from San Francisco to Phoenix. The next leg is from Phoenix to Tucson by means of bicycle. Then at Tucson, the trip continues by jet to Ft. Worth. From Ft. Worth, a bicycle ride is taken to Dallas, where the trip continues by jet to Atlanta, and so forth. It is clear that the speed of the trip is a function of the number of times stops must be made and the speed of the bicyclist between stops. Engaging a faster jet will have only a miniscule effect on the length of the trip. The speed of the jet corresponds to the execution inside the processor, and the speed of the bicyclist corresponds to the mechanical activity required to do an I/O.

DATA TRANSFER

Because it is relatively slow to access data when an I/O is required, special handling occurs. The special handling is best described in terms of the way data is organized. Data is organized in two basic units: records and blocks. The term **record** refers to the data that is requested by a program within the processor. Other common terms for a record are a **segment,** a **tuple,** and a **file.** For example, when a programmer in COBOL issues a read statement, the request is to see a single record of data. When a user issues a SQL* statement, the request often is for a set of records. Records are physically stored in a **block,** which is nothing more than a collection of records. These basic relationships are shown by Fig. 2.2. When the request is made to access a given record, the address of the record is located and *all* the physical block is transported from DASD to the computer, including the record that was desired. The block is loaded into a special place in main storage, called a **buffer.** This transfer is shown by Fig. 2.3. While the transfer of more data than requested (i.e., the transfer of an entire block instead of just the record that was requested)

*SQL is a major component of IBM's relational language DB2.

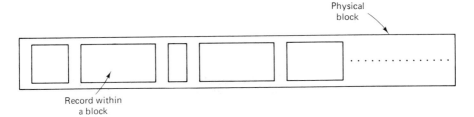

Physical block

Record within a block

Figure 2.2

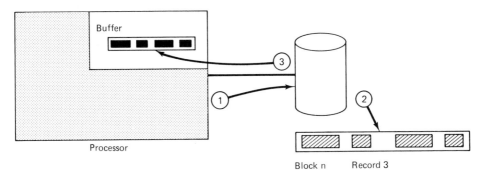

Buffer

Processor

3

1

2

Block n   Record 3

1. Record 3 of block n is requested.
2. The block is located on DASD. Record 3 is in the block.
3. The entire block, with record 3, is transported across the communication channel into a part of main memory called a *buffer*.

Figure 2.3

may seem wasteful, in fact it is not wasteful, and in the long run such a transfer can save much I/O.

Consider what happens when a program executing inside the computer needs to access data, but the data already exists in main memory (in the buffer). As long as the DBMS knows to look inside the buffer before issuing a read for more DASD, no I/O is required to retrieve the data that is already in the buffer area. The access of data that already exists in the buffer area (i.e., already in main memory) is shown by Fig. 2.4. By transporting and storing more data than called for when an I/O occurs (i.e., by transporting the whole physical block of data), there is a saving in I/O when a data request can be handled by data already in the buffer area. Of course, if there is no request for data that is already in the buffer area, then there is no saving.

The amount of space that is available in a computer for buffers is limited because buffers reside in main memory. When all the space in the buffer is full and another block needs to be loaded, there are several choices, as seen in Fig. 2.5. One choice is to make the block to be loaded into the buffer wait until space is available, but this means that an I/O effectively takes even longer and is a very unpopular alternative. Another choice is to expand dynamically the space available for buffers in main memory. This, too, is an unpopular choice, since dynamic alteration of the

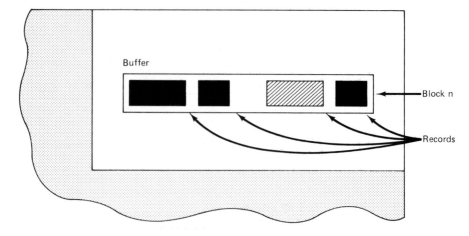

1. Block n was retrieved into the processor because of record 3.
   All records in the block were transported and stored.
2. While block n is in the buffer, another request is received for
   record 1 in block n. No I/O is needed, since the block is already
   in the buffer.

Figure 2.4

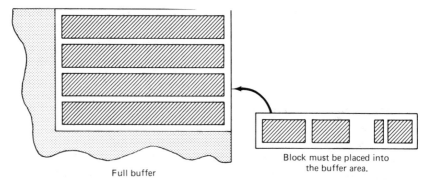

Full buffer

Block must be placed into
the buffer area.

Figure 2.5   When the buffer is full and there is another block to be loaded into the
buffer, either the block to be loaded must wait or one of the existing buffers must
be flushed. Another option is to allocate more buffer space in main memory.

areas of main storage creates complexity for the program that manages the space
of main storage. The usual choice is to remove one of the existing blocks from the
buffer space to make room for the block that must be entered into the buffer. Typically, a buffer is removed when data in the buffer is being retrieved, not updated.
If a record is in the process of being updated and is subsequently removed from
main storage, then the record and its block must be read again for update to occur.

The principle of transporting multiple records in a block holds true for the
case where records are being written as well as being read. For example, suppose
the computer is writing multiple records, each of which is to be stored in the same

block. The records are collected in the buffer area one at a time, and—once collected—are physically written, as shown in Fig. 2.6. The ability to write (i.e., do an I/O) once per block instead of once per record saves much I/O.

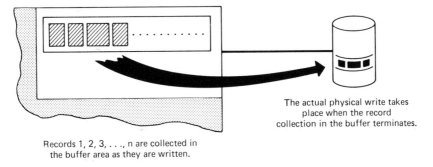

The actual physical write takes place when the record collection in the buffer terminates.

Records 1, 2, 3, . . ., n are collected in the buffer area as they are written.

Figure 2.6

ACTIVITY TYPES

There are four basic types of activities that must be done to use data in a data base:

— Insert/creation
— Deletion
— Update
— Retrieval

Insert activity occurs when a record that has not previously existed is created. New physical space is required as the newly formed record flows from the processor to DASD. **Deletion** occurs when a record is to be removed from the system. In the case of deletion, strictly speaking, there is no movement of data from DASD to the processor. In a few cases the physical location where the data formerly resided is blanked out. Most often, the space is logically deleted by removing all references to the data, thereby making the data inaccessible. In the case of logical deletion, the existence of the record is removed insofar as its ability to be located by the user, DBMS, or anyone else, but the actual physical contents remain intact. Of course, when the space is reused and is written over, the previous contents are destroyed.

In the case of **update activity,** data is retrieved from DASD. Some of the data in the record is changed, and the new contents of the record are rewritten. This activity requires movement from DASD to processor and then back to DASD. There is one type of data that cannot be updated, key data. **Key data** is data that uniquely identifies a record. As an example, Fig. 2.7 shows personal records that are identified uniquely by employee number.

The key of a record cannot be updated (it can be inserted or deleted but not modified) because the key uniquely identifies a record. If the key were altered, it would identify some other record that belonged in some other location. Not all records have keys (although most records do). A few types of records are merely

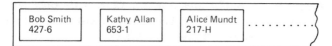

Figure 2.7 Personnel records are uniquely identified by keys. In this case, the employee number serves as a key for personnel data.

sequentially inserted into a block and, when read, are sequentially accessed. These records cannot be accessed directly by means of a key, as their only distinction is their physical order of appearance.

The final form of data transfer is **retrieval,** which occurs when a record needs to be accessed but not updated or deleted. The key of the record establishes which block is to be transferred into main storage, and data flow goes from DASD to the processor.

DATA TRANSFER TO THE PROGRAMMER

Once a block has arrived in the buffer area, data must be transferred to the program that had initiated the activity. Only the record that has been requested will be sent to the program, not all the data in the block. This activity is shown by Fig. 2.8. There are several ways data can be loaded into the program area from the buffers. One way is for the data to be directly transferred, as it has been stored on DASD. This is shown by Fig. 2.9. In this case the contents of the data in the buffer are not

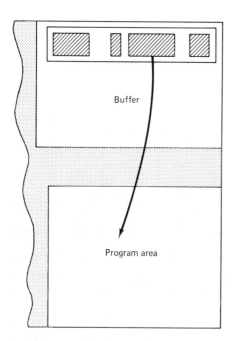

Figure 2.8 The requested record is sent to the program after the block is placed in the buffer area.

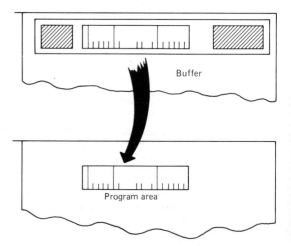

Figure 2.9 Literal movement of data from buffer to program area. This is a common method of transferring data.

rearranged, translated, or modified in any way as they are moved to the program area. This mode of transfer is the most widely used. As an example, suppose a record contains space for three data fields, one for name, one for social security number, and one for number of dependents. A record is defined to be 20 bytes. The first record to be considered contains the following values:

Social security number—4507899999

Name—Bill Inmon

Dependents—02

The twenty bytes allocated to the record are filled and the record in the buffer looks like 450789999BillInmon02. The next record in the buffer contains the data for Kay Jones. Kay has not let her employer know how many dependents she has. Her record in the buffer looks like this:

Social security number—396400121

Name—Kay Jones

Dependents—Null values

(Null values indicate that no dependent information has been determined for Kay Jones. Null values can be physically represented in a variety of ways, depending upon the particulars of the DBMS.) The 20 bytes allocated to the record are filled and the record looks like 396400121KayJonesBBB. Note that space is allocated for 9 bytes of name even though 8 bytes are used and that space is allocated for dependents even though Kay has not indicated any dependents (although she may have some even if she has not so indicated to the system). The records exist in this form on DASD, in the buffer, and in the program area, as shown by Fig. 2.10.

A second form of data transfer occurs when fields may have variable lengths. A typical use for variable-length fields is text or name storage. Where variable-fields are stored a control value that indicates the length of the field is needed. The use of variable-length fields is best illustrated by means of an example. Suppose two records exist for a person's name. In one record, the name Ann May exists; in another, the name Samuel Joachim Friedman exists. In the first record, there are

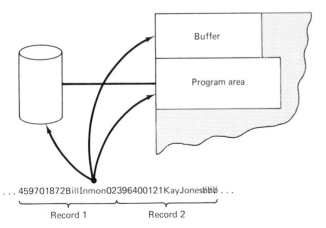

. . . 459701872BillInmon02396400121KayJonesⴺⴺⴺ . . .

Record 1   Record 2

Figure 2.10 Records 1 and 2 as they exist on the DASD, in the buffer, and in the program area.

two fields, one telling the length of the field (the control field) and another for the field itself. The record looks like this:

Length—06

Value—AnnMay

The same two fields exist for the same record (as they do for all variable length records). The second record looks liks this:

Length—21

Value—SamuelJoachimFriedman

The actual physical representation is

record1-06AnnMay
record2-21SamuelJoachimFriedman

As shown in Fig. 2.11, the record exists physically on DASD and in the buffer. But as the record moves into the program area, the physical form of the data may or may not be altered. One option is to translate the name into a standard format as it moves from the buffer to the program area, as shown by Fig. 2.12. In this case

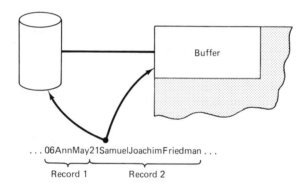

Figure 2.11

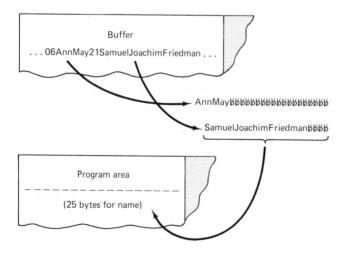

Figure 2.12

the program receives 25 bytes of information regardless of the length of the name. The program sees no difference between Ann May and Sam Friedman, as far as the data is presented. Each presentation of the data is consistent, and the program does not concern itself with the fact that the data is internally stored and transported more compactly than is apparent to the programmer or the user.

A second option in managing variable-length data is to let the program do its own field-length translation rather than masking the processing from the program. In this case the data is presented to the program exactly as it is stored, and the program does the field translation, as shown by Fig. 2.13.

Another data transfer option is that of variable fields (which may or may not be variable length). In this case only the fields containing nonnull values are stored at DASD and in the buffer area. This requires a field identification field to specify properly how the program should determine with which field it is dealing. In addition, a field length field is required if the field can be variable length. There are two types of variable fields, as shown by Fig. 2.14.

The usage of a variable field storage of data is best illustrated in terms of an example. Suppose a data base has records that can contain four fields, name, address, salary, and length of service (in years). There are two variable length fields—name and address—and two fixed length fields—salary and length of service. For the purposes of an example, there are four employees who will exist in the data base, Mary Jones, William Johnson, T. F. Chang, and Sergio Linda Martinez. The appropriate data for each of them is shown at the top of page 32.

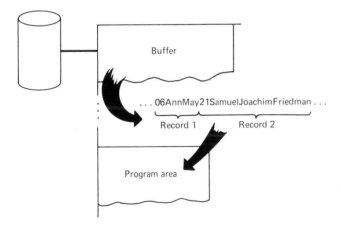

Figure 2.13 Where the application program manages the variable-length field, the data is presented to the program exactly as it is stored on the DASD and as it exists in the buffer.

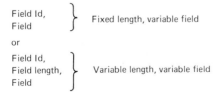

Figure 2.14

Chap. 2   Basic Concepts and Basic Operations

Mary Jones	William Johnson	T.F. Chang	Sergio Linda Martinez
1211 Willow	256 Baker	Salary—$1700	Service—14
Salary—Null	321 Wilson	Salary—$2500	Service—1
Service—12	Salary—$1400		
	Service—10		

As a word of explanation, Mary Jones has not divulged her salary to the system. William Johnson works from two locations. T. F. Chang does contract work and receives different rates of pay for the work he does. Sergio Linda Martinez is no longer employed but has a work history in which she stayed with the company for 14 years, left, and then returned for 1 year. The first field in the record is name, the second field is address, the next field is salary, and the last field is length of service. Both name and address have variable length field indications.

The physical record for each person is shown by Fig. 2.15. The data shown in Fig. 2.15 is tightly compacted. To make sense of a record, the field identifier is first located. Once the identifier is found it is determined whether the field is variable or not. If the field is fixed, the field data is located and the next field is translated. If the field is variable, its length is calculated and the field data is located. Knowing the length of the variable field allows the next field to be located. This process of field translation can be called **decompaction.** Decompaction is the reverse of **compaction,** which is done as the data is loaded onto DASD. Decompaction is normally done as the data flows from the buffer to the program area, as shown by Figs. 2.16 and 2.17.

So far, the discussion has centered around how data is stored on DASD, how it enters the buffer, and how it is transferred to the program area. Of course, there is the reverse direction for data that is being written, not read. Where data is decompacted and translated upon reading, it is correspondingly compacted and translated upon writing.

Record 1: 109MaryJones2101211Willow412
Record 2: 114WilliamJohnson208256Baker209321Wilson31400410
Record 3: 107TFChang3170032500
Record 4: 119SergioLindaMartinez414401

Figure 2.15 The compacted form of variable field data.

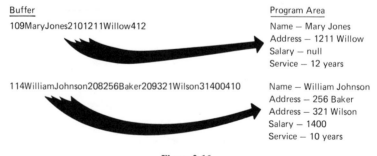

Figure 2.16

Basic Concepts   Section I

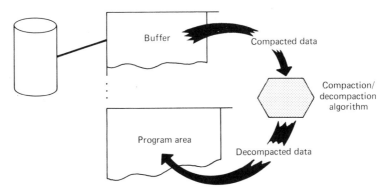

Figure 2.17

STORAGE AND TRANSFER TRADE-OFFS

It is apparent that when variable field length and/or variable fields are used, space is saved on DASD and more data can be moved for any given I/O. In other words, data that is defined with variability can be greatly compacted as opposed to data that is stored literally. By compacting the data, more data can be transported for any given I/O, thus minimizing the amount of I/O that is to be done. In this light, the conclusion can be drawn that *every* data base should be defined with variable length fields or variable fields. But many data bases are not defined that way because data variability can *cost* I/O in some cases. The case where data variability can cost I/O is best illustrated by an example. Suppose a record contains a variable length field for the quantity on hand. Four records of quantity on hand are stored on DASD.

    Record 1: 1416
    Record 2: 36
    Record 3: 136
    Record 4: 141367

Adding the field lengths for the records, the following (very compact) data is stored: 4141623631366141367. As long as there is no change in quantity on hand (more precisely, as long as any field does not exceed its current order of magnitude), then there is no problem. However, when the quantity on hand for record 2 goes to 121, the individual record needs to be written as 3121, but that value needs to be placed over the value 236. Unfortunately there is not enough space to write 3121 over 236 because 3121 occupies more space than 236. Either record 2 must be moved to some other location where there is space or all the data that currently exists must be reordered to allow room for the rewrite of record 2. In either case there is a large potential for I/O. I/O will occur if record 2 must be rewritten out of the current physical block or if the reordering of the block causes data to be rewritten elsewhere. In any case, changing the *length* of data when data is variable length has the potential for a great deal of I/O.

When record 3 goes from a value of 136 to a value of 8, the individual record goes from 3136 to 18. However, 18 requires a reordering of data, which may be tedious to do. Of course, the value could be rewritten as 3008, which does not require a reordering of data but does waste space. When data is static, a minimum amount of I/O is required for update (where data is variably defined). However, when data is volatile, so that the value in individual fields changes often, or when the existence of the data fields is constantly changing, then removing data variability can save a lot of I/O. The issue of data variability is resolved then by the *nature* of the data being stored—its usage and its physical profile—not by any inherent virtue of the storage of data.

KEYS

A *key* is one of the most fundamental concepts of data processing. It applies to both physical data bases (data as it physically exists) and to conceptual data bases (data as conceptualized by the user). A **key** is a data element that serves to identify some unit of data. The unit of data may be a segment, a tuple, a record, a file, or whatever physical unit of data that is appropriate to the data base management system.

Keys are generally divided into two types, primary keys and generic keys. A **primary key** is one that uniquely identifies a record. The key employee number is an example of a typical primary key for the personnel records of a company. Each employee has a unique employee number. A **generic key** is one that serves to classify the record rather than identify the record uniquely. Sex, age, salary, and department number are all forms of typical generic keys for a personnel record. There can be at most one primary key for a record, but there can be many generic keys. It is not necessary for every unit of data to have a primary key, although most do. In some cases, data is simply accumulated in the data base in the order in which it is entered. In this case one unit of data is physically placed next to the unit of data that was previously inserted (i.e., data is inserted and written in chronological order of entry). Bank teller activity collected throughout the day is often treated this way. Once the day is finished, all the data is stripped off the data base, written onto another medium or data base, and then transacted, edited, merged or otherwise used elsewhere. If a given record must be located when the records of data do not have a key, then each record must be sequentially accessed, which is a tedious thing to do if there are many records or the records are stored in many different physical blocks.

Keys are used to interconnect data from one data base to the other. Because keys are used to interconnect data bases, the keys are stored redundantly in many different places. Whereas redundancy of data is usually something to be avoided (for many good reasons), redundancy of keys that are used to interconnect data bases is normal, necessary, and perfectly acceptable.

The discussion of update versus retrieval of data has centered around variable length data. A similar argument can be made for variable field data. When data is stored on DASD, where the contents of the data will never or very seldom change, then the compaction that is possible with variable field data is attractive. However, when data fields are being added or deleted on a regular basis, then the I/O inherent to update may mean that it is more efficient to define the data literally.

ENCRYPTION

In the case where data is sensitive (that is, should be made very secure) it can be encrypted by means of an algorithm. When data is **encrypted,** it is stored on DASD in an irregular form. If an unauthorized person happens to gain access to the data, it will not be possible for that person to make sense out of the data without the encryption algorithm. As a simple example (so simple it would probably never be used!) of encryption, consider the case where values are complemented. For example, a three-digit number is encrypted by subtracting the actual value from 999.

Complement 703: $999 - 703 = 296$

Complement 1956: $9999 - 1956 = 8043$

Complement 21: $99 - 21 = 78$

Instead of storing the actual value, the encrypted value (in this case, the complemented value) is stored. The dynamics of encryption are shown by Fig. 2.18. When an unauthorized person stumbles upon the data found in the data base, the value 573 is read. But 573 is nonsensical. The encrypting algorithm is needed to make sense of the value. Thus the data enjoys a high level of protection as long as the encryption routine is protected. There is a drawback to encryption, however: To use the data on DASD in every authorized case, the decryption algorithm must be applied. Whereas encryption and decryption normally do not cause unnecessary

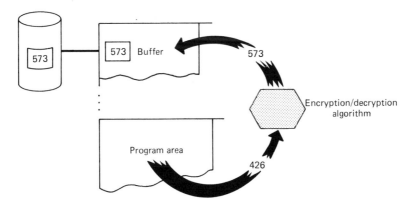

Figure 2.18 Encryption. (1) The value 426 is fed to the encryption algorithm. (2) The encryption algorithm yields 573, which is sent to the buffer. (3) The value 573 is stored in the data base.

I/O, they do require machine resources (i.e., machine cycles, or central processing unit (CPU) power). If encryption is used indiscriminately, there may be a large waste of CPU resources.

DATA BASE ACROSS DIFFERENT MODES OF OPERATION

A **mode of operation** is a related body of systems that execute in a similar fashion and have distinctive operational characteristics from other modes of operation. Modes of operation are most easily understood in terms of actual cases. Typical modes of operation are the *operational* mode, the *decision support* mode (dss mode), the *archival* mode, and the *development* mode.

OPERATIONAL MODE OF OPERATION

In the **operational mode** computer systems *run* the company. Data is stored and used at a detailed level. There is usually much operational data and many users of operational systems. Operational systems may be batch or online, with online systems the norm. Online response time is measured in terms of seconds (1 to 5). Typical operational systems include banking teller systems, airline reservation systems, manufacturing control systems, and so forth. When operational systems malfunction, there is an immediate impact on the day-to-day activities of the company. Usually some function of the company is disabled when there is a problem with operational systems.

DSS MODE OF OPERATION

In the **dss mode** are found systems that *manage* the company. Data is stored and used at a summary level, for the most part. Once data is in the dss environment, it is freely resequenced, refined, merged, and so forth. There is a relatively small amount of data per dss system and relatively few users doing dss activity. The nature of dss activity is analytical. Response time in the dss environment varies widely, depending on what kinds of activities the dss processing is doing and what other activities there are in the system. Response time may vary from a few seconds (20 to 30) to 24 hours. Normally data is managed and viewed in a *snapshot* mode, where operational data has been stripped at some point in time and then shipped to the dss environment. Because the data has been frozen in its entirety at one point in time, it is in essence a snapshot of the data. Typical dss systems include monthly account analysis (analysis of the highlights and trends of this month's account activity as compared to last month's or last year's activity), demographic analysis (analysis of customers or potential customers and their habits), and modeling activities (projections based on certain assumptions, where the assumptions can be easily changed to allow What if? questions to be posed).

ARCHIVAL MODE OF OPERATION

In the **archival mode** data is stored in machine readable form for future undefined processing requests. Data is kept at a detailed level wherever possible, given the uncertainty of future needs. There is usually a large quantity of data (usually much larger than either dss or operational data). Data can be stripped off of the operational systems or dss systems to feed the archival mode. Activity that processes the data generally takes very long periods of time. Since data is being stored for very lengthy periods of time, the media on which archival data is stored becomes a very important issue. The reliability of the media in the face of aging is a large issue. The archived data may be stored for a finite amount of time or stored indefinitely (of course, in reality there is some final boundary to the length of time the data is stored). Typical archival environments exist for government records, for records of past financial activity, for historical accounts of telephone-conversation billings, and so forth.

DEVELOPMENT MODE OF OPERATION

In the **development mode** of operation are found the activities of designing, programming, implementing, and testing systems. As such, there is very little data compared to the other modes of operation. Furthermore, what data there is is not live and can be destroyed by an errant program and restored at will with no ill effects on the running of the shop. There are usually relatively few users in the development mode of operation. Development aids are typically found in the development mode, such as IBM's TSO or VM/CMS. Response time may be very quick or very slow depending on what activities are transpiring and what other activities there are in the system. Typical activities of the development mode of operation are compilations, testing, manipulation of source text, and execution of design aids.

DATA BASE PRACTICES

Most of the data base theory and practices center around data base as it applies to a single mode of operation. Indeed, such concepts as distributed data base apply to a single mode of operation. In reality, however, data crosses the boundaries of different modes of operation on a daily basis. The concepts that apply to data base in multiple modes of operation may or may not apply to data base in a single mode of operation. For example, consider the practices that surround data base redundancy. In a single mode of operation, it is highly undesirable to have a high degree of redundancy. For example, redundancy in the operational mode of operation means that the salary of Ms. Jones is $35,000 in one place and $25,000 in another. This inconsistency of values is unacceptable both to Ms. Jones and her company. As another example, redundancy in the dss mode of operation means that dss group A makes their decisions on one copy of data and group B makes their decisions on another copy of the same or related data. But the decisions rendered by group A are diametrically opposed to the decisions made by group B. So redundancy within the same mode of operation is seldom, if ever, desirable.

However, redundancy across different modes of operation not only is not bad, but it is usually necessary and beneficial. There is, however, more than one school of thought on this subject. The two schools of thought can be tabbed the **dual** data base approach and the **truth** data base approach. The dual data base approach mandates that redundancy between different modes is a valid approach, whereas the truth approach mandates that there should be one data base for all uses, even across different modes of operation. IBM's DB2, IMS Fast Path, and RAMIS, FOCUS, and NOMAD are examples of DBMS software in support of the dual data base approach. Cincom's TIS, Cullinet's IDMS coupled with IDMS/R, and ADR's Ideal are examples of DBMS software in support of the truth approach. Each approach has its own merits.

TRUTH DATA BASE APPROACH

The truth data base approach dictates that there will be one and only one copy of the data base for all uses. Certainly there is no redundancy of data within the same mode. The idea of a single source of data is very appealing and blends well with the 1970's approach of integrating sequential master files. With a single data base, there is never any worry about synchronization of updates against redundant data. Since there is only one copy of the data and that copy is kept up to date, any analytical activity against the data base must reflect as accurate a view of the data as possible. There is great intellectual appeal to the simplicity of a single, truthful data base for all purposes.

However, there are some practical difficulties with the truth data base approach. The difficulties arise in the areas of performance. If the data base is being used heavily in the operational mode (and in particular, if there is much online update against the data base), then it is inevitable that there will be contention between different users of the system. When contention occurs, the entire system slows down. Online response times get progressively worse. The slowdown is magnified when there is a volume of dss activity that operates concurrently on the data. In essence there is a single source of data whose integrity must be tightly controlled where there are many and diverse users of the systems at the same time. Only a finite number of resources can be used to get at the data at any moment in time. As long as these precious resources are already being used (such as at peak processing periods), every user must queue to get at the resources. While queuing may not be too bad for the casual dss user, it spells real trouble for the operational user. So, when operational data bases exist in an environment that is response-time sensitive (and not all operational environments are highly response-time sensitive), the truth data base approach is questionable. In addition operational processing uses data at a very detailed level while dss uses data at a summary level.

DUAL DATA BASE APPROACH

The dual data base approach gets around the difficulties of performance that can occur in the truth data base approach. In the dual data base approach the operational data base is periodically scanned and stripped of data. The stripped data is then shipped to the dss data base environment. The scan of the operational data base is done at a time when there will be a minimum of interruption to the operational system, so performance is preserved. Off-peak hours such as 2:00 A.M. are favorite times for operational data base scans. Once the data is in the dss data base mode of operation, the data is manipulated by dss software at no expense to the operational mode of operation. In fact, dss systems are often run on completely separate processors. So the dual data base approach does not have the difficulties with performance that the truth approach had. But there are some disadvantages to the dual data base approach. Once the data is stripped off of the operational data base, it is current only up to that moment in time. There are now fully redundant data bases in different modes of operation.

Since there are fundamental differences in the usages of data in the different modes of operation, the dual data base philosophy is quite acceptable in terms of the consequences of the stripping of the data. In the operational mode, data must be managed at a very detailed level, by many users, and in a very response-sensitive manner. In the dss mode, data is managed at a summary level, is often refined, resequenced, redefined, and is manipulated quite easily. In the dss mode of operation, the up-to-the-minute accuracy of the data is not a factor. Because of the nature of dss processing, the dual data base approach is quite adequate to meet the needs of dss processing.

There are some practical considerations to the implementation of the dual data base approach. Some considerations are

- Scanning operational data bases once to satisfy all dss needs. There should be a single scan of any given operational data base to service all dss requests, not a separate scan of an operational data base for each dss request. This strategy ultimately saves on the total amount of I/O needed to satisfy dss requests.
- Gathering as much data as is needed. The scan of operational data bases should gather data that is known to be needed and data that is likely to be needed. On the average this prevents many rescans of data where only a little more data was needed than was originally thought.
- Saving the scanned operational data once used in the dss mode of operation. Once the scanned data is used in the dss mode of operation, it is prudent to save the scanned data until the next dss scan is done. If an analytical activity needs to be rerun (as is often the case), it will not be necessary to rescan the operational data base.

Another major consideration of the dual data base approach concerns the physical environment in which the different modes of operation will be executed.

In almost every case the operational data comes from the mainframe processor environment. When the data is transported to the dss environment, there are some very powerful reasons for removing it from the same physical environment that runs the operational systems. Typical of such an arrangement is the removal of data from the operational mainframe environment to the micro based dss environment. While there are unquestionably some limitations in the microprocessor environment, the micro environment gives the dss analyst most of the requirements for dss processing and at the same time frees the operational environment from a large processing load.

The dual data base approach makes one fundamental assumption: that there will be a single *system of record,* even though there is a duplication of data across modes of operation. A **system of record** is the final authority of the value of any given data element. As long as there is a single system of record (which 99% of the time will be in the operational environment), there is no problem with the dual data base approach. But where there is an attempt to maintain two (or more!) systems of record (either within the same mode of operation or across different modes of operation), there are a plethora of problems. Updates must be synchronized, recoveries become complicated, the total work done by the system multiplies, and so forth. (Note that in the distributed data base environment it is possible to have multiple systems of record. However, the systems are in the same mode of operation and such things as the management of updating are done at the DBMS software level, not the application level.)

SUMMARY

In summary, the major components of a data base environment are DASD (direct access storage devices), the processor, the line connecting DASD and the processor, the DBMS (data base management system), the buffer, and the program area. Data is divided into units of records and blocks. Records have many different names, depending on the DBMS. Entire blocks are written to and from DASD and the main processor rather than individual records. Buffer usage and allocation is a large issue in that the throughput that is possible within a system is largely dependent upon proper usage of those resources. The single most important factor in total system throughput is I/O, or input/output activity. I/O is crucial because the main processor operates at very fast electronic speeds and DASD operates at slower mechanical speeds.

Once the block of data arrives in the buffer, the individually requested record is sent to the program area, where it is able to be operated on by a program. Data can be transmitted to the program area in three modes—literally, in variable length fields, or by variable fields. The translation of variability can be done between the buffer and the program area or entirely within the program area. Variability of data—variable field length and/or variable field—works well when data is nonvolatile (i.e., when data, once inserted, changes very infrequently). Literal data works well when data is frequently updated. Finally, encryption can be used to protect data on DASD but at the cost of machine power (even though encryption normally doesn't cause I/O to occur).

An important consideration of data base is in which mode of operation it operates. Different modes of operation have different requirements. The principal modes of operation are the operational, the dss, the archival, and the development. Some data base concepts apply within a single mode of operation but do not necessarily apply across different modes of operation. One such concept is the usage or existence of redundant data. Within a single mode of operation, redundancy is a uniformly undesirable trait, whereas across different modes of operation, redundancy may well be a very desirable trait.

QUESTIONS

CPU

1.1. What is a CPU?

1.2. Is a CPU a mainframe? a microprocessor?

1.3. What types of CPU are there?

1.4. At what speeds does the CPU run?

1.5. What are the components of a CPU?

Memory

2.1. What is memory?

2.2. How does memory relate to the CPU?

2.3. At what speeds does memory run?

2.4. What types of programs, data, etc., are held in main memory?

2.5. Who allocates how main memory is to be divided? What program controls the allocation of main memory?

2.6. When is that allocation made?

2.7. What happens if that allocation is made improperly?

2.8. Is memory important in the micro environment? Why or why not?

DASD

3.1. What types of DASD are there?

3.2. What is a track?

3.3. What is a cylinder?

3.4. What is a read/write head?

3.5. Trace the activities of the usage of DASD from the moment it is known that data is needed until the data is actually located.

3.6. How many bytes of data will a spindle hold?

3.7. How fast does a spindle move?

3.8. Are spindles of data removable?

3.9. Who allocates DASD?

3.10. How does the system know where each data set is physically located?

3.11. What is a secondary extent?

3.12. What happens when an insert is made to DASD and there is no space available?

3.13. What monitors are there to determine the contents of DASD?

3.14. What advances have there been made in the past 10 years in DASD speed?

3.15. What advances have there been made in the past 10 years in DASD capacity?

3.16. What advances have there been made in the past 10 years in DASD costs?

3.17. What kinds of DASD are available for microprocessors?

Lines

4.1. What is a communications line?

4.2. Describe the different pieces of hardware that are connected to the mainframe by means of a line.

4.3. What capacity measurements are there for lines?

4.4. What costs are associated with lines?

4.5. How many lines can be connected to a mainframe? to a microprocessor?

4.6. Is the number of lines that can be connected to a mainframe a constraint?

4.7. What is a line concentrator?

Data Base Software

5.1. What is a DBMS?

5.2. Name 10 vendors of DBMS and their products.

5.3. Do all DBMS have online capabilities? batch capabilities?

5.4. Are DBMS interchangeable? Why or why not?

5.5. List 10 factors that affect the interchangeability of DBMS.

5.6. What are the differences between DBMS?

5.7. What criteria should be used in the selection of a DBMS for a shop?

5.8. What programming languages can be used in conjunction with a DBMS?

5.9. What are the practical limitations of a DBMS?

5.10. Do all DBMS have practical limitations?

5.11. Are there any DBMS without practical limitations?

5.12. Who installs a DBMS?

5.13. Who determines when a data base application should be built?

5.14. Who determines if a data base application is built properly?

5.15. What are the consequences of building a data base application improperly?

I/O

6.1. Why is I/O the limiting factor in most DBMS environments?

6.2. Is it possible to change the orientation of a DBMS so that I/O is not the limiting factor that it is?

6.3. How does I/O affect the design of a system?

6.4. Is I/O as important in batch systems as in online systems?

6.5. Describe the anatomy of an I/O.

Records and Blocks

7.1. What is a record?

7.2. What is a block?

7.3. How do records relate to blocks?

7.4. Is the data in all DBMS divided into records and blocks?

7.5. Where are record and block sizes defined?

7.6. Who defines record and block sizes?

7.7. What happens if the sizes are not properly defined?

7.8. What relationship is there between a block and the capacity of a track?

7.9. Do all DBMS access one record at a time? one set at a time?

7.10. What DBMS process one set at a time?

Basic Activities

8.1. What are the four basic activities in the life of a data base?

8.2. Why are there only four?

8.3. Describe how each activity is accomplished from the time a call is issued until data is accessed? Who issues the call?

Variable-Length Fields

9.1. What is a variable-length field?

9.2. What is a fixed-length field?

9.3. Do all DBMS support both types of fields?

Variable Fields

10.1. What is a variable field?

10.2. Do all DBMS support variable fields?

Data Compaction

11.1. How compactly can data be stored without variable-length fields and variable fields?

11.2. Where are the places compaction/decompaction can be done as data is transferred between DASD and the programmer's work area?

11.3. What are the considerations of compaction/decompaction at each place it can be done?

11.4. When are variable fields useful? variable-length fields? When are variable fields not useful?

Encryption

12.1. What is encryption?

12.2. What is the difference between encryption and compaction?

12.3. Is encryption a proper choice for every data base design?

12.4. Where are the places encryption can be done?

12.5. What are the considerations of encryption at every place it can be done?

12.6. Who should be in charge of the encryption algorithms?

12.7. What are the costs of encryption?

Keys

13.1. What is a key? What types of keys are there?

13.2. Where is a nonunique key valid? invalid?

13.3. Does all data have to have a key?

13.4. What criteria are there to determine the physical characteristics of a key?

13.5. Once a system is built, is a key easily changed? able to be changed?

13.6. Is the physical form of a key important? Why or why not?

EXERCISES

1. At what speeds do channels run? What different kinds of channels are there? At what speeds does memory operate? At what speeds does DASD operate?

2. All DBMS are not described in terms of blocks and records. Give several examples of different terminology. Does the difference in terminology reflect a fundamental difference in the way the DBMS work?

3. Some DBMS run in the online environment, some DBMS run in the interactive environment, some DBMS are designed for unstructured, fourth generation environments, and some DBMS run batch systems well. Which DBMS run well in which environments, and what are the essential differences in the different DBMS?

4. Pick a DBMS and determine the hardware requirements for it. Determine the total costs associated with the DBMS.

5. Give five rules of thumb for determining how online response time can be estimated *prior* to building the online system.

6. For a convenient DBMS and operating system, determine how many buffers are available. What size are the buffers? Can more buffers be allocated? What happens to blocks of data that exceed the size of the buffers? Determine where block size is set. Determine where record size is set. How can the systems programmer determine whether more buffers would enhance performance? How can the systems programmer determine if buffer space is being wasted? How can the systems programmer determine which are the most active buffers?

7. Name a DBMS that uses variable-length fields and one that uses fixed-length fields. Name a DBMS that uses variable fields and one that uses fixed fields.

8. Trace each step from the issuance of the data base call to the loading of the program work area for a compacted variable-length field data base.

9. Define unique keys for the following:
   (a) A person
   (b) An inventory record
   (c) A university
   (d) The payment of a bill
   (e) A ticket to a football game

CHAPTER 3

Data Management*

An understanding of the data base environment begins with a basic knowledge of the workings of the basic components of the data base environment, of the importance of I/O (input/output), and of the basic organization of data into blocks and records. But there is much more to the data base environment. Exactly how data is organized and accessed plays a huge role in the success or failure of the data base environment. The next level of understanding is that of data management—of how data is stored, retrieved, updated and deleted. There are two basic ways data is stored on DASD (direct access storage device): it is either randomized or it is indexed.

RANDOMIZATION

When data is randomized, the key (or whatever other unique characteristics the data possesses) of the data is used to establish a unique physical address on DASD. The act of key translation into an address is shown by Fig. 3.1. In Fig. 3.1, the key of Mary Smith's data is social security number. The key is used as input into the randomizer, which is nothing more than a piece of code (or an algorithm). The code of the randomizer translates (or maps) the input into an address, in this case disk

(*Note: Data management refers to the activities of the DBMS (data base management system) in storing, locating, and organizing data. The term *data management* has long been used in this context. In recent years there has been much discussion about data resource management, which refers to the managerial and organizational implications of control and usage of data within the enterprise. Data resource management should not be confused with data management.)

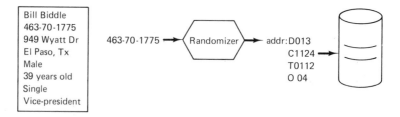

Bill Biddle
463-70-1775
949 Wyatt Dr
El Paso, Tx
Male
39 years old
Single
Vice-president

463-70-1775 ⟶ ⟨ Randomizer ⟩ ⟶ addr:D013
                                           C1124 ⟶
                                           T0112
                                           O 04

Figure 3.1

013, cylinder 1124, track 0112, and offset 04. To locate Mary Smith's data, only the key and randomizer are required. Note that I/O is needed only to access the data on DASD (i.e., going through the randomizer does not require an I/O). Also note that Mary Smith's data exists in record form within a physical block on DASD, as was shown in Chapter 2. There are at least five factors that determine the effectiveness of a randomizer (or a "mapping" algorithm):

1. DASD space available
2. The physical block of space available on DASD
3. The number of records to be randomized
4. The physical record size
5. The ability of the randomizer to spread the keys effectively.

DASD SPACE AVAILABLE

The most fundamental factor in effective randomization is the amount of space that is available on DASD. If there is inadequate space on DASD, then all other factors are moot because there is nothing that can be done to randomize the data effectively. When there is more data to be randomized (or *mapped*) into DASD then there is space for, it is inevitable that some data is randomized into the same location as other data. When there are many collisions, the internal order of the data is very disorganized. To use an analogy, when 60 students are forced into the space where 30 normally belong, then there is a great deal of chaos. The importance of mapping data into enough DASD space is illustrated by Fig. 3.2.

The significance of enough space is best illustrated by how randomization works. For a simplified example, suppose there is enough DASD to support 20 records (i.e., DASD is divided so that a maximum of 20 records can be inserted). The addresses of DASD are then divided into 20 locations. Suppose there are 1000 bytes available on DASD. Then the randomized locations or addresses would be address 1, address 51, address 101, and so forth, as seen in Fig. 3.3.

The randomizer is given the amount of DASD and the addressibility information. Next the randomizer is given a key to be randomized. As a simple example, suppose that the key is the social security number 463-70-1133. One randomization technique is to divide the number of records that can be randomized into the numeric value to be randomized (this works only for numeric values), producing a

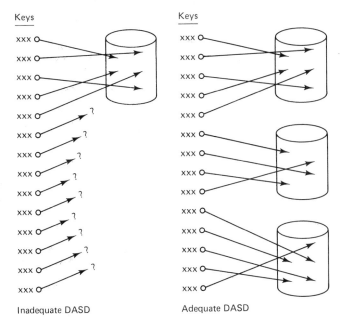

Keys

xxx
xxx
xxx
xxx
xxx
xxx
xxx
xxx
xxx
xxx
xxx
xxx
xxx
xxx

Inadequate DASD

Keys

xxx
xxx
xxx
xxx
xxx
xxx
xxx
xxx
xxx
xxx
xxx
xxx
xxx
xxx

Adequate DASD

Figure 3.2 On the left there is inadequate DASD space on which to map the data. The inevitable result is poorly organized data and many collisions. On the right there is adequate space on which to map the data. The data base on the right is much more efficient to traverse and operate on.

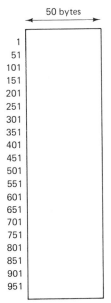

50 bytes

1
51
101
151
201
251
301
351
401
451
501
551
601
651
701
751
801
851
901
951

Figure 3.3 Twenty records in DASD, 1000 bytes of DASD addressibility every 50 bytes.

remainder, or **modulo** value. In this case 463-70-1133 modulo 20 yields a value of 13. Thus address 601 (derived by $(13 \times 50) - (50 - 1)$) is selected for social security number 463-70-1133, as seen by Fig. 3.4.

Such a limited amount of space and a limited number of records are appropriate only to an example that serves the purpose of explaining how randomization works. In practice, the number of records and the amount of DASD available are much larger. Figure 3.4 shows that if more than 20 records are to be randomized, more DASD will be required. But there are other factors in randomization than the amount of DASD, even though space is the single most important factor.

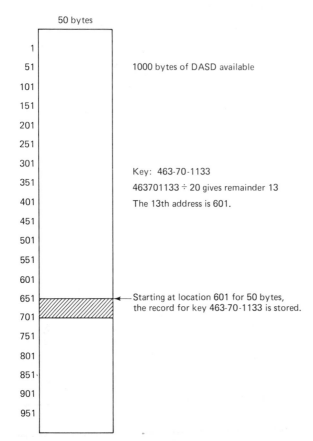

50 bytes

1
51   1000 bytes of DASD available
101
151
201
251
301
351   Key: 463-70-1133
401   463701133 ÷ 20 gives remainder 13
451   The 13th address is 601.
501
551
601
651   Starting at location 601 for 50 bytes,
701   the record for key 463-70-1133 is stored.
751
801
851
901
951

Figure 3.4

RANDOMIZATION: OTHER FACTORS

Other factors that are relevant to effective randomization include the length of the record to be randomized, the physical blocks into which randomization occurs, and the number of records to be randomized. The physical blocks into which DASD can be broken are a major factor because randomizers usually operate at the block/offset level. In other words, the lowest level of address (beyond disk, cylinder, and track, which are gross physical measurements of DASD) is addressibility to a block and an offset within the block. Suppose the space available for user data on a disk were divided into blocks of 100 bytes (which for practical purposes usually makes little sense because the overhead associated with each block would use nearly the same amount of space as would be available for regular data in the block). Then records of a maximum length of 100 bytes could be placed in a given block, which is a severe restriction. However, the addressibility of DASD by block would be very fine because there are so many blocks. At the other extreme, suppose a physical block were defined to be 10,000 bytes (which is usually as impractical as a 100-byte physical block!). Almost any reasonable record would fit into the block, but DASD would contain very few blocks. Figure 3.5 shows the extremes of physical block size and DASD.

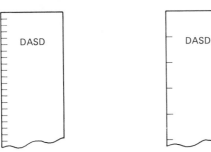

Many small blocks;
Many addresses to which to randomize but a limited amount of data is in any given block.

Few large blocks:
Any reasonable record can be inserted, but there are few addresses to which to randomize.

Figure 3.5 The trade-offs between large and small physical blocks.

The physical block size of DASD is an important factor of effective randomization as is total DASD. The next factor of importance is physical record size. If the record is small, then many records can fit into a block, but if a record is large, then fewer records will fit. In general, the smaller the record the better, as smaller records can be compacted nicely. Depending on block size, larger records may reduce much wasted space, as seen by Fig. 3.6. However, if records become *too* small,

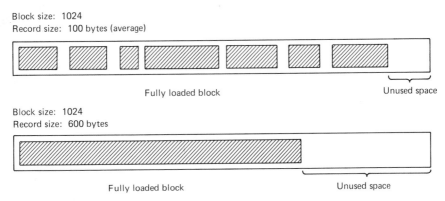

Block size: 1024
Record size: 100 bytes (average)

Fully loaded block   Unused space

Block size: 1024
Record size: 600 bytes

Fully loaded block   Unused space

Figure 3.6

then another factor must be considered. Records contain essentially two kinds of data, user data and system data. **User data** is data that is available to the program for data fields. **System data** is overhead data, data required by the system to determine the type of record, whether the record is deleted or not, what other data relates to the record, and so forth. Data in every system has some sort of overhead. In some systems this overhead data is called **prefix data.** Prefix data is independent of user data in that, regardless of the amount and format of user data, a certain amount of prefix data is required. Figure 3.7 illustrates the differences between user data and prefix data. When very small records are defined, the total amount of space occupied by prefix data becomes significant. For example, if a record is 15 bytes, of which 8 bytes are prefix data, it is likely that the overhead of prefix data is disproportionate. Thus the size of the record is a trade-off between the ability to place many records in a physical block and the overhead associated with each occurrence of a record.

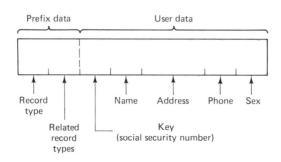

Figure 3.7 Prefix data is for the system; user data is for the programmer or user.

There is another factor relevant to record size and randomization, the variability of the record size. When the record size can vary, a new and very troublesome factor is introduced. As long as record sizes that vary in length have a small variance, then there is no major problem. For example, when the average record length is 150 bytes and 90% of the record lengths are from 140 to 160 bytes, it is easy to determine the behavior of records as they are inserted into blocks. But when records vary greatly in length, such is not the case. For example, when the average record size is 200 bytes, where 50% of the record sizes are between 125 and 275 bytes, and 90% of the records are between 10 and 2000 bytes, then fitting the records into blocks becomes very difficult.

Another factor relevant to randomization is that of the number of records to be inserted. If there are very few (or a fixed) number of records to be inserted, then the fit between records, block size, and DASD can be carefully measured. But when the number of records is unknown or is subject to wide variations, then effective use of the randomizer is questionable.

The final major factor in effective randomization is the randomization algorithm itself. In the simple case that has been shown, there were 20 addresses to which data could be randomized, and a modulo algorithm was selected. Assuming that the input to the randomizer was selected randomly, there would be an even distribution of keys across DASD. But consider the randomizer shown in Fig. 3.8. The randomizer will yield only three addresses. Address 1 is yielded for John Smith,

Input: "John Smith" address block 1
       "Bill Biddle" address block 2   **Figure 3.8** An unusual customized
       anything else address block 3   randomizer.

address 2 for Bill Biddle, and address 3 for any other input. Such a randomizer may be useful under a few very specialized circumstances. Under general circumstances, address 3 will share the same block for nearly all keys (hence nearly all records). Therefore, if the randomization algorithm itself does not spread data over DASD in an effective fashion, that randomization cannot be effective.

There are other factors that relate to the effective use of randomized data. Some of those factors are the pattern of growth of data, the pattern of insertion and deletion, the ability to redefine data and distribute it over a different amount of DASD, and so forth. However, the primary factors stated previously remain vital to effective randomization.

RANDOMIZATION: OVERFLOW

Consider the case where key A403 randomizes (i.e., is mapped) to address B35,014 as shown in Fig. 3.9. At a later point in time key ZK6352 is sent to the randomizer, and, as it turns out, it also randomizes to location B35,014. The record is to be inserted, but the data for key A403 already exists in the location, as shown by Fig. 3.10. This event is called a **collision**. It is true that both the data for A403 and ZK6352 cannot share the same location, and the space is already held by A403. Does this mean that the data for ZK6352 cannot be inserted? To the user there is absolutely no connection between the two records (since it is the randomizer that connects them), so it makes no sense to say to the user that record ZK6352 cannot be inserted because record A403 already exists. So space must be found for record ZK6352. The data for ZK6352 must be put into another location, and a connection must be made between B35,014 and the location of ZK6352. The prefix of A403 is a convenient place to use to make such a connection. There are essentially two choices as to where the collided record can be placed: in the same block to which it was originally randomized or in a physically separate block. The two options are shown in Figs. 3.11 and 3.12.

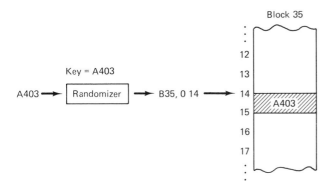

Figure 3.9 Data for record A403 is inserted into block 35, offset 14.

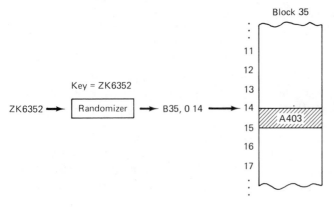

Figure 3.10 Both ZK6352 and A403 randomize to the same location.

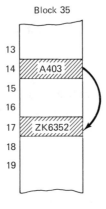

Figure 3.11 ZK6352 is stored in the same block to which it is randomized.

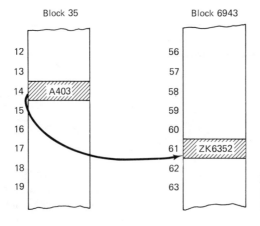

Figure 3.12 ZK6352 is stored in a physically separate location from the block to which it randomizes.

Basic Concepts   Section I

In one case ZK6352 has been placed into an unused space in the same block to which it originally randomized. When looking for ZK6352, block 35 will be retrieved, but A403 will be at offset 14. However, in the prefix of A403 is an indicator of the location of ZK6352, which is offset 17. ZK6352 can be found then in the same I/O. However, the data that will in the future randomize to offset 17 will not be able to be inserted, and another location will have to be used. The implication is that placing collision data in the randomized block may not be a good practice. The alternative is to place the collision record in a separate physical location (i.e., a separate physical block that has available space), called **overflow**, as seen in Fig. 3.12. When record ZK6352 is retrieved, first block 35 and then block 6943 will have to be accessed, thereby causing 2 I/O's. But the block to which ZK6352 first randomized will not become cluttered with misplaced records and will be able to handle future data directed to it. When more than two keys randomize to the same location or when data is to be inserted and the space it is directed to is already used, a chain of pointers is built, as shown by Fig. 3.13.

Overflow can be used under other conditions. Records may be of variable sizes and may be able to be added to or compressed. Consider the following case. A record, M3314, is being inserted, but there is not enough space to insert all of M3314 (Fig. 3.14). Data that cannot be placed in block 16, offset 5, is placed in another physical location. The record for M3314 now resides in the primary area of DASD (the location where it is randomized) and in overflow.

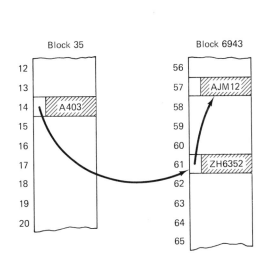

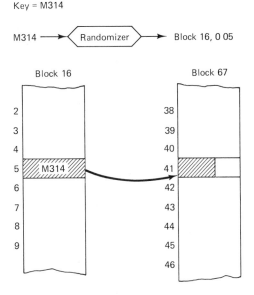

Figure 3.13 The result when A403, ZK6352, and AJM12 all randomize to block 35, offset 14: A chain is created through the prefix area of the records.

Figure 3.14 M314 randomizes to block 16, offset 5, but there is not enough space to place the data in the location. Extra available space is found in block 67, offset 41. The data for record M314 now exists in two physically separate locations.

AVERAGE RECORD SIZE: VARIATIONS

The importance of the variation of the record size fitting between reasonable norms can be illustrated in terms of a simple example. Suppose there are two types of records, A and B. Record A has an average length of 250 bytes and 90% of the occurrences of A are between 240 and 260 bytes. Such a record distribution is very well behaved. Record B has an average length of 400 bytes. Of B's records, 50% are between 250 and 500 bytes, whereas 90% of B's records are between 150 and 1000 bytes. The distribution of B's records are poorly behaved. Statistically, the standard deviation of A is much smaller than the standard deviation of B. Figure 3.15 shows the differences between A and B.

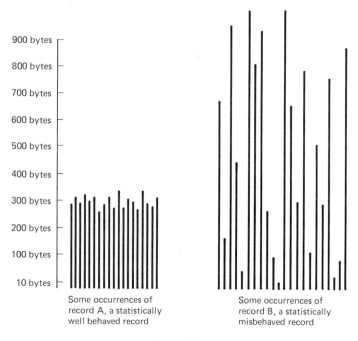

Some occurrences of record A, a statistically well behaved record

Some occurrences of record B, a statistically misbehaved record

Figure 3.15

Planning the physical block size for A is fairly simple. The number of records that need to be fitted into a block can be calculated in a straightforward fashion. For instance, suppose the designer wishes to place four type A records in a block. A block size of 1024K can be used with confidence. There will be a few unused bytes in the block, and, on occasion, only three records will fit in the block. But for the most part, four type A records will consistently fit into a 1024-byte block, as seen in a typical block shown in Fig. 3.16.

Now consider record B. Because of the variation in record sizes, a physical block size is hard to choose. Suppose the designer wishes to place five records on a 2048 block. Since there are, on the average, 400 bytes per record, it seems reasonable that there would be a snug fit. But because of the variability of the record size, such is not the case at all. Some blocks have large amounts of wasted space,

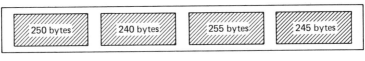

990 bytes used
1024 bytes available

Figure 3.16

whereas other blocks have records that overflow into other blocks. Were the records of a more uniform size, choosing a physical block size would not be a large issue, as there would be little wasted space and few records going into overflow. Figure 3.17 shows the case where record sizes vary widely.

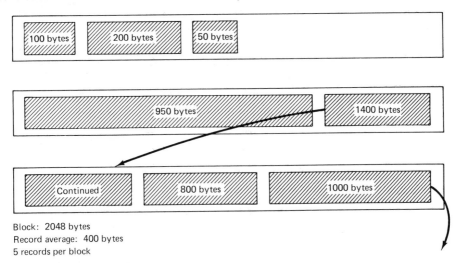

Block: 2048 bytes
Record average: 400 bytes
5 records per block

Figure 3.17

Suppose a block size of 2048, which is larger than necessary, is chosen to hold 2 records per block instead of 4 records per block, as shown by Fig. 3.18. In this

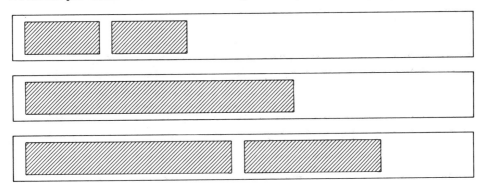

Block: 2048
2 records per block

Figure 3.18

Chap. 3   Data Management

case there is very little spillover from one block to another, thus reducing I/O. But there is also proportionately much wasted space. Now consider what happens when a smaller block size is chosen, say 4 records per 1048 block, as seen in Fig. 3.19. In this figure there is a minimum of wasted space and a maximum of I/O that must be done. So the designer is faced with two poor choices for physical block size in the face of a poorly distributed record size: either make the blocks too large and waste space or make the blocks too small and waste I/O.

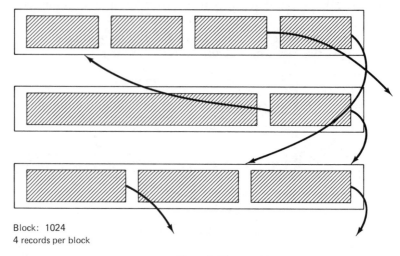

Block: 1024
4 records per block

Figure 3.19

INDEXING

In a randomized environment, data physically exists on the data base in an order that makes sense only to the randomizer. In an indexed environment, data exists in an order according to the sequence of the key of the record. The order may be

---

DBMS

A data base management system (DBMS) is the software that is at the heart of data base. From a very simplistic point of view, a DBMS makes the physical addressing of data very simple. Without a DBMS, a programmer or a user would have a difficult time locating and accessing data. But that simplistic view of a DBMS only scratches the surface.

Most full-function DBMS are large, complex pieces of code. A full-function DBMS must interface with *at least* the following components:

— The SCP (system control program, or operating system)
— The logical view of data
— The physical view of data
— Application programs
— The network

Each of these components is its own complex environment.

The SCP. The SCP is at the center of the operations of the computer. The DBMS must operate efficiently and in harmony with the SCP. When the SCP and DBMS are incompatible, either the DBMS cannot run at all, or the DBMS runs in an impaired state. An impaired state means the DBMS does not get the system resources it needs to run efficiently.

Application programs. These programs have a wide diversity of needs, from a large syntax of data base calls to a wide diversity in what, how and when activity is done. The allocation of resources to the application, the servicing of calls, the recovery considerations, the scheduling of executions—all these features are handled by the applications interface to the DBMS.

Logical view of data. The logical view of data can vary from program to program and within the same program. One program may want to look at data in an entirely different way than another program. It is the job of the DBMS to accommodate multiple views of the same data when requested.

Physical form of data. The physical form of the data is concerned with where data is physically located, how it is stored, how it can be transported, and how it can be physically manipulated—in other words, the problems of data management. In some cases the DBMS handles all data management by itself; in other cases the DBMS handles some aspects of data management and lets the other aspects be handled by a low-level access method, much as VSAM (IBM's virtual storage access method).

The network. The network is the facility for using data though a cathode ray tube (CRT), or online. The DBMS may manage the network entirely or may connect with a network manager, such as IBM's CICS.

With the complexity and diversity of the different functions of a DBMS, it is no wonder that it is large and complex. Each of the interfaces are very different, and the DBMS must blend them all together successfully. To complicate matters further, the interfaces are constantly changing. So the DBMS must hit not only a complex target but a moving target as well!

ascending or descending. In an indexed environment, data is directly retrieved through an index. For example, suppose a data base is ordered by social security number and the data base is indexed. To locate a given social security number, 459-70-1872, a search is made of the index. When the number is located in the index, an address to the physical location is determined and the data is located, as seen in Fig. 3.20.

Two I/O are required, one to go through the index, and another to go to the actual data. There are many ways to build an index. The simplest form of an index is one that points to the block and an address within the block for each record in

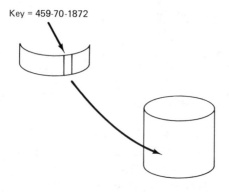

Key = 459-70-1872

Figure 3.20 The location for 459–70–1872 is determined through a search of the index.

the data base, as seen in Fig. 3.21. Note that the records are in sequence within the block, and the physical address within the block is stored in the index. A search for key 3 requires going through key 1 and key 2. There is a simple variation of the index in which only the highest key value per block is stored, thus saving much space in the index (see Fig. 3.22). In this figure there are no addresses within blocks

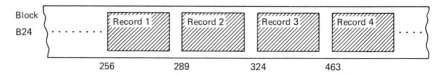

key1	key2	key3	key4	. . . .	Key
B24	B24	B24	B24	. . . .	Block
256	289	324	463	. . . .	Address (offset)

Block B24

Record 1   Record 2   Record 3   Record 4

256   289   324   463

Figure 3.21

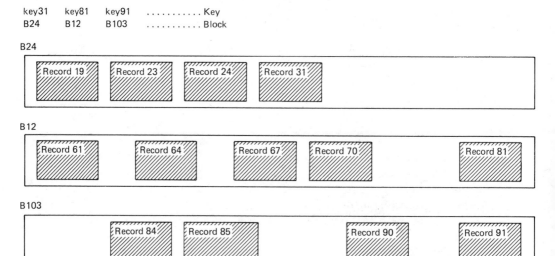

| key31 | key81 | key91 | . . . . | Key |
| B24 | B12 | B103 | . . . . | Block |

B24

Record 19   Record 23   Record 24   Record 31

B12

Record 61   Record 64   Record 67   Record 70   Record 81

B103

Record 84   Record 85   Record 90   Record 91

Figure 3.22

Basic Concepts   Section I

because each search of the index requires a physical block search. For example, to locate record 85, the index is searched. Key 31 (in the index) is less than 85, so record 85 is not in block 24. Key 81 (in the index) is less than 85, so record 85 is not in block 12. But key 85 is less than key 91 (in the index), so if record 85 is in the data base it is in block 103. Block 103 is searched sequentially and record 85 is located. Note that the sequence of the blocks—block 24, block 12, block 103—is irrelevant as far as the index is concerned. Also, if record 81 were to be deleted, the index for block 12 would have to be changed to show key 70 as the highest key for the block. Such an indexing technique is a form of **sparsely populated index.** In some cases this sparsely populated index points to a densely populated index, creating an **indexed** index (or "super" index).

Now consider the first index (Fig. 3.21). When the data is reordered, each of the addresses must be reset in the index. For example, if record 1 were updated by having 10 bytes added to it, then record 2 would need to be moved to location 299, record 3 to location 334, and record 4 to location 473 and the indexes adjusted accordingly. The overhead of adjustment could be minimized by creating a block prefix space (as opposed to a record prefix space), in which addresses of offsets are maintained within the data base block rather than in the index. Such an arrangement is shown in Fig. 3.23. The index contains an offset rather than an address. The usefulness of this indirection is shown when a record (record 2) is updated and its length is extended, but there is no space in the original location. It is a simple matter

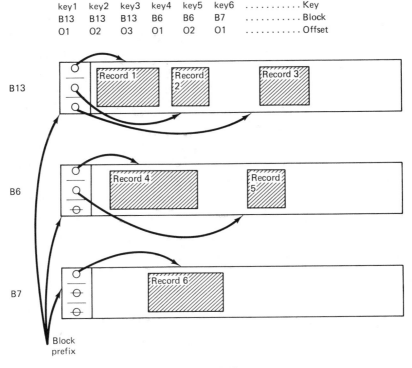

Figure 3.23

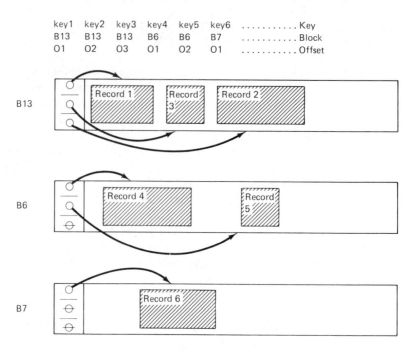

key1	key2	key3	key4	key5	key6	.... Key
B13	B13	B13	B6	B6	B7	.... Block
01	02	03	01	02	01	.... Offset

Figure 3.24

to relocate record 2, reset the address in the offset, in block prefix, as shown by Fig. 3.24. In this case the index remains untouched.

Another form of indexing occurs when the index itself is indexed, as when the sparsely populated index points to a densely populated index. When there is only a single index, it must be scanned sequentially to locate the desired key. Since the index itself is its own data base, this amounts to a sequential scan of data, albeit a limited scan; but it may amount to several I/O's. What can be done is to create a **super** index, as shown in Fig. 3.25. In the super index, the highest indexing is accessed first, to locate the proper index block. Once the proper index block has been located, then data is searched. Such a structuring of indexes saves sequential searching of an index. Because the super index is so compact and is so often accessed, it may be placed permanently in main storage, thus bypassing the need for an I/O to access it.

INSERTION/DELETION IN AN INDEXED DATA BASE

Suppose a simple (very simple!) indexed data base exists, as shown in Fig. 3.26. The index contains three entries, one for each key. All data is in the same block. The data is referred to by an offset, rather than an absolute, address. The first activity that happens to the data base is that record 39 is to be inserted. There is ample space in the data base and there is an available offset for the record, so insertion into the data base is no problem, as seen in Fig. 3.27.

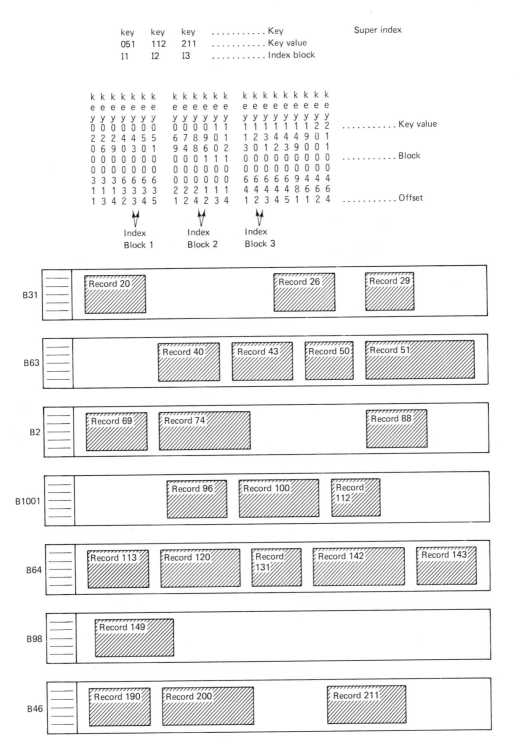

Figure 3.25

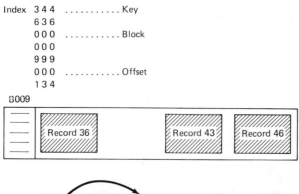

Figure 3.26   A very simple index data base.

Figure 3.27   Record 39 is loaded into the data base and the offset is loaded with record 39's address.

However, insertion into the index is not quite as simple. In the index in its unupdated form (as shown in Fig. 3.26), there is no space for insertion of entry 39. But that does not mean record 39 cannot be inserted (record 39 cannot be inserted only if it already exists). Instead, index entries for records 43 and 46 are moved into unused space, and space is made for entry 39, as shown in Fig. 3.28. Now suppose that record 44 is to be inserted. Logically it can be inserted (in that no other record 44 is in the data base). But physically there is no room for it, as seen in Fig. 3.29. However, this does not mean that the record cannot be inserted. There are two common techniques for insertion. One technique utilizes pointers. In this case, the index is inserted into the block where record 45 resides, and a physical pointer is

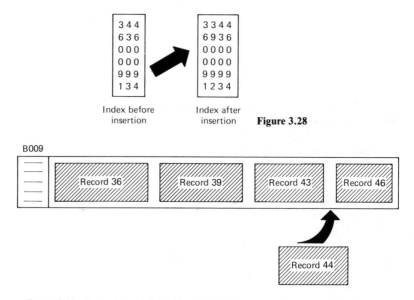

Figure 3.28

Figure 3.29   Record 44 is to be inserted, but there is no space for it in the block.

Basic Concepts   Section I

used to maintain the sequence of the records, as seen in Fig. 3.30. Using entry into another physical block and connecting the data by means of pointers does not require a reordering of data. Record 44 can be retrieved directly through the index (as it would be able to be retrieved in any case). The sequential order is maintained by use of pointers that direct the search to another block after record 43 is accessed. Note that one more I/O is required in going from record 43 to 46 than would be if the records were maintained in sequence.

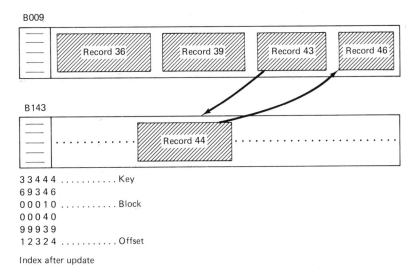

B009

Record 36   Record 39   Record 43   Record 46

B143

Record 44

```
33444 .......... Key
69346
00010 .......... Block
00040
99939
12324 .......... Offset
```

Index after update

Figure 3.30   Pointers exist from record 43 to record 44 and from record 44 to record 46. The pointers are in the prefix of the record.

The other option to inserting record 44 when there is no space in the block is to split the block. In this case some records are moved out of the original block and placed in a previously unused block. This split is shown by Fig. 3.31. More space is now available for future insertions, and the sequence of the data is maintained. Deletion of an indexed record is usually a simple process. It is not normal for deleted space actually to be deleted or written over. Instead, what happens is that the index pointer and the block offset are uninitialized and the space is left vacant. This has the effect of leaving space for future growth in that unused space can be reused. A deletion is shown by Fig. 3.32. The record 43 still is in the data base, but there is no way to access the record, since the record's index and its offset have been loaded with null values.

DUPLICATE INDEX ENTRIES

So far, all the index types shown have had unique keys, and there has been no possibility for duplication of key values. But is it mandatory that there be no key duplication? The answer is no; there are many valid cases when indexing is done

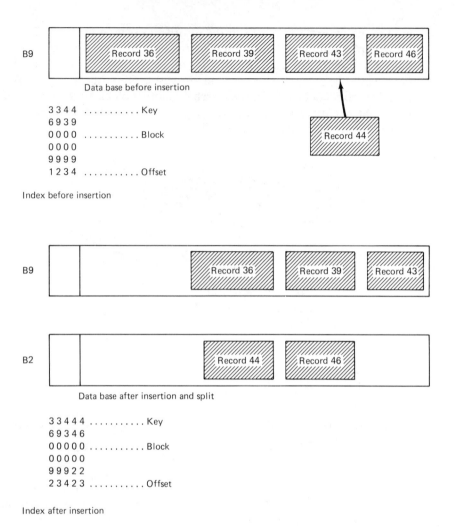

B9

Record 36   Record 39   Record 43   Record 46

Data base before insertion

Record 44

3 3 4 4 .... Key
6 9 3 9
0 0 0 0 .... Block
0 0 0 0
9 9 9 9
1 2 3 4 .... Offset

Index before insertion

B9

Record 36   Record 39   Record 43

B2

Record 44   Record 46

Data base after insertion and split

3 3 4 4 4 .... Key
6 9 3 4 6
0 0 0 0 0 .... Block
0 0 0 0 0
9 9 9 2 2
2 3 4 2 3 .... Offset

Index after insertion

Figure 3.31

on the same value. Such a case is illustrated by Fig. 3.33. In this case an index has been created for Smith, but there are several Smiths in the data base. There exists an entry for each Smith in the index, and there is no difference between the key of one record and the key of the other. The ordering of the entries is random. Each entry was created in the order that it was inserted. Should there be a desire to distinguish between one Smith and another, an artificial numbering sequence can be adopted, as seen by Fig. 3.34. The sequencing is usually done in the order that the records have been inserted into the data base. The usefulness of such an artificial index is in "remembering" where processing left off. For example, suppose the index of the first five Smiths is scanned and then the sixth Smith's record is read. If the scan of the index for Smith is to occur, it is convenient to remember to begin

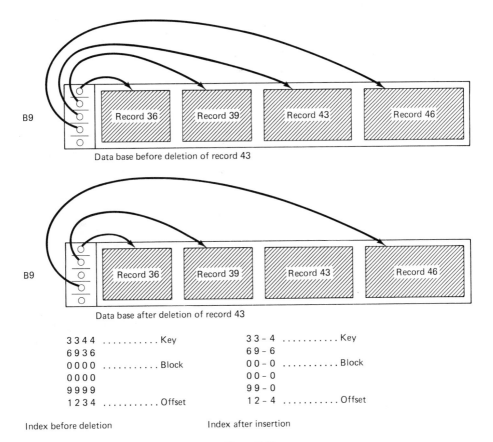

B9

Data base before deletion of record 43

B9

Data base after deletion of record 43

```
3 3 4 4  . . . . . . . . . . Key        3 3 - 4  . . . . . . . . . . Key
6 9 3 6                      6 9 - 6
0 0 0 0  . . . . . . . . . . Block      0 0 - 0  . . . . . . . . . . Block
0 0 0 0                      0 0 - 0
9 9 9 9                      9 9 - 0
1 2 3 4  . . . . . . . . . . Offset     1 2 - 4  . . . . . . . . . . Offset
```

Index before deletion   Index after insertion

Figure 3.32

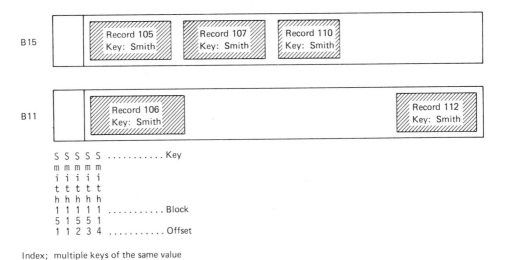

B 15

B 11

```
S  S  S  S  S  . . . . . . . . . . Key
m  m  m  m  m
i  i  i  i  i
t  t  t  t  t
h  h  h  h  h
1  1  1  1  1  . . . . . . . . . . Block
5  1  5  5  1
1  1  2  3  4  . . . . . . . . . . Offset
```

Index; multiple keys of the same value

Figure 3.33

Chap. 3   Data Management   **65**

```
S  S  S  S  S  . . . . . . . . . . Key
m  m  m  m  m
i  i  i  i  i
t  t  t  t  t
h  h  h  h  h
0  0  0  0  0  . . . . . . . . . . Artificial
1  2  3  4  5               numbering
1  1  1  1  1  . . . . . . . . . . Block
5  1  5  5  1
1  1  2  3  4  . . . . . . . . . . Offset
```

Figure 3.34 Artificial sequencing of
Smith.

the search at the seventh Smith and not to have to return to the first of the index
and rescan it.

HASHED INDEXES

Although the index itself is compact relative to the data base, a large index can still
contain much space. It is often desirable to compress that space as much as possible,
especially when the index is to be loaded into main memory. In this case the index
key itself can be compressed. This is done by hashing. **Hashing** in a simplified form
is shown by Fig. 3.35. In the simple hashing algorithm shown, the first three digits
of the last name are combined with initials to create a five-digit key. The key is
greatly compacted over a general-purpose name key. But note that the frequency
(or possibility) of duplicates is raised by this form of hashing. However, this does
not raise a problem as long as the duplicates are not too numerous. The net effect
of a hashed index is a much smaller, more compact index, which is efficient in the
face of I/O and space considerations.

Name Hasher

Input: last name, first name, initial
Output: first three digits of last name, first initial, second initial

Examples

James Bacon: BacJb
William H. Inmon: InmWH
Maryce Jacobs: JacMb
Merrill Jackson: JacMb
Venkatakrishnan: Venbb
Mehdi P. Ghadiani: GhaMP

Figure 3.35 A simple name hasher.

SINGLE RECORD BLOCKS

An even simpler form of data structuring occurs when a physical block can hold at
most one record. Such an arrangement is useful for very long records of widely
varying length (i.e., the standard deviation is large relative to the average length).
Figure 3.36 illustrates such an arrangement. In the figure, four records of widely
varying length are stored. Each record is directly addressed by its index (i.e., when
the index entry is located, it is a sure thing that at least the first part of the record
is going to be in the block pointed to). Some records are shorter than the block,

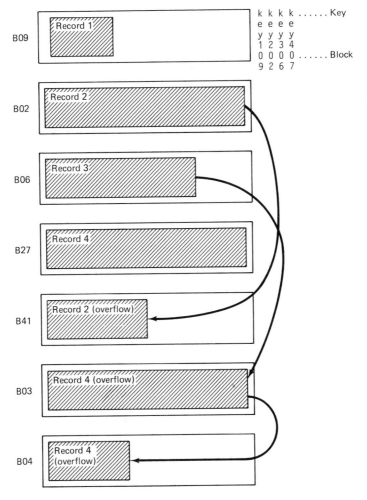

Figure 3.36

thus wasting space. Other longer records are dispersed over several blocks. It requires several I/O to retrieve those records. Single record blocks are one technique for handling widely varying record sizes.

ALTERNATE INDEXING

So far the indexes shown can be classified as primary indexes. A **primary index** is one that points to the key of a record. But there are indexes that can be made for the data other than those that index the key of the record. Consider a data base whose primary order is by social security number. An alternate index is created on two nonkey attributes of data, name and color of eyes, as shown in Fig. 3.37. The great usefulness of alternate indexes is their ability to enter a data base on a basis

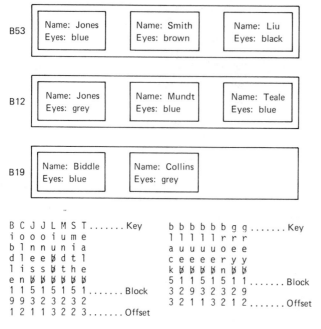

Primary order — social security number

B53 | Name: Jones / Eyes: blue | Name: Smith / Eyes: brown | Name: Liu / Eyes: black

B12 | Name: Jones / Eyes: grey | Name: Mundt / Eyes: blue | Name: Teale / Eyes: blue

B19 | Name: Biddle / Eyes: blue | Name: Collins / Eyes: grey

```
B C J J L M S T . . . . . . . Key        b b b b b b g g g . . . . . . . Key
i o o o i u m e                          l l l l l r r r
b l n n u n i a                          a u u u u o e e
d l e e ⌀ d t l                          c e e e e r y y
l i s s ⌀ t h e                          k ⌀ ⌀ ⌀ ⌀ n ⌀ ⌀
e n ⌀ ⌀ ⌀ ⌀ ⌀ ⌀                          5 1 1 5 1 5 1 1 . . . . . . . Block
1 1 5 1 5 1 5 1 . . . . . . . Block      3 2 9 3 2 3 2 9
9 9 3 2 3 2 3 2                          3 2 1 1 3 2 1 2 . . . . . . . Offset
1 2 1 1 3 2 2 3 . . . . . . . Offset
```

Alternate index on name   Alternate index on color of eyes   **Figure 3.37**

other than the primary key. This is an efficient and legitimate use of the feature. But consider what happens when the secondary index is used to process *all* the records in the order of the secondary index. For the purposes of illustration, take the name alternate index (assume for the purposes here that there is space for only one block in the buffer area). The first access is to Biddle, which costs an I/O to bring the block into the buffer area. The next access is to Collins, which happens to be in the same block as Biddle, so no I/O is required. The next access is to Jones, which is in block 53, so an I/O is required. The next access is to Jones in block 12, and another I/O is required. The next access is to Liu, and another I/O is required, and so forth. Unless there is a fortuitous occurrence of finding data in the buffer, one I/O will be required for every alternate index entry followed from the index into the primary data base. From the standpoint of I/O, then, it is very expensive to process lengthy amounts of data in other than its primary order.

However, there are other performance considerations for alternate indexes. Consider what happens when the field an alternate index is based on undergoes change, as seen in Fig. 3.38. In this case the record in block 31, offset 2, is an employee of Coopers and Lybrand, and the alternate index reflects this fact. But one day the employee decided to become an independent. Since the record is in other than employee-company order, only a change of company name from Coopers and Lybrand to independent is required in the data base. This change requires a minimum of I/O. But in the index, the old entry—for Coopers and Lybrand—must be

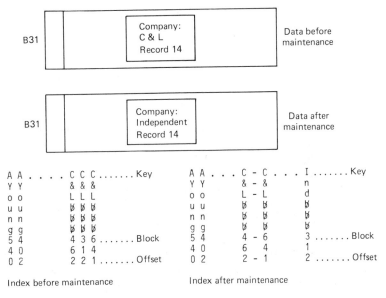

Figure 3.38

deleted and a new entry must be made for independent. At the very least this re-quires reordering of data. Usually it requires I/O to several blocks to maintain the index values properly.

INDEXING RANDOMIZED DATA

Although infrequently done, it is possible to index (alternately) a randomized data base. In such a case the data base records are randomly organized according to their key values in the normal fashion already discussed. Then, as the records are loaded en masse or inserted one at a time into the data base, one or more alternate indexes are created. As in the case of all alternate indexes, used improperly, alternate indexes can cause much unnecessary I/O. The proper design option is an indexed random-ized data base when there is much direct entry into the data base using the ran-domizer or alternate index and an absolute minimum of sequential access by means of the alternate index thereafter.

SUMMARY

There are two primary ways data is retrieved in a direct online fashion, by a *ran-domizer* and by an *index*. A randomizer is a piece of code that calculates an address based upon the key of the record. The record is placed in the address if there is no data already there. If data already exists in the location to which the data is ran-domized, another location is selection and a pointer is created to that location. Such a randomization to the same address is called a collision. The important factors affecting effective randomization are the total amount of DASD space, record size, the number of records to be inserted into the data base, physical block size, and the spread of keys. When an entire record cannot fit into a physical block or when a collision occurs, other storage, called overflow, is used.

In general, the more uniform the record size, the better the fit with physical blocks. Indexing involves the use of more I/O than randomization in that a direct retrieval to an index record requires calls to a physical index and the block in which the record is located. The index normally points to a block and an address from the beginning of the block, or use is made of a block prefix in which offset addresses are maintained.

Different levels of indexes can be created (i.e., an index of an index can be created to speed the search of the index). Deletion of an index usually requires only an index and offset deletion, not an actual physical record deletion. Variations on indexes include hashed indexes or sparse indexes. And finally, alternate indexes can be made on any data field, but access by alternate index should be limited because of performance reasons. Massive sequential access to data by means of an alternate index is a very expensive activity (in terms of I/O).

QUESTIONS

Randomizer

1.1. Create a randomizer for the names in the phone book. Minimize collisions but use space carefully.

1.2. What are the factors that determine successful randomization?

1.3. Under what conditions should data be randomized? not randomized?

1.4. Trace the steps in going from a key to an address as the randomizer is used?

1.5. What happens to data that has been randomized when the basic algorithm changes? the physical block changes? the number of records per block changes? the total space to which randomization occurs changes?

1.6. How can it be determined how much of a randomized data base is in overflow?

1.7. Who makes the determination whether a data base has too much data in overflow?

1.8. How much space should be left slack in a randomized data base?

Indexing

2.1. How much space should be left in an indexed data base?

2.2. When a collision occurs, what choices does the designer of the data management facilities have?

2.3. What is an index?

2.4. What are the differences between an index and a randomizer?

2.5. When should an index be used, as opposed to a randomizer?

2.6. When should both an index and a randomizer be specified?

2.7. When should a randomizer be used, as opposed to an index?

2.8. Trace the activities from the moment a key is located until the address is located in using an index. Point out where all the I/O occur.

2.9. When should an index be preloaded into main storage?

2.10. What is an alternate index?

2.11. Can any field be indexed alternately?

2.12. Under what circumstances should a field be alternately indexed?

2.13. Under what circumstances should an alternate index not be specified?

2.14. How much space does an index require?

2.15. Identify five different indexing techniques for translating a key into an address.

2.16. Can an index ever point to data that has collided? Should it?

2.17. When should an index be unique? nonunique?

2.18. How important is the decision whether to make a data base indexed or randomized?

2.19. Should data that is highly volatile be indexed?

2.20. Who should make the basic decision of indexing or randomization?

2.21. Once a system has been built, how easy is it to change the decision of indexing or randomization?

EXERCISES

1. Write a randomizing routine that accepts key values from 000 to 999, which randomize into 40 different physical locations. Now alter the algorithm to accept alphabetic as well as numeric input. Make sure the algorithm spreads the data evenly to different locations.

2. Write a randomizer such that additional record locations can be added to the data base after the data base has been initially loaded. What conventions must be adopted?

3. Obtain a copy of the code for a standard randomizer for your DBMS. Trace the logic through for the randomization of a variety of keys. Determine how your randomizer handles collisions. Change your randomizer to point all records to a single location (admittedly a silly thing to do). Suggest how the speed of execution of the randomizer might be improved.

4. Pick a common data base record in your DBMS. Determine its actual physical location.

5. Where is overflow in your DBMS? What code exists to manage overflow? How much data can be put into overflow? What happens when overflow is full and there is an attempt to add more data?

6. What tools do you have to determine how many collisions have occurred for a data base in your shop? What can you do to avoid future collisions?

7. Describe all the components of a simple index for a DBMS in your shop. Repeat for a sparse index and a super index. Give simple examples of each. When is each type of index appropriate? inappropriate? Can indexes be stored in main memory? When should they *not* be stored there?

8. Dump the contents of an indexed data base. Find the keys in the index. Find the pointers to data.

9. In terms of I/O consumed, describe a method for determining when it is cheaper to scan an index, using the index to look into every record that has been indexed, than it is to dump the entire data base and then sort it into the desired order. Are there other considerations than total I/O consumed? If so, what are they?

CHAPTER 4

Data Structuring

While the storage of data determines much about how it is best used, there are other measures of the usefulness of data. One of those measures is in how the data is structured. The **structure** of the data refers to the view the programmer or user has of the data as the data is inserted, retrieved, or deleted from the system. Of course, the structure of the data is ultimately embodied at the basic physical level, as has been discussed in earlier chapters. This means that at a lower level, data structures, however they are presented, consist of records, blocks, addresses, etc.

To illustrate the usefulness of a data structure, consider a simple relationship of data, as shown by Fig. 4.1. In this figure a part number and a supplier are shown to be related. There are several ways this relationship may be depicted. One way is for the relationship to exist from the part to supplier (or a $1 : n$ relationship). In this case, given a part number, the suppliers of the part number can be determined. Another form of the relationship is from the supplier's view (another $1 : n$ relationship). What parts does a supplier furnish? Still a third view combines both the part and supplier view, so that the relationship may be viewed from either perspective (an $m : n$ relationship). The part/supplier relationship can be described in at least four ways: hierarchically, inverted, networked and relationally. To make better use of the part/supplier relationship, more detail needs to be added to the relationship, as seen in Fig. 4.2.

Figure 4.1

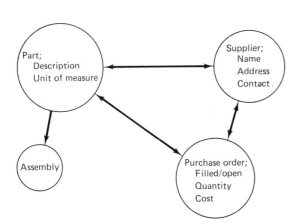

Figure 4.2 The entity part has data attributes of description and unit of measure. Where one or more assemblies exist that produce the part, a relationship is made. The entity purchase order is listed by reference number. Each supplier contains name, address, and individual contact. The purchase order exists as a result of a part being ordered. Once the order is placed, the entity purchase order exists. Once the order is filled, the supplier changes the filled/open data attribute from an *O* to an *F*. All the purchase orders for a part as well as the supplier for each of the orders can be accessed. All the purchase orders that are being serviced by a supplier as well as the part data for each order can be accessed. The relationship between part and supplier can also be accessed from either part or supplier.

HIERARCHICAL MODEL

The **hierarchical model** will be described in terms of *segments,* a term from IBM's IMS. A **segment** is a collection of data elements, one of which may be a key. To create the hierarchical model, two segments are defined—one for the part and one for the supplier. The key of the part segment is part number and the key of the supplier is supplier identification, as seen in Fig. 4.3.

Figure 4.3 Two segments, part and supplier, are defined and are keyed by their respective numbers.

This figure shows that in addition to the keys part number and supplier number, data elements are added to the segment. Now, the assembly is added to the part number, as seen by Fig. 4.4.

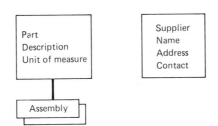

Figure 4.4

The only data in the assembly segment is an assembly number. There may be zero or more assembly numbers for a part. The assembly segment is called a **dependent segment** because the existence of the assembly segment depends on the existence of the part segment. If the part segment does not exist, there can be no assembly segment. But if a part segment exists, it may have zero, one, or multiple assembly segments. The part segment is referred to as the *parent,* and the assembly segment is the *child.* Next a segment must be defined for the purchase order. Since the purchase order can be accessed from *either* part or supplier, it is defined in two places, as a dependent of part and as a dependent of supplier, as seen in Fig. 4.5. In this figure the data exists twice, or is *physically paired,* so when retrieval is to be done, both part and supplier have their own data. Of course, when update (or insertion or deletion) is to be done, redundant activity will occur (both dependent segments must be updated when the data element filled/open changes, for example).

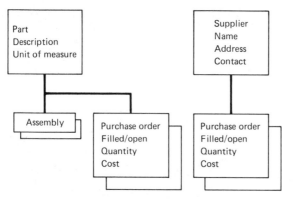

Figure 4.5

The final relationship to be fulfilled is the part/supplier relationship. Note that the part/supplier relationship is different and separate from the part/purchase-order/supplier relationship. For example, the fact that there is no part/purchase-order/supplier relationship does not imply that there is no part/supplier relationship. The fact that there are no purchase orders for part XYZ and Ace Hardware *does not mean* there is no part XYZ—Ace Hardware relationship. Ace Hardware may well be the sole supplier of part XYZ. The lack of existence of the relationship merely means that no XYZ parts are on order from Ace. Thus the hierarchical design as depicted by Fig. 4.5 satisfies the data relationships originally presented.

INVERTED DATA STRUCTURES

The first step in creating an **inverted data structure** from the part/supplier relationship as depicted in Figs. 4.1 and 4.2 is to create flat files for part and supplier, as shown by Fig. 4.6. In the case of flat files, all the parts and then all the suppliers are laid end to end, in order, one at a time onto a DASD (direct access storage device). The first occurrences of part, description, unit of measure is followed by the next occurrence, which is followed by the next, and so forth. The data is *flat-*

Part	Description	Unit of measure		Supplier	Name	Address	Contact

Figure 4.6   Inverted list flat files.

tened (i.e., reduced from a hierarchical structure to a flat file structure) as it is written out (in the sequence of the key). After it is laid out, indexes are created, as shown in Fig. 4.7. After the key indexes are created, nonkey (alternate) indexes are created. For each part number an index is created for unit of measure, as seen in Fig. 4.8. Next, a flat file is created for assembly. It contains part number as a key and assembly as data. The file can be used to go from part number to assembly. Then two indexes are created. The primary index is in part number order, as is the data. The alternate index is on assembly. Figure 4.9 illustrates this part of the inverted model.

Part	Description	Unit of measure		Part	Description	Unit of measure		Part	Description	Unit of measure
AAA	screw1	lb		AAC	screw2	lb		AAF	nut1	kg

Flat file

```
A A A A A A  . . . . . . . . . . Key
A A A A A A
A C F G M R              Index of a
1 1 0 0 4 9  . . . . . . . . . . Block     flat file
9 9 4 4 6 6
1 2 1 2 2 1  . . . . . . . . . . Offset
```

Figure 4.7

```
C C C . . . K K K . . . L L . . . T T T T . . . .  . . . . . . . . . . Key – U/M
A A A . . . I I I . . . B B . . . 0 0 0 0 . . . .
R R R . . . L L L . . . S S . . . N N N N . . . .
Ø Ø Ø . . . 0 0 0 . . . Ø Ø . . . Ø Ø Ø Ø . . . .
1 2 4 . . . 4 1 2 . . . 6 7 . . . 5 5 4 8 . . . .  . . . . . . . . . . Block
9 6 5 . . . 2 7 6 . . . 6 1 . . . 6 6 2 0 . . . .
1 4 3 . . . 2 1 1 . . . 4 3 . . . 4 3 6 2 . . . .  . . . . . . . . . . Offset
```

Figure 4.8

Part	Assembly	Part	Assembly	Part	Assembly	Part	Assembly	. . .
AAA	25102	AAG	46135	AAN	79110	AAP	25130	. . .

```
A A A A A A A  . . . . . . . . . . Key (part)      0 0 0 0 0 0 0 0  . . . . . . . . . . Key (assembly)
A A A A A B B                                       0 0 0 0 0 0 0 0
A G N P Q 1 4                                       1 1 1 1 1 1 1 1
1 1 2 2 4 4 1  . . . . . . . . . . Block            2 3 3 3 4 4 4 5
9 9 6 6 1 1 3                                       0 1 3 6 1 3 9 2
2 1 1 2 1 2 1  . . . . . . . . . . Offset           4 9 0 9 9 1 1 6  . . . . . . . . . . Block
                                                    6 9 3 7 7 4 9 3
Part index                                          1 2 1 6 4 3 4 2  . . . . . . . . . . Offset

                                                    Assembly index
```

Figure 4.9

Finally, the purchase order flat file is created. The file can be in part order or supplier order but not both at the same time. For the example shown, the records are in part number sequence, although a supplier index is to be created. In addition, other nonkey indexes—filled/open and amount—are created on the data elements as shown in Fig. 4.10. To implement the part/supplier relationship, two flat files are created that consist of part/supplier and supplier/part relationships. The only difference between the files is their physical sequence. Every entry in one file has a corresponding entry in the other file. Whenever an insert of part/supplier is done in one file, a corresponding insert of supplier/part is done in the other. The same parallel activity is done for deletes. In all, six flat files (and assorted indexes) are created, as shown by Fig. 4.11.

Part	Supplier	Purchase Order	F/O	Amount	Cost	
AAA	Ace	M24890	f	65610	231.00	Entry 1
AAD	G&K	JJ6511	f	21000	421.43	Entry 2
AAG	Ace	011246	o	41010	19.97	Entry 3
AAK	Ace	QD1142	o	3200	459.12	Entry 4
AB1	Smith	S11241	o	1800	19.81	Entry 5
ABA	G&K	F01611	f	69663	5616.07	Entry 6
ABC	Ace	JQR2	f	1266400	401.62	Entry 7
.	.	.	.	.	.	.
.	.	.	.	.	.	.

```
A A A A . . .  . . . . . . . . . . Key
A A A A . . .
A D G K . . .
0 0 6 6 . . .  . . . . . . . . . . Block
3 3 5 5 . . .
1 2 1 2 . . .  . . . . . . . . . . Offset

Part number index (primary)
```

```
A A A . . . G G . . . S S . . .  . . . . . . . . . . Key
c c c . . . & & . . . m m . . .
e e e . . . K K . . . i i . . .
Ø Ø Ø . . . Ø Ø . . . t t . . .
Ø Ø Ø . . . Ø Ø . . . h h . . .
6 7 0 . . . 4 4 . . . 6 4 . . .  . . . . . . . . . . Block
9 1 3 . . . 3 9 . . . 7 1 . . .
1 3 2 . . . 4 1 . . . 3 2 . . .  . . . . . . . . . . Offset

Supplier index (alternate)
```

```
f f f f . . . o o o . . .  . . . . . . . . . . Key
2 1 6 7 . . . 1 1 2 . . .  . . . . . . . . . . Block
6 3 9 2 . . . 3 9 6 . . .
1 4 5 2 . . . 3 2 2 . . .  . . . . . . . . . . Offset

Filled/open index (alternate)
```

```
0 0 0 0 0 0 0 0 0 0 0 0 0 0  . . . . . . . . . . Key
0 0 0 0 0 0 0 0 0 0 0 0 0 0
0 0 0 0 0 0 0 0 0 0 0 0 0 0
0 0 0 0 0 1 1 1 1 1 1 1 1 1
0 1 1 1 1 1 1 3 5 5 5 6 6
1 0 0 1 1 0 2 2 4 8 9 2 4
0 2 3 0 4 2 3 5 5 1 0 3 2
1 4 2 6 7 4 7 9 0 3 4 5 1  . . . . . . . . . . Block
2 4 5 4 7 8 9 2 5 8 1 0 8
1 2 5 5 3 6 2 5 3 5 4 5 1  . . . . . . . . . . Offset

Amount index (alternate)
```

Figure 4.10 The physical layout of a parts data base with three alternate indexes. The primary index is keyed on part number. There is a filled/open index that is keyed on the filled/open field. There is another alternate index on supplier, which is keyed on the supplier field. The last alternate index is keyed on amount.

Part	Description	Unit of measure		Supplier	Name	Address	Contact		Part	Assembly

Part	Supplier		Purchase order	Filled/open	Amount	Cost		Supplier	Part

Figure 4.11 The inverted structure of part/supplier data.

NETWORK STRUCTURE

In order to create a network structure from the data relationships portrayed in Fig. 4.2, the first step is to create a part number and supplier schema. The schema is shown in Fig. 4.12. After the schemas are defined, the assembly is defined as a dependent of part, much as the relationship was defined hierarchically (see Fig. 4.13).

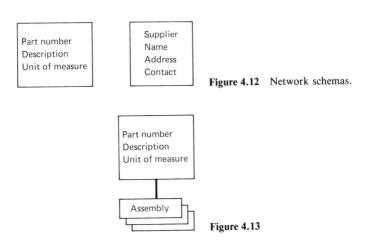

Figure 4.12 Network schemas.

Figure 4.13

There is one difference between the network and the hierarchical structure as far as an assembly is concerned. In the network environment, the last assembly within the assembly set points to the first, whereas in the hierarchical environment, the last assembly simply ends the chain. For example, suppose three assemblies, A214, A219, and A61, exist beneath part XYZ. The part data is accessed. Then assembly A214 is accessed. Next A219 and then A61 are accessed. In the network environment, A61 points back to A214, in the hierarchical environment, no such connection is made. The next step is the creation of the purchase order data. In terms of Cullinet's IDMS, such a record can be called a **junction record,** which is nothing more than a record that has two or more parents (i.e., the record is dependent for its existence on two records). There are several steps in the creation of a junction record. One step is to create the data of the junction record. Another step is to create the pointer to the appropriate supplier and another pointer to the appropriate part. Note that each purchase order has one and only one part and one and only one supplier with which it associates. At the same time, pointers from part data and supplier data must be built. Like a dependent segment, a part or supplier can have zero or more purchase order pointers. Also, for every purchase order there exists one pointer in the part schema and one pointer in the supplier schema. Figure 4.14 illustrates the basic definition of the network definitions of junction records. An actual implementation of junction records is shown by Fig. 4.15, where data elements (name, address, contacts, etc.) have been omitted to show the relationship between data. Unlike a dependent segment in the hierarchical model, a junction record has two (or more) parents.

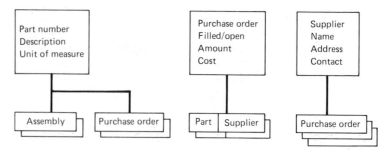

Figure 4.14

Finally, the part/supplier relationship is added to the network model. This relationship is added by means of pointers from part to supplier and supplier to part, in the same fashion as that found in the hierarchical environment. The basic form of the data is shown by Fig. 4.16. An implementation is shown by Fig. 4.17. In this case a part/supplier relationship is established, as well as a purchase order relationship. Note that only (application) program logic prevents a purchase order for part ABC to be established from ACE hardware. There is nothing in the DBMS preventing the creation of a purchase order segment when no part/supplier relationship exists.

THE RELATIONAL MODEL

The fourth type of structure to be analyzed is called the relational model. The **relational model** views data as a series of tables, much like the flat file presentation of the inverted file. To represent the data found in Fig. 4.2 relationally, the first step is to create tables based on part and supplier, as seen in Fig. 4.18. To create the part/assembly relationships, another table is created. The part/assembly table allows the part/assembly relationship to be made. Figure 4.19 illustrates the part/assembly table.

The creation of the purchase order table is done with the purchase order data and a **connector** (or common data) to back the part and supplier that belong to the purchase order. At a later moment in time when the connection between purchase order and part or purchase order and supplier is to be made, this data will be used to join the two tables. A **relational join** is the table that is created as a result of the intersection of the data in one table matched with the data in another table based upon some common field. The purchase order data is shown by Fig. 4.20.

Next, tables are created to allow the part/purchase order and the supplier/purchase order relationship to be made. These tables consist of nothing but connecting data, and one is shown in Fig. 4.21. Finally the $m : n$ part/supplier relationship is constructed by the creation of two tables, a part/supplier table and a supplier/part table, as shown in Fig. 4.22.

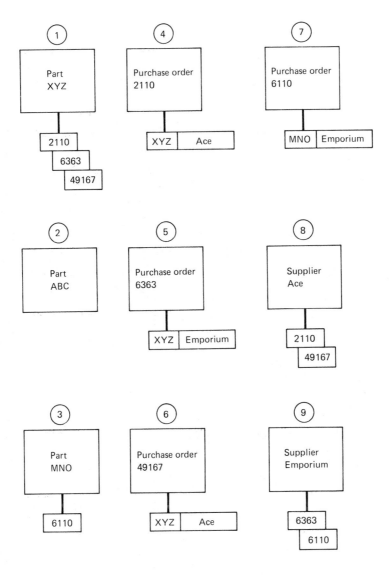

1. The purchase orders for part XYZ are 2110, 6363, and 49167.
2. Part ABC has no purchase orders.
3. Part MNO has one purchase order, 6110.
4. Purchase order 2110 is for part XYZ and is from Ace Hardware.
5. Purchase order 6363 is for part XYZ and is from Emporium Hardware.
6. Purchase order 49167 is for part XYZ and is from Ace Hardware.
7. Purchase order 6110 is for part MNO and is from Emporium Hardware.
8. Ace Hardware has purchase orders 2110 and 49167.
9. Emporium Hardware has purchase orders 6363 and 6110.

Figure 4.15

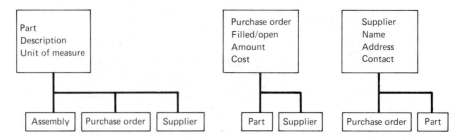

Figure 4.16

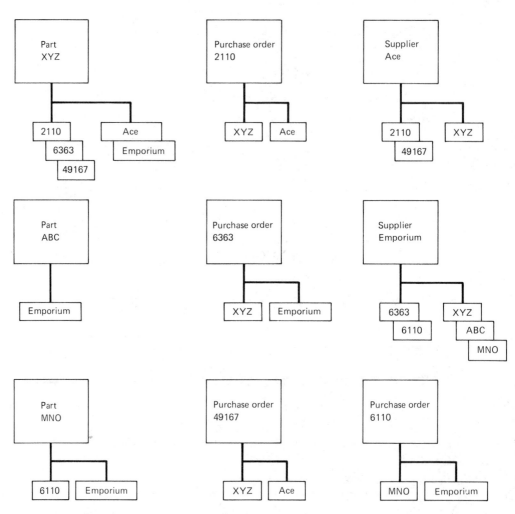

Figure 4.17 The junction relationship (purchase order) and the *m:n* nonjunction relationship (part-supplier).

Basic Concepts   Section I

Part	Description	Unit of Measure		Supplier	Name	Address	Contact
ABC	screw	lb		Ace	Ace Hd	James Rd	Ed Smith
MNO	nail	lb		Emp	Empor	121 1st	Wilson Picket
XYZ	nut	bins					

Figure 4.18

Part/Assembly

ABC/AJ2632
ABC/K14
ABC/K196
XYZ/M1413
.   .
.   .   **Figure 4.19**
.   .

Purchase Order	Part	Supplier	Filled/Open	Amount	Cost
2110	XYZ	Ace	O	16	$140
6110	MNO	Emporium	F	24	$136
6363	XYZ	Emporium	O	16	$210
49167	XYZ	Ace	O	1100	$6310

Figure 4.20

Part/Purchase Order		Supplier/Purchase Order	
MNO	6110	Ace	2110
XYZ	2110	Ace	49167
XYZ	6363	Emporium	6110
XYZ	49167	Emporium	6363

Figure 4.21

Part/Supplier		Supplier/Part	
ABC	Emporium	Ace	XYZ
MNO	Emporium	Emporium	ABC
XYZ	Ace	Emporium	MNO
XYZ	Emporium	Emporium	XYZ

Figure 4.22

In all, the data relationships shown in Fig. 4.2 have been created by a combination of flat tables and joining tables. The flat tables principally hold data, and the joined tables are used for joins and data. The data and data relationships shown in Fig. 4.2 can be structured in many ways. Each method of structuring shares certain similarities with the other methods but at the same time having distinctive characteristics. Interestingly, each method of structuring is capable of the same functional representation, with the difference lying at the implementation level. Lying beneath each type of structuring, in one form or another, are the familiar basic data management fundamentals of indexes, randomizers, overflow, records, and physical blocks.

ADDRESSING

The most fundamental aspect of locating data is in determining its address. Whether data resides in main storage or DASD, it is located at some unique address. The physical address is the most basic vehicle by which data is managed. In DASD, data is typically located at a device, a cylinder, a track, and an offset. In main memory, data is located at a fixed address or an offset from some location. In any case the addressibility of data is at the heart of being able to use a computer. Addressibility is achieved in two basic ways at the data base level, either *directly* or *symbolically*.

DIRECT ADDRESSING

Direct addressibility of data is achieved by the usage of an actual hard address. The location of the data is carried precisely as it is physically known throughout the system. The great advantage of direct addressibility is that it allows data to be located with an absolute minimum of overhead. No index, randomizer, or overflow is encountered when data is directly addressible. In that sense direct addressing is quite efficient. The disadvantage of direct addressibility is that if the location of the data needs to be changed, all pointers or direct references to the data must be changed. Such a change is usually awkward and inefficient to make. Figure 4.23 shows a set of data and pointers that are implemented directly. The data can be used to relate a part to the supplier's address very quickly. But if the key of a supplier is desired (or any other data, for that matter), the pointer must be followed to the supplier's location. In other words, even though a direct pointer is efficient in terms of directing the system where to go, *only* the direct address of the data is

Part/Supplier Address

```
ABC   d01 cy43 t18 of 03      (Note:  d = disk, cy = cylinder, t = track, of = offset)
MNO   d01 cy43 t17 of 05
XYZ   d26 cy13 t36 of 89
XYZ   d57 cy28 t51 of 25
```

Figure 4.23 Part/supplier relationship implemented with pointers (or direct addressing); the appearance of a direct address on DASD.

available, not any other information about the data. Furthermore, to locate the data, an I/O must be done when following a direct pointer.

SYMBOLIC ADDRESSING

The other major type of addressing found in the data base environment is **symbolic addressing.** In the case of symbolic addresses, the key of the data to which we are pointing is stored, not the address of the data. Using the hierarchical model as an example, Fig. 4.24 illustrates a symbolic pointer. To go from part to supplier using symbolic pointers requires converting the symbolic pointers to a physical address. This is done in the same fashion—through an index or a randomizer—as if an actual call had been made against the supplier data base. The mechanics of using a symbolic pointer that points into a randomized data base are illustrated by Fig. 4.25.

In this case one I/O is generated (the equivalent of a direct pointer). The only difference between using a direct pointer and using a symbolic pointer into a randomized data base is the overhead of going through the randomizer (and the possibility that the record in question has collided with another record). The advantage of a symbolic pointer into a randomized data base is that the data in the data base being pointed to can change locations independently of the symbolic pointers that point to it. For example, supplier ACE could be moved to location disk 13, cylinder

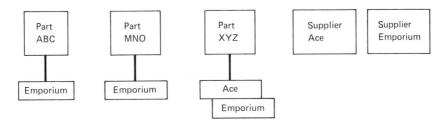

Figure 4.24   A hierarchical implementation of symbolic pointers.

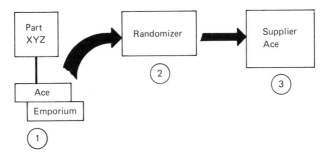

1. The Ace symbolic pointer is selected from part XYZ.
2. The key value Ace is fed to the randomizer and address d26 cy13 t01 of 03 is generated.
3. An I/O is done to the location generated by the randomizer.

Figure 4.25

21, track 13, offset 09, and as long as the randomizer knows where to find the data, the symbolic pointer need not be touched. In the case of direct pointers, whenever the direct pointer changes locations, *all* pointers to it must be reset. Another advantage of symbolic pointers is that if *only* the key information needs to be accessed, then there is no need to do I/O into the data base being pointed into. For example, if all that is needed is part/supplier information, then a simple scan of part ABC, supplier Emp; part MNO, supplier Emp; part XYZ, supplier Ace; and part XYZ, supplier Emp can be made. Since *all* the data exists in the same location, only the I/O used to scan the data is needed, not an I/O to each unit of data being pointed to.

The other use of symbolic pointers is to point into an indexed data base, not a randomized one. Such a case is shown by Fig. 4.26. Two I/O are required to point symbolically into an indexed data base, as opposed to one I/O to point symbolically into a randomized data base. When pointing symbolically into an indexed data base, more I/O is done than if direct pointers were used. However, data can be relocated in the indexed environment without an adjustment being made to the symbolic pointer.

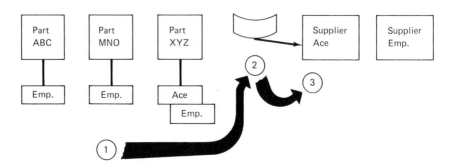

1. Part MNO is selected and the supplier —Emp— is found.
2. The key Emp is run through the index pointing into the supplier data base, the index generates the address — d01 cy43 t18 of 03 to find the supplier.
3. Location d01 cy43 t18 of 03 is located and the data is found.
4. Note that two I/Os were required: one to go against the index and one to go against the data base to actually find the data.

Figure 4.26

COMBINING SYMBOLIC AND DIRECT POINTERS

It is possible to combine both symbolic and direct pointers into the same addressing schema (although there is rarely a legitimate reason for doing so). Suppose the supplier data base were indexed and that on occasion there was a need to process the relationship at the key level only. Then it might be useful to specify both symbolic and direct pointers at the same time. Figure 4.27 illustrates such a case. The advantage of specifying both direct and symbolic pointers is that no I/O to the index will be done when crossing from the part to supplier data base, and that when only

CONTENT ADDRESSABLE MEMORY

Nearly all commercial processors use memory that is location addressable. **Location addressable memory** allows data to be stored and retrieved by a unique location—an address. One limitation of location addressable memory is that it must be processed serially. To determine the contents of the data that reside at the address, the processor goes from one location to the next, in some cases finding data that meet the search criteria and in other cases not finding data that meets the criteria. The serial processing of location addressable memory is one of the fundamental limitations of commercial processors. It is possible to have another kind of memory, **content addressable memory** (or **associative memory**). To date the commercial success of content addressable memory has been limited. **Content addressable memory** contains data that can be accessed by the content of the data, not the location of the data. The use of content addressable memory is best illustrated by an example. Suppose memory contains 100 records, as shown in Fig. CAM.1.

	Account No.	Amount	Date	Teller
Record 001	014690	231.43	03/01/82	JM
Record 002	296110	361.47	06/19/83	KT
Record 003	961163	35.22	06/29/83	JF
⋮	⋮	⋮	⋮	⋮
Record 100	671103	493.63	06/03/82	SH

Figure CAM.1 Main memory is loaded with 100 records.

Now suppose a search is to be done to locate all records whose account number lies between 751012 and 967103. The search is done on all records at once, since each record is content addressable. The results of the search are shown in Fig. CAM.2. Even though memory can be searched by content of data, with existing processors it must be serially processed—i.e., a record at a time. The great advantage of content addressable memory is that it allows searching to occur in parallel; all records are searched by content at once. The disadvantages of content addressable memory are that it normally utilizes serialized processing once the records are addressed and the cost of content addressable memory is very high.

	Account No.	Amount	Date	Teller
Record 003	961163	35.22	06/29/83	JF
Record 013	770112	493.63	10/23/83	CH
Record 046	841169	575.21	12/31/83	SF
Record 047	891163	966.69	11/14/83	CH
Record 053	936972	433.21	10/30/82	KJ

Figure CAM.2 Each of these records satisfies the search criteria. The records are located by a single machine instruction simultaneously.

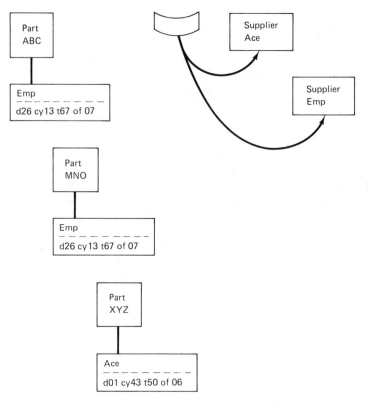

Figure 4.27 Both direct and symbolic pointers have been specified.

keys are needed, the part/supplier key is kept in the same location. However, the disadvantages are that the direct pointer needs to be reset whenever a supplier changes address and that the two pointers (the direct and the symbolic) require more space than if only one or the other pointer has been specified.

ADDRESS INSERTION, DELETION

Whenever symbolic or direct addresses are specified, care must be taken with their maintenance. Consider what happens when the relationship part MNO and supplier Ace Hardware is to be created, as seen in Fig. 4.28. To create the relationship sym-

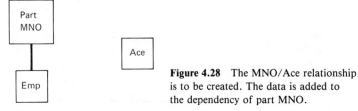

Figure 4.28 The MNO/Ace relationship is to be created. The data is added to the dependency of part MNO.

bolically requires an insertion into the part data base, which uses I/O. If the relationship is direct, the I/O to the part data base must be done in addition to I/O to the supplier data base to determine the location of the data (see Fig. 4.29).

However, deletion can cost even more I/O, depending on how many data bases address the segment being deleted. For example, suppose Emporium Hardware is to be deleted. Of course, no part/Emporium relationship can exist if Emporium does not exist. So all pointers to Emporium as well as Emporium itself must be deleted. Such activity can create much I/O.

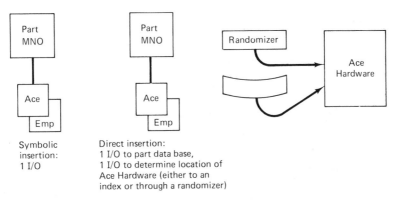

Symbolic
insertion:
1 I/O

Direct insertion:
1 I/O to part data base,
1 I/O to determine location of
Ace Hardware (either to an
index or through a randomizer)

Figure 4.29

HIGHER LEVEL STRUCTURING

So far data bases have been discussed at two levels: the physical level, where data existed in records and blocks on DASD, and at the systems level, where data had a basic structure, either hierarchic, inverted, network, or relational. But data bases have structure at an even higher level as well—the user level. The basic levels of data structuring are shown by Fig. 4.30. As an example of the user view of data, from the relational model, a view is defined is shown in Fig. 4.31. In this view data is drawn from two tables- the purchase order table and the supplier table. The two tables can be connected because of the existence of supplier key in both tables (see Fig. 4.32). The user looks at the data as if it were defined as the user sees it, not as it exists in the actual tables known to the system. To create any given tuple in the user view requires the merging of two tuples at the system level. The same sort of user structuring of data is applicable to the other forms of data; the user is able to view the data as the user desires, not as the data is actually constructed. However, to accommodate the user view requires behind-the-scene work by the system to present the data as the user wants it.

There are limitations, of course. The user is limited to the data that already exists at the system level. For instance, the user will not be able to include the receipt data for field purchase orders in the user view because the data does not exist in the system. If the user adds the data to the system, then it can be included.

Another limitation concerns the joining of data. Data can be joined only if

Physical level — blocks, records

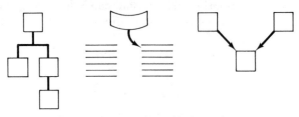

System level — hierarchic, inverted,
relational, network

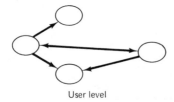

User level

Figure 4.30 The levels of data structuring.

Purchase Order	Filled/Open	Cost	Supplier Address	Supplier Contact
M24890	F	231.00	216 1st Street	Pete Zoll
JJ6511	O	421.00	Main & Broadway	Kathy Allan
O11246	O	10192.72	1st	Pete Zoll
QD1142	F	46002.91	1st	Pete Zoll
A11241	O	19.81	Williams Tower	Bob Smith
F01611	F	30.35	Main & Broadway	Kathy Allan
JQR2	O	401.62	216 1st	Pete Zoll

Figure 4.31 A user-defined view made up of composite tables that can be connected (or joined).

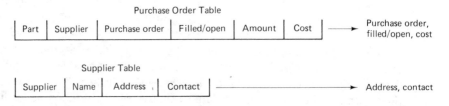

Purchase Order Table

| Part | Supplier | Purchase order | Filled/open | Amount | Cost | → | Purchase order, filled/open, cost |

Supplier Table

| Supplier | Name | Address | Contact | → | Address, contact |

Figure 4.32 The two tables are joined on supplier.

there is a common data field over which the join can be made. Throughout the discussion on levels of data structures, it must be kept in mind that however data is structured at the system level, it first exists at the physical level; however data is structured at the user level, it has an underlying structure at the system level. The implication is that the usefulness and power of data is a product of its embodiment at all three levels. If a data base environment is created with disregard for one or more of the levels, then it is unlikely that the resulting product will be satisfactory in the light of practical application.

ACCESSING DATA

The simplest way that data can be accessed is by physical block and record. In this case a position in the data base is attained and records and blocks are simply read sequentially. In Fig. 4.33 block *m,* record *n* is located, and sequential process begins there. Note that processing is very efficient. Depending upon the average number of records in a block, only a fraction of the number of I/O needed if the records had been scanned separately is necessary to scan the data. The reason is that once position in the data base is established, it is not necessary to use the index to do a physical scan. Only the physical blocks, one after the other, are scanned. A randomized data base can likewise be scanned with one difference, as shown in Fig. 4.34.

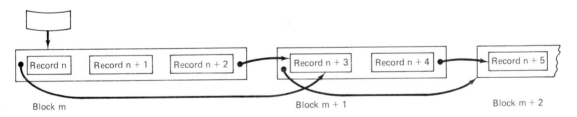

Block m   Block m + 1   Block m + 2

Figure 4.33 Records have their own sequencing, which is achieved by either physical juxtaposition or pointers. Blocks have their sequencing by means of pointers that exist in the block prefix area.

Figure 4.34 Even though there is a physical ordering of records, the ordering is random, i.e., nothing can be inferred about the sequence of the records in physically passing from one to the other. The physical sequencing is done by means of pointers from one record to the next.

As the scan proceeds from block to block and record to record, there is no order to the records. This means that the key of any one record may follow the key of any other record with no regard to key value. The data base is randomized, and a sequential scan of the records reflects that fact.

Another way that data can be scanned sequentially is by means of an alternate index, as previously discussed. Figure 4.35 shows such an index. However, if the extent of the scan involves more than a few records, the I/O involved is calamitous because each record being accessed is in a different location and requires its own I/O.

An interesting exception occurs in the case of inverted file systems. In the case of inverted files, the selection of records can be made by comparison of data within the index, so that when a record is accessed it is *known* to satisfy the selection requirements. To better illustrate the differences between inverted list index processing and other types of processing, consider the following problem. A user wishes to find all records for bank withdrawals between May 9, 1983, and June 12, 1983, that were for over $5000 and that were from noncommercial accounts. In a typical hierarchical environment, where an index exists to separate commercial and noncommercial accounts, a scan is done on noncommercial records only. But even then, each noncommercial record must be accessed to determine if a withdrawal of over $5000 was made and if it was made between the specified dates. All noncommercial records have to be scanned when only a fraction (perhaps only 5% or 10%) satisfy the request. Such activity is inefficient.

Now consider an inverted file that has an index on noncommercial accounts, data, and dollar values. All of the selection of records is done in the index. If only 5% of the withdrawals satisfy the criteria, then only 5% of the records are accessed. In this case inverted list processing is highly efficient. Of course, if an index did not exist on one of the fields being used as a search criteria, then inverted file processing is no worse than regular record selection.

Now consider random accesses to a data base. As has been stated, going through an index requires two I/O, one for the index and one for the data. Random retrieval requires one I/O by means of a trip through the randomizer and a search of the data. (*Note:* The case presented here is the simplest case. It assumes no index is moved to main storage and it assumes no data has collided as it was randomized.) Thus the difference between the indexed environment and the randomized environ-

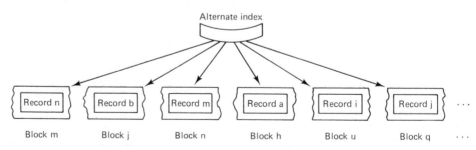

Figure 4.35 In general, each sequential entry in the alternate index points to a different physical location.

ment is a doubling of I/O—the indexed environment requires twice the I/O of the randomized environment. The significance of the difference is best illustrated by looking at the environments globally. For a single transaction, there is little or no difference between one and two I/O. But if there are many transactions, the differences mount. If a data base environment supports 1,000,000 direct access calls a day, then it makes a great deal of difference whether one or two I/O are done per call. If, on the other hand, a data base environment supports 100 direct access calls a day, then it probably does not matter at all how many I/O are being done.

IMPLIED ORDERING OF DATA
THROUGH PHYSICAL STRUCTURING

The structuring of data as presented to the programmer—hierarchical, network, or otherwise—is accomplished by a variety of techniques of arrangement of data at the physical level. Each technique has its own peculiar advantages and disadvantages. The trade-offs usually center around the issues of performance and flexibility.

Figure 4.36 shows a very simple form of physical data structuring to achieve an implied order. In this figure the **physical occurrence** of one record type implies an ordering of data. For example, reading the data from left to right, the key of the record on the left will always be less than or equal to the key of the record on the right. In other words, there is an implied order in moving from left to right as the records are physically stored. This type of ordering is what one might expect to find in a sequential tape file. To insert a record between existing records requires a great deal of movement of data, as many occurrences of data must be moved at one time. Since the physical order of data implies a logical ordering, much CPU is consumed by data management activities.

Figure 4.36 Physical juxtaposition of like occurrences of data imply an ordering. Much data manipulation occurs if an insert is made for a record such as Clark.

Figure 4.37 shows a similar but more complex case. In Fig. 4.37 **physical juxtaposition** is used to indicate ordering of data as well as ownership of data. All the family names (Adams, Akers, etc.) appear in order, but given names are (Bob, Mary, Susan, etc.) between family names. When a given name follows (i.e., comes to the

Figure 4.37 Physical juxtaposition of different types implies an ordering and ownership of data. For example, Mary belongs to Adams, as do Bob and Susan. The order of family names has an implication as well. Adams appears before Akers, which appears before Brown. Given names have an implied order as well. When inserts and deletes are made, much manipulation of data occurs.

right of) the family name, the implication is that the given name belongs to the family. For example, Bob, Mary, and Susan belong to the Adams family. Furthermore, physical juxtaposition is used to show the order of given names within a family. The problem with this kind of implied order is that much data management activity occurs when inserts are done. Much I/O is consumed when entire blocks of data must be rewritten. Furthermore, space may or may not be made available upon deletion of a record, depending upon algorithms and the size of the record to be inserted.

Thus physical juxtaposition uses space efficiently in that no overhead is required to imply an order or ownership of data. But tremendous amounts of CPU and I/O overhead are required for data management in the face of volatile data.

A third way to give data an implied order is through **pointers,** as seen in Fig. 4.38. Figure 4.38 shows the same data managed under a pointer scheme. Each record has an overhead area to indicate the address of related data, thus using more space than physical juxtapositioning. Each family record has a pointer that indicates where the next family record is (i.e., Adams points to Akers, which points to Brown, etc.). The family record also points to the first occurrence of a given name record (i.e., Adams points to Bob, Brown points to Abe, etc.). Each given name record points to other given names in the same family (i.e., Bob points to Mary, Mary points to Susan, etc.). The given name record is also shown as having is a parent pointer. Using this pointer Mary points directly to Adams. This means that the owner of Mary's record can be determined independently of any other pointer chain. Note that physical positioning means nothing—there is no implication of physical ordering of data.

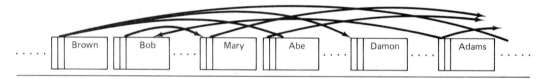

Figure 4.38 Pointers that are attached to each occurrence of data are used to create the implied ordering of data. The physical appearance of data means nothing. Family names point to family names in the logical order of occurrence. Family name points to the first occurrence of given name and the first given name points to the next given name to maintain that ordering of data.

Data management with pointers uses much less data management processing upon the occasion of an insert. When data is deleted, the space can be easily reused, assuming the inserted record will fit into the available space.

A fourth possibility for managing the implied order of data is shown by Fig. 4.39. Figure 4.39 shows that data occurrences are stored separately from each other and that data relationships are stored independently as well in a **relationship** data base. There is an implied order to the records as shown in each of the three data bases. However, to change a family/given name relationship requires only a change to the relationship data base.

Data management suffers from the same problems noted in Fig. 4.36. A con-

Basic Concepts   Section I

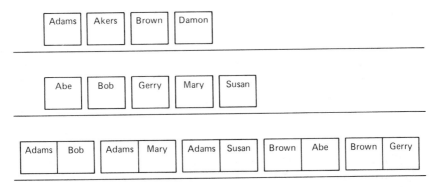

Figure 4.39 The data bases exist. One data base holds the family name in order of occurrence. One data base holds the given names in order of·occurrence. A *relationship* data base holds the data that ties a family name to a given name. The relationship data base is in physical order by family name.

venient way to circumvent some of the problems of data management is to introduce block prefix data, which allows the records to be placed randomly within the block (Fig. 4.40). Data can be inserted randomly within a block. The implied ordering of data is kept in the block prefix. As new data is inserted or as data is deleted, the block prefix is adjusted, but the data is not physically moved within the block. The relationship between family and given names is stored by means of a separate relationship data base. Even though data within the block does not move upon insertion or deletion, the indexes that point into the block must be adjusted as relative positioning of the records change.

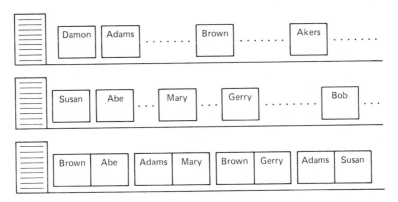

Figure 4.40 As in Fig. 4.39, data in this figure is stored separately by occurrence type, but there is no implication of data ordering based on physical juxtaposition. Instead, data is inserted randomly within a block (thus easing the data manipulation activity). The implied ordering of the data is stored in a block prefix area. Upon insertion, the block prefix is manipulated to keep the table of entries in sequence. Because there is only one size record in a block, space reusability is not a large issue.

SUMMARY

Data is structured at three levels, the physical, the system, and the user levels. At the physical level data exists in blocks and records. At the system level data can be structured in (at least) four ways: hierarchically, inverted file, network, and relationally. All four structures can support the same data and data relationships. At the user level, data is fashioned to the users needs and is supported by system data structuring. Two types of addressing are possible in a noncontent addressable machine, direct addressing and symbolic addressing. Each form of addressing has its own set of advantages and disadvantages. And finally, the issue of whether data is better defined randomly or indexed depends upon the global nature of the processing that is to occur.

QUESTIONS

Hierarchical Structures

1.1. What is a hierarchical structure?
1.2. Which DBMS support a hierarchical structure?
1.3. How many levels down into the hierarchy can the structure go?
1.4. How many different types of dependents can exist beneath a parent?
1.5. How many physical twins can exist for any occurrence of a dependent?
1.6. How is a hierarchical structure stored on DASD?

Prefix Data

2.1. What is a prefix?
2.2. What kinds of prefixes are there?
2.3. Can the programmer directly access prefix data?
2.4. Should the programmer access prefix data?

Inverted List Structures

3.1. What is an inverted list structure?
3.2. Describe a structure in terms of the names in the telephone book.
3.3. How does an inverted list differ from a hierarchical structure?
3.4. Describe the index of an inverted list structure.
3.5. What processing is more efficient: hierarchically than inverted? inverted than hierarchically?
3.6. Describe how an inverted list structure is placed on DASD.

Relational Structures

4.1. What is a relational structure?
4.2. How does a relational structure differ from a hierarchical structure? from an inverted structure?

4.3. How is a relational structure stored on DASD?

4.4. What can a relational structure be used for more efficiently than a hierarchical structure? an inverted structure?

4.5. How are relationships formed between data bases using a relational structure?

4.6. Must a relational structure be indexed?

4.7. Do all relational fields need to be indexed?

Addressing

5.1. What is symbolic addressing?

5.2. What is direct addressing?

5.3. How do the forms of addressing differ? How are they the same?

5.4. Which form of addressing is more efficient?

5.5. Which form of addressing is more flexible?

Content Addressable Memory

6.1. What is content addressable memory?

6.2. Why is content addressable memory not widely used?

6.3. How fast are searches in content addressable memory?

6.4. What happens when basic application changes need to be made to keyed data in the face of content addressable memory?

EXERCISES

1. For a bill of materials and for bank account activity, describe a suitable data structure using the hierarchical model, the relational model, the inverted model, and the network model.

2. How are keys described in your DBMS? How are they physically stored?

3. Part/supplier is usually an $m : n$ relationship. Draw simple structures (hierarchical, relational, inverted, and network) for the following pairs: screw/Ace, nut/Ace, bolt/Ace, ax/Ace, screw/Jones, nut/Jones, screw/Emporium, bolt/Emporium, hacksaw/Jones, blade/Ace, wheelbarrow/Jones, bolt/Wilson.

4. For the structures built in Exercise 3, define them with indexes. Now trace the I/O needed to access the different relationships. Next define the supplier data base as being randomized. Repeat the I/O analysis. Based on this exercise, is any one model more or less efficient with I/O? Why or why not?

5. For your DBMS, identify where direct or symbolic addressing is specified. Are both allowed? at the same time? When would you want to use both?

CHAPTER 5

Program Execution

In the mainframe data base environment, programs operate in one of three modes: *batch, online,* or *interactive.* Each mode has its own set of characteristics and its own set of advantages and disadvantages. The **batch** mode of operation is characterized by sequential processing, usually of entire data bases. The lengths of jobs run in the batch environment typically involve many I/O (input/output). There is usually little or no direct user interface with the system (i.e., the user normally does not use a CRT (cathode ray tube) to access the system in batch). Input is collected and at specified intervals—overnight, hourly, weekly, etc.—the input is transacted en masse against the data base. The term *batch* stems from the collecting and batching together of the input to be processed. The **turnaround time** (i.e., the length of time from the user's input submission until the user can see the results of the processing) is gauged in hours or sometimes days. The batch mode of processing optimizes the use of the computer, not the time of the user.

The **online** mode of operation is one where processing occurs in short bursts. The basic unit of processing in the online environment is called a **transaction.** In many respects an online transaction is similar to a batch program (they are both programmed, both do computation, both do data base calls, etc.), but there is an essential difference. Online transactions run for a very short amount of time and are absolutely stingy with I/O. Depending on the online environment and the applications being run, as few as 2 or 3 or as many as 15 or 20 I/O's are done by an online transaction. The result of limiting the I/O that a transaction can do is a consistently quick performing system. Online transactions do not do data base scans (unless of course there are only a very few records in the data base being scanned). The turnaround (or response) time for an online system is measured in seconds.

(*Note:* There are two standard measurements of response time, *internal* and *external* response times. **External response time** is that amount of time from when the user depresses the enter key until output is returned. **Internal response time** is measured from when the DBMS (data base management system) inside main memory receives the request until output is sent from main memory. Internal response time does not measure line time, i.e., the time spent going to and from the terminal and computer. An internal response time of 2 to 3 seconds would be disastrous, while an external response time of 2 to 3 seconds would be quite satisfactory for most shops. Unless otherwise stated, response time refers to external response time.) The user normally has access to the system by means of a CRT and so has direct access to the data. Whereas the batch mode involves a preponderance of sequential processing, the online mode is almost exclusively randomized, or direct access, processing. The online data base environment is very sensitive to the amount of I/O done. Most online systems are I/O-bound (i.e., the central processing unit (CPU) operates at less than full capacity while waiting for I/O to be completed).

The third environment is the *interactive time-sharing environment*. The **time-sharing environment** shares some of the characteristics of the online *and* the batch environment. The user can operate in the interactive environment by means of a CRT. The user can also initiate batch jobs to be run. The user can both selectively access data (as in the online environment) and run data base scans (as in the batch environment). The turnaround time in the interactive environment is a function of the work being processed. If the system is lightly loaded, a selective access of data (e.g., What is the balance in Ms. Jones' account?) can take a matter of seconds, as if the environment were online. But if the system is fully loaded with processes that scan one or more data bases (e.g., with many requests about the average balance in all accounts), then turnaround time may be in terms of hours. There is usually a peak processing period in interactive systems when *all* processing slows down considerably. Figure 5.1 illustrates the differences between the three environments from a queue and a machine perspective. The size of the processes running within the machine is measured primarily by the number of I/O's the process requires, although there are other important criteria, such as total memory required and CPU utilization.

BATCH PROGRAMS

Programs that operate in the batch data base environment are often written in COBOL or PL-1 (or a nonprocedural language). A typical batch update program will accept input (that has been batched) and will use the input as a basis for updating, analyzing, or manipulating a data base. Then the next update input record will be read and the processing continues for data base records accessed by the transaction. The batch update environment is shown by Fig. 5.2. The proceedings of the update are recorded in a report, which serves as a verification to the user that what has been transacted is, in fact, what the user wanted to be transacted. The updated data base is not available to the rest of the system while it is being updated, much as a tape master file is not available for access while it is being

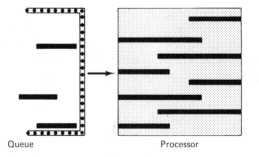

Online Environment:
Many small transactions in queue and in system. Turnaround: 2–3 seconds.

Queue   Processor

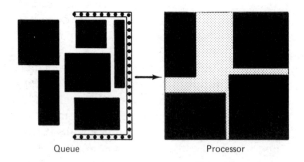

Batch Environment:
Many large programs in queue and in system. Turnaround: 2–12 hours, perhaps overnight.

Queue   Processor

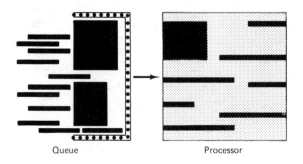

Interactive Environment:
Lightly loaded; a mixture of long and short running jobs in system. When lightly loaded response time varies greatly, from 2–3 seconds to 30 minutes or more.

Queue   Processor

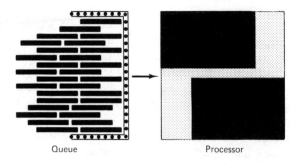

Interactive Environment:
Heavily loaded; a mixture of long and short running jobs in the system. Queue time, especially for short running jobs, becomes a major factor. In this case turnaround may be from 30 minutes to 12 hours.

Queue   Processor

Figure 5.1

Basic Concepts   Section I

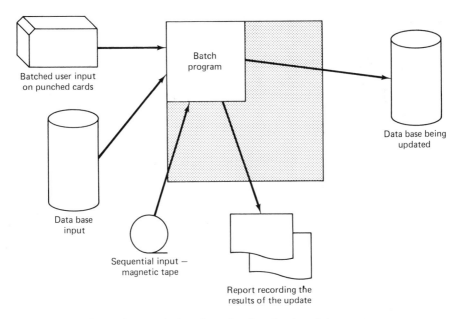

Figure 5.2 Typical configuration for a batch update program.

updated. Another common form of a batch data base program is the data base scan and report. A simple form of a scan and report program is one that starts at the first of the data base, strips records (either all records or selected records), and produces a report. In some cases the records are reported in the same order as they occur; in other cases the records are sorted after they are stripped and reported in a new sequence. Figure 5.3 illustrates the configuration of a simple scan and report

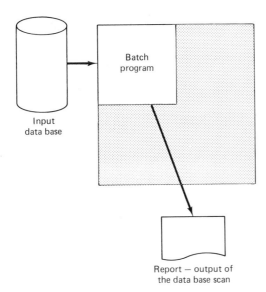

Report — output of
the data base scan

Figure 5.3 A simple batch data base scan and report.

program. Now consider the program that is written. (The following roughly approximates the flow of a program. Precise COBOL, PL-1 or other syntax is not intended or necessary.) Figure 5.4 shows a simple skeleton of a program. To understand what really happens as the batch program is run requires an outline of the underlying system activity that occurs as a result of the program execution. The first step in unmasking the underlying activity is to view the configuration in which the program runs, as seen by Fig. 5.5.

```
Initialize
Do Until End of Records
    Get Record
    If.....
    Then.....
    Else.....
    Add.....
    Subtract.....
    Write Report Record
```

Figure 5.4 The skeleton of a simple report program. Records are read sequentially and written onto a report.

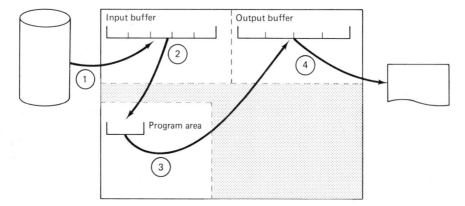

1. Data blocks are organized sequentially. There are five records to a block.
2. The buffer holds one blocks worth of data. The appropriate record is fetched from the input buffer area into the program work area to satisfy the data base call.
3. The program work area holds one record's worth of data. Upon the condition of writing an output record, data is sent from the program area to the output buffer.
4. The output buffer holds four records' worth of data, which is written onto a report.

(*Note:* These sizes are for the purpose of an example only. In actual practice there are usually many more buffers, with blocks and record sizes that are much larger.)

Figure 5.5

Now consider the execution of the program, as portrayed by Fig. 5.6. Four types of activity are of interest: the code that is executed, the activity of the machine, the I/O that is done, and the speed of execution. The first thing that becomes apparent is that electronic (i.e., nanosecond) speeds are achieved throughout the program execution except during I/O (which occurs at mechanical, or millisecond, speeds). The second observation is that I/O is done only on every third call on input and every second call on output. The frequency of I/O depends on two things—

Basic Concepts   Section I

Program Code	Machine Activity	I/O	Speed
Initialize	Data variables initialized, files opened.	Yes	e
Get Record	Buffer searched, data not in buffer.	–	e
	Block located on DASD.	Yes	m
	Block fetched into buffer.	–	e
	Record in buffer located.	–	e
	Record shipped to program work area.	–	e
If.....	Program logic.	–	e
Then.....	Program logic.	–	e
Else.....	Program logic.	–	e
Add.....	Program logic.	–	e
Subtract.....	Program logic.	–	e
Write Report	First output buffer loaded.	–	e
Get Record	Buffer searched, data found in buffer.	–	e
	Record shipped to program work area.	–	e
If.....	Program logic.	–	e
Then.....	Program logic.	–	e
Else.....	Program logic.	–	e
Add.....	Program logic.	–	e
Subtract.....	Program logic.	–	e
Write Report	Second output buffer loaded.	–	e
Get Record	Buffer searched, data found in buffer.	–	e
	Record shipped to program work area.	–	e
If.....	Program logic.	–	e
Then.....	Program logic.	–	e
Else.....	Program logic.	–	e
Add.....	Program logic.	–	e
Subtract.....	Program logic.	–	e
Write Report	Record sent to output buffer, buffer full.	–	e
	Write output block.	Yes	m
	Load first output buffer.	–	e
Get Record	Buffer searched, not in buffer.	–	e
	Block located on DASD.	Yes	m
	Block fetched into buffer.	–	e
	Record in buffer located.	–	e
	Record shipped to to program work area.	–	e
If.....	Program logic.	–	e
Then.....	Program logic.	–	e
Else.....	Program logic.	–	e
Add.....	Program logic.	–	e
Subtract.....	Program logic.	–	e
Write Report	Second output buffer loaded	–	e

Figure 5.6 Program execution for (1) an input buffer area that holds three records; (2) an output buffer area that holds two records. (*Note:* e = electronic, m = mechanical speed.)

the number of records a block can hold and the dependency on the buffer not to be flushed. The third observation is that even though the programmer assumes the program executes at an even pace, in fact it does not. (However the pace of execution is not a factor in the logic executed by the program.)

In some cases flow goes quickly from one of the programmer's instructions to the next, and in other cases flow is actually impeded rather severely, although this impediment has no impact on the validity of the code written by the programmer. Another assumption is that the program has control of the data base. For the report to be correct, other programs should not be able to alter the data base while the report is being generated. And finally, there are two levels of data structuring that are occurring. As the data is physically read, the DBMS accesses it in its most primitive form, at the raw physical level. Then, as the data is transcribed from the buffer to the program work area, the system level of structuring is imposed on the data and presented to the program accordingly.

There are other uses of the DBMS than the purely sequential mode in batch processing. Data can be accessed in what can be termed the *skip sequential* mode. The **skip sequential mode** occurs when data is accessed randomly to some point (e.g., the record for Amy Jones). Then, once the record is located, sequential processing is done (e.g., for the records for Ann Jones, Arthur Jones, Ashley Jones, Bill Jones, Bob Jones, and Carrie Jones). After processing a number of records sequentially, another random skip is done (e.g., to the record for Mary Landers). By the same token, data *can* be accessed randomly in the batch data base mode, even though data is sequentially accessed most of the time.

ONLINE EXECUTION OF A PROGRAM

Most of the concepts that apply to a batch execution of a program also apply to online program execution. When data is read, it is read into a buffer area and is read in blocks. The record is stripped out of the block and presented to the program's work area. Records are buffered and blocked upon output. If a record already exists in the buffer area, it is not reread, and so forth. But the online environment involves another set of considerations as well. It is not desirable for an entire data base to be locked up when being operated on by an online program. This is true for several reasons. One reason is that the online program most likely will be interested only in a very small part of the data base—a few records at most. But the most important reason is that if the entire data base were locked up, as is the practice in batch, then other programs would not be able to get to the data base at the same time, thereby greatly increasing the amount of time it takes to make the program execute. So in the online environment, data lockup occurs at the lowest level possible—at the record or even the system-structuring level—thereby allowing as many programs as possible to get to as much data as possible in the data bases. But the control of which program is accessing which records (and when is the program finished) requires that all online programs be under a centralized control. Such a control program is called (not surprisingly) an **online controller.** The online environment is depicted by Fig. 5.7. Programs share common buffers, both input and output. The terminal activity is also controlled by the online controller. Consider now the amount of activity that must occur to achieve 2 to 3 second response time (i.e., 2 to 3 seconds for external response time). For the simple program flow, as shown in Fig. 5.8, there is a remarkable amount of activity, as shown in Fig. 5.9.

The program execution is very similar to that of batch, with the following exceptions. The input comes from a terminal and is received by the online controller. The read and write activity is done from a buffer area that is shared with *all* other online programs. While the online controller is managing a data base, no other processing can be done against the data base. For the activity that is being con-

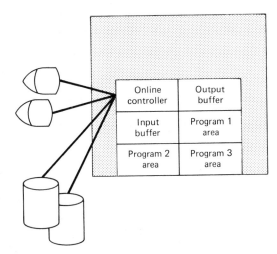

Figure 5.7 Configuration of a typical online program environment.

```
Initialize
Get Record
If.....
Then.....
Else.....
Add.....
Subtract.....
Write Record
End of Program
```

Figure 5.8 Simple program flow for an online transaction.

Program Code	Machine Activity	I/O	Speed
	Operator depresses enter button at terminal.	–	e
	Transaction is shipped down the line.	–	e
	Transaction is received at the host.	–	e
	Once scheduled, transaction is dequeued and is sent into execution.	Yes	m
Initialize	Program logic.	–	e
Get Record	Buffer is searched, record not in buffer.	–	e
	Block is located.	Yes	m
	Block is fetched into buffer.	–	e
	Record in buffer is located.	–	e
	Record is protected by controller (integrity).	–	e
	Record is shipped to program work area.	–	e
If.....	Program logic.	–	e
Then.....	Program logic.	–	e
Else.....	Program logic.	–	e
Add.....	Program logic.	–	e
Subtract.....	Program logic.	–	e
Write Record	Record is sent to output buffer.	–	e
End of Program	Protected records are released by controller.	–	e
	Input buffer is freed.	–	e
	Output buffer is written.	Yes	m
	Transaction reply is shipped up the line.	Yes	m
	Transaction is received at the terminal and is available for display at operator's request.	Yes	m

Figure 5.9 The anatomy of online execution of a transaction.

Chap. 5   Program Execution

trolled, the online controller protects records from being used and updated concurrently by two or more programs. Part of the online controller function is to ensure that the system is able to be restored in the eventuality of a breakdown. Looking at Fig. 5.9, it is a wonder that response time in the 2- to 3-second range is even possible. There are basically three components that are of interest in achieving consistent high response time:

— Line time
— Queue time
— I/O time

Line time is the amount of time a transaction spends in traversing to and from the terminal to the processor. **Queue time** occurs as the transactions arrive at the processor and wait to enter into execution. When transactions arrive faster than the processor can handle them, they are queued. When queuing occurs, response time can grow drastically. Furthermore, if transactions are arriving too quickly, there is little the designer can do. The issue becomes one of capacity, not design, at this point. Finally, **I/O** are the number of physical I/O generated by the program once into execution. Any of these three factors can prevent adequate external response time from occurring.

INTERACTIVE PROGRAM EXECUTION

The third common data base environment is the **interactive environment.** The interactive environment shares many characteristics with both the batch and the online environments. A typical flow of events is shown by Fig. 5.10. A terminal may either be on or off the system, and it is the terminal operation that controls that aspect of the system. Also observe that when the terminal is under the control of the terminal operation space, the system appears to be an online system, except that no data bases are allocated automatically to the terminal operating space. The other point in time at which the system appears to be online is when a data base is allocated. Then the terminal has access to the data base as if the terminal were online. However, note that only *one* terminal can own a data base at any one point in time (assuming full integrity under update processing), so only one terminal can appear to be online at once, as far as any given data base is concerned. The nature of programs that run in the interactive environment can be anything from a single record update to multiple data base scans. Also note that the terminal that initiates an interactive program may or may not have to be signed onto the interactive controller for the program to run. Indeed, in some interactive systems, a user at a terminal can log on, initiate a program, and sign off without ever allocating the data base the program is to run on. In this case the program that has been initiated will be queued and will be run when there are available machine resources to which the data bases that the program needs to use can be allocated.

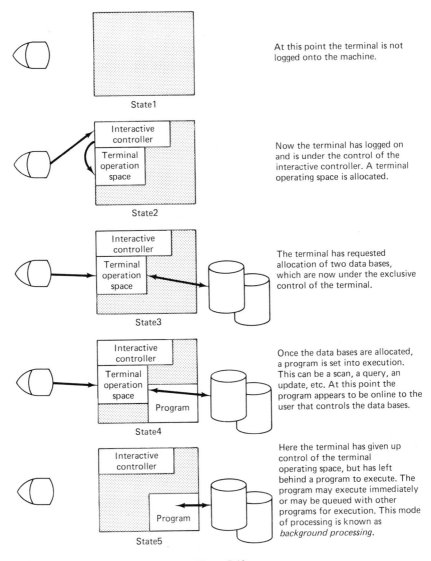

At this point the terminal is not logged onto the machine.

State1

Now the terminal has logged on and is under the control of the interactive controller. A terminal operating space is allocated.

State2

The terminal has requested allocation of two data bases, which are now under the exclusive control of the terminal.

State3

Once the data bases are allocated, a program is set into execution. This can be a scan, a query, an update, etc. At this point the program appears to be online to the user that controls the data bases.

State4

Here the terminal has given up control of the terminal operating space, but has left behind a program to execute. The program may execute immediately or may be queued with other programs for execution. This mode of processing is known as *background processing*.

State5

Figure 5.10

DATA BASE AND TELEPROCESSING

The first step in understanding data base is to envision the inner workings of the DBMS as manipulated by an application program—how it locates data, stores data, how it manages data. But data management and program execution constitute only one aspect of the data base environment. Another important aspect of the environment is the method by which an end user views the data. In the batch mode the end user normally views reports, which are the output of long-running batch programs. While there is nothing wrong with reports, at best reports represent the status of data only up to some moment in time. After that the report may or may not be accurate. Also, reports are typically bulky and hard to manage. The distribution of reports is another less-than-ideal aspect.

A much more effective way for users to view their data is through a CRT (i.e., a terminal, video display unit, etc.). While there are many variations on the mechanics of allowing a user direct access to data, the three most common ways— online, interactive, and microprocessor—will be discussed.

ONLINE USAGE OF CRT

The typical path to data from a terminal in the online mode begins at the terminal, where a user enters a request to access and/or change data. The request is called a **transaction** in the online mode. As the user enters data on the CRT, the input from the user is collected in the CRT in a buffer area. Figure 5.11 illustrates the initial

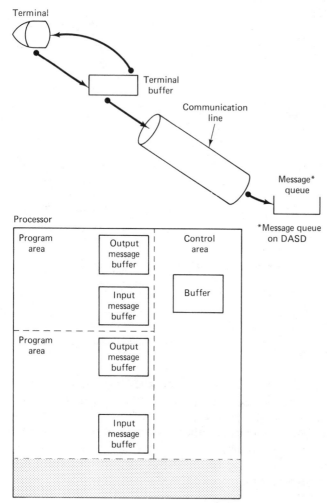

Figure 5.11 At this point, the input message has gone through editing at the terminal and has passed to the message queue.

Basic Concepts   Section I

activities of the transaction. The buffer for the terminal is finally fully loaded, and the user depresses the ENTER or RETURN key to signal to the system that the buffer is ready for transmittal. At this point one of two actions occur. If the terminal is a "smart" terminal, a certain amount of editing of the data in the buffer will occur. Usually the editing is fairly superficial. If sex were entered as x instead of m or f or if age were entered as -31, then the terminal editor would return the screen to the user for correction.

If the terminal is not a smart terminal or if the smart terminal has successfully edited the data in the buffer, then the data in the buffer may be compacted before transmission. **Compaction** insures that a minimum of data is sent down the line. Once compacted, the data (sometimes called a *message*) enters the network and flows across the lines, arriving at the processor in a place called the *message queue*. The **message queue** is the place where all incoming messages are collected (on DASD) prior to execution in the system.

After arriving in the message queue, the transaction signals its arrival to the control area (Fig. 5.12). The name of the transaction, the sender, and the time of arrival are all typical pertinent information that is sent to the control area. Based upon the particulars of a given transaction and what other transactions are in the system and sharing the message queue, the arriving transaction is prioritized and is scheduled for execution. When it comes time for the transaction to go into execution, the message is sent to a buffer in the program area. The arrival of the input message is logged. The executable machine code of the program must either be brought in from DASD, or the code needs to have been preloaded into the program area. Systems optimized on rapid performance usually have the executable machine code preloaded into the program area. After the message is loaded into the input message buffer, any initialization of the program area that is needed must now occur.

Now the programmer's code goes into execution, driven by the message entered by the user at the terminal (Fig. 5.13). Note that a data base call goes to the control area, and from the control area the call is actually executed against the data base. Once the call is made, the data (or other output of the call) is passed to the control area, and from the control area it is passed to the program area. The handling of data base calls through the control area represents the means by which multiple users can use the same data base at the same time. It is the responsibility of the control area to assure data integrity across all online users.

As updates are made against a data base, the update activity is stored in a special buffer. Once the transaction terminates, the buffer is written to a log (either on tape or DASD) indicating a successful update. If the update processing is not successful, the contents of the buffer are used to determine the data base activity that must be backed out. After the program is through doing its data base activity and doing whatever other calculations and manipulations are required, the output of the transaction is ready to be sent out of the program area. The output is collected in an output message buffer in the program area (Fig. 5.14). Once the transaction is complete, the output is shipped to a general-purpose output buffer in the control area. Other output is collected there until it is time to do a physical write.

Note that the flow depicted shows a single output message being shipped back

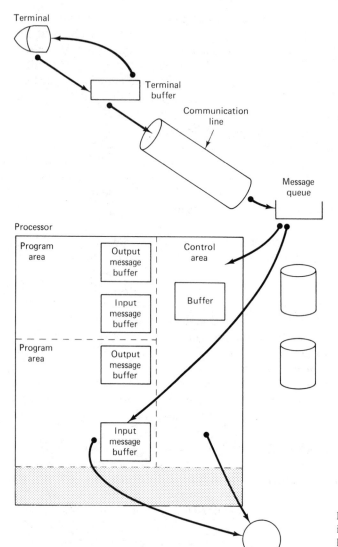

Figure 5.12 The message has signaled its appearance to the control area and has been scheduled. It has been loaded into the program area.

to the originating terminal, which is a common event. However, more than one output message may be sent, and the destination may be other than the originating terminal. When the output in the general-purpose output buffer is ready to be written, the output is written and shipped up the line. Once into the communication line, the output message is received at the terminal's buffer (Fig. 5.15). The message is decompacted and formatted and is then displayed to the user. The sequence discussed has depicted many of the important features of a typical online flow. Many technical details have been omitted to avoid interrupting the flow of the discussion. The architecture inside the processor described is only one such possibility, although

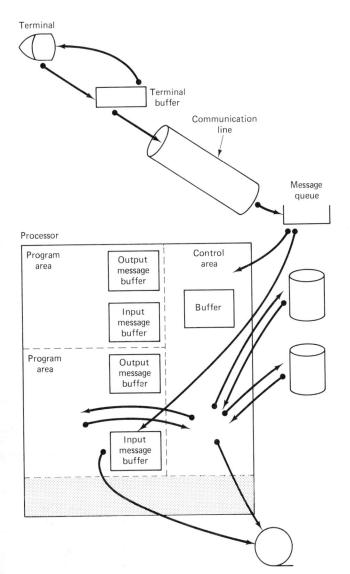

Figure 5.13 Now the transaction is in execution. It is doing data base calls through the control area. The output message is being built in the output message area.

its functions, in one form or another, represent most online architectures. However, it is not meant to specifically portray any particular architecture.

More than one terminal is able to use the online facilities, as shown by Fig. 5.16. The terminals share all the same common facilities except, of course, for the terminal itself. Data, communication lines, buffers, and message queues are all commonly shared resources. Bottlenecks may occur in many places, given the number of facilities shared. Typical bottlenecks include the message queue (when the transaction arrival rate exceeds the amount the system is able to handle or when the control area is being inundated by long-running transactions that use much I/O).

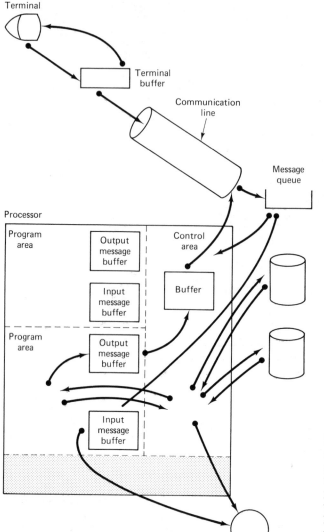

Figure 5.14 The output message is ready to be sent. It is sent to the general-purpose output buffer area in the control area. Once the general purpose output area is ready to be written out, the output is sent up the line, headed for the output destination, which in this case is the originating terminal.

Other bottlenecks include the common buffer areas, the program areas, or specific data upon which transactions happen to be enqueued. On occasion, bottlenecks occur in the communication lines.

INTERACTIVE USAGE OF CRT

Online systems can handle many users and much data with very quick response time and still maintain data integrity. Now consider another type of system that can access data directly through a CRT, the **interactive system.** The interactive environ-

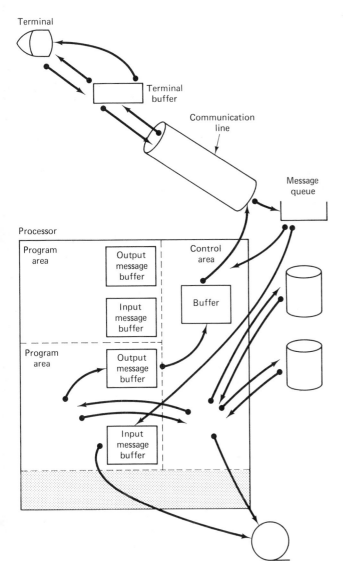

Terminal

Terminal
buffer

Communication
line

Message
queue

Processor

Program
area

message
buffer

Control
area

Input
message
buffer

Buffer

Program
area

message
buffer

Input
message
buffer

Figure 5.15 The message is sent through the communication line and arrives at the terminal buffer. In the buffer it is decompacted and prepared for display. The output is then displayed on the screen.

ment shares some of the characteristics of the online environment and does not share other characteristics. Consider the environment depicted in Fig. 5.17. In the interactive environment a user decides to log him- or herself on using a terminal that is attached to the interactive network. The log-on message is placed in a terminal buffer and undergoes some very basic edits. If the log-on message and format are not correct, control is returned to the terminal for correction. Once the log-on message is proper, the message is passed from the terminal buffer down the communication line. Through the communication line the message arrives at the processor and encounters system control. System control recognizes the log-on and password and determines what space is appropriate in memory for the terminal. The space

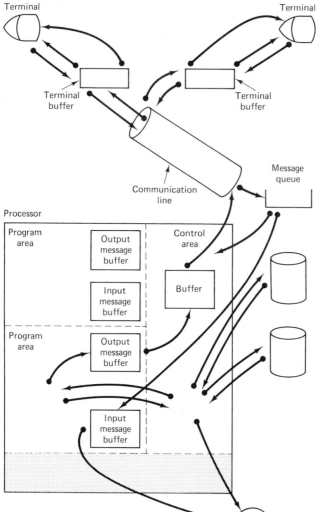

Figure 5.16 More than one user is able to use the online resources. Data is shared through the control that is achieved by passing all calls to the control area. The control area then assumes central responsibility for data base integrity.

requested by the terminal is then allocated by the system controller (Fig. 5.18). The space allocated is roughly divided into two spaces: a control area and a program area. The control area in the interactive environment contains some of the function found in the control area of the online environment; the system control area contains the remaining function.

Once the control area and the program area are allocated, a certain amount of initialization occurs in preparation for the first user commands. After the control area has been allocated and initialized, as shown in Fig. 5.19, the user actively begins the session. Typically one of the first things the user does is to allocate data. At this point in time all data and data bases are under the control of the system con-

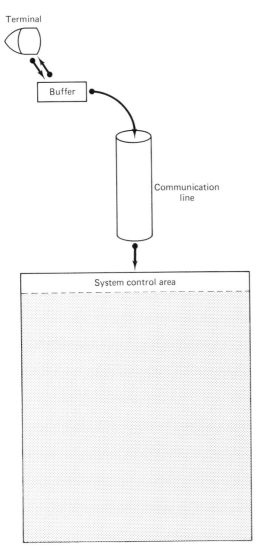

Terminal

Buffer

Communication
line

System control area

Figure 5.17 The terminal initiates a
session by informing the system-control
area.

troller. When the system controller receives a request for data allocation, there is
no problem as long as the data is not already allocated exclusively. Data is allocated
exclusively to a program area when the program area needs to update the data. If
a program area wants exclusive allocation for data already in use or if a program
area wants to use data nonexclusively when that data is already being exclusively
used, then there is a conflict. Otherwise, the program has the data allocated to it.

Once the data is passed to a user, it is up to the user to do such control functions as opening and closing the data space (Fig. 5.20). At this point the system
controller is nothing more than a traffic controller, directing who can and can't
have data.

Once the user possesses the data, the user can manipulate, change, or access

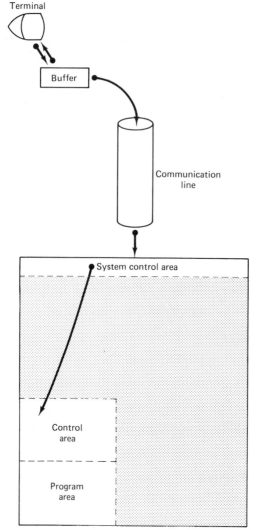

Terminal

Buffer

Communication
line

System control area

Control
area

Program
area

Figure 5.18   The system control area allocates space if it is available for the session.

the data at the user's leisure. The user typically uses predefined programs, nonprocedural code, or menus to process the data. At this point, as far as the user is
concerned the data is online (see Fig. 5.21). But the full implications of the interactive environment are not easily seen in looking at a single user. Consider Fig. 5.22,
which shows two terminals in session. Each terminal has its own separate program
space (or work space). There is a sharing of communication lines and processors,
as found in the online environment. But there is no sharing of data (when data is
being used exclusively). Control of data integrity comes from the individual control
areas. The only central control comes from the system controller, and the control
at that level is very crude. The types of processes that are run in the program areas
tend to have wide variability in terms of resources used, from a limited query of a

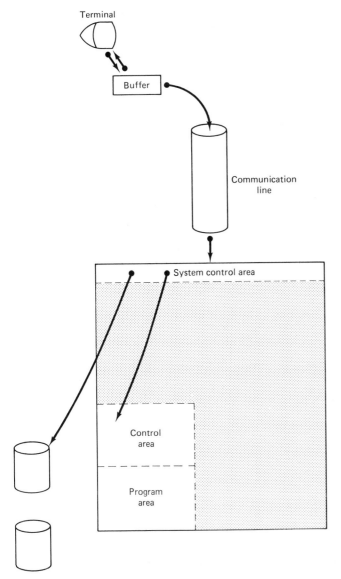

Figure 5.19 Once the space is allocated, the user requests some data. The data is requested exclusively.

data field to a scan of many data bases. The variability in the processes run in the interactive environment is a change from the processes run in the online environment. In the online environment, the processes are all short-running. Furthermore, the length of time a session holds a program area in the interactive environment is longer by orders of magnitude than the time a program space is held in the online environment. The online environment is typified by many users sharing many common resources, whereas the interactive environment is typified by users sharing a few resources and having exclusive rights to their own selective resources.

One of the limiting factors of the interactive environment is the amount of

DEADLY EMBRACE

One of the online issues outlined in Chapter 5 is that of lockup (or contention) for data base access. When an online transaction ties up an entire data base online for any length of time, (1) it is wasteful in that *all* the data is not being used at once and that other online transactions cannot access the data base while it is being held by the original transaction and (2) it has the effect of slowing down the entire system. So the effects of a data base lockup were minimized by reducing the amount of data locked up at once, (i.e., tying up only a portion of the data base rather than the entire data base). Integrity control was reduced to a lower, much finer level, such as to the record, tuple, or segment level. But there is another problem with lockup that can occur even when data is controlled at a very fine level. Consider the situation in Fig. DE.1. At the moment in time for which Fig. DE.1 was depicted, terminal 1 controls record A and terminal 2 controls record B. A few moments later, another snapshot of the online system is taken, as shown in Fig. DE.2. In this case terminal 1 must access record B to complete its processing. In the meantime it holds onto record A. But terminal 2 holds onto record B, and it needs record A to complete its processing. Unless there is some way of resolving this conflict, the terminals will sit and stare at each other ad infinitum, *really* slowing up the system. In practice, what happens is that the system (the online controller) recognizes that a deadly embrace has occurred and backs out one of the transactions so the deadlock can be resolved. Once one of the transactions is backed out, the other can execute in a normal fashion.

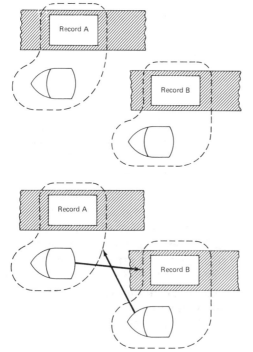

Figure DE.1 Terminal 1 has access to record A and terminal 2 has access to record B.

Figure DE.2 To complete processing, terminal 1 must access record B while holding control of record A. At the same time, record B must access record A while controlling record B. This is known as *deadlock* or *deadly embrace*.

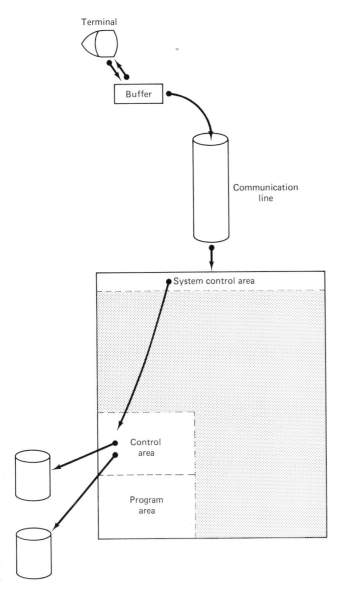

Terminal

Buffer

Communication line

System control area

Control area

Program area

Figure 5.20 Once the system control area loses control of the data, it is up to the control area to maintain local responsibility for integrity.

memory that is available. Only a finite number of people can be logged on at any moment in time. Another limitation of the interactive environment occurs when many users are actively using the system. The entire interactive system experiences long periods of slowdown.

MICROPROCESSOR USAGE OF CRT

It is a temptation to say the micro environment solves the problems of online and interactive processing. There is some truth to that view, but there are also some

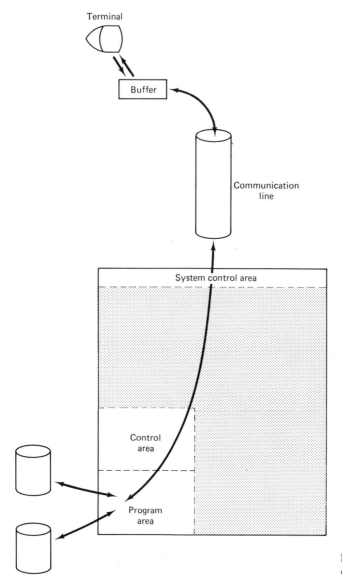

Figure 5.21 The data is updated directly from the program area.

inherent limitations to the micro environment. Figure 5.23 depicts one perspective of the micro environment. Interestingly, in one form or another the functions found in the online and interactive environments are likewise found in the micro environment, although the functions are implemented quite differently and in different places. There is no need for a communication channel to handle multiple terminals because there is only one terminal. But there is a need for communications to other microprocessors and to the mainframe, if there is a mainframe link.

Inside the micro are buffers, file-control areas, program areas, and system-control areas that roughly serve the same purpose as they did in the online and

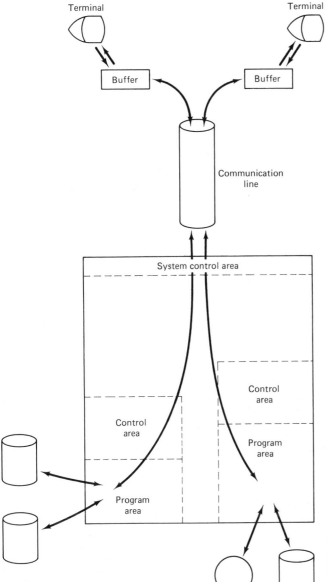

Terminal

Terminal

Buffer

Buffer

Communication
line

System control area

Control
area

Control
area

Program
area

Program
area

Program
area

Figure 5.22 Multiple terminals share many resources, but the terminals act independently. The sessions look as if the terminals were entirely different machines.

interactive environments. However, the complexity inside the micro is much, much less than that found in the mainframe processor because the micro is essentially one program (or set of programs initiated by a single user) that is in execution. Thus issues such as data integrity are simplified. The micro environment is very similar to an interactive session after the interactive session has been initiated.

If the issues of data integrity and contention for resources have been greatly alleviated by going to the micro environment, other issues have arisen. Consider

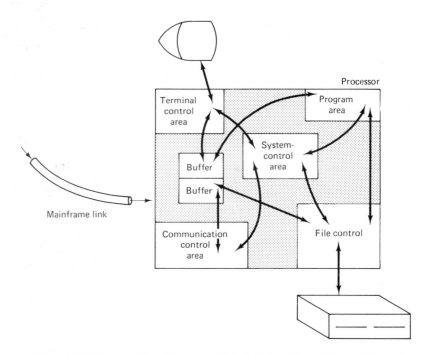

Figure 5.23 The many functions accomplished in the online and interactive environments are also accomplished in the microprocessor environment. There are some substantial differences of scope and implementation, but the basic functions remain.

Fig. 5.24. Although it is possible to transmit data from one microprocessor to the next in this figure, there are many drawbacks. The most obvious is that of performance. If user A wishes to access data owned by user B and user B has the data stored on a floppy disk, then user A must wait for user B, and it could be a long wait (in fact, it could be an indeterminate amount of time). Another major issue is that of data consistency. Since each owner of a micro is solely responsible for his or her data, there is no guarantee that that data will be meaningful when another user shares the data. Data may have undergone significant edits and refinements under one user's process unbeknownst to another user. Another problem with Fig. 5.24 is in the amount of data that may be transmitted and received. The limitations occur because of the number of buffers that are available and the speed and amount of transmissions of data to the computer. And so the problems continue.

Micros are often used in a stand-alone mode, where all communications, data manipulation, and system control occur inside the micro. But micros can be connected to other micros, and a network can be formed. When the network—commonly called a **local area network** or LAN—the tasks of communication control and data integrity take on new perspectives.

There are basically three ways that micros are linked to each other: through a *ring,* through a *star,* or through a normal communication line (a *bus*), as shown by Fig. 5.25. In a **ring,** communications are passed from one processor to the next using a technique called *token passing.* When a token is passed to a processor the

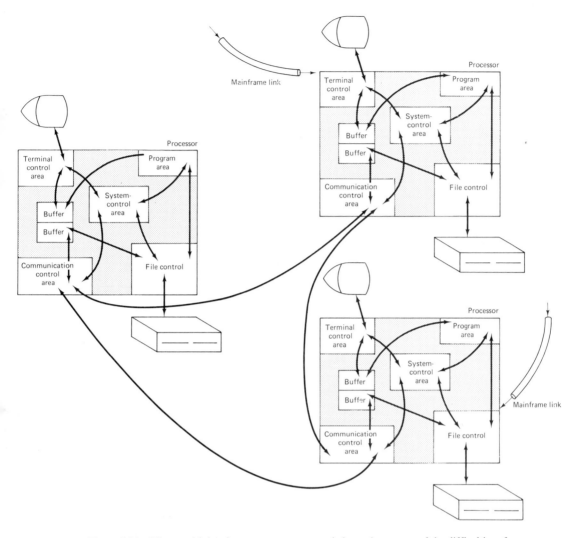

Figure 5.24 When multiple microprocessors are coupled together, many of the difficulties of the mainframe environment are solved, but new difficulties arise and old problems take a new form.

processor may proceed if it wishes to initiate a communication. One of the limitations of the ring is that if any processor becomes dysfunctional, the network is broken. Data integrity from a network standpoint is based on ownership of data at each processor. Consequently, if network wide update is to occur (i.e., if processor A can update processor B), then the operating system of each processor must be synchronized with all processors in the network. If only access of data, not update of data, is required throughout the network, then a much less elaborate data control architecture is required.

The second network configuration is the star network. The **star** configuration

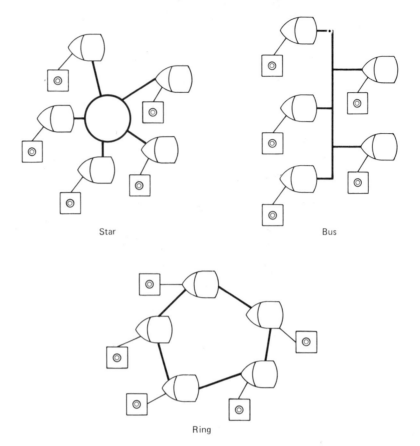

Star

Bus

Ring

Figure 5.25

has a central controller that manages the network. The star network is only as powerful as the central controlling unit. The capacity and availability of the central unit becomes the limiting constraint of the star network. The central control unit typically controls only data communications, not data integrity. Since data is owned by each processor, the data integrity of the network remains at the individual processor level. From a data integrity standpoint, there is no difference between a star network and a ring network as long as the central controller of the star network does not participate in data management.

The third configuration is the bus network. The **bus** network is the most common and the most flexible network. The bus network is realized by using standard communication equipment. The tasks of network management are done by the *interface card* that is found in each processor. As in the star and ring networks, the data integrity of the network lies at the individual processor level, since data is owned by each individual processor. One major advantage of the bus network is that no central controller is necessary. This results in greater availability, since the network does not have a processor as a single failure point.

Basic Concepts   Section I

TABLE 5.1

	Online	Interactive	Micro
Response time	2–5 seconds	2 seconds–5 hours	2 seconds–5 minutes
Length of activity	Consistently short	Variable: short to very long	Variable: short to long
Shared data?	Yes	No (not exclusively)	No
Amount of data	Much	Much	Relatively little
Number of users	Many	Many	One
Data integrity	High degree	Low degree	Strictly up to owner
Operational/dss	Operational	dss	dss
Flexibility	Poor	Fair to high	Fair to high
Typical software	IDMS/CICS, IMS/DC	TSO, VM/CMS	dbase II, FOCUS/PC

There are many different modes and variations on the direct access and usage of data through a CRT. Each mode has its advantages and disadvantages, its costs and its benefits. Table 5.1 summarizes the different modes in which CRT are used to access data.

SYNTAX

The syntax of data base is divided into two types of syntax—data manipulation syntax and data definition syntax. **Data manipulation syntax** is the language used actually to access and use data. The manipulation language is commonly entered into execution in two modes, the programmed mode and the interpretive mode. In the **programmed mode,** syntax is compiled and prepared for execution prior to execution. The programmed mode is used where there is a need to control data base activities, such as online processing. The **interpretive mode** is free-form; the user decides what is needed at the terminal and enters instructions to that effect into the system. The user has the freedom to access whatever data is available through interpretive syntax.

DATA MANIPULATION SYNTAX

Immediately after entry from the user, the interpretive instructions are turned into executable code, and operations against the data base commence (as opposed to the programmed mode, where syntax is translated into executable code at the moment of compilation). However data manipulation language is entered into the system, there are some basic activities that must be done: data insertion, deletion, access, and update. In addition to the basic data manipulation features, most data manipulation languages have more advanced functions, such as the summing of data, the averaging of data, the verification of relationships, the merger of data based on data relationships, and so forth. While it is necessary to understand the syntax for data manipulation in order to use a language, the *effective* use of a language requires an understanding of the underlying work being done by the system as a result of the commands entered by the user or programmer. In particular, the designer, programmer, and—to a lesser extent—the user need to be aware of the work being done by the system.

LANGUAGE AND I/O

Data manipulation languages come in two forms, procedural language and nonprocedural language. **Procedural language** derives its name from the way the code functions. Procedural language tells the computer how to proceed in the execution of instructions and in the location and manipulation of data. Procedural code is typified by COBOL or PL-1 programs, where the programmer, line by line, directs the activity of the process. Some sample (pseudo) procedural code might look like this:

```
OPEN...
A: READ...
IF...
THEN...
ELSE...
GO TO...
B: ADD...
IF...
CLOSE...
```

Nonprocedural language does not tell the program *how* to proceed but instead tells the processor *what* is needed. The processor then determines how to proceed. Nonprocedural code is typified by SQL, ORACLE, and INGRES. Some sample nonprocedural code might look like this:

```
SELECT BNAME, AGE
FROM B
WHERE AGE>31
```

RECORD/SET RETRIEVALS

Procedural syntax usually operates on one record at a time. The programmer directs the processor to find a specific occurrence of data. Part of the procedural specification is to qualify exactly what data is required. As an example of a procedural record request, consider the following IMS PL-1 call:

```
DCL EMP CHAR(21) INIT('EMPLOYEE(EMPNO=2465)');
DCL SAL CHAR(24) INIT('SALARYbb(YYMMDD
    =790713)');
CALL PLITDLI (FIVE, GU, PSPCB, SALWKAREA, EMP,
    SAL);
```

This PL-1 call will go to the employee data base and will find the employee whose employee number is 2465. Next, the salary data for that employee will be searched, looking for the pay record for July 13, 1979. This is an example of a procedural language searching for a single record.

Whereas procedural syntax usually operates on single records, nonprocedural syntax operates on sets of records at a time. (There is the case where a set contains exactly one record, at which point record and set processing are equivalent. Normally it is assumed that a set contains an indeterminate number of records.) As an example of a nonprocedural language that operates on sets, consider the following example from Model 204:

```
OPEN CENSUS
BEGIN
1. FIND ALL RECORDS FOR WHICH
SEX=FEMALE
STATUS=HEAD
2. COUNT RECORDS IN 1
3. PRINT COUNT IN 2
END
```

In this case the census data is being searched for *all* population records where the head of the household is a female. The search is done in terms of a set of records, not a record at a time.

There is no doubt that nonprocedural code can cause many more machine instructions to execute than an equivalent amount of procedural instructions. The power of nonprocedural language is very helpful when there is a need for flexibility, such as in the dss environment. But because of the potential number of resources used by nonprocedural languages, care must be taken when using them if there is to be any regard for the hardware budget. Nonprocedural languages must be handled *very* carefully in the operational environment, which is much more sensitive to machine resources than the dss environment. The differences between procedural languages and nonprocedural languages is best illustrated by a look at the data base calls issued as a result of the call and the I/O consumed by the call.

PROCEDURAL DATA BASE PROCESSING

For the purposes of this illustration, a simple, small data base will be used. Consider the data base depicted by Fig. 5.26. This data base is an indexed data base, where there are three primary data blocks and two overflow blocks. There are three records per block. The value of the key is shown inside each record. The data has arrived

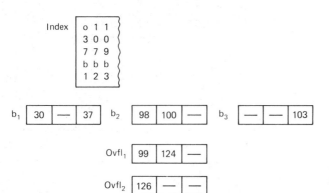

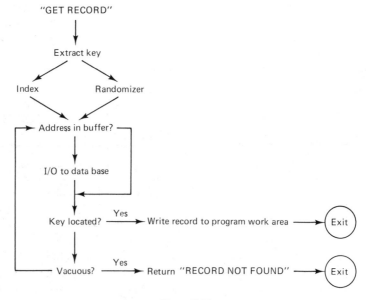

Figure 5.26   A simple data base for illustrating differences between set and record call.

at its current state of organization by the following relevant activity. Records 98 and 100 have been inserted in the same block as record 105. Then record 99 was added and was put into overflow. Later record 105 was deleted. Record 109 was inserted as the high-order record in block 3, which at that time contained records 106 and 108. Then record 126 was added and was put into overflow. Later, record 124 was added, and then records 106 and 108 were deleted. The index is sparse, showing only the high-order entry in each block. The search algorithm knows to search the overflow chain beyond the high-order record value in the highest block if that record has an overflow pointer.

The simple search algorithm that services the procedural call is outlined in Fig. 5.27. The algorithm operates as follows: First, the call is passed to the parser, or language translator. What the call wishes to have done is determined, along with

Figure 5.27

Basic Concepts   Section I

the values of the search to be done. Next the key is translated into an address by means of an index or randomizer, depending on the data base. In the data base shown, an index is used. After the key has been translated into a block address, the next activity is to determine whether the block is already in the buffer in main memory. If the block is in main memory, there is no need for an I/O. Otherwise an I/O is done to retrieve the block. Once the block is retrieved, it is put into the buffer in main memory for processing. Once in the buffer, it is determined whether the record is in the block or not. If the record is not in the block, a message is returned to that effect. If a pointer chain to overflow must be followed, then the search process is repeated for the overflow block until either the record is found or the record is determined to not be in the data base. To envision how the algorithm works, suppose the programmer has issued a procedural call to locate the record whose key is equal to 100. Figure 5.28 schematically shows the activity taken. The figure shows that the index is read and the record being sought is in block 2. Block 2 is read and the record is located. Two I/O are required, one to the index and one to block 2.

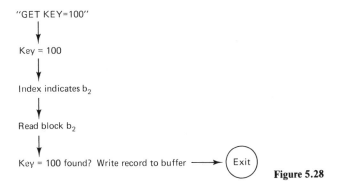

Figure 5.28

Now consider a read to record 126, as shown by Fig. 5.29. This figure shows the logic initiated if the high-value index entry of the highest block shows a value lower than the value being sought. Instead of actually assuming the record being sought is not in the data base, a search is initiated. The overflow chain is followed from record 109 to record 124 and then to record 126. In all, four I/O are done: one to the index, one to block 3, one to overflow block 1, and one to overflow block 2.

Finally, consider the search for a record not in the data base, as shown by Fig. 5.30. In Fig. 5.30 the record for key = 76 is sought. The index indicates to look in block 2. Block 2 is retrieved, and the first record found is record 98. Since record 76 is less than record 98, it is inferred that record 76 is not in the data base. In all two I/O's were done, one to the index and one to block 2. There is an important function that is not taken into account by the search algorithm, data integrity. The algorithm *assumes* it can access data. While this may certainly be true for *some* types of access processing, this algorithm would be at fault if there is a desire to protect data exclusively. While some aspects of data integrity may be passed up in

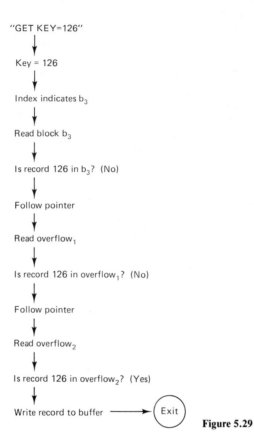

Figure 5.29

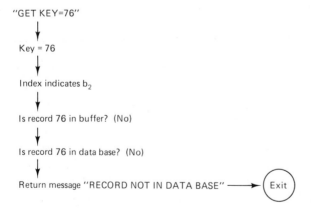

Figure 5.30

doing purely access processing, data integrity cannot be bypassed in doing such activities as inserts, deletes, or changes to data.

Now consider the I/O needed to service nonprocedural calls. Consider the simple data base depicted by Fig. 5.31. The data base shown is an inverted file data base, indexed only on social security number, a field not shown. Now suppose the nonprocedural statement is issued to find all records where sex is male and age is greater than 31. The algorithm that processes the call is seen in Fig. 5.32. The algorithm first parses the request, determining what is to be done and against what data. After the parsing, the algorithm determines the optimal strategy for processing the data. The blocks are first retrieved sequentially; then the records within the block are retrieved. Having retrieved all blocks in the data base, the algorithm terminates. Each record is queried as to whether it applies to males over 31. When a hit is made, the record is passed to the output buffer. One I/O is done for every

"GET ALL RECORDS WHERE SEX=MALE AND AGE GT 31"

b_1	Name = Jones Sex = m Age = 36 Sal = $1000	Name = Smith Sex = m Age = 29 Sal = $775	Name = Wilson Sex = f Age = 31 Sal = $1050

b_2	Name = James Sex = m Age = 31 Sal = $775	Name = Johnson Sex = f Age = 24 Sal = $1550	Name = Inmon Sex = m Age = 39 Sal = $1965

b_n	Name = Mohr Sex = f Age = 39 Sal = $2060	Name = Ives Sex = m Age = 24 Sal = $679	Name = Klein Sex = f Age = 26 Sal = $755

Figure 5.31

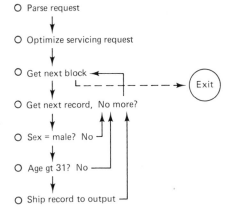

O Parse request

O Optimize servicing request

O Get next block

O Get next record, No more?

O Sex = male? No

O Age gt 31? No

O Ship record to output

Exit

Figure 5.32

```
b b b b b b . . . .
1 1 1 2 2 2 . . . .
r r r r r r . . . .
c c c c c c . . . .
d d d d d d . . . .    The index for the
1 2 3 1 2 3 . . . .    personnel data base
m m f m f f . . . .
3 2 3 3 2 3 . . . .
6 7 1 1 4 9 . . . .
```

Figure 5.33

block and every record in every block that is accessed. The entire data base is scanned. There are *n* blocks, and *n* I/O are done.

Now consider what happens when there is an index on the data fields of sex and age, as shown by Fig. 5.33. In this case there is no need to go to a block unless there is a record in the block that meets the search criteria. It is known *before* going to the block whether a record will meet the criteria, because the index has been previously searched. And searching the index is quite efficient, since the data in the index is quite tightly packed. If the question "How many men over 31 are in the data base?" is asked, there is no need to go to the primary data base at all in the face of the index shown. The question can be answered by processing the index independently of the primary data.

DATA DEFINITION SYNTAX

The other type of syntax that is common to a DBMS is the **data definition language** (DDL), which is used to define the form and structure of the data in the data base. Most data base users neither see nor become aware of DDL. Usually DDL is executed by a data base administrator or data base designer. DDL is usually executed as the system goes into implementation and occasionally as changes are made to the structure of the data in the system.

As an example of DDL, consider the following example from IMS:

```
DBD  NAME=PERSONDB
SEGM NAME=EMPLOYEE,BYTES=256,PARENT=0
FIELD NAME=(EMPNO,SEQ),BYTES=6,START=1
FIELD NAME=LNAME,BYTES=25,START=36
SEGM NAME=SALARY,BYTES=92,PARENT=EMPLOYEE
FIELD NAME=)SDATE,SEQ),BYTES=6,START=1
  .   .   .   .   .   .
  .   .   .   .   .   .
  .   .   .   .   .   .
```

This example of data definition language has defined a view of a data base, the PERSONDB data base. The root of the data base is 256 bytes long and is keyed by EMPNO (employee number), which is 6 bytes long and starts in column 1. The root segment can also be accessed by a field known as LNAME (last name), which is 25 bytes in length and starts in column 36. There is a dependent segment, SAL-

ARY, that is 92 bytes in length and is keyed on SDATE (salary pay date). This language is given to the DBMS prior to the building of the data base so that the DBMS can interpret and use the data, once the data base is built. As a rule, IMS is rather rigid in its data definition language. There is little room for default specifications or dynamically invoked options (thus giving IMS its reputation of inflexibility).

As another example of DDL, consider the following language from Model 204:

```
CREATE FILE PERSONL
PARAMETER ATRPG=1,FVFPG=1,MVFPG=10,ASTRPG=345
PARAMETER BSIZE=704,BRECPPG=23,BRESERVE=268
PARAMETER CSIZE=78,DSIZE=470
END
OPEN PERSONL
INITIALIZE
  .  .
  .  .
  .  .
OPEN PERSONL
DEFINE SOC.SEC.NO(KEY,BINARY) NAME(KEY)
DEFINE DEPT(KEY,FRV,FEW-VALUED)SEX(KEY,CODED,
    FEW-VALUED)
```

The first few statements tell Model 204 what the name, physical size, and structure of each of the different tables for the data base are. Then the data sets are initialized. The next lines of DDL define different fields and the physical attributes of those fields. Once the data is physically allocated and structured and the fields are defined, the data base is ready to be used.

SUMMARY

Program execution occurs in one of three modes, batch, online, or interactive. The interactive mode shares both online and batch characteristics. Online program execution is characterized by the execution of many very short running processes, while batch program execution is characterized by long running processes. Online execution optimizes the time of the user of the system, whereas batch processes optimize the throughput of data through the system. Interactive processing offers some advantages of both online and batch processing.

Online program execution is greatly concerned with data and transaction integrity. The emphasis on integrity allows many transactions to pass through the system and do updates without compromising the data bases. Teleprocessing operates against data bases in three modes, the online mode, the interactive mode, and the microprocessor mode. The activities done by the system in each mode are essentially the same. However, the activities are packaged differently and result in very different environmental characteristics. Data base syntax is divided along lines of data manipulation language and data definition language. Data manipulation language is executed in two modes, the programmed mode and the interpretive mode. Data definition language is used to determine the structure (and in some cases the contents) of the data base.

QUESTIONS

Program Types

1.1. What is a batch program?

1.2. What is an online program?

1.3. What is a time-sharing program?

1.4. In what programming languages are programs written?

1.5. Who writes programs for data base systems?

1.6. What is a procedural language? a nonprocedural language?

Program Differences

2.1. What is the difference between a batch program and an online program from a language standpoint? from a design standpoint?

Functional Differences

3.1. Why do batch programs accomplish as much function as possible?

3.2. Why do online programs accomplish function a small amount at a time?

I/O Read/Writes

4.1. Does every read or write by a programmer cause an I/O? Why?

I/O Reads

5.1. Can a read cause more than one I/O? If so, how?

5.2. Can a write cause more than one I/O? If so, how?

I/O's and the Programmer

6.1. How can a programmer determine when an instruction will cause an I/O?

6.2. Does a programmer need to determine how many I/O's are used? under what circumstances?

Code and I/O Speeds

7.1. What is the difference, in terms of speed, between the execution of programming code and the execution of an I/O?

7.2. Why is the difference between the two speeds so important?

8.1. What is meant by a program's path length?

8.2. How can path length be determined?

8.3. In what cases is it useful to determine path length?

Programming Efficiencies

9.1. Is program efficiency of execution (as far as programming code is concerned) an issue in terms of system performance? How much of a factor?

Teleprocessing

10.1. What is meant by up the line? down the line? local? remote?

10.2. Where does a modem fit between the terminal and the processor? a concentrator?

10.3. Is message compaction important? If so, how important, and where?

10.4. Describe the differences in sessions in the online environment, the interactive environment, and the microprocessor environment?

10.5. What are the difficulties in linking microprocessors to each other? to the mainframe?

10.6. What are the advantages in using microprocessors? the disadvantages?

10.7. Name two pieces of online software, two pieces of interactive software, and two pieces of microprocessor software.

10.8. What bottlenecks are there in the online environment? in the interactive environment? in the microprocessor environment?

Syntax and I/O

11.1. What is a procedural language? a nonprocedural language? Give six examples of both.

11.2. What is a record call? a set call? Is there such a thing as a set call in a procedural language? Is there such a thing as a record call in a nonprocedural language?

11.3. What I/O does a procedural call use? a nonprocedural call? Does a nonprocedural call use more or less I/O than a procedural call?

11.4. Write a nonprocedural call (in SQL, Model 204, etc.) to find the number of men making more than $20,000 per annum in a personnel data base. Now write the equivalent code in a procedural language such as COBOL.

11.5. How important is it for the end user or the programmer to be aware of the resources used in doing processing? in the operational environment? in the dss environment?

11.6. What is the effect on I/O in using an index (as opposed to not using an index) in a nonprocedural language?

EXERCISES

1. What happens in the online environment when a transaction does too many I/O? Who determines that too many I/O have been done? Once into execution, what can be done about an online transaction that is running too long? Does the limitation on the usage of I/O pose major restrictions to the online designer? Does the limitation of I/O have

an impact on the type of program logic that can be executed? For your DBMS, what is an appropriate upper limit for the I/O's that a transaction should do?

2. How can you determine internal response time on your DBMS? external response time? How reliable are the measurements?

3. Name three or four operating systems that support the interactive environment.

4. Is CPU utilization an issue in determining response time? How can you tell how much CPU was used by a job or a transaction? If the same (identical) transaction is run with the same input against the same data several times throughout the day, will the transaction use the same amount of CPU? the same amount of I/O? Why or why not?

5. Where can you go to determine how much I/O your DBMS uses in the execution of a given job? of a transaction?

6. Where can you go to determine that a given CRT is down? that an entire line is down?

7. A shop is having poor response time. They are running on a 5-mip (million instructions per second) machine. Keeping the same configuration except for the processor, they upgrade to a 10-mip machine. What can they expect in the way of improved response time?

8. A typical progression for the tuning of a DBMS is as follows: the first tuning effect nets a fair amount of improvement of response time. The next tuning effort several months later yields much less improvement. The next week a tuning effort is undertaken, and no visible improvement is made. Why do these phenomena occur? What are the limits of improving a system? Is it possible to tune a system and actually hurt response time? As a long-term strategy, does it make sense to keep a system well tuned?

9. What impact does increasing real memory have on performance? Why? Where can real memory best be used to enhance performance? What limitations are there to adding real memory? What implications are there for virtual memory for system performance? When can virtual memory hurt performance?

10. In your shop give two examples of skip sequential processing.

11. Describe the basic components of the online controller in your shop. How does it interface with the SCP? with the data bases? with application programs? What is the maximum transaction arrival rate that your online controller can sustain? What happens when your controller experiences a greater arrival rate?

12. Do you have smart or dumb terminals in your shop? Can you program a personal computer to look like a smart terminal and then send the transaction on the online controller? What are the issues here?

13. What amount of traffic can your communication lines bear? What is a local terminal? a remote terminal? How many remote terminals can your processor handle? how many local terminals?

14. Where does a programmer learn about the I/O caused by his or her program? Does a programmer need to learn about I/O? in online systems? in batch systems? in interactive systems? in micro based systems?

15. Is all procedural code done a record at a time? Is all nonprocedural code done a set at a time? Give examples.

16. For your DBMS, identify the data manipulation language. Identify the data definition language.

17. How does your DBMS detect deadly embrace? What does it do about it once detected? Is there an integrity exposure?

18. Take a batch and online program from your production system. Identify the I/O done by every instruction. Suggest design and programming efficiency improvements.

19. For an online transaction in your system, trace the flow from the moment the transaction is entered until the response is returned. Include interactions with all buffers, control areas, program areas, internal integrity protection mechanisms, and any other major operating facilities. Suggest improvements for efficiency.

20. Repeat Exercise 19 for the interactive environment.

21. For your DBMS locate the code that does the parsing. Trace a simple transaction through your parser and examine the output.

CHAPTER 6

Utilities

Data bases, like most other parts of a data processing system, require both normal care throughout the life cycle and a certain amount of specialized handling. For the most part, a well-designed DBMS (data base management system) handles most circumstances quite adequately. But there are a few special cases that are handled by utilities:

— Data base initialization

— Data base recovery

— Data base reorganization

In addition a periodic monitoring is necessary for

— The data base itself

— The data base environment

Each of these special cases can be handled by a utility piece of software. In most cases, the utility comes with the DBMS. In some cases the software must be custom written on an application-by-application basis. Each of these utilities will be described.

DATA BASE INITIALIZATION

Data base initialization occurs for at least two levels, the physical and the system level. At the physical level, initialization causes

— Allocation of data to occur

— Formatting of the space (DASD—direct access storage device) into physical blocks

Allocation of physical data is not a trivial matter for most DBMS. The primary concern is that most physical DBMS spaces purposely are not easily extendable (certainly not those that use randomizers). Were DBMS space extendable, the extension would amount to an overflow of overflow, which surely would cause undue I/O (input/output) and other undesirable data management problems. In addition, due to randomizing algorithms most data bases require space to be meticulously accounted for, and the general capability of extending data capacity does not fit. Therefore, the initial allocation of space is not to be taken lightly because it is the amount the application will have to live with for some period of time. If space is overallocated, as is the practice in some shops, then the data base may not run out of space any time soon, but there is an automatic waste. If, on the other hand, not enough space is allocated, either the data base runs out of space or much internal thrashing occurs, as data collides often during randomization.

The actual allocation utility merely claims the space in the physical catalog and/or index and removes anything currently occupying the space. It may be desirable to allocate the space over more than one disk pack so that line traffic can be spread throughout the system. Once the space is allocated, the next step is to format the space. This simply amounts to fitting the physical blocks that are specified into the tracks that are available and formatting the block prefix space and initializing it. Normally the actual newly allocated space is not reset to a given value (such as all 0s), although it can be if there is some reason to do so.

From an I/O standpoint, it is easy to see that much I/O will be required for initialization. However, since the data base is being initialized and there is nothing in it, the I/O done is not a concern because the initialization and formatting is done well out of the way of the online environment. On a few occasions a special record will actually be inserted into the data base during initialization. Often the record is the first or last record in the data base and as such carries a key that gives it that unique identification. Data base initialization at the system level (i.e., initialization of actual data values, as opposed to initialization and structuring of space) may be optional and may or may not be done by a utility that comes with the system. In some cases data bases are loaded by a conversion program. In other cases data bases are loaded by actual usage of the data bases. When conversions occur, they may be from a card file, a tape file, another data base, or from many other sources at the same time. The system-level initialization involves nothing more than a long series of inserts into the data base. Records are inserted as if they were being actually transacted online against the data base, except that they are inserted sequentially and they are all inserted at once.

DATA BASE RECOVERY

Data base recovery is applicable to both the online and the batch environment, but in practice it is most frequently used for online recovery (*Note:* the practical experience of the authors indicates that approximately 60% of recovery is for online systems, and 40% is for batch systems). The net effect of data base recovery is to restore the data base to some prior point in time so processing can resume. Consider the following case (which is *very* typical). An online environment is brought up at 7 A.M. Clerks, managers, users, and others operate vigorously against the data base all morning. Records are inserted, deleted, updated, and queried. At 11:30 A.M. a power surge occurs and the mainframe processor goes down. The online system is lost. Operations is faced with a decision about how to proceed. One option is to turn the clock back and restore the data bases to their state as of 7 A.M. This is operationally easy (a quick copy restore of the data as of 7 A.M. is an easy thing to do). But that obliterates all the data manipulation and transactions that have occurred between 7 A.M. and 11:30 A.M. As far as the business of the enterprise is concerned, turning back the clock may not be an option even if it is convenient to do. Customers will not be happy to learn that their account was not credited with payments or that their acknowledged order has been discarded. So the activity from 7 A.M. to 11:30 A.M. must be recovered.

The usual approach to recovery is to log each transaction as it occurs. The log is kept on tape or disk. The actual writing to the log represents a commitment by the system that the transaction is completed. Once the log tape is written (and usually time stamped), it is a fairly straightforward matter to run it through a utility, with the net effect of restoring the data base to its state immediately prior to 11:30 (or when the failure occurred). But what about data that is sitting on the output buffer but has not been written to the log? Such data is in a state of limbo. It is not on the log, so it has not been committed. The data base has been changed (so the user thinks), but when the data base is restored to its 7 A.M. state, the change will not be reflected. So, the data in the buffer must also be restored. One possibility is to send a message to the user that the transaction must be resubmitted. Since there is relatively little data in the buffer, this may not be a particularly onerous task. Another choice, if the buffer is able to be restored, is to go ahead and transact the data (i.e., commit it to the log tape) and rewrite the data base record as if logging had normally occurred.

DATA BASE REORGANIZATION

Data base reorganization is a conceptually simple process. The first part of the reorganization is the unload step, in which data is simply read in its logical order and written to another location (on DASD) or on another medium (on magnetic tape). The tape is then reread into the second step, the reload step (see Fig. 6.1).

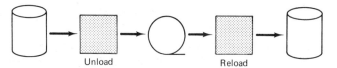

Unload   Reload   **Figure 6.1** Data base reorganization.

Because of the utility's simplicity, it is known as an *unload/reload* as well as reorganization. There are basically three reasons why unload/reload is done:

- To internally clean up the data base, or to increase the data base space
- To restructure the data base
- To serve as a recovery tool

Figure 6.2 shows part of an indexed data base that is internally unclean. The data base has reached this state by means of many data management activities such as inserts and deletes which over time have caused the data to be very poorly organized, insofar as the logical order of the data is concerned. By rearranging the data, the logical order can be made consistent with the physical order, thereby saving many I/O when traversing the data base physically. Note that an indexed data base is shown, but reorganization is equally valid for randomized data bases. In the case of randomized data, the frequency of collisions, the order and length of the chain formed when collision occurs, and parameters to the randomizer can be changed upon reorganization. Figure 6.3 shows the data after reorganization. Note

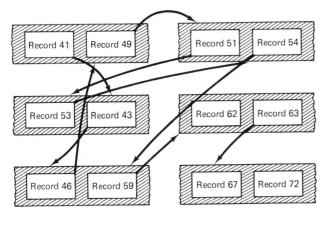

Figure 6.2 The logical sequencing of data is unclean. Many I/O are required to access the data in its logical order because the logical order does not coincide with the physical order.

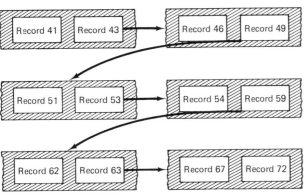

Figure 6.3 Data after reorganization. Many fewer I/O are required because the logical order of the data matches the physical order.

that the logical sequencing of the data (the sequence formed by the key of the record) matches the physical sequence. Now the data base can be most efficiently processed.

Another reason for reorganization is to extend the physical space that a data base has available. This can include such activity as lengthening or shortening the physical block size, increasing or decreasing the offsets available for each block, distributing free space throughout the data base, changing the ratio of primary space and overflow space, and so forth.

Some DBMS have facilities for partial reorganization. Partial reorganization of a data base is a real advantage over full reorganization in that full reorganization requires that the entire data base be removed from any kind of processing while being reorganized. If the entire data base must be reorganized all at once and if the data base is large, then the amount of time for which the data base is unavailable may be very long. This may be especially disturbing to the online user, who cannot conduct business while reorganization is occurring. So a partial reorganization facility allows only a fraction of the data base to be disabled, thus enhancing total system availability.

Partial data base reorganization is done on a partitioned data base basis. Either the data base is physically divided into partitions at the point of design, or a utility is run to determine which locations are needed to be reorganized, thus forming a basis for partitioning. In the first case, where the data base is divided into partitions, only the partition being reorganized goes down. In the case where artificial partitions are set, the entire data base goes down, but only a portion of the data base actually undergoes reorganization, thus shortening the time spent during reorganization. Note that all other data bases that directly point into the data base being reorganized must have their pointers altered when the data base being pointed into is reorganized. Figure 6.4 shows one data base, A, pointing directly into another data base, B. When the data in B is altered, the pointers in A must likewise be altered.

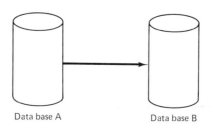

Figure 6.4   Direct addressing from data base A into data base B. When the addresses in B change, the direct pointers of A must be reset.

Data base A   Data base B

In the case of a partial reorganization, even if only a fraction of the data base is reordered, all direct addresses into the data base must be rectified. In such a case, the rectification may require considerable resources. A final point about partial reorganization is that it is valid only for internal cleanliness of the data. It is not valid for restructuring the data base. (If a data base were to be restructured by a partial reorganization, then at some moment in time, part of the data base would be in one form and part would be in another form.)

Reorganization for restructuring a data base occurs in the same steps as re-

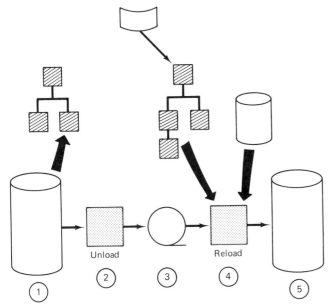

1. The data base is unloaded in its old format.
2. The unload is done in logical sequence order.
3. The unloaded data is placed onto another medium.
4. The data base is reformatted and defined as such to the DBMS. The reload program accepts old data in the old format, reformats it, and writes it out in the new format. It also accepts new data to be loaded into the new format.
5. The load is done under the new format.

Figure 6.5

organization for performance, with one exception. The data base is unloaded under its old format, a new format is defined, and the data is reformatted, as seen in Fig. 6.5. Because the structure of the data base must remain consistent, a data base that is partitioned must still be reorganized all at the same time. If the data base is large, this may cause the user some inconvenience. Note that structural reorganization applies only to nonvariable field, fixed-length data. Although variable field data sometimes needs to be reorganized for one reason or the other, structural reorganization is not a normal occurrence.

Reorganization for recovery is not a frequent or normal event. Recovery procedures usually are adequate. But on occasion it is more convenient simply to reorganize a data base than it is to try to recover it. Of course, this would apply only to small data bases that could be quickly reorganized.

DATA BASE MONITORING

Data base monitoring is necessary over the life of a data base because most data bases are dynamic. The number of records, the length of the records, the distribution over the physical block, the nature of overflow, the number of collisions are

UTILITIES: VENDOR OR INDEPENDENT SUPPLIED?

Most vendors of data base management systems supply the necessary utilities as part of the software package that comes with the data base software. But many data base shops choose to use utilities that have been written either in the shop itself or by outside independent software vendors. There are two reasons why tailor-made or independent software may be desirable:

Function. The vendor-supplied utilities perform only the basic functions. Other software may be more sophisticated.

Efficiency. The vendor software must be built to handle *all* cases in which the data base may be used, whereas no shop exercises all the options of a DBMS. Thus by tailoring a piece of software to a particular subset of a DBMS, greater efficiency may be achieved. The independent software can be written at one or all of three levels, the physical level, the system level, and the application (or user) level. When the software is written at the physical level, the software is very sensitive to the slightest change in the basic DBMS package. At the physical level, the software addresses the "bits and bytes" of the DBMS at the lowest possible level. Any new release of software by the vendor makes the utility vulnerable.

When the vendor changes the DBMS at the physical level in a new release, the non-vendor-supplied utility may not work anymore. The utility then must be changed to account for the vendor changes. At the system level the same considerations hold true, except that vendors normally include standard *user exits,* where independent vendors (or anyone) are free to enter the system level and execute a certain type and amount of instructions. If independently supplied software uses only standard user exits, then changes from release to release of the DBMS should have little or no impact on the utility. However, if the utility goes beyond these exits and modifies the basic DBMS package, then the utility is subject to the same difficulties encountered at the physical level.

The third level of the software is at the application level. In this case only standard calls are used throughout the language interface. The change of releases by a vendor should not affect the utility. If an independent version of a utility is desired, it must be remembered that the vendor has no responsibility for non-vendor-written software written below the application level. It is not reasonable for a vendor to account for software compatibility over which it has not control.

all aspects of a data base that constantly change. As a data base changes, it is good data base management practice to ensure that inefficient activity is not regularly occurring. To this end data base utilities are needed to determine the characteristics of a data base. The following are some of the essential things a utility should monitor:

— *Structural integrity.* Is the structure of the data base being violated? Do indexes exist that point to nonexistent data? Does data exist that should be indexed but is not? Is the integrity at the system level secure. (Do all hierarchical children have parents? Do all network junction records have two or more parents?) One major function performed by the utility is the verification of all symbolic and direct addressing. Does any symbolic or direct pointer exist for which no data correspondingly exists?

— *Data characteristics.* How many records are there? How are they structured? How much of the data is in overflow? How much is in the primary area? How often do collisions occur? How much space is unused? What is the average record size? the standard deviation? How are the keys distributed? How is the unused space that is available distributed? These questions are the *minimum* that should be answered by a utility. Knowing the proper answers to these questions allows the data base administrator to do two things: to see how the data base is changing over time and to plan for optimum use of space. Without a utility to trace data base characteristics, the data base administrator is effectively blindfolded.

— *Online data base environment characteristics.* Another utility that is necessary is one that will outline minute-to-minute changes and the characteristics of the online environment. The utility is helpful both as an online facility to give an up-to-the-second snapshot of what is going on in the system and a more comprehensive hard copy journaling of what the entire environment looks like. Some of the online characteristics that are useful are percentage utilization of critical pools and buffers, percentage utilization of program work areas, transactions that are queued, the length of time of execution of active transactions, and a list of active transactions.

In addition, these characteristics and others are useful for analytical purposes in hard copy form. Both online and hard copy are invaluable in analyzing the problems that arise on the occasions that the online computer slows down. For the sake of comparisons it is useful to have a series of normal snapshots so that the sloweddown, or abnormal, snapshots of the online system can be compared to a base.

THE REORGANIZATION/RECOVERY ENVIRONMENT

What determines whether or not reorganization or recovery is necessary? There are two basic modes of determination: an **anticipatory mode** (i.e., a proactive mode) or a **reactive mode.** The basic tool of the anticipatory mode is regular system monitoring, as has been discussed. The data base monitor can be used to determine that either reorganization is necessary or a system failure is imminent. As such, monitoring is the first line of defense of good data base administration. In other cases a reorganization is predictable. Such a case might occur when a new phase of a project is implemented and much more data and/or activity is being processed.

However, the need to execute a utility cannot be anticipated in every case. In such cases, the utility is run in a reactive mode. Typically, a user is executing a program and the program **abends** (i.e., abnormally ends) and ceases to execute. Or, suppose the master terminal operator notices that one or more data bases have been shut down by the system. When errors like these occur, the utilities are run in re-action to the problem. As a rule a shop that runs utilities in an anticipatory mode is able to minimize the ill effects of having to run the utility. The utility can be run when least noticeable and when it can be anticipated. But when utilities are run in a reactive mode, in almost every case they are run under extreme pressure because the execution of the utility causes major disruption to the system. In the worse case the entire system—all transactions, all data bases, and all programs—become in-operable until the utility can be run. In other cases the online (or interactive) system experiences a severe slowdown.

In the case of recovery (which is the normal reactive utility), there are usually several options. One option is actually to solve the problem. A solution implies the problem must be analyzed, that there is a solution, and that solution can be effected. But in some cases the solution to the problem cannot be determined, or even if it is determined, it is not able to be effected. In those cases (which are far from rare), either a bypass or a temporizing solution is effected. A **bypass** allows the system to continue execution with some part of the system being inoperable. A **temporizing solution** is one that does not solve the problem but allows the system to remain operable in a somewhat impaired state. Both bypass and temporizing solutions are in effect until the proper solution can be applied.

As an example of a problem where a solution can be analyzed and effected, consider a data base that has run out of space. All transactions running against it are stopped when the out-of-space condition is encountered. The operator brings the data base down, allocates more space, loads the appropriate catalog entry, and, if necessary, reloads the data into the new space. Then the data base is brought online, and transactions are able to process against it again.

Now consider a data base where a particular record is misplaced (for any num-ber of reasons). In this case an index points to a record that doesn't exist. When a user attempts to access the record through the index, an error condition is raised, and the transaction terminates abnormally. A quick investigation does not reveal the cause. Instead, a message is broadcast throughout the system not to access the improperly constructed record until further notice. This gives the data base admin-istrator time to analyze why the problem occurred. The system is then brought up even though it is known that at least one record is incorrectly established. Such a case is an example of bypassing an error until a solution can be found.

The third type of solution, a temporizing one, is illustrated by the following example. Suppose a data base is loaded with a different type of data than the de-signer originally intended. Because of overflow problems and a poor design, more I/O is done than was ever intended. The system slows down significantly. The prob-lem is analyzed, and the long-term solution is a rework of the data base design. Unfortunately, a rework will take at least a month. So a short-term solution is adopted until a long-term solution can be effected. The short-term solution is to allocate much more space than is necessary with much larger physical blocks than were originally specified and reorganize the data base into the new space. This par-tially alleviates the I/O problem at the expense of wasted space. Such a solution is temporary and at least allows the function to be accomplished even though it is wasteful of DASD.

SUMMARY

An essential part of the data base environment are the utilities that are occasionally required. One such utility is the data base initialization utility, which prepares space at both the physical and system levels. Another important utility is the recovery utility, which allows the online activity of the system to be restored in the eventuality of a failure. The recovery is done by means of a log or journal of online activity that has been kept as the data base is updated. A third important utility is that of reorganization. Reorganization occurs for performance, restructuring, and infrequently as part of the recovery strategy. Another useful utility is the data base monitor, which measures many aspects of the data base environment that would be difficult to otherwise ascertain. A final utility discussed is the online environment monitor, which measures many internal aspects of the online environment.

QUESTIONS

General Considerations

1.1. Are utilities necessary?

1.2. What function is served by utilities?

1.3. Could the function be served some other way? If so, how?

1.4. Is a utility necessarily an efficient piece of code?

Basic Utilities

2.1. Describe four basic utilities.

2.2. What function is accomplished by the utilities?

2.3. Could the function be accomplished if the utilities didn't exist?

2.4. Would the data base system function without the utilities?

Availability Considerations

3.1. Is it necessary for a data base to be taken off-line while it is being reorganized?

3.2. Is it necessary for a data base to be taken off-line while it is being recovered?

Home Grown Utilities

4.1. What are the advantages of a shop building their utilities? the disadvantages?

Application Supported Relationships

5.1. If a shop builds its own data relationships by means of application pointers, is it mandatory that the shop build its own utilities to verify the integrity of the relationship?

Recovery/Reorganization

6.1. What is the biggest factor in the length of time necessary in the execution of a recovery or a reorganization of data?

6.2. What can be done to minimize that factor?

Data Base Monitoring

7.1. What different aspects of a data base should be monitored? when? by whom?

7.2. How can it be determined that more space is necessary for a data base?

Archiving Data

8.1. Can archival activity be done by a utility? If so, how?

8.2. Is there archival activity that cannot be done by a utility? If so, what?

Data Base Initialization

9.1. What is meant by physical initialization of data? by structural initialization?

9.2. Is initialization of data the same thing as a load of data?

Loading a Data Base

10.1. List three ways data can be loaded into a data base.

EXERCISES

1. For your DBMS identify the utilities you have. Who is in charge of initiating the utilities? Are the utilities all vendor supplied? If not what is the origin of the utilities?

2. How are raw areas of data initialized in your data bases? Who determines block sizes? record sizes? What effort is there in changing these sizes once set?

3. How can more space be added to your data bases? Describe all the necessary steps.

4. What are the drawbacks of overallocating space for a data base? the advantages? Are there certain types of data bases where overallocation is a sound strategy?

5. How much free space is there in your most common data bases? in your largest data bases? How is free space allocated? How is it distributed?

6. Do you have a randomized data base that is also indexed? What is the data base being used for? What is the index being used for?

7. Does your DBMS reclaim space after deletion has occured?

8. What recovery procedures do you have in your shop? Are they routinely exercised so that there is no emergency when they must be actually used? How long does it take to exercise the recovery procedures? Is the down time acceptable for the users? Who is in charge of recovery in your shop?

9. Do you have facilities for temporizing solutions in your shop? Have they been exercised? What impairment is there in using temporizing solutions?

10. Do all data bases need to be reorganized? under what conditions?

11. Is reorganization as simple as an unload/reload? Explain extenuating circumstances when reorganization might not be so simple.

12. Does a reorganization always clean up data internally?

13. Can the amount of time needed for reorganization be determined by using the amount of time needed for reorganization for another data base and extrapolating? What are the pitfalls with this approach to estimation of reorganization time?

14. What part of a reorganization takes longer, the unload or the reload? Why?

15. Under what circumstances can a reorganization be used for recovery? When should a reorganization *not* be used for a recovery?

16. What facilities are there in your shop for monitoring the contents of a data base? What key indicators are there that a reorganization needs to be done?

17. Can recovery be planned? How can the test environment create errors that necessitate the use of recovery utilities? Is this a sound testing strategy?

CHAPTER 7

Miscellaneous Topics*

In many ways the primary limitation of data base is I/O (input/output). I/O limits how much data can be processed by a transaction or program. An option that minimizes the effects of I/O is storing the data base in main memory—not in a buffer area that is constantly being flushed, but in a regularly specified portion of main memory set aside for such data (see Fig. 7.1).

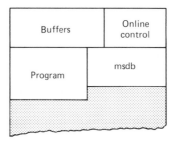

Figure 7.1 Here msdb exists in main memory along with other occupants.

Having the main storage data base (msdb) in memory means that no I/O must be done to access the data, thus enabling the program to operate at electronic speeds, not mechanical speeds. Such data is very quick to access and is widely available.

(*Note:* The following discussion on main storage data bases is not to be confused with IMS Fast Path main storage data bases (MSDB). If IMS MSDB are to be referenced, they will be referenced in capitals. The discussion applies to the generic case of main storage data bases, of which MSDB are one type.)

Typical uses of such a data base are installation wide tables, statistic gathering, security, application control, and so forth. A typical example of an msdb is for *conversational control,* as illustrated in Fig. 7.2. In this figure only a small amount of information is managed by any transaction. Such is the nature of online processing. The msdb is built up a piece at a time until the business transaction can be processed. The use of the msdb means that the information does not have to be entered at once. In the case shown, only a limited amount of data is entered; in actual design the conversation may go on for an extended amount of time and may involve much processing.

The main design criteria of msdb is that they be critical to access and limited in size. Data that is not critical to access should be placed in less expensive and slower storage. Voluminous data that is critical to access should be placed in DASD (direct access storage devices). Only limited amounts of data should be placed in main storage. Main storage represents a very precious resource of the computer that is used for many important purposes, such as buffers, the system control program (or SCP), and the nucleus of the DBMS (data base management system). Unfortunately, the available space in memory varies so much from one environment to the next that no rough guidelines can be set. So there must be a balance made between the space reserved for msdb and the actual utility of that space. In a virtual

```
))Tx1 - enter account, name
)J431, Tippett
))Tx2 - enter amount desired
)$45,00
))Tx3 - enter account to be credited
)MR645
))Entry has been made for J Tippett
   transferring money from account
   J431 to MR645 in the amount of $45,00
```

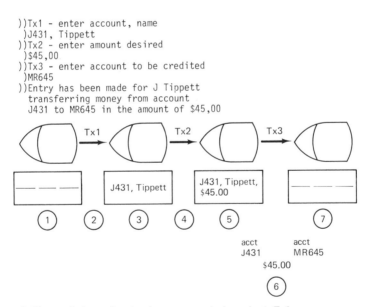

1. The terminal scratch pad main storage area is clear prior to Tx1.
2. Tx1 causes data to be written to scratch pad area.
3. The terminal scratch pad msdb holds J431, Tippett as a result of Tx1.
4. Tx2 causes data to be added to scratch pad area.
5. The terminal scratch pad msdb holds J431, Tippett, $45.00 as a result of Tx2.
6. Tx3 causes $45.00 to be transferred to acct MR645 from acct J431 and the scratch pad area is cleared.
7. Terminal msdb is ready for further activity.

Figure 7.2

Chap. 7   Miscellaneous Topics

memory system, one of the issues will be whether to page fix the msdb or not. (When a page is not fixed in virtual memory, it means the page can be rolled out onto DASD if the page is not being frequently accessed. Memory that is page fixed cannot be rolled out to DASD even if the memory is not being accessed at all.) When the msdb is not page fixed, it can be removed from main memory because it has been paged out. When it is needed again, it must be paged back in main memory, and in doing so I/O occurs.

A sample layout of an msdb record is shown by Fig. 7.3. There are several things to note here. The data portion of the record is pointed to by an offset pointer, which is located by a key value. Note that the key value is not repeated in the data portion of the record, in the interest of saving space. (In the case of records stored on DASD, the key is usually repeated in the index and on DASD.) The second point of note is a protection bit in the record itself. The protection bit is used in conjunction with one type of main storage data—online update data. Nononline update data is data that is updated strictly in batch, such as a table that is updated only during the nightly run. Online update data can be updated by the online system during the running of the online environment. The protection bit applies only to the online update data. If the bit is turned on (i.e., equals 1), then no program can access the online update data. If the bit is off (i.e., equals 0), then online update data can be accessed. If an online program wants to update the data, it turns the protection bit to 1 and then takes the data to its program work area. When the program returns with the updated value, the updating program resets the bit to zero after the data has been updated. Nononline update data can be accessed online (but not updated) as needed. Update of the nononline update data occurs typically at a system checkpoint, when the entire data base is read to DASD and deleted from main storage. Once on DASD, update occurs in the normal fashion. Once the update on DASD is finished, the entire data base is reread into main storage. Such stringent data management creates an absolute minimum of slack space once the data base is in main storage. Other typical data management controls are indexing only on the records key, fixed-length entries, a limited number of inserts (where inserts are allowed), and so forth.

Backup and recovery are done by means of a roll in/roll out procedure in which the entire data base is restored from DASD. Because the data base is small, such quick restoration techniques are possible. Of course, data base changes must be replaced on the online update part of the data base.

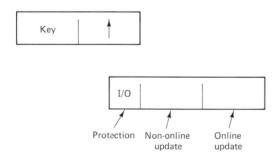

Figure 7.3 A typical layout for an msdb data base.

Basic Concepts   Section I

Data base integrity refers to the property of data bases such that, once formed or given value, they maintain that form or value until legitimately altered by facilities of the DBMS. Without integrity, data bases are fairly useless. They are unreliable and unable to be accessed or used with confidence. Thus data base integrity is one of the cornerstones of the data base environment. The following aspects of data bases become important from an integrity standpoint:

— Structural integrity
— Index integrity
— Addressing (direct, symbolic) integrity
— Individual record concurrency integrity
— Data base concurrency integrity

Structural disintegrity occurs when the basic format and structure of the DBMS has been violated, as is illustrated in terms of a hierarchical data base (Fig. 7.4). In this case a set of sibling segments (or children) exists with no physical parent. This is a violation of the normal rules of hierarchical segmentation.

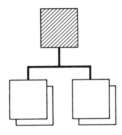

Figure 7.4 A set of dependent segments where the parent is deleted.

Figure 7.5 shows an index for which no data exists. Such a form of structural disintegrity may be appropriate to an inverted list environment (or an indexed environment, for that matter). A third case of structural integrity collapse is shown by Fig. 7.6, where a network structure is shown addressing (either direct or sym-

Figure 7.5 An index entry that points to a nonexistent record.

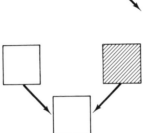

Figure 7.6 A junction record for which no complete set of owners exists.

bolically) a junction record that does not exist. In all cases such a break in integrity should not occur, but, for a various assortment of reasons, it occasionally does. Some of the reasons might be a DBMS code failure, an application-code quirk, an SCP failure, a CPU failure, or an operations failure. What is of interest is not where the failure lies, but the nature of the problem and what can be done to resolve it.

Another class of integrity exposure occurs when online data bases are updated. As has been seen in main storage data bases, a protocol and level of protection has been created for online updated data. The same sort of protection (although at a much more sophisticated level) exists for regular online updates on DASD. Consider Fig. 7.7. In this figure a balance is accessed under faulty integrity control. The balance is increased by $100 to $428. However, before the record is replaced it is also accessed by another transaction. Now the balance is replaced at $428. In the meantime, however, transaction 2 has subtracted $25.00, but the $25.00 is subtracted from $328, the balance when the record was accessed. When the record is replaced, it is replaced by $303. This represents an online update integrity exposure. What should have happened is that as the record was being updated from $328 to $428, no other transaction should have been able to access the record. Instead, access was allowed and a faulty balance resulted.

Time		Record 1
n	Tx1 accesses record 1.	Balance = $328.00
n + 3	Tx2 accesses record 1.	Balance = $328.00
n + 4	Tx1 adds 100 to balance, returns record after update.	Balance = $428.00
n + 8	Tx2 subtracts 25 from balance originally retrieved.	Balance = $303.00

Balance is $303.00
Balance should be $403.00
The transaction that added $100.00 was in essence wiped out by online disintegrity.

Figure 7.7

Another form of integrity failure occurs at a higher level, the data base level. In practice this failure rarely occurs. When it does, the results are no less catastrophic. Figure 7.8 illustrates such a change, which—when an error occurs—occurs

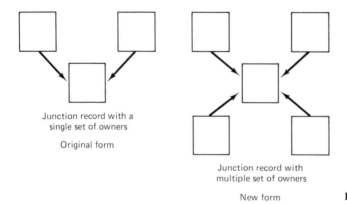

Junction record with a
single set of owners

Original form

Junction record with
multiple set of owners

New form

Figure 7.8

at the data base level. In this figure a network data base is being reorganized so that a junction record has multiple sets of owners instead of one set. Halfway through the conversion run, an error occurs and only half the data base is converted. In this case one-half of the data base can be accessed as one structure, and the other half of the data base has another structure. Such a rarely occurring error is at the data base level and is not tolerable.

Still another level of data base integrity occurs at the application level. At this level only the application program has knowledge that an integrity exposure has occured. For example, suppose in a personnel file an employee's record is listed as sex = K and age = -31. Of course Sex must be male or female, and age must be positive. What has happened is that patently incorrect data has entered the system, and there is no way for the operating system or DBMS to know it. It is up to the application solely and entirely to correct this error.

For each type of integrity there is a corresponding mechanism to ensure that data can be restored to a proper state. Structural integrity is often verified by independent utilities. Both audit and restore utilities exist for this purpose.

A concept central to the integrity of a data base system is the level of integrity. The **level of integrity** refers to the level of structuring for which integrity control is kept. For example, if the level of integrity is the data base itself (as was the case in some early systems), then when a transaction is accessing any part of the data base, the entire data base is reserved for that transaction. It does not require a large imagination to see that if there is much activity on the system at all, then many transactions will be waiting on each other as they access data bases. So, in the interest of performance, most DBMS have a very low level of integrity at the record level or physical block level. This means that there is a small probability of many transactions holding up other transactions because the granularity of the data is protected by the integrity mechanism of the system.

SELECTING A DBMS

The selection of a DBMS is a very far-reaching decision. Once a DBMS is selected and once application code is written for the DBMS, it is very difficult and/or expensive to convert existing applications to another DBMS, although such a conversion can be done. A conversion from one DBMS to another requires very strong motivation. Historically, there have been attempts at writing application code that was independent of the DBMS, so that all that needed to be changed within the application code was the actual syntax of the calls made to the DBMS. But the strategy of addressing the interchangeability of DBMS at the syntax level has been an almost universal failure for a variety of reasons:

- The logic of the application code is as closely tied to the DBMS as the syntax is.
- The underlying physical structure of one DBMS is so different from another that even if the syntax of the calls are the same, the results produced by the calls are not the same.

- The calls in one DBMS are only generally similar to the calls in another DBMS, and the small differences turn out to be more than trivial.

Therefore, once a DBMS is selected, it is usually in use for a long time.

If a DBMS is difficult to replace, it is a simple matter to add another DBMS when needed. However, from a strategic management perspective, adding many DBMS is highly undesirable. Each DBMS introduces its own technology, which in turn requires its own support. Strictly from a support and usage standpoint, it does not make sense to have many DBMS in the same shop. Most shops wish to avoid supporting many different types of hardware and hardware vendors for the same reasons. Furthermore, the degree of compatibility of different DBMS is usually fairly low, so that skills learned in one DBMS environment are not immediately transferrable to another DBMS environment.

The original notion of DBMS was that a single DBMS served all needs. The notion of a single DBMS has its appeal and was widely accepted in the early days of data base. But over time the different needs in the usage of DBMS grew so rapidly and in such a varied fashion that a single DBMS had a very difficult time in satisfying the many needs. The primary division of needs occurred along the lines of dss (decision support systems) and operational systems. Operational needs are characterized by much update transaction processing against a data base that holds data at a very detailed level with a high degree of integrity. In general, operational transactions are characterized by a series of short-running activities against the system, whereas dss systems are characterized by a combination of short-running and long-running programs that easily manipulate data, usually at a summary level.

In selecting a DBMS, it is a temptation to base the selection on the requirements of the first major system to be constructed. Since DBMS tend to be around for a long time and since a shop would like to have as few DBMS as possible, the criteria for selection ought to include ALL the systems that will go data base, not just the first system. The major differences in the two environments mean that most shops have different DBMS for different environments—i.e., one DBMS for operational systems and another for dss systems. The criteria that make one operational DBMS more suitable than another are not the same criteria that apply to suitability of a dss DBMS.

Operational Criteria for Selection

The criteria for operational systems can be divided into two categories, criteria that apply to all operational DBMS and criteria that apply only to online DBMS (operational DBMS may be purely batch).

General Criteria

- *Data structuring.* Does the structure of the data supported by the DBMS in general fit with the needs of the structure of data found in the shop? For example, if a shop has bill-of-materials processing, will the data structuring under the DBMS handle the required recursive forms of the data?

- *Flexibility.* How easy is it for the data and processes built by the application developer to change? What levels of changes are needed?

- *Security.* What security features are there? Can the data be encoded? Can the data be protected at the record level? field level? data base level? What audit trails are there? What logging is there?

- *Application development facilities.* What automated tools exist to enhance the design process? the coding process? testing?

- *Package availability.* What commercial application software is available? financial packages? manufacturing packages? modeling packages?

- *Utilities.* What utilities are supplied by the vendor? What utilities exist commercially external to the vendor? What functions are there for which no utilities exist? Can the utilities be tailored? enhanced?

- *Data dictionary.* Does the DBMS come with its own data dictionary? Will the DBMS work with commercially available data dictionaries? To what degree is the data dictionary integrated with the software?

- *Multiprocessor support.* What capabilities are there for communication between different types of the DBMS running on a processor of the same size (e.g., mainframe to mainframe)? on processors of different sizes (mainframe to micro)?

- *Resource utilization.* What machine resources are required by the DBMS? Can more machine resources be easily added when needed? At what point will processing have to be split across different processors?

- *Documentation.* What documentation currently exists? What is needed but doesn't exist?

- *Support personnel.* How many people are needed to support the DBMS? data base administrators? designers? training? technical support? operational? others? Are personnel generally available on the marketplace?

- *Direct cost.* What is the license cost? What about licensing for test machines? for multiple machines?

- *Education.* What education facilities exist? by the vendor? by outside agencies? Is there a level of education that exists but is not available?

- *Vendor stability.* What reputation does the vendor have? Is the vendor financially stable? Are there other local sites serviced by the vendor?

- *Data base size.* Is there a finite limit to the amount of data that can be handled by the DBMS? If so, what is that limit?

- *Dss compatibility.* What dss software exists that can access or otherwise use the data of the DBMS? How easy is the transfer of data from the DBMS to the dss environment?

Online DBMS Selection Criteria

- *Recovery/restart.* What recovery/restart facilities are there? What options does the operator have at the point of failure? Will recovery/restart procedures be able to be run quickly enough to satisfy the availability requirements?

- *Performance management.* What performance tuning options are there? How easy are those options to exercise? How easy is diagnosis of performance problems? How effective are the performance tuning options?
- *System interfaces.* Can other online copies of the DBMS or teleprocessing monitor be accessed? Can other types of DBMS or teleprocessing monitors be accessed? What are the technical considerations of interfacing two separate DBMS? the economic considerations?
- *Availability.* How "fail soft" is the system? Can part of the system go down without taking the entire system down? What diagnostics are available to the operator to help bring the system back up? How long does it take to bring the system back up? What are the integrity exposures in the running of the system in a partially disabled state?
- *Maximum transaction throughput.* What is the maximum number of transactions per second that can be handled by the system? Is the shop going to surpass that limitation?
- *Integrity control.* At what level does transaction integrity control exist? How recoverable are lost transactions? Can integrity control be bypassed if desired?
- *Test facilities.* What online testing facilities are there? What online simulation testing facilities are there?
- *Operational support.* What level of individual is needed for operational support? how many people? What operator functions can be automated? How sensitive is the system to operational support?

Dss DBMS Selection Criteria

While many of the criteria of the selection of dss and operational DBMS are the same, there is a difference in emphasis. Some of the selection criteria for a dss DBMS are as follows:

- *Direct cost.* What is the software licensing cost? for multiple copies? for different processors?
- *Hardware.* Does the dss DBMS run on a mainframe? on a micro? on both? Is it useful to have the dss DBMS on both?
- *Mainframe-micro link.* Is it possible to move the data from the mainframe to the micro easily? at all? Is it possible to move the data from the micro to the mainframe easily? at all?
- *Ease of use.* Can an unsophisticated user use the dss DBMS in a day? What training is needed? What is available?
- *Documentation.* What documentation exists? What is available? at what costs?
- *Speed of operation.* How fast does the software operate? Will the speed be adequate for the needs of the user?
- *Program size.* What is the minimum storage needed? What is the maximum storage that can be used?

- *Data limitations*. Is there a maximum amount of data that can be accessed or managed? Are there types of data that cannot be handled by the dss DBMS?
- *Browse capabilities*. Does the dss DBMS have browsing capabilities? If so, how easy are the browsing capabilities to use?
- *Data dictionary*. Does the dss DBMS have a data dictionary? Is it a passive dictionary? an active dictionary?
- *Record limitations*. What physical record limitations are there? How big is the maximum record? the minimum record? Are there types of data that cannot go into a record? How many records will fit into a block?
- *Vendor stability*. What reputation does the vendor have for support? Is there a hotline? What do other users of the dss DBMS say about the vendor? Does the vendor have a sound financial foundation?
- *Menu capabilities*. Must queries be programmed? Can queries be driven by menu selection?
- *Data transfer to other dss users*. Can data be transferred to other dss users? easily? What sort of communication between users is possible?
- *Report-writing facilities*. Does the dss DBMS have report-writing facilities?
- *Data management*. What data management facilities are there? How are files named? Can they be renamed? Can files be scratched easily? Can they be restored easily?
- *Application software*. What application software exists for the dss DBMS? Is there a body of users with whom data and programs can be shared?
- *Operational software*. Is there an interface to receive data from operational software? to pass data to operational software?

TESTING

The importance of proper testing of newly developed data base systems is best illustrated by examining the results of inadequate testing. When a system is inadequately tested (and there are errors, which all test personnel assume that there are), the result is system malfunction. The malfunction may be as minor as an improper formatting of a report or as major as the disabling of the online system. In any case testing brings out the errors so they can be corrected *before* their negative impact is felt. The first consideration of testing is for the environment in which the system will run—either batch or online (for the purposes of testing, the interactive environment will be considered to be the equivalent of the batch environment).

Testing in the batch environment is relatively easy because programs and data can be isolated in the batch environment, even to the point of putting data and processes off onto another machine. Typically, a large production data base is selectively stripped of its data (i.e., 10% or 15% of the production data is stripped to produce a representative sample of test data), and the stripped data is used for testing. If a data base is to be created from scratch, a creation program is written to build a representative data base (sometimes called a *living sample* data base). The creation of the batch test environment is shown by Fig. 7.9.

One difficulty with the batch environment occurs when more than one system is being built and/or tested at once and both systems are using common data and programs. In this case great care must be taken so that the existing system *and* the new system are accounted for during testing. The following are the primary concerns of testing in the batch environment:

— Is the programming done properly? (e.g., are data exceptions and functional program logic checked)?
— Have the data definitions been properly defined and has change been coordinated?
— Have the volumes of data been accounted for?

The online environment is much more difficult for testing because, in addition to the above test criteria, the online environment also addresses the following:

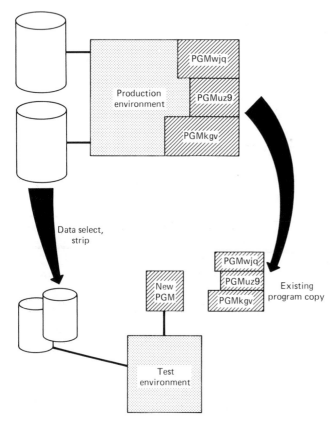

Figure 7.9 Creating and insulating the batch test environment from the production environment.

- *Performance.* What kind of response time will the system being tested have? What kind of impact will the new system have on existing response time? What resources will be used up?
- *Availability.* What kind of availability characteristics will the new system have? What kind of impact will the new system have on existing availability postures?
- *Batch window impact.* Will there be available capacity to run the new system in the batch window?

For these reasons the online environment is much more difficult to test than the batch environment because the online environment involves the entire community of data and programs. The isolation that is normal in the batch environment (which makes testing easy) is not possible in the online environment without giving up some degree of validity. Furthermore, when there is a problem with such fundamental issues as performance or availability in the online environment, there usually is no quick cure, such as a change to a line of code. Performance and availability are determined by the architecture of the application design and are impossible or impractical to retrofit.

The online environment, like the batch environment, is stripped and recreated into a physically separate environment. This allows individual programs to be unit tested, proving the validity of their code. But this stripping and recreation necessarily makes stress testing for performance and availability very difficult. And when a shop uses nonstandard DBMS exits, the test environment must be *identical* to the online environment; otherwise the tests will not be valid. As long as there is a single application being tested, the coordination of the test and production environments may not be too difficult, but in an environment where more than one major application is being tested, the coordination of different system generations become difficult.

Once the system is unit tested (making sure it works in a stand-alone environment), it must be tested for integration. This test is to make sure that the interfaces with other programs are solid and that the data that the system changes and uses is in synchronization with other parts of the system. The most difficult part of the online test is for performance and availability. The true performance and availability characteristics of a system are not known until the system is operating in the production environment under a full volume of data and transactions and is competing with other systems for shared online resources, such as buffers or main storage space. Availability can be analyzed by means of determining the length of recovery or reorganization, as has been discussed. One way performance can be analyzed is by a full re-creation of the production environment. This approach yields valid results although it is *very* expensive because of the duplication in machine, DASD, and technical support costs. A less expensive approach to performance testing is through simulation. This approach involves modeling the existing environment and then adding on the new system to produce an expected performance profile. Although this approach can be done by hand (i.e., by a paper-and-pencil analytical approach), existing software packages are more precise and more efficient to use.

TUNING

Data base tuning achieves optimal system performance using existing resources without changing application code. Tuning is done after the application is up and running. There are two major limitations to tuning. One limitation occurs when more resources, such as DASD, main storage buffers, channels, and regions, are needed. When the problem of performance is *purely* one of a lack of resources, there is very little the tuner can do, once the optimal configuration is established. The second limitation to tuning is that tuning is done to optimize some static configuration of a machine—a processor of a certain size doing a certain amount of work against a specified amount of data. Unfortunately, when any of those factors change—the processing environment, the work being done, and/or the data on which the work is done—the system generally needs to be retuned. So tuning is like shooting at a moving target. The normal method of determining that a system needs to be tuned is through monitors, although a cruder method is to wait until the online system experiences a slowdown. The monitors generally give much information, such as where the bottlenecks are, what resources are being enqueued upon, and where data is widely scattered into overflow.

The sort of tuning activities for data bases include the physical placement of data (so that the spread of popular data is over multiple locations rather than concentrated in a single location), the allocation and reallocation of DASD as data bases grow and change, the reorganization of data to enhance the internal cleanliness of data, and the redefinitions of physical space parameters to accommodate data base changes. On occasion a change of randomizers is required.

Tuning in the online environment requires a mixture of data base, system programming, and network administration skills. It is normal in this environment to push one thing down in one place and have something pop up elsewhere. Furthermore, the tuning activities in the online environment are very visible; if a mistake is made it is very quickly obvious to everyone using the online system. Some of the typical online tuning activities are the analysis and modification of buffer pool usage, the prioritization of activities and transactions as they are routed through the system, the allocation and page fixing of main storage, the interface with the SCP (system control program), queue monitoring, and starting and stopping of the internal control program. The job of the tuner is closely related to the job of the master terminal operator (MTO). Whereas tuning is an absolutely useful and necessary activity, it is not the key to online performance. A poor design ties the hands of the tuner to the point that there simply are no system options. Tuning enhances performance; design is essential to performance.

DATA DICTIONARY

A **data dictionary** is a repository of the definitions of data (the semantics) that are stored in a commonly accessible library. There are two kinds of data dictionaries, active dictionaries and passive dictionaries. An **active dictionary** is one that is not optional and is usable in an interactive fashion. An example of an active dictionary is the dictionary used by Cullinet's IDMS. A **passive dictionary** is one that is optional and is not normally used in an interactive mode, such as IBM's data dictionary.

When a dictionary can be used interactively, the user is able to call up the definitions of data directly and then to use the definitions to do some activity, such as select elements for retrieval. For a passive dictionary, the contents of a data base are examined in a listing, and if the user wants to select data elements for display, he or she must use a conventional means, such as writing a COBOL program or using a query language.

The sort of definitions that are typically (but not necessarily) stored on a data dictionary are COBOL or PL-1 data layouts, control block definitions, conceptual design documentation (entity relationship diagrams, etc.), procedures (job runs, job steps, overrides, etc.), program source code, and miscellaneous documentation. As a shop grows and these vital pieces of documentation concurrently grow, there is a need to keep the documentation in a central repository. In that sense a data dictionary is an inventory of data, or a "data base for data base." In a small environment, a data dictionary may be kept informally in an assortment of libraries and in an assortment of forms. But as a shop grows and there is a need for shared data and shared resources, the need for a formal data dictionary grows.

The care and tending of the data dictionary generally comes from a joint effort of data administration, data base administration, and applications that have data on the data dictionary.

QUESTIONS

Msdb Considerations

1.1. What are the differences between a msdb and a data base on DASD?

1.2. Under what conditions should a data base be put in main storage?

Msdb: Advantages and Disadvantages

2.1. What is the advantage of very quick access to data such as that stored in a msdb? the disadvantages?

2.2. What are the special recovery considerations of a msdb?

2.3. What are the special structural design considerations of a msdb?

Data Integrity

3.1. What is meant by data integrity?

3.2. What are the different kinds of integrity?

3.3. Who is responsible for data integrity?

3.4. How can data integrity be monitored?

3.5. What are the consequences if data integrity is not ensured?

Testing

4.1. What needs to be tested in a data base environment?

4.2. Who should do testing? when?

4.3. What role should the user play in testing?

4.4. Why is testing important? how important?

4.5. What documentation should be produced as a result of testing?

4.6. What is a stress test?

4.7. What is an integrated test?

4.8. To what extent can online systems be tested in batch?

Tuning

5.1. What is meant by data base tuning?

5.2. List 10 things the tuner can do to tune a system.

5.3. What is the result of a tuning effort?

5.4. How can it be determined that a tuning effort is necessary?

5.5. How can it be determined that a tuning effort was successful?

5.6. Who should tune a system?

5.7. Is there such a thing as detuning a system? If so, describe such a procedure. What rationale is there for detuning a system?

5.8. What besides tuning should be done to ensure good system performance?

Data Dictionary

6.1. What is a data dictionary?

6.2. Is it mandatory that a DBMS have a data dictionary?

6.3. What is a passive dictionary?

6.4. What is an active dictionary?

6.5. What is a formal data dictionary?

6.6. What is an informal data dictionary?

6.7. Who should control the contents of a data dictionary?

6.8. Does the existence of definitions on a data dictionary mean that data is under control?

6.9. Is data redundancy controlled by a data dictionary?

6.10. What types of data can be put on a data dictionary?

6.11. What besides data can be put on a data dictionary?

EXERCISES

1. Is a DBMS needed to create and manage an msdb? What requirements would you place on software responsible for managing an msdb? Write a piece of software that fulfills your requirements.

2. Describe six different types of data and structural disintegrity. Describe how each can be detected and repaired.

3. Data structures can be created and maintained by either the DBMS or by the application. Describe the different integrity exposures for each. From an operational viewpoint, describe the options available for recovery in each environment. From a development viewpoint describe options and differences in each environment.

4. Does the basic data model (hierarchical, relational, inverted, network) have any inherent relationship to integrity exposures? (For example, is the inverted environment any more or less susceptible to integrity exposures than the network environment?)

5. For each data model, describe three or more different levels of integrity. Describe how each level might be violated. Describe the consequences of a violation.

6. Is data base integrity the same problem in the dss environment as it is in the operational environment? Why or why not?

7. Describe the differences between data base integrity and transaction integrity. Which is more important?

8. Describe 10 different tuning activities that you can do in your DBMS environment. How can you measure the effectiveness of these activities? Who is charged with tuning your system?

9. Why is tuning always a temporary activity? Is there such a thing as a permanent tuning effort? Why or why not?

10. Why is the first major tuning activity that a shop does usually the most effective? Why do subsequent tuning efforts usually give marginally less satisfaction? Is this always the case?

11. What impact on performance would doubling your transaction load have? doubling your maximum transaction arrival rate? doubling the data managed by your system? How can increases in volume be predicted? be monitored?

12. What data dictionary do you have? What is meant by an informal data dictionary? by a formal one? What are the advantages and disadvantages of each? What procedures do you have for the usage and control of a data dictionary? How rigorously are they followed? How do you keep definitions current? What types of definitions do you have on your data dictionary? Are those definitions the final authority in your shop? Is there a more current version elsewhere?

CHAPTER 8

Data Base Design[*]

System design is made up of **process design** and **data design.** At the conceptual level these two activities are inseparable. The design of data in the absence of process considerations and the design of processes in the absence of data considerations inevitably yield unsatisfactory results. The details of process design as it is interwoven with data base design are discussed at length in *Information Systems Architecture**. The reader is invited to inspect the discussions of process design as found in that book. The importance of conceptual data base design is best understood in terms of the environment that is created where conceptual data base design is not done. Consider a hypothetical shop that has many tape-oriented sequential systems. The shop eventually tires of the limitations of the sequential environment and decides to "go data base".

To go data base the shop takes its sequential systems (dominated by the *master file* concept) and converts the systems to data base (where each master file is converted into a data base). The conversion of each system is done under a local perspective. A **local perspective** is one that considers only the immediate set of system requirements, without looking at the broader requirements of a shop. In a local perspective a designer does not recognize that many parts of the system at hand are recreated in other systems throughout the shop. The conversion of each individual sequential system amounts to the replacing of the magnetic tapes of the shop with direct access devices. Surprisingly, there are several advantages to this type of con-

(**Note:* This chapter is a condensation of material from two books previously published by the author, *Information Systems Architecture* (Prentice-Hall, 1986), which addresses conceptual system design, and *Effective Data Base Design* (Prentice-Hall, 1981), which addresses many aspects of physical data base design.)

164

version. One advantage is that data can be addressed directly. There is no longer a need to pass records 1, 2, . . . , n to get to record $n + 1$. Another advantage of a transparent conversion of sequential systems to direct access systems is that one program can access data concurrently with other programs, something that is not possible with magnetic tapes. In the sequential mode only one program at a time can access a magnetic tape. But direct access devices under the control of a DBMS (data base management system) allow multiple programs to access data at the same time. Still another advantage of a simple conversion of sequential systems to direct access devices is that, once on DASD, the data is capable of going online. The user is no longer tied to reports but has the capability of looking at and using data as it is directly stored. Yet another advantage of a series of simple local conversions of systems from a sequential mode to a direct access mode is that such conversions are straightforward to do. They require a minimum of planning and are often politically expedient. Fewer designers and programmers (in the short run!) are required and the resulting system looks very similar to what the user is used to seeing. Because the system has undergone only a superficial transformation, there is an absolute minimum of impact on the users.

Because of these immediate advantages of a series of direct system-by-system conversions from the sequential environment to the direct access data base environment, many shops choose such a policy. Such a conversion requires little or no conceptual design. However, from a long term perspective such a conversion—a local, system-by-system conversion—has *major* drawbacks. The local approach continues the practice of building and maintaining many separate, redundant systems. The redundancy of systems was one of the strong motivations for going data base in the first place, but merely placing data in a data base that can be accessed directly does nothing about the issue of redundancy.

Redundancy of data and of processing across many systems wastes many resources. The most obvious resource wasted is that of development resources. It is obviously more efficient to develop a system once than many times. The next obvious resource wasted by system redundancy is system maintenance. It requires many fewer resources to maintain one system than it does to maintain the same system in multiple parts. Where there are multiple systems a single change in the user's environment must be reflected throughout all redundant systems. The work of changing the system, synchronizing the changes, ensuring the changes are made consistently, converting all data, and locating where changes should be made is a time-consuming, complex task. The result of a series of local conversions is a collection of redundant systems that mirror the preceding redundant sequential systems. In such a case a shop is deriving only a fraction of the potential advantage of going data base. When a simple local conversion is done, data base is only being used as an alternative access method to magnetic tape.

What is required to unlock the full potential of data base is a change in perspective. A *global* approach is required (as opposed to the local perspective). A **global perspective** is one that considers *all* the requirements of a shop, not just the limited set of requirements of a single system. *All* system needs are analyzed in relation to the totality of needs of other systems. In such a fashion nonredundant data base systems can be created. To be effective, a global perspective must be taken *long* before physical design begins. Global design must begin with a solid conceptual design, upon which ultimately all physical systems will be built. Global design does not depend on or otherwise relate to any particular DBMS. The physical implementation of a global design can come in many forms. There is a large degree of independence of physical design and global (or conceptual) design.

Global system design encompasses both data and processes. The focus in this book is on the aspects of data design. The essence of conceptual data design is to recognize commonality of data across all requirements and still allow for individual data differences. The importance of recognizing commonality is best illustrated in terms of an example. Consider an insurance company that desires to build systems to serve its auto policies. The data processing department sets off building systems as quickly as possible. An auto policy system for Texas is built, then one for Colorado, one for Kansas, and so forth. Individual systems are built for each state for two reasons. One reason is that there *are* differences in the laws governing each state. The other reason is that of expediency. Building a global system requires much more effort initially in design than quickly building a system for an individual state.

After a period of time the company has 50 auto policy systems, one for each state. The maintenance effort is no small task. Then one day a non–data processing executive asks why there are 50 unique systems, since each system is functionally very similar to each other system. Essentially, the systems manage policy expenses, premiums, and losses. While no two systems are truly identical (as the laws of any two states are not identical), there nevertheless is a tremendous amount of commonality among the various systems. It would be much more desirable for the insurance company to have a single system that accounts for the differences, where appropriate, between states. Unfortunately, once the systems are built, management is very reluctant to rebuild them, however onerous the maintenance. A local approach that resulted in 50 separate systems has been adopted when a global approach that would have resulted in a single, unified system was necessary. The system designers failed to recognize the commonality of data across all requirements. To adopt a global posture, a conceptual design was necessary prior to the physical building of the first part of the system. At the heart of recognizing commonality across large systems is the ability to abstract data and structures. Figure 8.1 shows

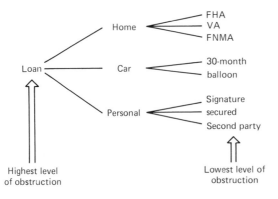

Figure 8.1 Much common information is shared by all loans, although there is unique information about FHA loans, 30-month car loans, and signature personal loans. Abstraction allows these differences and commonalities to be accounted for.

how different levels of abstraction both account for differences in data and recognize commonality of data across a broad range of requirements.

The building of a conceptual design is like the building of a blueprint (see Fig. 8.2). The conceptual design is useful to the programmer, the user, management, data base administrator, and anyone else using the system. The conceptual design or blueprint can be used for estimation, communication, clarification, and planning. The blueprint encompasses both data and processes. The commonality of both data and processes is recognized *before* the system is physically built.

The recognition of commonality allows the designer to build processes *once* and data and data structures *once.* The source code that defines a program and the data base definitions that define a data base exist nonredundantly. Once compiled, the machine usable form of the code may exist in many places, and data base definitions, once transformed into a computer usable form, may exist in many places. But the source of the code and the data definitions exist, nonredundantly in a single place. Because control of the system is at the source level, conceptual design is independent of any physical implementation. The nonredundancy of data and processes occurs because the commonality has been recognized at a global level. While a conceptual blueprint recognizes and combines commonality, individual differences

Figure 8.2 A skyscraper requires a blueprint; a shanty does not. Complex information systems require a blueprint; a simple report does not.

in data and processes are likewise taken into account. If conceptual design recognized only commonalities, then the resulting system design would indeed be nonsensical.

DIFFERENT LEVELS OF MODELING

The model of data that is built during conceptual design must address different levels of understanding of the systems that are based upon the model. The different levels of modeling that are appropriate depend on the size and complexity of the system being designed. A very large, complex environment may require five or six levels of conceptual modeling, while a simple environment may require only two or three levels. Three levels of modeling are presented in this book, but the reader is alerted to the fact that in practice there may be more or fewer, depending on the particulars of the data being modeled.

The need for different levels of modeling during conceptual design is illustrated by three levels of maps, as shown by Fig. 8.3. At the highest level is a globe that shows the relative position of the seas and countries on the different continents. At the midlevel is a state map showing the borders of the state, the major highways, and the different cities within the state. At the lowest level is the city map showing streets, buildings, churches, railroads and the like.

Each level of mapping has its own uses. One would not use a globe to find the nearest police station, nor would one use a city map to find the way to China (unless of course, one is in Tibet!). So different, yet related, maps are needed to describe the conceptual architecture of a shop's information systems. At the highest level of the conceptual architecture are found the major and most basic elements in a shop and how they relate. At this level these elements are often called **entities.** At the lowest level of the conceptual architecture is found the data elements that are required physically to build data bases, sometimes called the **model** for a subject data base. And throughout all levels of the conceptual architecture there is a relationship between the different levels of modeling.

COMPONENTS OF MODELING

The basic components of data modeling are as follows:

- Definition of the scope of integration
- Identification of dimensions
- Identification of different data views
- Creation of entities and relationships between entities
- Creation of data item sets (dis)
- Creation of the physical model
- Identification of attributes

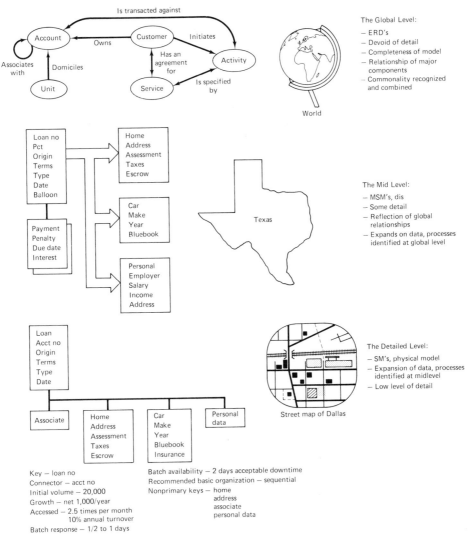

Figure 8.3 Different levels of modeling.

- Identification of data characteristics
- Identification of keys

SCOPE OF INTEGRATION

The **scope of integration** is the definition of what is and what is not to be in the conceptual architecture. It is an English language description outlining what data and processes are to be included in the model. The scope of integration is perhaps the most important part of the modeling process in that a proper definition of the scope of integration ensures a proper focus throughout the building of the conceptual architecture. The importance of a proper scope of integration is best understood in terms of an example. Suppose a modeling effort is begun and a model is created for a manufacturing environment. After the model is created, management asks where personnel and payroll are in the model. The entities of parts, suppliers, orders, and the like do not represent personnel or payroll. So the modelers are left in an awkward situation. Had management wanted personnel and payroll included in the model and had a scope of integration been formally defined that had included manufacturing, personnel, and payroll, then management's criticism would have been valid. But without a formal scope of integration, it is ambiguous whether personnel and payroll should have been included in the model. Without a formal outline of the boundaries of the model, the modeling process has a way of never ending. In addition to outlining what should be included in the conceptual model, the scope of integration should also specifically outline what is not to be in the conceptual model.

In many ways the scope of integration is like a contract between the system modeler, the end user, and management. The modeler is liable for everything within the scope of integration and for nothing outside of the scope. If the user or management wishes to change the scope at a later point in time, then the user or management must understand that there is a cost associated with the change, and it is the responsibility of the user or management, not the modeler, to bear the costs.

Over time the scope of integration changes, even in the most stable and well-thought-out environments. But in a properly modeled environment, the changes in the scope of integration come in small degrees. Because the changes are small, they are relatively easy to accommodate. If a change is monumental, then the scope of integration has not been properly defined from the outset.

As a matter of practice, it is wise to begin a modeling effort with as large a scope of integration as possible and then narrow the scope down as the modeling process progresses. It is always easier to narrow the scope of integration then it is to expand the scope of integration. However, if the scope is too large, the modeler should be aware that the model may never be complete and that the resulting systems are impractical to build. So the size of the scope of integration should be a trade-off between what a shop would like to model and what the shop is actually able to implement, with a tendency to err on the side of largeness.

DIMENSION

A **dimension** is a broad view of some part of the business or enterprise that is being modeled. A dimension represents the collective of all the different parties engaged in the same business activity. As such there are usually multiple dimensions in the scope of integration. In any case there is always one dimension within the scope of integration, the primary business-based dimension, and there may be other dimensions. For example, the primary business-based dimension of a manufacturer typically includes parts, orders, suppliers, bill of materials, shop floor control, and so forth. Other nonprimary business-based dimensions of the manufacturer might include other data that is relevant to the development engineer, the plant auditor, the payroll department, and personnel. While each of these nonprimary business-based dimensions views some of the same data as the primary business-based dimensions and other nonprimary business-based dimensions, each dimension is unique. The scope of integration is comprised of all the different dimensions that are appropriate. All the dimensions combine to define completely the contents of the conceptual architecture. Figure 8.4 illustrates the basic relationship between the scope of integration, dimensions, and other levels of data modeling.

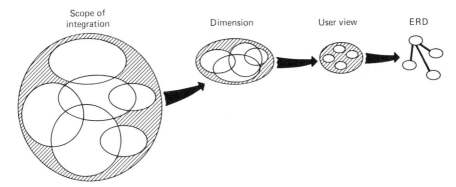

Figure 8.4 The scope of integration is made up of different dimensions; different users' views make up dimensions; data views are a part of user views; entity relationship diagrams (ERDs) are made up of data views.

DATA VIEWS

A dimension is made up of one or more user views (usually several). A user view is composed of data views and process views. A **data view** (dv) is the view of data within a dimension by a single user. If a dimension represents a single user, then there is only one dv for the dimension (an unlikely event). If more than one user is represented by the dimension then there will be multiple dv. A dimension encompasses process views as well as dv.

For example, consider the primary business-based dimension of a manufacturer. Some of the different users that participate in that dimension are engineers, production control personnel, purchase order processing personnel, and the foreman on the assembly line. The engineer views the data in the primary business-based dimension in terms of parts, bill of materials, material requirements processing, and so forth. Production control personnel view the data in the primary business based dimension in terms of inventory, orders, parts rejected, lead times, and so forth. Purchase order processing personnel view the data in the primary business-based dimension in terms of orders received, quantity on hand, quantity discounts, parts explosions and substitutions, and so forth. The supervisor on the assembly line views the data in the primary business-based dimension in terms of scheduling, parts explosions, suppliers, manufacturing orders, rejects, and so forth. In total, these people (and other relevant users that are included in the scope of integration) form the basis for the data that belongs in the primary business-based dimension. The dv of the users are collected and merged together to form the model of data for the conceptual architecture. Other dimensions within the scope of integration are created in the same manner.

ENTITIES AND RELATIONSHIPS

From the collected dv in a given dimension, an **entity/relationship diagram** (ERD) is created. An ERD consists of the entities that are found in the dimension and any relationships between the entities. The entities are derived from the various dv that belong in the dimension. The ERD represents the modeling of the data at its highest level within the conceptual architecture. Entities are usually void of detail; i.e., there is very little added to the ERD other than the identification of what the entity is. As an example, consider the primary business-based dimension of a manufacturing company. Typical entities would include parts, orders, and suppliers. Figure 8.5 illustrates a simple manufacturing entity. Entities within the same dimension should be in the same level of abstraction. The level of abstraction refers to the breadth of the classification of the entity. Some entities encompass very much data, whereas some other entities represent a limited amount of data.

For example, the entity–demand–probably does not belong in the same dimension as parts (even though there is undoubtedly a demand for parts). While demand may be an entity that applies to the dimension of an economist and part is an entity that applies to a shop supervisor, it is unlikely that an economist and a supervisor would ever be common users in the same dimension. As an example of keeping the level of abstraction of different entities consistent, the dimension of the economist would include demand, supply, goods (including parts), and so forth, and the dimension of the supervisor would include parts, orders, and the like.

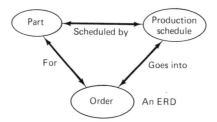

Figure 8.5

All the data that is viewed collectively by the users in a dimension must be represented by some entity (i.e., a user in a dimension cannot view data that is not represented by one or more entities). Such things as the parts of an engineer, the routing of goods on the shop floor, the inventory of precious goods, and orders for a finished product are *all* represented by entities. Every type of data represented by the user is accounted for by the entities in a dimension, as symbolically shown by Fig. 8.6. Furthermore, no data is represented by more than one entity in a dimen-

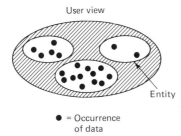

User view

= Occurrence
of data

Entity

Figure 8.6 Every occurrence of data in the user view is encompassed by an entity. No occurrence of data is encompassed by more than one entity.

sion. If an engineer views a part as belonging to a bill of materials, then within the same dimension the part cannot also belong to a separate inventory entity. Within the same dimension there must be *one* part in the dimension that serves all users. This consolidation within a dimension ensures that the commonality of data is recognized at the highest level.

There may be (and usually is) some duplication of entities across different dimensions. The same entity may exist in multiple dimensions. This apparent anomaly is rectified as the different dimensions are merged to form the resultant subject data base. Once the entities of a dimension are identified, the relationship between any two entities is identified. The relationship between the entities may be $1:1$, $1:n$, $m:n$, or nonexistent. For example, consider a part/order relationship. For a given order there may be multiple parts (i.e., the order may be for more than one part). By the same token, for a given part there may be multiple orders. So the part/order relationship is $m:n$. Now consider another relationship between a supplier and a part. A given supplier may supply more than one part, but a given part can come from only one supplier (in the case being considered). Such a supplier/part relationship is $1:n$.

Now consider a special relationship, the manufacturing bill of materials. In this relationship a part is made up of other parts. Such a relationship is **recursive,** where an entity has a relationship with itself. Typical recursive manufacturing relationships include what parts go into other parts, what parts are made from other parts, and what parts are substitutes for other parts. These recursive relationships are indicated by an arrow pointing into the entity from which it originated (i.e., back into itself), as shown by Fig. 8.7.

Relationships at the ERD level of modeling typically are accompanied by verbiage. The verbiage describes something meaningful about the relationship, such as "is made from", "supplies", and "owns". The verbiage is optional, even though it is well advised. The output of the highest level of modeling is the ERD, which is simply the aggregation of the entities and relationships for the different dimensions that belong to the scope of integration.

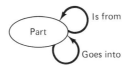

Is from

Part

Goes into

Recursion of an entity   **Figure 8.7**

DEFINITIONS

One of the most important aspects of high-level modeling for a conceptual architecture is the definition of entities. A proper definition is essential if the entity is
to apply to *all* the occurrences of data within the scope of integration. Without solid
definitions, it is normal for systems at the implementation level to have the same
name for data and yet have the data mean different things (or different shades of
the same thing). Another variation of data inconsistency occurs at the implementation level when the same data exists in different parts of a system under different
names. Data inconsistency and ambiguity is greatly minimized by a sound definition
of the data at the highest level of modeling, the ERD level. The criteria for quality
of definition of the entities that are inside the ERD are as follows:

- Does the definition of the entity encompass *all* it ought to encompass?
- Does the definition of the entity encompass *only* what it ought to encompass?
- Is there any occurrence of data in the scope of integration that is not included
  in the definition of an entity?
- Has every business-specific term used in a definition been previously defined?
- Is there an occurrence of data in an ERD that has been defined by more than
  one entity?
- Is the verbiage used in the definition comprehensible?
- Do the user and data processor understand and concur with the definition?

The criteria for quality of definition are best illustrated in terms of an example.
Suppose the modeler has defined a part as basic material. Does this definition encompass *all* it ought to encompass? Isn't a finished product also a part? The definition is refined: A part is basic material or a finished product.

But does this definition encompass *only* what it ought to encompass? The
answer is no. If the manufacturing process being modeled is for a bicycle factory,
then there are many basic materials, such as clay, balsa wood, plasma, and tree
bark, for example, that do not belong in the definition. So the definition is refined:
A part is a finished product or basic material used in the manufacturing process.

The next criteria for quality of definition asks if there are occurrences of data
not covered by the definition. In the definition there is no allowance for assemblies
that are not yet finished products. So the definition is once again refined: A part
is basic material used in the manufacturing process, an assembly, or a finished product.

Now the criteria for quality of definition requires that every business-specific
term used in the definition be previously defined. In this case manufacturing process
is used and has not been previously defined. A definition for manufacturing process
might be an arrangement of work in order to change raw goods or subassemblies
into an assembly.

Now it is necessary to ask if an occurrence of data is included in more than
one definition. Suppose there were separate definitions for parts and assemblies.
An analyst might ask if a cam shaft is a part or an assembly. It is both, so part and
assembly need to be combined into the same definition. The next criterion for a

sound definition is whether the verbiage is proper. Suppose an engineer had defined a bill of materials as the relationship of parts in a recursive unidirectional or bidirectional form from which the traversal of the manufacturing process can be derived by means of static relationships. While this definition might mean something to an engineer, there are many people who need to use a bill of materials that will not clearly understand what is being said. A simpler definition of bill of materials might be the structure of the data in a manufacturing process.

The final criterion for quality of definition requires that the user and data processor understand and concur with the definition. This mutual agreement on the definition ensures that the activity of defining the entities has not been either a purely data processor activity or a purely user activity. To be successful, the definitions must be meaningful to both data processors and the users.

MIDLEVEL MODELING

Once the ERD has been constructed, each entity is then expanded into a greater level of detail, which includes keys, attributes, and other characteristics. A **key** is a data element that is used to separate a given occurrence of data from other occurrences of data. For example, the key of an entity for a person might be social security number or employee number. A key may be unique or nonunique. Sex, age, and color of hair are nonunique keys of an entity that represents a person.

Data elements that are not keyed are called **attributes.** The attributes for an entity that represents parts might include part description, unit of measure, quantity on hand, and so forth. At the midlevel of modeling, most common attributes are identified. The midlevel of modeling below the ERD is sometimes called **dis modeling.** The terminology **minimum structure model** (msm) is also used. At the midlevel the different types of entity are introduced. The notation for *is a type of* is used. When a dis is broken into its separate types, all types of the dis are delineated. For example, the dis representing a car manufacturer's parts may be broken down by the general category in which it belongs, such as motor block, transmission, carriage, or body. Once the breakdown begins, it must be continued to include *all* types of parts. Figure 8.8 illustrates an example of breaking an entity down into its component types.

As a rule only unique data is associated with a given type. If all types of data have a common attribute, the attribute should be placed at a higher level within the modeling of the dis. For example suppose an entity representing a part is broken into airplane tail parts, airplane engine parts, airplane body parts, airplane wing parts, and airplane interior parts. Now suppose each of the types of parts has an attribute, quantity on hand. The attribute quantity on hand should be represented at the higher part level (i.e., the more abstract level), since it applies to all types of parts, not at the level of each individual type. What belongs at the level of each type is the data unique to the type. As an example, for the model representing the interior contents of the airplane is found the attribute *removable,* which indicates whether the part is removable from the aircraft or not. Such an attribute applies to the food dolly or fire extinguisher in the aircraft but most certainly does not belong

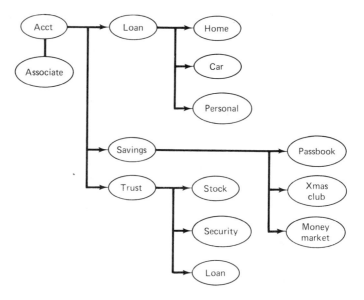

Figure 8.8 The entity account has been broken down into its more detailed component parts.

to the wing assembly. So the type of data for the airplane's interior has a unique attribute that does not belong to the other types of airplane parts. The next step in creating the midlevel model is shown in Fig. 8.9. The dis level of modeling of the conceptual architecture is the midlevel of modeling. It represents a transition of modeling from the ERD to the lower level detailed modeling, the physical model.

PHYSICAL MODEL

After the dis (or midlevel) model has been built, the physical model is ready to be built. The **physical model** is the lowest level of modeling prior to the actual data base design. The physical model includes the following:

- All data elements
- Physical attributes of the elements
- Identification of the keys (unique and nonunique) of the model
- Order of appearance (and any other internal structuring) of the model
- Grouping of the data elements based on the dis reference to their commonality and uniqueness
- Connectors to other data

As an example of how the physical model is built for the dis, consider the dis shown in Fig. 8.9. A physical model for the dis is shown by the two physical data base models in Fig. 8.10. The figure depicts two data base models, a home loan data base model and a car loan data base model, two very different, yet integrated, data

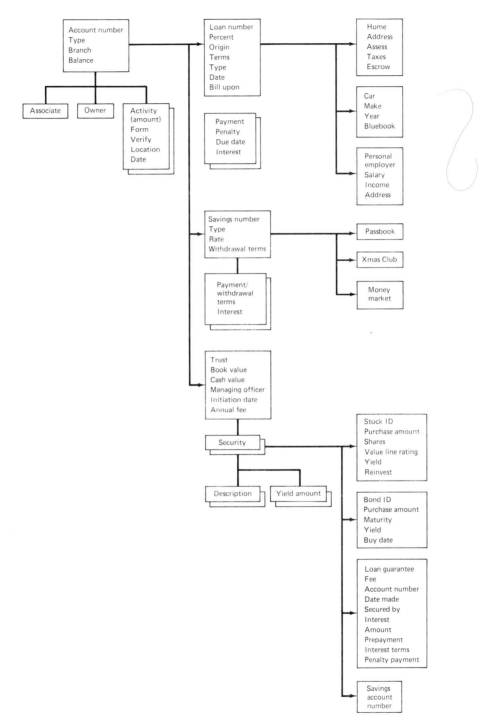

Figure 8.9 From the entity breakdown shown in Fig. 8.8, the more detailed dis is drawn. From the dis, the physical model is created.

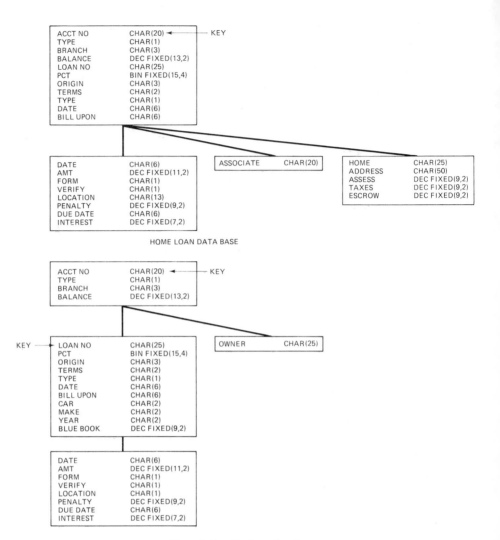

Figure 8.10 Car loan data base.

structures. Note that all common data elements have like physical characteristics in their different data base models (e.g., type is described by CHAR(1) in both the car loans and the home loans data base). Also, like data elements are grouped together in the same order (e.g., ACCT NO, TYPE, BRANCH, and BALANCE are grouped together wherever they are found). The grouping of data elements corresponds to the groups indicated by the dis.

Also of interest is that some data appears in one model but not the other. ASSOCIATE appears in the home loan data base but not the car loan data base, for example. Some data is grouped differently from other data. ACCT NO data and LOAN NO data are grouped together in the home loan data base, whereas ACCT NO data and LOAN NO data are separated in the car loan data base model.

The difference in the grouping of data implies that for home loan data there is one loan per account and for car loans there may be more than one loan per account. Also, the physical model can be implemented in a variety of ways: hierarchically, relationally, or by a network. To this point there is no implied physical implementation.

While the integrated data structures may look very similar to unintegrated structures, there are some major differences. Consider the amount of source code needed to implement the data bases as shown (Fig. 8.11). This figure shows that

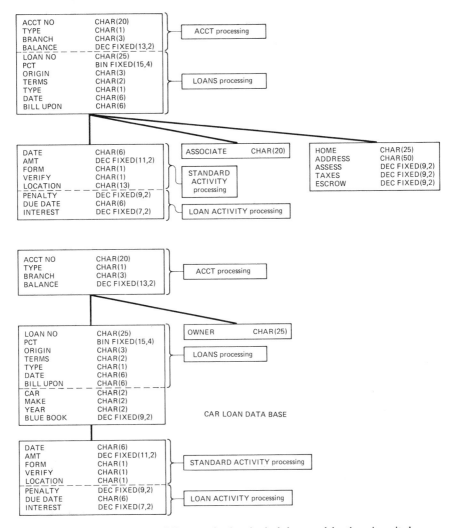

Figure 8.11 Despite the differences in the physical data models, there is a single source code that handles the activity for each piece of data. The data layouts are arranged so that there is no need for multiple source codes to manage the same types of data.

only one set of source code is needed to handle account processing, one set is needed to handle standard banking activity, one set is needed to handle loans, and one set is needed to handle loan activity. While there is some savings of coding in developing the two data base systems as shown, consider the savings in the development of personal loans (and all sorts of other related banking activities). Because of these savings, the development costs are reduced. And by the same token, consider changes to account processing. When account processing code needs to be modified, the modification is made to a single set of source code, not to many similar sets of source codes widely scattered around the bank.

Finally, consider another advantage of integrated systems—the foundation upon which dss systems are based. When dss systems access car loan data or home loan data, there is no question as to the data's consistency and to the processing that has manipulated the data.

NORMALIZATION

One of the foundations of data analysis and the building of the conceptual architecture of integrated systems is the normalization of data. Normalization of data is the process by which data elements are organized in a fashion optimized to produce as stable a data structure as possible. The origins of normalization are steeped in an academic setting, and much theory and conversation exist on the academic viewpoint of normalization. But normalization has a practical as well as an academic basis.

A commonly held view about normalization is that data has several forms of normalization: first normal form, second normal form, third normal form, and so forth. Most data analysis recognizes the need for three levels of normalization. Data arranged in third normal form is often presumed to be in a very stable form. There are at least two approaches to building normalized data structures: the classical bottom-up approach and the nonclassical top-down approach. Both approaches to achieving normalized data structures will be discussed.

Classical Botton-Up Normalization

Bottom-up normalization is best illustrated by the normalization of a typical flat file data structure. Such a structure might be found in the COBOL layout for a file existing on magnetic tape. Consider the flat file structure as shown in Fig. NORM.1. In this figure many data elements have been congregated. The flat file structure can hold up to three occurrences of loan data and payment information for three payments for each loan. The first form of normalization requires that occurring groups be removed, as shown in Fig. NORM.2. After the occurring groups have been removed, data is organized so that elements that depend on keys for their existence are related to those keys. The grouping of data around keys is shown by Fig. NORM.3.

Once the keys of the structure have been identified, the relationship of keys to each other is identified, along lines of existence, as shown by Fig.

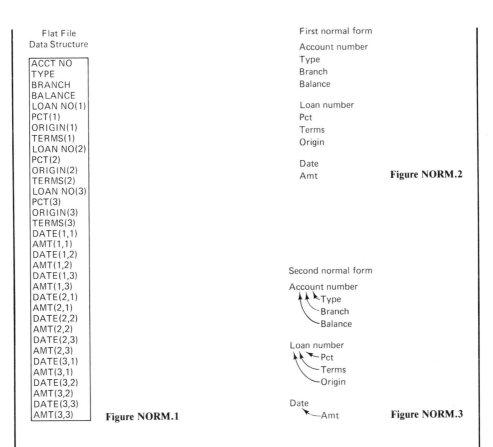

Flat File
Data Structure

```
ACCT NO
TYPE
BRANCH
BALANCE
LOAN NO(1)
PCT(1)
ORIGIN(1)
TERMS(1)
LOAN NO(2)
PCT(2)
ORIGIN(2)
TERMS(2)
LOAN NO(3)
PCT(3)
ORIGIN(3)
TERMS(3)
DATE(1,1)
AMT(1,1)
DATE(1,2)
AMT(1,2)
DATE(1,3)
AMT(1,3)
DATE(2,1)
AMT(2,1)
DATE(2,2)
AMT(2,2)
DATE(2,3)
AMT(2,3)
DATE(3,1)
AMT(3,1)
DATE(3,2)
AMT(3,2)
DATE(3,3)
AMT(3,3)
```

Figure NORM.1

First normal form

Account number
Type
Branch
Balance

Loan number
Pct
Terms
Origin

Date
Amt   **Figure NORM.2**

Second normal form

Account number
Type
Branch
Balance

Loan number
Pct
Terms
Origin

Date
Amt   **Figure NORM.3**

NORM.4. The data structure shown in Fig. NORM.4 shows data in third normal form, where every nonkey element relates to its key.

Nonclassical Top-Down Normalization

Now consider another way to achieve the same normalized structure, as shown by Fig. NORM.5. At the highest level of modeling is the ERD, where a basic entity is identified. From the ERD a dis is described, in which the major types of the entity are identified. The dis is further refined into a physical

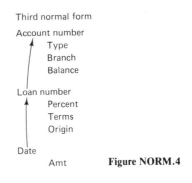

Third normal form

Account number
Type
Branch
Balance

Loan number
Percent
Terms
Origin

Date
Amt   **Figure NORM.4**

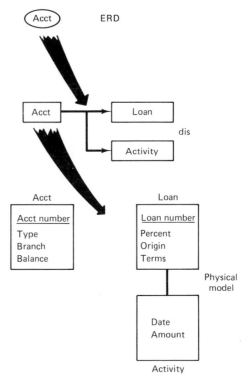

Figure NORM.5

model by adding appropriate major data elements. The result is the same normalized structure that was achieved by classical bottom-up normalization. The primary difference in the data structures produced is not in the content but in how the structures were derived.

Top-Down versus Bottom-Up

Normalization can thus be achieved in a top-down or a bottom-up fashion. Bottom-up normalization begins with all the details that will appear in the system. There are great amounts of detail to begin with in bottom-up normalization. Top-down normalization entails the derivation of data and data structure through a rigorously defined process. The process used to derive the structure naturally makes the overall relationships of the different parts of the data easy to see. An advantage of the top-down approach is that it is easy to verify that all the data that belongs in the model in fact is there. Top-down and bottom-up normalization complement each other. A purely bottom-up approach, while addressing much detail, often neglects major structural aspects of the data. A purely top-down approach nicely defines the structure of the data but often omits or overlooks much detail. The most effective approach to achieving a complete, well-structured normalized data structure is to do a combination of top-down and bottom-up normalizing.

MARRYING THE PHYSICAL DATA MODEL
AND THE PROCESS MODEL

Once the detailed modeling of the data is completed, the system is ready to go into physical design. But before going into physical design, cross-check between data and processes must be made. The cross-check ensures that all data needed to support a process and all processes needed to support data are present.

The result of physical modeling and the consolidation of different dimensions with each other is subject data bases. **Subject data bases** are important because they represent a shop's legitimate effort to integrate data. Common data is collected in a single place, which frees a shop from redundant development and maintenance. When a subject data base does undergo change, the impact of the change is minimized because the change is localized to a limited amount of data. Upon implementation of subject data bases, a shop has a foundation for future growth.

USING THE BLUEPRINT

An information systems architecture is a blueprint. As such it serves as a tool for a variety of people who have a variety of needs. But the blueprint is not static; it changes as the user's environment changes. Over time, every user's environment changes. The only difference in users is the rate of change. If the blueprint has been properly constructed, the changes in the user's environment will be able to be accommodated with a minimum of fuss; such is the nature of integration. So the architecture that is built must constantly be modified. While the activities of the initial building of the blueprint are time consuming and intensive, the ongoing maintenance of the blueprint is much less demanding.

PHYSICAL DATA BASE DESIGN

As the transition is made from the physical model to the actual physical data structure (i.e., the data structure as the DBMS knows it), the general issues of design are divided into two classes—the issues of transition and the basic issues of physical design.

The first transition issue is how to conform to the physical model in its most basic form and how the physical model corresponds to the physical data structure. In some cases the data item set and the physical model will appear to be very similar; in other cases they will be quite different, as in Fig. 8.12.

The next transition issue is how the key structures are to be represented. The primary issue is the scope of representation of the keys. This issue (which relates directly to the scope of integration, as defined in the conceptual model) must be decided before the proper physical form of the key can be decided. Figure 8.13 shows three different key structures for a parts data base. If the system being built is for office supplies and a key structure of xxx9 is adopted, the key structure will accomodate only office supplies, since other types of parts have a much expanded

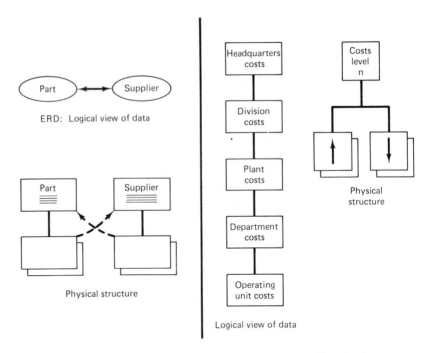

ERD: Logical view of data

Physical structure

Logical view of data

Physical structure

Figure 8.12 The physical data structure on the left—part-supplier—has been patterned after the logical view of the structure, as shown in the entity relationship diagram. The physical structure on the right—a recursive cost structure—logically satisfies the views of the end user but is not physically patterned after the logical view of the data.

Airplane parts key structure —   xxx9999999
Office supply key structure —   xxx9
Tooling and maintenance key structure — xxxxxxxxxxx

where 9 = numeric, x = alphanumeric

A limited part key definition —   xxx9
A universal part key definition — xxxxxxxxxxx (where office supplies are preceded by 7 blanks
                                                                    and where airplane parts are preceded by 1 blank)

Figure 8.13

key structure, as shown in the figure. It will never be adequate for other types of parts. But if the key structure adopted is xxxxxxxxxxx, as defined in the figure, it will fit the most general case of parts.

The next transition issue in going from the physical model to the actual physical structure of the data is the determination of the search criteria on other than the key of the data. In some cases searches will be quite efficient and simple to execute, such as when determining the first and last name of a person whose data is keyed by social security number. Such a search is easy to make because the data is normally carried in the same locale.

But other nonkey criteria may not be so straightforward, such as occasional searches through the entire data base based on multiple nonrecurring criteria. As an example a search may be done for employees who have an advanced degree in engineering, who speak French, and who are not married. The same request may not ever be issued again.

Data elements must be identified before the transition from the physical model to the actual physical structure is complete. As in the case of key definition, care must be taken so that *all* elements that are needed to satisfy the search criteria within the scope of integration are properly accounted for. A general definition of the volume of data is necessary to make a transition from the physical model to the actual physical data structure. Data volume is important to the designer for many reasons. For example, if there is to be a small amount of data, the designer may feel free to include some slack space for future expansion in the actual physical data structure. On the other hand, data volumes that are very large may be physically partitioned into several units and probably will contain absolutely no slack space whatsoever. The medium on which data resides is decided in no small part on the volume of data and its criticality. Large amounts of data may be put into an archival file or on photo-optical storage. Less voluminous data may reside on DASD, and highly critical small amounts of data may reside in main memory. Each of these media greatly influences the ultimate physical design of the data.

A final issue involving the transition from physical model to actual physical data structure is the interface with other data. The interface is laid out in its most basic form by the ERD. The interface must satisfy long-term goals (i.e., the scope of integration) and must be as simple and straightforward as possible. When the interface is complex and cumbersome, it is a sign that the logical relationships between the data have not been abstracted properly. Complexity at the interface level leads to unnecessary development and maintenance complexity. In summary, the transition issues of general data base design are as follows:

— General structure of the data
— Key structure
— Other search criteria
— Data element definition
— Data volume
— Medium on which data will reside
— Data interfaces

GENERAL PHYSICAL ISSUES

Once the transition issues are settled, it is safe to proceed with general physical design issues. (As a note, general physical design issues *can* be addressed without having fully resolved *all* transition issues. However, the result is usually a waste of work on a grandiose scale. When a major transition issue is not decided and physical issues are being set in concrete, it is a matter of coincidence if the physical design fits with the transition resolution when the transition issue is finally decided.) The first physical issue to be resolved is the selection of the DBMS. The selection of the DBMS depends greatly on the way the system will be used. For example, a large automated teller system would not fit well on a relational DBMS, and a highly flexible personnel system would not fit well on a hierarchical DBMS. Greatly influencing the choice of the DBMS is whether the system has dss or operational characteristics. Once the DBMS is (or are) selected, the framework for the other system criteria is laid.

The most basic physical design issue after the selection of the DBMS is a determination of the structure of the data. There are two criteria here: *Can* the DBMS represent the data at all? *Can* the DBMS represent the data well? The distinction between these two questions is not trivial. Many DBMS *can* represent data in many forms but, for some forms, do so in an awkward and/or inefficient fashion. For example, relational systems usually represent bill-of-materials data awkwardly because the user must personally retain all the level-by-level explosions for a part. In relational systems, it is the user that is in control of data relationships, which gives relational systems great flexibility. However, that flexibility is bought at a price. Another example of an awkward representation of data is the $m : n$ relationship of data in the hierarchical environment.

Another very important issue is that of the teleprocessing monitor and how well the monitor works with the DBMS. Is a large amount of telecommunication needed? If so, the DBMS and teleprocessing monitor must be able to handle the load. A large amount of teleprocessing activity usually implies a need for a low level of data integrity. These fundamental considerations must be accounted for in the selection of the DBMS.

OPERATIONAL DATA BASE DESIGN

The following general design guidelines apply to all operational systems, both batch and online. Access paths are an important physical design issue. An access path refers to the ability of the user of the system to proceed from one part of the data structure to the other with a minimum of effort. As in the case of data structures, there are two issues: Does the path exist at all? If the path does exist, is it awkward to use? As an example of access paths, consider Fig. 8.14. In this figure data is designed to be able to go from part to supplier but not from supplier to part. There is no problem as long as an access path from supplier to part is not required. As the data exists now, there is only a single access path.

A related issue is the creation of access paths where the path may not be warranted. An access path always entails a certain amount of overhead, both in terms of data and processing. If an access path is very infrequently used, it may well be that it is most efficient not to create the path for everyday, ongoing usage. For example, if the path from supplier to part is only rarely used, then the design shown in Fig. 8.14 may well be acceptable. In the few instances where the path from supplier to part is used, then the part data base can be scanned to determine which paths can satisfy the desired relationship. Of course, such a scan requires many

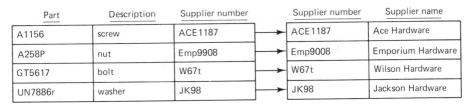

Part	Description	Supplier number		Supplier number	Supplier name
A1156	screw	ACE1187	→	ACE1187	Ace Hardware
A258P	nut	Emp9908	→	Emp9008	Emporium Hardware
GT5617	bolt	W67t	→	W67t	Wilson Hardware
UN7886r	washer	JK98	→	JK98	Jackson Hardware

Figure 8.14

resources and should only be done very infrequently. The usage of access paths, then, is the determining factor in which paths should and should not be built. Another important, basic physical decision is whether the data base is to be randomized or indexed. This is in part dependent on the DBMS and in part dependent on the usage of the data. If the data is to be used sequentially a predominance of the time (as in payroll processing), it makes sense to organize the data base in a sequentially oriented manner (i.e., with an index). If the data is to be used randomly a predominance of the time (as in automated teller processing, where requests are received randomly and asynchronously), then it makes sense to organize the data randomly.

While the choice of the basic access methods is very fundamental and is almost obvious, it is, nevertheless, a very important consideration. If the wrong access method is chosen, then much unnecessary I/O is used. Furthermore, once the wrong access method is chosen, there is very little that can be done by the system tuner.

Another important physical decision is the recovery strategy for the data base. In some cases recovery is entirely up to the DBMS, so the designer and programmer do not have to concern themselves. But in other cases recovery (or different degrees of recovery) must be designed and programmed into the system from the outset. If that is the case, the designer must be aware of the recovery requirements from the outset.

The final general physical design issue is that of functional satisfaction. Functional satisfaction of the user's requirements refers to the right data elements being available to the user in the form the user wishes and in the timeframe the user wishes. If the design does not satisfy both the immediate user requirements and the long-term requirements of the system, then the design will not be satisfactory. If a system is to be built in phases, the first physical structure that is built may not include data that satisfies all functional requirements. However, the physical structures that are built should anticipate future requirements and not preempt them. In other words, the physical structure that is built in the first phase(s) of a project serves as a stepping stone for later phases.

ONLINE DATA BASE DESIGN

The criteria for success in the online environment include *all* the general criteria for data base design as well as the criteria for performance and availability. The performance and availability characteristics of a system are designed into the system from the outset; they are not retrofitted after the fact. It is a mistake to think that since a system operates on a very fast computer with a high degree of reliability, the application system that runs on that computer will likewise have good performance and will be available a high percentage of the time.

Certainly if a computer cannot process quickly and is not available a high percentage of the time, then the system will not perform well or be available as desired. But the computer is only one component of the system. Even though computers operate very quickly, there is much competition within the computer by the transactions operating within it for resources, which move the online transactions through the system. If there were only a few transactions, then the internal competition would not be a factor, but there are usually many transactions (such is the nature of the online environment), so the speed of the computer is needed to keep the entire workflow moving.

By the same token, just because the computer is up and running does not mean the application programs are likewise up and running. Most online system downtime is caused by factors other than the computer going down, such as I/O errors, application code failures and operational failures.

PERFORMANCE

Online performance is achieved as a combination of *both* transaction and data base design. It is not sufficient to address *either* transaction design or data base design; *both* aspects of design are essential to the achievement of online performance.

ONLINE TRANSACTION DESIGN

The backbone of online transaction design is the standard work unit concept (SWU). (*Note:* The SWU concept is adequately described in the literature. See the references for this chapter for detailed discussions. This section serves as a summarization.) The SWU refers to a standardization of the amount of work accomplished by any given online transaction. In the online environment, there is no limit to the amount or type of activity that can be accomplished, only to the way that the activity is accomplished. In the online environment, activities are accomplished a small step at a time. To understand how design under the SWU differs from that of batch design, consider a businessperson making plane reservations to Florida from Los Angeles.

The businessperson goes to a travel agent and requests a booking. The first leg is from Los Angeles to Phoenix and is first class. The agent enters that flight and receives a confirmed booking. In Phoenix the businessperson is to stay overnight, so another related transaction is entered, booking a hotel. Another transaction for the same trip, booking a rental car in Phoenix, is entered. The businessperson wants a compact car. The next day the businessperson is to go from Phoenix to Dallas, so a transaction is entered making that arrangement. Separate hotel and rental car transactions are entered for an overnight stay in Dallas. The next day the businessperson goes from Dallas to Atlanta and then on to Miami. An online transaction confirms the flight to Atlanta, and another transaction settles the flight to Miami. In all, the agent has accomplished much function in an online environment, and the online system has exhibited response time in seconds. The agent has accomplished the function a small piece at a time. Had the agent been operating in the batch mode, all the booking requests would have been entered at once, and the system response time might have taken hours to confirm the bookings. The difference between the online and batch way of packaging function is shown by Fig. 8.15.

The rationale for the necessity of separation of function in the online environment is illustrated by a classic analogy (originally presented by MCAUTO years ago), when an hourglass represents the online system, in which the transactions in the system correspond to the grains of sand in the hourglass. The bottleneck of the hourglass represents the precious resources of the online system, as illustrated by Fig. 8.16. The flow of sand through the hourglass is representative of online throughput. As long as the grains of sand are small and uniform in size, the flow is smooth. But if pebbles are mixed with the grains of sand, then the flow becomes irregular. In addition to the time required for a large pebble to get through the bottleneck of the hourglass, the large pebble holds back many small grains of sand

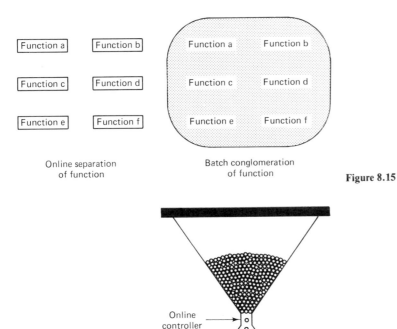

Function a	Function b		Function a	Function b
Function c	Function d		Function c	Function d
Function e	Function f		Function e	Function f

Online separation
of function

Batch conglomeration
of function

Figure 8.15

Online
controller

Figure 8.16 Grains of sand are like online transactions. The grains are small and uniform in size, creating a smooth, efficient, and continuous flow.

that are behind it and that could move through the bottleneck much more efficiently.

The analogy to online systems is almost perfect. Slow, long-running transactions that use many system resources slow the entire system down.

The online system runs at the speed of the slowest transaction.

The hourglass analogy dictates that online transactions use as few resources as possible. The primary measure of resource consumption is the number of I/O done, but there are other important resources such as CPU cycles, load module size, and total number of data base calls.

DATA BASE DESIGN FOR ONLINE PERFORMANCE

The second critical success factor for online response time is data base design. The primary goal of data base design is to use I/O efficiently. There are several places where I/O and data base design are a consideration:

— Data occurrences
— Control data bases
— General access overhead
— Application blocking of data
— General structural overhead
— Data driven processes
— General misuse of the DBMS

Each of these topics is addressed separately.

DATA OCCURRENCES

Data occurrences come in two types, **physically bound data** and **physically separate data.** In either case the goal is to use the minimum of I/O in the satisfaction of the requirement to process the occurrences of data.

Physically Bound Data

An example of physically bound data is the number of records stored in a single physical block, such as the segments in an IMS data structure or the tuples in the physical unit of storage of a relation. The problem with many occurrences of physically bound data occurs when the occurrences of data in a single physical unit spill over into multiple physical units, requiring an I/O for each new location being accessed. Figure 8.17 illustrates a case where the tuples of a relational data base have been scattered over multiple physical locations. The amount of I/O that is used to get from the first tuple to the last tuple is considerable. The designer could have reduced this I/O by

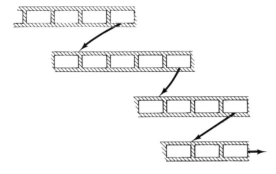

Figure 8.17 Tuples scattered over many different physical locations. Note that I/O is required to access all the tuples.

— Defining larger physical blocks so that more tuples could have been placed in a given physical unit of data.
— Reducing the number of tuples that are physically bound together. This could be done by placing the same amount of data into multiple tables, thereby creating multiple entry points into the tables.

The second option is illustrated by Fig. 8.18. A third design option is to reduce the physical amount of data in each tuple, thereby allowing each physical unit of data to hold more tuples.

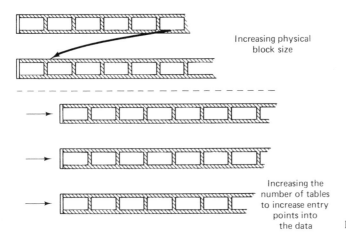

Increasing physical block size

Increasing the number of tables to increase entry points into the data

Figure 8.18

Physically Separate Occurrences of Data

The second type of processing in which I/O occurs frequently is where data is disconnected physically but bound together logically. As an example of this condition, consider an IMS logical relationship or a relational data base that has been joined (Fig. 8.19).

Two data bases exist physically, but their union allows the user to look at the data bases in a combined fashion, based on a common data field shared by both

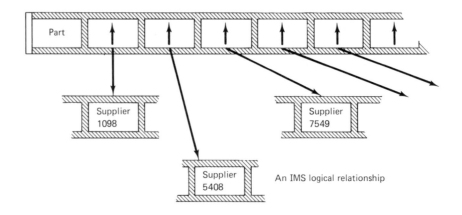

An IMS logical relationship

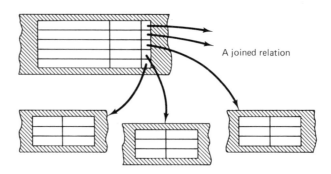

A joined relation

Figure 8.19 Forms of physically separate occurrences of data.

data bases. Using one data base as a reference into the other costs I/O because every reference to the data base being pointed to is in a different location and thus requires an I/O.

As a rule, only a finite amount of logically related data should be processed (five or six occurrences) in any given online transaction. This implies that entry points into the logically bound occurrences of data should be frequent, so that an online transaction will not require many I/O for the data being sought. As an example of breaking a table into smaller tables to reduce I/O, see Fig. 8.20. Figure 8.20 shows two tables of data, a policy table and an agent table. The tables are joined on agent number. The specified query requires much I/O, both in the searching of the policy table and in the searching of the agent table. Figure 8.21 shows the same data divided into smaller units. In Fig. 8.21 the work done by the system to satisfy the query is substantially less than the work required for the data as originally portrayed in Fig. 8.20.

Policy Table

Policy Number	Name	Amount	Agent Number	Type
0012-1	J Jones	12,000	12-698	Life
0012-3	B Goodwin	35,000	13-880	Life
0023-1	K Karlstrom	36,000	13-880	Auto
0024-2	J Goetz	30,000	13-558	Life
0025-1	R Ladd	18,000	90-991	Auto
0027-2	S Smith	23,000	90-112	Home
0034-1	B Carpenter	21,000	45-113	Auto
0045-2	J Moffatt	56,000	90-330	Life
0046-2	K Hines	34,000	90-220	Home
0046-4	K Ives	23,800	90-331	Life
0048-2	K Klein	34,950	90-112	Life
0049-2	E Bersak	56,000	13-881	Home
0051-2	E Bersak	34,000	13-885	Life
0051-3	J Brown	36,000	45-114	Auto
0051-4	B Graham	45,975	27-500	Home
0052-3	T Graham	67,750	27-889	Auto
0053-1	B Wallace	75,990	13-993	Auto
0054-2	D Buttorf	12,500	45-121	Auto
0054-3	T DeVane	15,000	90-007	Life
0055-2	M Winstead	13,500	90-011	Auto
0055-7	G Dodge	50,000	90-033	Life
0058-3	W Stillwago	12,500	13-887	Auto
0059-2	K Jones	14,500	27-798	Home
0063-2	D Staron	13,575	45-188	Auto
⋮	⋮	⋮	⋮	⋮

Agent Table

Agent Number	Name	Town	State
12-698	M Davis	Santa Fe	N Mex
12-980	S Davis	Albuquerque	N Mex
12-989	D Martin	Albuquerque	N Mex
13-558	J Bishop	Denver	Colo
13-880	F Sinatra	Colo Spgs	Colo
13-881	J Carson	Denver	Colo
13-885	G Frey	Greeley	Colo
13-887	D Henley	Las Cruces	N Mex
13-993	D Felder	Socorro	N Mex
13-995	T B Schmidt	Ft Carson	Colo
13-999	J Walsh	Denver	Colo
27-500	B Leadon	Provo	Utah
27-668	R Meisner	Salt Lake C	Utah
27-798	D Bunnell	Denver	Colo
27-889	G Peek	El Paso	Texas
27-901	G Beckley	Van Horn	Texas
45-113	S Nicks	El Paso	Texas
45-114	M Fleetwood	Boulder	Colo
45-121	C Perfect	Roswell	N Mex
45-136	L Buckingh	Artesia	N Mex
45-188	G Slick	Dallas	Texas
⋮	⋮	⋮	⋮

Figure 8.20 Servicing the request "For all life insurance policies greater than $25,000, how many are serviced by an agent from Denver, Colorado?" requires much work by the system and many I/O. The request could be serviced much more efficiently by breaking the data up into finer units and by logically organizing the data in a different way.

193

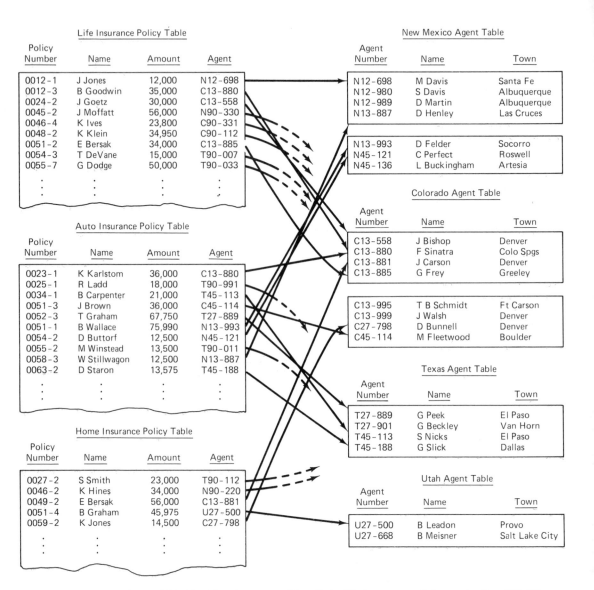

Figure 8.21 Servicing the request "For all the life insurance policies greater than $25,000, how many are serviced by an agent from Denver, Colorado?" requires a minimum of resources because data has been broken into fine physical units and because the physical units of data are organized along the lines of geographical division.

CONTROL DATA BASES

Control data bases are data bases that serve a utilitarian function rather than contain data that directly relates to the business of the system. Some examples of control data bases are terminal data bases, security data bases, audit data bases, and tables data bases. There is nothing inherently wrong with control data bases; in fact they are necessary. But the *implementation* of control data bases usually leaves a lot to be desired.

Control data bases, implemented improperly, hurt performance in that they cause unnecessary contention for data. For example, suppose a system is designed so that every online transaction updates a control record before it attends to the business of the transaction. It does not matter whether the transaction is for inventory, accounting, or marketing. Consider what happens when traffic on the system builds, as shown by Fig. 8.22. In this case the control data base becomes a single thread through which all online activity must first pass. The system can process requests only as fast as the requests can access, update, and then release the control data base. The performance implications are clear.

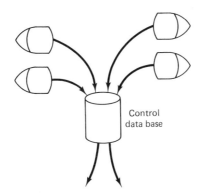

Control
data base

Figure 8.22

A second difficulty with control data bases occurs when the control data base goes down. Since every online transaction first accesses the control data base, every transaction is, in essence, disabled when the control data base becomes unavailable.

There are several implementation techniques that can be used to avoid severe problems of contention or availability. The first technique is to ensure that data is broken into as fine a physical unit as possible within the control data base. The integrity control features of the DBMS determine the level of physical granularity that is appropriate. By breaking the data within a control data base into small physical units, the number of transactions that desire exclusive control of the data at any moment in time is greatly lessened. Figure 8.23 illustrates two organizations of data (which, for practical purposes, are equivalent): One organization contains a table in which 1000 entries are defined, and another table contains 100 tables, where 10 entries are defined in each table. The two organizations of data are functionally identical, although they are physically arranged differently.

Consider what happens when a terminal needs to update a single entry in the large table, as shown by Fig. 8.24. Assuming that the online data integrity facilities protect the table as a whole, concurrent online activity cannot access any data in the table as long as the current online activity has control. Figure 8.25 shows what happens when the tables are split up. When an online activity "grabs" a table, as shown in the figure, it holds only a limited amount of data. Other online activities are free to access other tables at the same time. By breaking data into small physical

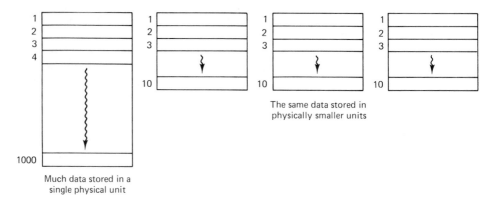

The same data stored in physically smaller units

Much data stored in a single physical unit

Figure 8.23

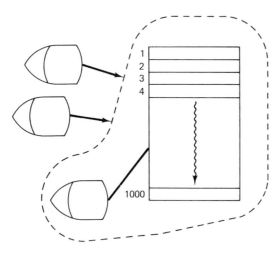

Figure 8.24 When data is tied up in large physical units and an online activity has tied up the data, other online activities cannot be transacted against the data until the activity currently using the data has finished.

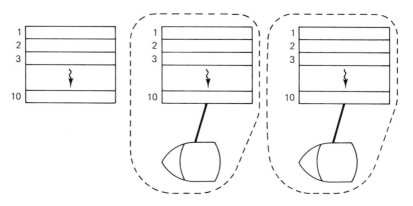

Figure 8.25 When data is divided into physically smaller units, the chance of two or more online activities using the data at the same time is reduced.

units, the problems of contention (i.e., the single threading of online transactions) are greatly reduced. The next implementation technique for managing control data bases is to split the data bases into physically separate data bases. In this case, the definition of the data remains identical across all data bases, but the contents of the data bases differ from one data base to the next.

Figure 8.26 shows a control data base that has been broken into four physically separate control data bases based on the usage of the data: marketing, personnel, inventory, and accounting. As an example of how data is physically separated, only accounting control data exists in the accounting control data base. Accounting control data does not exist elsewhere, so the contents of the different control data bases are nonredundant. What is redundant is the format of the data bases—i.e., how the data is defined to the DBMS. The importance of the redundant format across all physical iterations of the data base is that the same code can operate on one data base as it would on any other; i.e., the development and maintenance of the code that supports the control data base must be done once and only once.

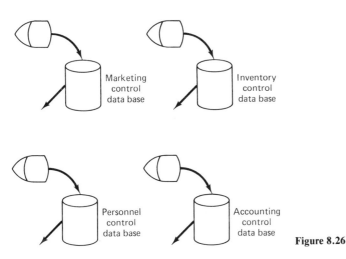

Figure 8.26

The physical splitting of control data bases results in a higher degree of online system availability *and* performance. Performance is enhanced because there is a separation of traffic going into a single data base. Availability is enhanced because when one data base goes down, the entire system does not come to a halt. Figure 8.27 shows a marketing data base that has gone down. Its demise has no effect whatsoever on the other parts of the system. Only marketing is affected.

Another benefit of physically separating control data bases is that the processing workload can be split easily at a later point in time. When control data bases tie many different applications together, it is very difficult to split any part of the processing workload off to a separate machine. For example, if inventory control, accounting, and personnal share a common control data base—such as a terminal control data base—then splitting the accounting processing off to another machine becomes a difficult task. But if inventory control, accounting, and personnel each

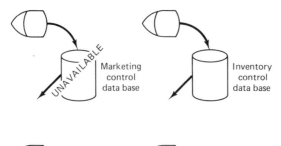

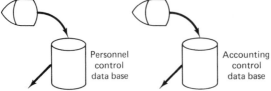

Figure 8.27 A control data base exists for different applications. When the marketing control data base goes down, the availability of the other applications is not affected.

have their own physically separate control data bases, then there is no problem if it is desirable to split accounting off to another machine.

As a shop makes the decision to split its control data bases physically, the question arises concerning the lines along which the split should be made. One popular choice is along functional lines, such as accounting, inventory control, and personnel. Another popular choice is geographically: by southwestern region, northern region, and western region. There are other choices and mitigating factors as to which choice is correct. In any case, a shop should choose a single consistent criteria for dividing data bases. Some systems should not be divided along lines of function and other systems divided along geographical lines. Multiple criteria lead to chaos.

There is another solution to the implementation problems of control data bases. The solution *applies only in very limited cases. It is not a general solution and when applied improperly has very negative consequences.* It is, nevertheless, a solution under some circumstances. The solution is to duplicate control data bases. This solution applies only where there is a limited amount of data that is nonvolatile, i.e., not updated. If a control data base meets these criteria (and occasionally one does), then a raw duplication of data greatly enhances both availability and performance. But there are many problems that arise in using this approach, such as

---

DESIGN REVIEW

Online performance and availability are designed into the basic architecture of a system. They are not retrofitted. One way for a designer to determine if the design will be a good one or if the system is going to flop is to build the system, implement it, then see what happens. Many large corporations adopt this philosophy. But too often the result is that the system is a failure and must be rebuilt. This attitude is similar to spending 40 million dollars to build a plane and then stepping into the cockpit and hoping it flies.

If the airplane buries itself in the ground, the pilot is out of luck. A much more sensible (and economical) approach is to test the design *before* it is built. This is the analogical equivalent of building a model of the airplane and placing it in a wind tunnel. If the model buries itself in the earth, at least $40 million won't have been wasted, not to mention a test pilot.

Design review is the tool that is used to test online systems before they are built. When used properly, design review can save companies *much* wasted development work by pinpointing system deficiencies before the system is built. To be effective, design review must be done in at least three places in the life of the project: as the physical model of the system is formulated from the logical model, as the physical data bases are designed, and as the program specifications are written. The earlier this occurs in the life cycle of the design of the system, the easier basic design flaws are to correct.

Design review does not replace management; instead design review is a tool by which management receives the best information on which to make decisions. As such design review is a fact-finding mission. *Any* topic is open to review. Some topics of discussion will be applicable to the data processing environment in general. Some topics will be specific to the project being reviewed. Some topics will be political in nature. Other topics will be technical. There should be no limitation on the topics discussed. *Anything* that will inhibit the success of the project is fair game. The more critical and sensitive the topic, the more worthy it is for discussion.

Those involved in a review are all who are affected by the development, operation (computer operations), management, or usage of the project. It is mandatory that the user attend the architectural review (the review as the system passes from the logical to the physical model). Those involved are generally divided into two classifications for the purpose of the review: the committee and the observers. There should be a maximum of 12 people on the committee; there may be any number of observers. The committee is led by the design-review leader. The design-review leader must be as objective as possible. For this reason the design review leader *must never* have a connection with the project being reviewed. For many reasons, design reviews are not effective when run by people staffed from the project being reviewed. To this end design review is often run by outside consultants.

The output of design review is a report listing the important points brought up during the review that goes to management. The report is most effective when open to the general public—i.e., anyone attending the review, anyone involved in the project, the user, management, etc. The report should not be a secretive document. The report is prepared by the *recorder.* The recorder works in tandem with the leader and filters points that are being discussed. The recorder does not merely take down notes on every discussion; only notes on those discussions that management needs to hear are entered. Many discussions are very technical or are irrelevant and are filtered out by the recorder. The final report should be returned to management in a timely fashion, within a week or two of the review.

synchronization of updates when data values must be changed, that must be carefully weighed.

APPLICATION BLOCKING OF DATA

One option facing the designer is where and how to store iterations of the same type of data. This decision can save or cost a substantial amount of I/O. The correctness of the decision (like almost every other data base design decision) depends on the data (its form, its volume, its volatility, its insert/delete/update characteristics) and how the data is used (randomly, en masse, first in/first out (FIFO), first in/last out (FILO), etc.).

The two options facing the designer are to let the DBMS block the data (i.e., allow the normal DBMS storage and access activity to occur) or to let the application programmer block the data (i.e., force the application program to take on certain data management activity), as shown by an example taken from IBM's IMS in Fig. 8.28. On the left-hand side of Fig. 8.28 the DBMS is shown blocking the data. Whenever an occurrence of data is inserted or deleted, the data is stored and transported separately from other occurrences. Each of the occurrences of data is retrieved, one at a time. On the right-hand side of the figure, the designer has placed n logical occurrences of data into a single physical occurrence of data (i.e., a physical occurrence of data has been blocked by the application programmer). When blocked, all logical occurrences of the data are retrieved at once; i.e., if any one logical occurrence of data is retrieved, then all logical occurrences are retrieved.

The most obvious savings from application blocking of data comes in the

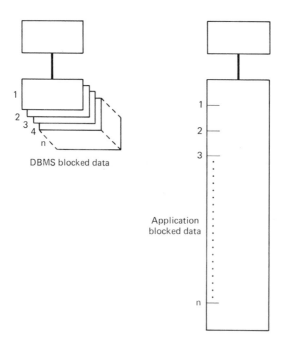

DBMS blocked data

Application blocked data

Figure 8.28 On the left, the DBMS manages the blocking of data. There are n separate occurrences of data beneath the parent data. On the right, the application programmer has blocked the data so that n occurrences of data exist in the same record.

Basic Concepts   Section I

number of calls issued to process the data. It requires *n* calls to retrieve data normally handled by the DBMS and only 1 call to retrieve application-blocked data. Prefix space is also saved (i.e., the overhead associated with every occurrence of data is minimized). Here, *n* prefixes are required for data handled under normal data management of the DBMS, whereas only 1 prefix is required for application-blocked data. But the real savings potential comes in the I/O used, as shown by Fig. 8.29. In this figure DBMS-blocked occurrences of data are shown to be strewn over many physical locations. Application-blocked data is not. In application blocking, once the 1st occurrence is reached, the 2nd to *n*th occurrences are sure to be in the same physical location.

It is thus apparent that application blocking of data can save I/O and other online resources in the cases where application blocking of data is appropriate. The following are the criteria for the appropriateness of application blocking of data:

— Number of occurrences of data and the regularity of their occurrences
— Insertion/deletion pattern of the data
— Access pattern of the data
— Occurrence (or unit of data) size
— Usage of query language

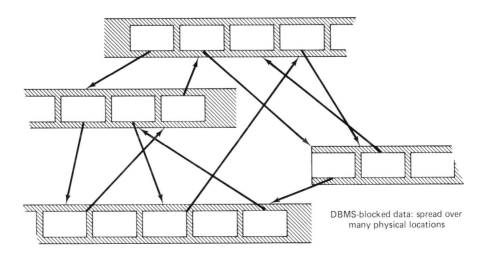

DBMS-blocked data: spread over many physical locations

Application-blocked data: Once the first occurrence is located, the remaining data is sure to be in the same location.

Figure 8.29

Number of Occurrences

If there are a variable number of occurrences of the data, then DBMS blocking is appropriate. If there are a fixed number of occurrences, then application blocking is appropriate. As an example of a variable number of occurrences of data, consider the checks written on a checking account. One month, one account will have 35 checks, another account will have 76, and so forth. Furthermore, the number of checks written on one account one month will differ greatly from the number of checks written the next month. The number n to be set for blocking is very difficult to determine given data whose number of occurrences are highly variable.

But consider a payroll application, where people are paid weekly. There will be 52 paychecks a year, every year. In such a case the number of occurrences is set and is not likely to change. This case may be a candidate for application blocking of data.

Insertion/Deletion Pattern

In cases where the insertion/deletion pattern is random, DBMS blocking of data is appropriate. In cases where the pattern is set, then application blocking of data is appropriate. Consider Fig. 8.30, where a segment is blocked to hold five occurrences of data and four occurrences are filled. An insertion is to be made between occurrences 2 and 3. Can the insertion be made? Should slot 5 hold slot 4's data, then slot 4 hold slot 3's data? What happens if all the slots are filled? These questions can be answered but are a real burden (a data management burden) on the appli-

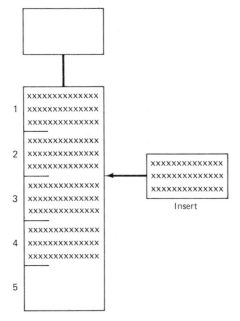

Figure 8.30

cation programmer. It is clear that if application blocking is to be used, insertion needs to be done in an order of the next physically available slot.

An even more insidious case occurs where there are five slots in an application blocked record and those five slots are filled and another occurrence is to be added. Does an existing occurrence already blocked have to be discarded? Does a record for another five occurrences have to be allocated? If it is to be allocated, where is it to be placed?

Now consider deletions. Figure 8.31 shows a filled application-blocked segment. A request is made to delete the third entry, as shown. The questions that arise are: Should the data be blanked out? Can a delete bit be set? Should data in slot 4 be moved to slot 3 and then data in slot 5 be moved to slot 4? These questions can be answered, but again they place a burden on the application programmer. In the interest of efficiency and simplicity of development and maintenance, the application programmer's role should be as simple as possible. If deletion were to occur all at once (i.e., all occurrences deleted at once), then there is no great application programming problem, and the data is a candidate for application blocking.

Access Pattern

The access pattern of data that is blocked is important but not as important as the insert/deletion pattern. If data is to be accessed sequentially (i.e., from occurrence n to $n + 1$ to $n + 2$, etc.), then application blocking is appropriate. However, if the data is to be accessed randomly, then DBMS blocking of data is appropriate. When data is blocked by the application, it is natural to proceed from occurrence

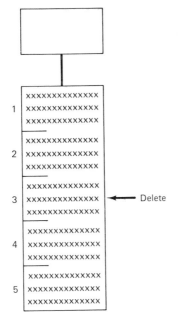

Figure 8.31

1 to 2 to 3, and so on. But the DBMS has no problem in locating the randomly organized data, assuming key information is available.

Occurrence Size (or Data Unit Size)

A rather quixotic restriction is that of the physical size of the occurrence or unit of data. If the physical unit of data that holds the occurrence is small, then it makes sense to block the data by the application. But if the unit is large, then it makes sense to let the DBMS block the data.

For the criterion of physical size, the largeness or smallness of a unit depends entirely on the basic physical characteristics of the system. For instance VSAM (IBM's Virtual Storage Access Method) has finite physical boundaries over which units of data are best defined. Any design based on VSAM and going over these boundaries invites unnecessary I/O caused by VSAM native data management facilities when those physical boundaries are exceeded.

Usage of Query Language

A final consideration of application blocking of data is the usage of a query language. If data is blocked by the application, then that blocking must be described to the query language. This may not amount to more than an inconvenience, but it is just one more level of complexity. Some query languages handle application blocking of data quite well; some handle it quite awkwardly. If no query language is to be used to access the data, then the occurrences can be blocked by the application.

Thus a series of factors determines if application of DBMS blocking of data is appropriate. Very few cases fit all of the criteria, either one way or the other. The usual case is for three or four criteria to fit. It remains up to the designer to use good judgment in choosing the correct design option.

GENERAL STRUCTURAL OVERHEAD

General structural overhead occurs as a result of elaborate data structures or because data has been placed awkwardly within the structure. As an example of general structural overhead, consider an oversegmented data base, as shown by Fig. 8.32, which shows a data base with many hierarchical levels and many segments at each level. Whether the structure is appropriate is not the question; in any case, the structure will require significant amounts of resources just to be traversed. Accessing a lower-level segment requires going through the pointers from the root to the segment being accessed.

In addition, because of the different segment types, it is likely that much of the data will be in overflow. As a rule, if 20% or more of a data base is made up of overhead, then it is a good bet that the data base is oversegmented. This rule of thumb does not apply to certain data bases, such as control or tables data bases, that may contain small amounts of user data.

Basic Concepts   Section I

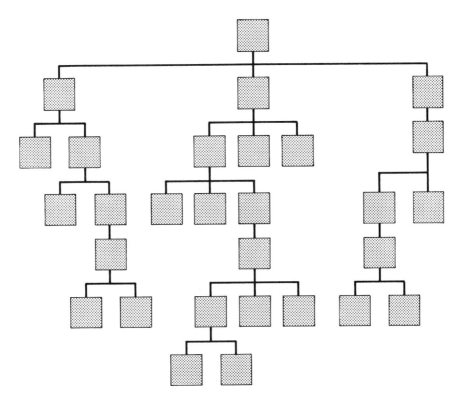

Figure 8.32 An oversegmented data base.

The second problem with general overhead arises in the placement of data. In general the data that stands the greatest chance of being accessed often should be structured in the place that stands the least chance of going into overflow. The rules for proper placement of data vary from one DBMS to another.

DATA DRIVEN PROCESSES

Data driven processes encompass both process design and data base design. They are one of the most common and, at the same time, most unrecognized problems. **A data driven process** is one whose resource consumption depends on the amount or configuration of data on which it operates. This bookish-sounding definition can be illustrated by an example. A data driven process is shown in Fig. 8.33. In the first example the account activity for credit card charges for Joe Foster is sought. Joe has had only 3 pieces of activity and requires only a few (2 or 3) I/O. The next request is for Melba Nowak's activity. She has had 7 pieces of activity and requires a few I/O. But the next request is for the activity of the IBM corporation. IBM has had 15,000 pieces of activity and requires 2000 I/O. In looking at the request prior to execution, there is no way to determine how many I/O would be required. The

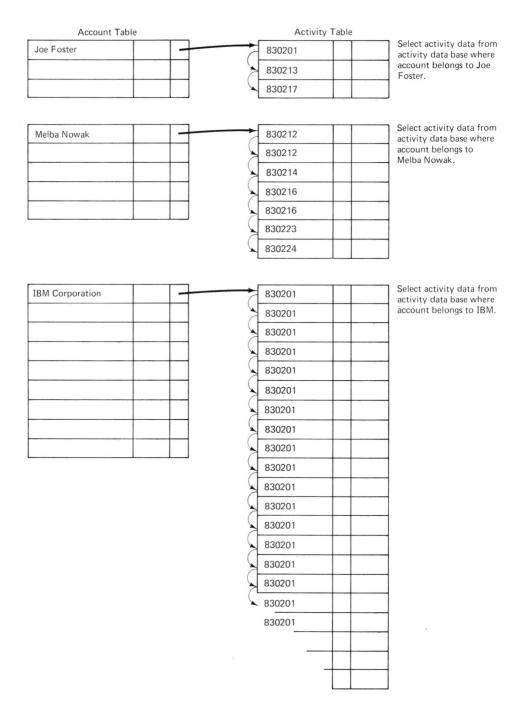

Figure 8.33 An example of data driven processes.

only difference in each of the requests is the data on which the request operates. Such a request is a form of a data driven transaction.

One of the insidious difficulties with data driven transactions is that they normally do not show their true colors in the test environment. Most test environments are not sophisticated enough to cause the problems that come with data driven processes to surface. Test environments only carry limited amounts and types of data. Because there is only a small amount of data, the difficulties of data driven processes are not apparent in the test environment.

There are several approaches to solving the problems of data driven processes. The most obvious is to address the problem as if it were a problem of data occurrences, as discussed earlier in this chapter. But often that approach is inappropriate because there are mitigating factors. The following are some other approaches:

— Operating on only a finite number of occurrences and reporting back to the terminal operator when the limit has been reached. At that point the terminal operator has several options: to continue the processing where it had been interrupted, to terminate the process, or to continue the process in another mode, such as batch or overnight.

— Separating data according to function. In the example discussed, separating private data from commercial data and then processing the two different types of processes differently would solve some of the difficulties of data driven processes. Unfortunately, such a separation cannot always be made.

— Classifying data into two classes, small and large, based on the number of occurrences. Then an attribute is created in an appropriate table, so the processing can examine the field to determine what the characteristics of the data are *before* processing the data online. This approach works when there is a clear-cut distinction between the classes of data. Furthermore, the field that is set to determine the class of the data must be set offline. Unfortunately, this type of processing is not often convenient to do.

In practice, data driven processes are addressed by a combination of solutions unless there happens to be a single solution that addresses the problem.

GENERAL MISUSE OF A DBMS

Most DBMS have lots of capabilities. But within their range of capabilities some things are done efficiently and well, and others are done inefficiently and awkwardly. As an example of a misuse of a DBMS capability, consider the inverted structure shown in Fig. 8.34. Indexes exist for three of four data fields. As long as queries go against the indexed fields, processing is efficient because most of the processing is done in the indexes. But if part of the search criteria includes the fourth, nonindexed field, then the search is slow because each individual record must be searched, causing unnecessary I/O. Such a use of a data base capability is inefficient. Proper use of the DBMS facility would be either to index the fourth field or not to use the fourth field for search criteria.

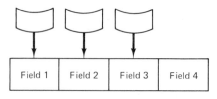

Figure 8.34 An inverted data structure that is indexed on three fields.

PROPER USE OF AN ALTERNATE INDEX

Another inefficiency in data base design occurs when alternate indexes are used improperly. There are two pitfalls to alternate indexes: the wholesale accessing of the index and the overhead associated with update, creation, and deletion of the index.

The worst abuse of an alternate index is in the wholesale accessing of data via the index. Every time the alternate index is used to go into the primary data base, an I/O is required because, in general, the data being accessed in the primary data base is in different blocks. If 100 entries in the primary data base are being accessed, then on the average 100 I/Os will be required. Thus the online programmer can quickly raise the number of I/O consumed by his or her transaction simply by spinning down a secondary index and looking into the primary data base.

But the accessing of data by means of an alternate index is not the only concern with alternate indexes. Another concern is the I/O used in the altering of the primary data base. Suppose a data base has four alternate indexes (nonsparse) pointing into the data base. Then at least five I/Os are required when a record is entered into the data base, one I/O is needed for insertion in the primary data base, and four I/O are required for insertion into the alternate indexes. If a field on which the data has an alternate index is altered, then one I/O is required for alteration of the primary data base, one I/O is needed for deletion of the entry in the alternate index where the record formerly was, and one I/O is required for insertion of the entry into the alternate index where the record is now positioned.

DATA BASE DESIGN FOR AVAILABILITY

The design techniques for a high degree of data base availability are covered in depth in Chapter 7 of *Effective Data Base Design* by W. H. Inmon, Prentice-Hall, 1981. This section summarizes the concepts presented there. The primary issue of availability is the **mean time to recovery** (MTTRc) and the **mean time to reorganize** (MTTRo). Both MTTRc and MTTRo are primarily a function of data base size. As a rule, the larger the data base size, the longer MTTRc and MTTRo are. The strategy, then, is to break data bases into smaller physical sizes. The total amount of the data remains the same, but the physical units over which the data bases are defined change.

Typical criteria for the physical separation of data include split by key range, split by function, or split by geographical location, as seen in Fig. 8.35. One of the foundations of good data base design is the assumption that *every* data base will

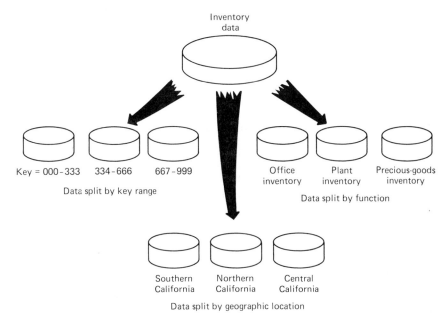

Inventory
data

Key = 000-333   334-666   667-999

Data split by key range

Office
inventory

Plant
inventory

Precious-goods
inventory

Data split by function

Southern
California

Northern
California

Central
California

Data split by geographic location

Figure 8.35

fail at some time. Designing a data base for the online environment under the assumption that it will never fail is an outright and unqualified mistake. The questions that must be asked are: What else will fail when the data base fails, and how long will it take to bring the data base back to life?

Finally, the issue of reorganization for the purpose of restructuring must be addressed. If a data base cannot be (either easily or at all) restructured, then it is a matter of time before the changes in the user's environment will not be able to be accommodated.

DSS DATA BASE DESIGN

The needs and goals of the dss environment are entirely different than those of the operational environment. The criteria for success for the two environments are very different because of the fundamental differences in the nature of the environments. In the dss environment, it is the end user (or someone speaking for the end user) that is writing and running the dss applications. In operational systems, it is the professional programmer who is writing code.

In dss systems, the user has a great amount of control of the operations and usage of the dss systems, such as determining naming conventions, back up activity, and the initiation of runs. In operational environments, these decisions have been made long ago and are out of the control of the end user. In dss systems the user is free to shape and change data and data structures at will, whereas those same decisions in the operational environment are monumental and are well beyond the control of a user. Because of the great differences in the environments, the activities of data base design are very different.

DSS SYSTEMS: DATA SOURCES

Very few dss systems operate on data that is generated in toto by and for the dss system. Far and away the majority of dss systems operate on data that is foreign to them. The foreign data comes from an extract of operational data, from archival data, or from an external data base. In addition, data that has been previously manipulated by a dss system and has been stored for future reference may provide a source of input for dss systems.

Extracted Operational Data

The most common data source for dss systems is data extracted from the operational environment. **Extracted data** has been selectively taken from the operational environment as of some moment in time. As such it represents a snapshot of data. The data that is sent to the dss environment is usually at a very detailed level. The lower the level of detail, the more flexible the data is, as the data can serve a wide variety of purposes. The strip may or may not contain a snapshot of all the records in the data base. Some data base records may have been selectively omitted. The data that is sent to the dss environment is usually sent in the form of a flat file. Very often there is a large amount of data sent to the dss environment.

Archival Data

On occasion dss systems need to access archival data. **Archival data** is the historical preserve of data processing. As systems age, data often needs to be weeded out. Rather than simply being discarded, the data is archived. Archival data is invariably voluminous. Archival data is almost always stored at a very detailed level (for the same reasons that extracted data is passed to the dss environment at a detailed level). The format of the archived data may have changed over the years (as well as the meaning of the contents!), which plays havoc with the analysis of the data. Archival data may or may not represent a complete logical set of data (i.e., there is no guarantee that all occurrences of a given type of activity will be present). Archival data is notorious for being unable to be accessed due to the aging of the media on which it is stored. Resequencing or otherwise massaging archival data usually takes massive amounts of resources. The usage of archival data in the dss environment should be as selective as possible.

External Data

External data refers to data found and used externally to the company. External data is usually purchased or leased from outside sources. Market profiles, customer lists, and mailing lists are all forms of external data that might be used by dss systems. Like operational data, external data represents a snapshot of a data base. Usually the volume of external data is much less than that of operational extracts or archival data. Demographic analysis, "what-if" analysis, and market projections typically use external data. Generally the physical medium on which external data is presented is highly reliable, given that the data is presented as a paid resource.

Recycled Dss Data

As dss activities are done, it often makes sense to store the data or output of the dss processing. Once saved, the data can be used for future needs, such as trend analysis and projections. The amount of data coming from this source is usually limited, as compared to other sources. Since the data is already in the realm of dss systems, the format of the data is no problem.

INFORMATION SYSTEMS ARCHITECTURE AND DSS DATA BASE DESIGN

Once the source of the data has been established (or at least inventoried), the next step in data base design is to decide what data is appropriate to the dss process at hand. The first place to look is the conceptual architecture that has been created as a result of modeling the information systems. The information systems architecture (ISA) is the result of conceptual design and forms the foundation for dss systems, just as it forms the foundation for operational systems. The different levels of modeling found in the ISA form a basis for what data dss systems ought to be using, where to find the data, and how the data relates to the enterprise as a whole. Without an ISA, the dss analyst has a difficult time in deciding what data to use. Typical of a dss process that must be constructed in the absence of an ISA is the rummaging through five or six related files of data, with selected data being plucked out in a haphazard fashion. The degree of confidence the dss analyst has in the non-ISA environment is low because of the subtle differences in the redundant data and the inconsistency of the data, which is almost always undocumented. But with an ISA, the dss analyst has a road map by which to proceed.

Once the analyst has determined the proper source of the data, there is another entirely different set of considerations. These considerations center around the physical aspects of the data: the volume of data, the existing structure, the current sequencing of data, how the data needs to be refined, what the data needs to be merged with, and so forth. The physical decisions become fairly apparent once the source of the data is determined. One physical issue is the compatibility of different sources of data. If the data is to be captured and analyzed, then the major compatibility issue is whether all the data that needs to be captured in fact has been captured. For example, suppose dss work is to be done on all the account activity for a bank for a month's time. The operational data is stripped and sent to the dss environment. Analytical work commences. But someone notices that only teller account activity has been captured, not the bank's automatic teller machine activity. Doing an analysis on only one type of account activity will probably lead to faulty conclusions.

The issue of compatibility looms even larger where there is more than a single captured stream of data that is involved. Suppose a shop is comparing this month's sales against the same month's sales for the last 3 years. The basis of the comparison is warped by such questions as these: Should inflationary adjustments be made? Were last year's sales for the same product base? for an equivalent sales force? Was there less or more competition 3 years ago than today? The issue of comparative compatibility is even more difficult when dealing with large masses of undefined archival data.

SOME DSS SPECIFIC DESIGN PRACTICES

Dss data bases should deal with data at the lowest level of detail that is feasible. When data is stored at the lowest level, there is the greatest flexibility for future unknown processing requests. As an example, suppose an analysis is being done on the hours of work spent on a given project. Each person tracks their hours by project and reports the hours weekly. At a summarized level, the data could be stored by project. But suppose at a later point in time an analysis must be done by hours spent by department, not by project. If the data is stored at a summarized level, such an analysis by department cannot be done. But if hours spent on a project are stored at the individual level and the information relating to a person's department is also carried, then such an analysis can be done at a later point in time.

Once data has been captured and put in a usable form by dss systems, the data should be kept for as long as it might possibly be used. Along with the data should be stored a careful description of the format of the data and any refinements or qualifications that apply. If the data is to be effectively reused at a later point in time, the dss analyst needs to know exactly what data is at hand. While it is important to store basic dss data, it is equally important to get rid of work, trial, or holding data bases. Incomplete, unrefined, or partially merged data will only confuse future dss efforts. It is better to have no data at all than to have ambiguous or incomplete data. In addition to the saving of data, it is often useful to save processing specifications. If processing steps have to be retraced, data tells only part of the story.

In deciding what data to put into dss systems, much thought should be given to how the data relates to other data. The interrelationships of data should be one of the foremost considerations in determining the selection criteria of data. Even if a specific dss process does not need a major identification for its own needs, future flexibility will be enhanced by carrying additional data.

For example, suppose an analysis is being done on hours worked by project. People report hours worked by their project and department. At the same time, employee number can be attached even if the data is not needed for immediate requirements. At a later point in time the question of the skill mix required by a project may be raised. The analysis can be done by using employee number for a project and analyzing the personnel data base for skills based on an employee's number. The collection of major data elements, even when not needed for immediate requirements, enhances the later usability of the data for a variety of purposes.

Whenever possible, data should be exchanged by many users. The exchange of data promotes data consistency and reduces the total amount of work that needs to be done.

Finally, because the end user must also double as the computer operator in many dss environments (especially in the personal computer environment), there are some mundane practices that greatly enhance the usability of the data. One practice is to employ consistent data labeling schemes. Nothing is worse than going through a rigorous analysis and then finding out that improper data has been used. External documentation greatly helps to alleviate the mystery of what data is where. Finally (especially in the micro environment), data must be backed up in *every* case.

SUMMARY

There are two major activities of data base design, conceptual design and physical design. Conceptual design involves the recognition of the commonality of data across all system requirements while still allowing for individual data differences. Conceptual design and modeling are done on different levels, which accounts for both the great amount of detail and the structure of the data.

At the highest level of modeling is the ERD, at the midlevel is the dis, and at the lowest level is the physical model. Once conceptual design is complete and a conceptual architecture has been created, physical data base design can begin.

There are two types of physical design, operational physical data base design and dss data base design. The issues of operational data base design are the performance and availability of the online environment. These issues revolve around access paths, recovery and reorganization, the standard work unit, the number and type of data occurrences, the general organization of the data, control data bases, application blocking of data, and data driven processes.

The issues of physical data base design for the dss environment are concerned with the source of data, the volume of data, the compatibility and homogeneity of the data, the storage of data, future uses of data, and the level at which the data is viewed.

QUESTIONS

Performance

   1.1. What is meant by performance?
   1.2. What is the single most important factor in determining performance?

Availability

   2.1. What is meant by availability?
   2.2. What factors are important to availability? Why?

Online and Batch Environments

3.1. Are the issues of performance and availability relevant to batch systems?

3.2. Are the issues of performance and availability relevant to the online environment?

3.3. To which environment are the issues of performance and availability most relevant?

Tuning

4.1. Can performance be tuned into a system?

4.2. Is more hardware a long term solution to the issue of performance?

4.3. When will tuning a system help?

4.4. When will buying more hardware help?

Conceptual Data Model

5.1. What is meant by a conceptual data model?

5.2. Describe the components of a conceptual data model?

5.3. Why is a conceptual data model important?

5.4. Is a conceptual data model mandatory?

5.5. What happens if there is no conceptual data model?

5.6. What is the relationship between the conceptual model and the physical data model?

5.7. Who should build the conceptual data model?

5.8. Who should build the physical data model?

5.9. What role does the user play in the building of the two models?

Design Differences

6.1. What differences are there between batch data base design and online data base design?

Data Base Size

7.1. What is a large data base?

7.2. Why is data base size an issue?

7.3. What can be done to minimize the negative effects of a large data base?

Standard Work Unit

8.1. What is the SWU?

8.2. Why is the SWU important?

8.3. How important is the SWU?

8.4. Does the SWU apply to all online systems?

8.5. Does the SWU imply that some activities not be done online?

8.6. Who should design online transactions?

8.7. When in the life of the design of a system should online transactions be designed?

8.8. Can the SWU be retrofitted onto an existing system?

8.9. How can the SWU be measured?

8.10. List five ways of designing transactions according to the SWU.

Data Occurrences

9.1. Why are many occurrences of data a problem?

9.2. Are there conditions where many occurrences of data are not a problem?

9.3. List 10 design techniques that can be used to minimize the problem of many occurrences of data.

9.4. Describe the relationships between the SWU and many occurrences of data.

Control Data Bases

10.1. What is a control data base?

10.2. How does a control data base differ from a subject data base?

10.3. How does a control data base hinder performance?

10.4. Are control data bases necessary to the data base environment?

10.5. How does a control data base hinder availability?

10.6. How can control data bases be implemented to minimize their negative effects?

Data Duplication

11.1. What are the problems of raw duplication of data?

11.2. What problems does raw duplication of data solve?

11.3. How can the problems of raw duplication of data be minimized?

11.4. Is raw duplication of data ever justified?

11.5. Why is the design technique of raw duplication of data seldom used?

Data Base Overhead

12.1. What is meant by data base overhead?

12.2. How can data base overhead be minimized?

Application Blocking of Data

13.1. What is application blocking of data?

13.2. How can application blocking of data enhance performance?

13.3. Can application blocking of data hinder performance?

13.4. What criteria are there to determine whether application blocking of data is appropriate?

13.5. What happens if a design fits some criteria for blocking but not all?

13.6. How can application blocking of data save I/O?

Data Driven Processes

14.1. What is a data driven process?

14.2. When can the designer determine whether or not a process will be data driven?

14.3. Why is a data driven process bad for performance?

14.4. List four design techniques that can be used to minimize the effects of or eliminate data driven processes.

14.5. What is the relationship between data driven processes and many occurrences of data?

14.6. Why do data driven processes display their true operating characteristics in the production environment but not in the testing environment?

14.7. How common are data driven processes?

EXERCISES

1. Normalize the following data into third normal form:

    (a). Age, sex, height, name, social security number, weight, hair color, employer, department, job description, salary, pay records, dependents, address, college education

    (b). Part, supplier, unit of measure, eoq (economic order quantity), description, supplier address, supplier contact, quantity on hand, expeditor, delivery point, supplier phone number, shipment date, quantity shipped

    (c). Policy, agent, liability limitation, claim amount, claim date, claim description, policy issuer, policy contact, agent name, agent address, reinsurer, policy riders, attached policies, prior claims, prior settlements

2. For a major application in your shop, create an ERD. If an ERD has already been created, verify that it has been implemented properly.

3. Take an entity for the ERD in Exercise 2 and create a dis. Indicate keys and all important attributes.

4. From the dis in Exercise 3, create a physical model. Include all physical characteristics, all keys, and all connectors.

5. For the physical model created in Exercise 4 show how the model can be implemented in each of the basic data models (hierarchical, relational, inverted, network).

6. Take several unintegrated but related systems in your shop. Identify common data. Identify common processes. What is the cost of maintaining separate systems?

7. Define and give examples for the following:

(a) ERD	**(f)** User view
(b) Entity	**(g)** Dis
(c) Relationship	**(h)** Physical model
(d) Dimension	**(i)** Key
(e) Data view	**(j)** Nonunique key

8. Take four major entities relevant to your shop. Define the entities. Now use the criteria for sound definitions to determine how good your definitions are. Refine your definitions if necessary.

9. Describe what belongs in a blueprint for conceptual systems architecture.

10. The physical model lays a foundation for most but not all issues of physical data base design. List 10 physical data base design issues that must be decided *after* the physical model has been built.

11. If you have online systems at your shop, what is your SWU? Was your SWU derived by design or default? Do you have online systems that do not fit the SWU? How are they managed?

12. What are the general online availability guidelines for your shop? the general online

response time guidelines? Who set them? How are they enforced? How are they monitored?

13. Take the function accomplished by one of your large batch programs. Break up the function into its component parts. Write specifications for online transactions that fulfill each of the functions. Make sure that each online function falls in line with your SWU guidelines.

14. There is a saying, The online environment runs at the speed of the slowest transaction. Is this true for *all* online environments? If transaction and data integrity are not issues, is the statement true?

15. Identify several different control data bases in your shop. Are they causing enqueue problems? availability problems?

16. How are commonly used tables handled in your shop?

17. IBM offers a common access method called VSAM, which has many internal data management facilities. What sets VSAM apart from a DBMS? How are they the same?

18. Give three examples of data driven processes.

CHAPTER 9

Data Base Machines

The preceding chapters have described a DBMS (data base management system) in detail. Conventional hardware and software implementations were used throughout.

The 1970s have seen the emergence of a new technology for implementation of DBMS. Specialized hardware and software subsystems have been conceived, designed, and built to implement some subset of the DBMS function. These specialized systems are usually referred to as **data base machines.**

The data base machine is an attempt to improve three specific characteristics of the DBMS:

- Performance
- Usability
- Availability

While sufficient facts are not available to assess the success of the data base machine in these areas, the possibilities will be discussed, with emphasis on the differences between this new environment and the conventional DBMS environment. It will be seen that the performance improvement is still an open issue, that the usability factors are due more to the data model chosen, and that the availability of data will be similar to that of distributed data bases, as described in Chapter 10.

In this chapter the nature and structure of the data base machine is discussed. The data base machine is compared and contrasted to a conventional DBMS. The processing efficiencies of the machine are explained, as well as other advantages and disadvantages. The associative processor, sometimes considered to be a data base machine, is described in the last section.

While data base machine research and technology are in their youthful stages, it is quite likely that these machines will become more and more prevalent in the DBMS environment in the years to come. At this early stage, it is difficult to find a consensus of what exactly constitutes a data base machine. After the architectural issues have been analyzed, a definition is offered.

CONVENTIONAL DBMS ARCHITECTURE

Before embarking on a discussion of data base machine concepts, it is important to understand the architecture of a conventional DBMS. A conventional DBMS is the typical implementation found in most commercially available products. The majority of these products, whether they be a mainframe, minicomputer or microcomputer DBMS, are fully implemented in software that executes on a general-purpose CPU (central processing unit) and the data itself resides on general purpose auxiliary storage devices such as disk drives. This architecture is shown in Fig. 9.1.

The basic functions of a DBMS can be divided into two groups. The first group relates to the data base itself:

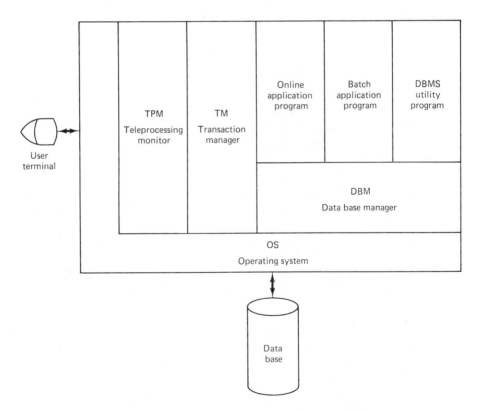

Figure 9.1 Conventional DBMS architecture: single centralized system.

- *Data definition.* Using a data definition language (DDL), data element characteristics are defined, redefined, displayed, and deleted.
- *Data access.* Using a data management language (DML), data is added, retrieved, updated, and deleted.
- *Data integrity.* The consistency of the data is maintained.
- *Concurrent data access.* Multiple users are permitted simultaneous access to the data base in a controlled and managed way.
- *Data base security.* Security clearance is checked before allowing a user to access data.
- *Data base recovery.* Media, software, and operational errors are recovered from by bringing the data base to a point where consistency is known to exist.
- *Data base access audit trails.* Data accesses are logged for audit control.
- *Data base distribution.* Movement of data between partner DBMS is accomplished in a controlled and reliable manner.

The second group of DBMS functions relates to the processes that use the data base:

- *Transaction integrity.* All resource modifications caused by a transaction are consistently applied.
- *Transaction recovery.* Transactions are never lost across system or application failures.
- *Transaction audit trails.* Transaction usage is logged for audit control.
- *Network access.* Terminals and other I/O devices are given direct access to the transaction management function.

The CPU in Fig. 9.1 may be any general-purpose processor of any size. In what follows, the CPU is considered to be a mainframe.

An operating system (OS) controls the operation of the CPU. The hub of the DBMS is the data base manager (DBM). The DBM is charged with the fundamental data management responsibilities. It maps the calls from the application programs to an internal format and executes the appropriate data accesses to retrieve and update data base records. Data security and integrity are controlled and preserved by the DBM.

The DBM services the requests of three general types of users. All these users are actually application programs acting on behalf of the DBMS and user. Some DBM apparently accept requests directly from the end user, but in reality an application program is provided that accepts and processes these direct requests.

The first type of user, an **online application program,** is invoked when a user at a terminal submits a real-time request for data from the data base. The teleprocessing monitor (TPM) handles the communications protocols between the terminal and the host computer. The transaction manager receives an edited request from the TPM and schedules the online application program related to the request from the terminal. The online application program issues calls to the DBM to retrieve, update, or delete data in the data base.

The second type of user is the **batch application program.** Batch programs are scheduled by computer operations personnel to access the data base for purposes of reporting, scheduled offline updating, and other noninteractive processes.

The third type of user is the **utility program.** Often these programs are supplied as part of the DBMS by the vendor to perform routine data base maintenance such as backup, recovery, reorganization, and reporting. The DBM may view these utilities as a type 2 user (i.e., a batch application) or as a type unto themselves with special privileges and access paths to the data base.

Several observations important to the understanding of data base machines must be made about the conventional DBMS in the following areas:

- *Integrity.* Data base consistency is always maintained.
- *Concurrency.* Simultaneous access by multiple users must produce consistent results.
- *Data access granularity.* A single record, a subset of a record or sets of records are returned to the application program depending upon the DBMS itself.
- *Performance.* DBMS systems require substantial amounts of CPU power, but ultimately the performance of the DBMS is dependent upon the number and duration of the I/O requests.
- *Reliability.* The disk subsystem is the weakest link in the reliability of a DBMS.

Integrity

The DBM is responsible for the integrity of the data base. If an application program should fail while a transaction is inflight (i.e., being processed) or if the operating system or disk subsystem should fail, the DBM will guarantee the integrity of the data base. This responsibility may be carried out automatically or the DBM may require the execution of related utilities in an offline mode to restore integrity.

Concurrency

The DBM is responsible for the concurrent access and update of the data base by the three types of users. Some DBM assume this responsibility in a simple fashion by allowing only one program access to the data base at a time. Other DBM provide multiple-user concurrency by requiring that each type of user have his or her own copy of the DBM, wherein the individual DBM communicate with each other to maintain concurrency control.

If the DBM enforces a protocol that requires the DBM to respond to a data request from one program before another data request from the same or another program is honored, concurrency problems are not an issue. In essence, this approach answers the concurrency issue by refusing to let it happen and is, therefore, not interesting.

Other DBM require that all programs (online, batch, and utility) that wish to access a given data base channel their requests through a single copy of the responsible DBM. Concurrency control is maintained only within the domain of the controlling DBM, as shown in Fig. 9.2.

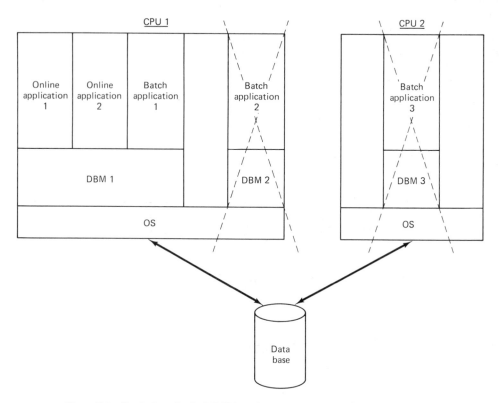

Figure 9.2 Single (nonsharing) DBM environment: Only one DBM has access to the data base.

Some DBM are capable of communicating with other DBM regarding the concurrent access to the same data base. Each participating DBM agrees to coordinate its accesses with the other DBM so that each application program, irrespective of its supporting DBM, is isolated from the affects of its concurrently executing peers. To help understand this multiple-DBM coordination, consider application program A issuing a request to DBM A for a particular data base record. DBM A understands that the target data base is also in use by other DBM. Consequently, DBM A sends a request-to-access message to the other DBM asking for their concurrence to proceed with the access. If none of the other DBM are using the specific data base record needed by program A, then they all return positive concurrence to DBM A. DBM A proceeds with the access knowing that none of the other DBM sharing the data base will access that data base record until DBM A frees it. The record is freed when program A explicitly tells DBM A that the record is no longer needed or when DBM A detects that program A has completed processing. The other DBM are then notified by DBM A that the record is available for access.

Figure 9.3 illustrates this case using the data sharing function of IMS. Here we see that the IMS DBM use an agent called the IMS *resource lock manager* (IRLM) to coordinate the concurrent accesses among themselves. The IRLM is a software

Basic Concepts   Section I

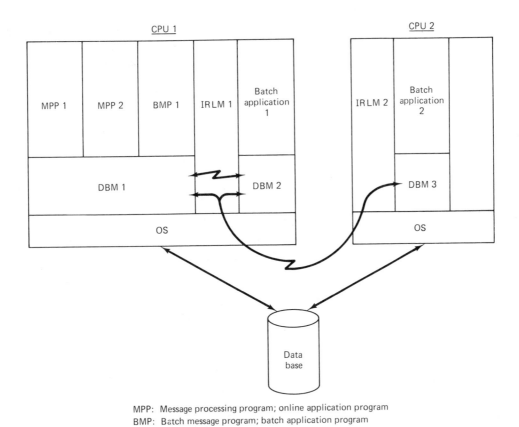

MPP: Message processing program; online application program
BMP: Batch message program; batch application program
IRLM: IMS resource lock manager

Figure 9.3 Multiple (sharing) IMS DBM's environment: Concurrent access with full integrity.

component of the IMS DBMS that communicates with the various copies of IMS that will share the data. Only a single copy of the data exists in this case. Each DBM has direct access to the data but communicates its actions on the data with the other DBM. All the DBM that have direct access to the data base have an equal role in the maintenance of data base integrity. In Chapter 10 we contrast this multiple DBM–direct access environment with the distributed data base environment.

The CPU where a DBM resides is called the **host** CPU. The system component responsible for concurrency control is actually software in the host CPU. If one of the hosts should fail, the other DBM executing on the other hosts would be unable to access the data base until the failing system recovered or until the failing system promised that the data base integrity was no longer compromised due to the failure. If the other DBM were to access the data base before the failing DBM was recovered, the data base could be corrupted. Consider the case where an active DBM updates a specific record in the data base before the failing DBM is recovered. Further, during the DBM recovery process, assume the failing DBM backs out a data base change to the same record. The change made by the active DBM would be partially or completely lost, thereby corrupting the data base. Had the active DBM waited until the failing DBM was recovered, data base integrity would have been maintained. Alternatively, had the failing DBM promised that no data base back-outs would be performed, the active DBM could proceed with the update without possibility of corruption. This example demonstrates that complex recovery scenarios are involved when multiple DBM on multiple hosts concurrently share the same copy of the data.

Data Access Granularity

The unit of data transferred between the host and the disk is a block of data. It may contain a portion of a data base record or one or more records of the data base. Disk drives in use today are accessed by physical address. The host requests a block of data with a certain address and the disk locates that address and transfers the data. The protocol used between the host and the disk in an IBM mainframe environment is a block at a time. The System/360 I/O (input/output) interface designed in the early 1960s is the same one in use today in even the most powerful of CPU from that vendor.

If the host-based DBM, such as IDMS, IMS, DB2 or SQL/DS, require a specific data base record that matches certain user-selection criteria, each possible data base record that might match the criteria must be transferred to the host for inspection by the DBM. Many data transfers may occur between the disk and the DBM in the host to support a single data transfer between the DBM and the requesting application.

The largest amount of data that a DBM is able to pass back to an application program in one call is the data access **granularity** of the DBM. When an application program requests data from the DBM, a *single* record or subrecord may be returned or the request may result in a *set* of records or subrecords to be passed back to the application. If the DBM is only capable of returning a single record or subrecord, then the DBM is called a **record-at-a-time DBM,** abbreviated **record DBM.** If more than one record or subrecord can be returned, then the DBM is termed a **set-at-a-time DBM,** abbreviated **set DBM.** Set DBM can significantly reduce the number of calls to the DBM from the application program and therefore reduce the DBM overhead.

The granularity of the transfer between the DBM and the application, whether it be record or set, is not directly proportional to the transfer between the DBM and the disk. Even if the DBM passes a set of records to the application in response to one call to the DBM, many individual disk I/O interactions may have been performed by the DBM to produce the set of records. In other words, although the application program interface (API) to the DBM may be optimized to return multiple records for one application request, the I/O operations initiated by the DBM may or may not be optimized depending on the actual capabilities of the I/O subsystem itself. The API optimization may pale in light of the lack of disk I/O optimization. This API optimization versus disk I/O optimization issue is important when considering the data base machine later in this chapter.

Performance

The conventional DBMS requires substantial amounts of processor cycles to achieve its goal. Catalogs must be searched to locate the data base records that are candidates for the user request. Data base pointers must be followed to retrieve the records. The records must be matched with the original selection criteria from the user, and data base and transaction concurrency, integrity, and accountability must continue to be maintained.

The DBMS is competing for the same CPU cycles as the other work on the host CPU. A shortage of CPU cycles could increase the length of time necessary to satisfy the request for data. The large number of I/O interrupts caused by all the data requests to the disk results in a substantial commitment of CPU cycles to the operating system software that initiates and terminates the I/O activity. The DBMS itself is preempted by the operating system during the I/O interrupts, and this has a negative impact on the performance of the DBMS.

Because of the richness in function of the DBMS and as a result of the need to service the high I/O activity, the demands for CPU cycles in a conventional DBMS are quite high. Consequently, a DBMS is generally viewed as a CPU-bound system. A **CPU-bound system** is a system whose performance is more dependent upon the CPU resource than any other resource.

Real-life DBMS applications may or may not emphasize this intrinsic CPU-bound characteristic of a DBMS. A well-designed DBMS application tends to reveal the CPU-bound nature of the DBMS. Other applications that, due to design, require inordinate numbers of I/O will tend to overshadow the CPU-bound factor with excessive I/O. Many existing applications are I/O bound because of data base design.

Reliability

Usually, DBMS-based applications are relied upon heavily by their users. Reliability of the total system is important. The overall reliability of the system is only as good as the reliability of the components that constitute the system.

There are two major components required for the access of data. The DBMS software executes in the host CPU. If the host fails, data access will not be possible (i.e., from that host). The data itself resides on disks. The CPU gains access to the data by sending a request to the disk drive. These components are shown in Fig. 9.4. Depending on the particular system studied, additional hardware may exist between the CPU and the disk to manage and control the CPU-disk communications; channels and disk control units are examples. For the purposes of this book, this additional hardware may be assumed to be part of the disk unit itself.

If the CPU fails, all data access by this host is prevented. However, if the disk itself should fail, all data access from all CPU would be prevented. Assuming, then, a multiple-host environment, the weakest link in the DBMS is the disk itself and its controller. This is an important observation in the study of the reliability of a data base machine.

CPU

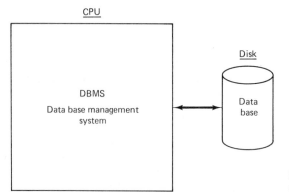

Figure 9.4 Data access components: Conventional DBMS environment.

As an aside, reliability of the hardware and software components is only one perspective. Another perspective deals with data availability. If the components, taken as a system, are reliable, the data will be highly available. If the data is highly available, the components must be reliable.

THE COMMUNICATIONS PROCESSOR ANALOGY

In a conventional DBMS, the host CPU assumes a large burden of the data base access. The application program issues simple requests for a certain subset of the data, the DBM passes simple data requests to the disk, and the DBM reduces the mass of data sent from the disk to the subset requested by the application.

In addition to the significant CPU requirements of a DBMS, the number of I/O performed to "chase the chains" to the required data base record can be quite high. Offloading some of these functions to a different processor may be a worthwhile endeavor.

The possibility of offloading repetitive, routine chores to specialized hardware has been explored and successfully implemented in other areas of computer technology. The communications processor is a good example.

In the 1960s, the majority of the protocol conversion and related editing required to communicate with an interactive terminal connected to a mainframe was performed by the host CPU. The communication control unit provided only the most basic of character assembly functions; the remainder was left to the host.

As communications networks grew in size and sophistication, it became clear that a considerable reduction in CPU usage could be realized by moving some of the message assembly functions, network management functions, and error recovery procedures outboard to the then-called communication control unit. With this outward movement of function, the microcoded and hard-wired control units were transformed into powerful processors, whose specialty was dealing with the unique world of telecommunications. The IBM 3725 Communications Processor of today, with megabytes of storage and its own software control program, is a far cry from its predecessor, the hard-wired IBM 2701.

Communications processors have become network nodes in their own rights with high-levels of autonomy from the host. They have relieved the CPU of the tasks of line-polling, data link control, transmission framing, and code translation. Time-consuming operations such as error recovery can often be totally handled in the communications processor without the aid of the CPU. When the network or host gets backed up, the communications processor can buffer the message traffic until the situation clears. As communications processors mature, it is becoming increasingly difficult to distinguish them from the host CPU in terms of power, size, and function.

The handling of communications lines is quite different than any other I/O device. It is an interrupt-intensive task, where the success of the communications processor can be measured on the machine's ability to sustain high interrupt rates and cycle-steal data in and out of memory.

Data base machines are to the 1980s what communications processors were to the 1970s. The feasibility of replacing a host-resident DBMS and low-level disk hardware with an intelligent machine is becoming a prevalent topic for academic research and discussion in data processing circles. The overall thrust behind the data base machine is much like the one that brought communications processors into existence.

Keeping this analogy in mind helps in the understanding of the motivations and goals of a data base machine.

DATA BASE MACHINE DBMS ARCHITECTURE

A data base machine is an intelligent, software-driven device that assumes some subset of the function of the DBMS. It may or may not utilize specialized hardware or software, but its primary raison d'etre is the execution of DBMS tasks. Just as the communications processor is referred to as a *front-end processor,* the data base machine is a *back-end processor.*

Referring to Fig. 9.4 again, the entire DBMS responsibility in a conventional DBMS resides in the host. Compare this with the configuration that incorporates a data base machine, as shown in Fig. 9.5. An additional component has been added and part of the DBMS responsibility has been moved from the host to this new component, the data base machine.

As already seen, the basic functions of a DBMS can be divided into data related functions:

- Data definition (define, redefine, inquire, delete) using a DDL
- Data access (add, retrieve, update, delete) using a DML
- Data integrity
- Concurrent data access
- Data base security
- Data base recovery
- Data base access audit trails
- Data base distribution

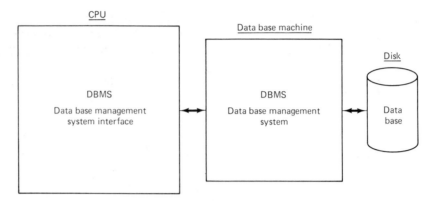

CPU

Data base machine

Disk

| DBMS | DBMS | Data base |
| Data base management system interface | Data base management system | |

Figure 9.5 Data base machine configuration; Three components instead of two.

Also, there are the following workload related functions:

- Transaction integrity
- Transaction recovery
- Transaction audit trails
- Network access

There is considerable controversy surrounding the question of which of these functions could and should be moved to the data base machine. Indeed, there are several implementations of the data base machine concept that have answered the question differently. The subset of DBMS functions offloaded from the host to the machine can be used to categorize the data machine type:

- *DBMP.* The majority of the DBMS functions—data access, integrity, concurrency, recovery—are moved outboard to the data base machine. The host-resident portion of the DBMS becomes a "pass-through" device funneling the data access requests to the data base machine.
- *Associative data processor (ADP).* The data addressing function is moved outboard to the data base machine. The DBMS remains predominantly host-resident, but it now looks at the disk as a content addressable store instead of a location addressable store. See the box on Content Addressable Memory in Chapter 4 for a definition of these terms.

Data base machine vendors and supporters usually give three primary reasons for moving some of the DBMS function to a dedicated processor:

1. *Performance.* Overall performance will improve.
2. *Usability.* The system will be easier to use.
3. *Availability.* The data will be more accessable to a greater variety of users.

The two types of data base machines will be analyzed with reference to these characteristics.

DATA BASE MANAGEMENT PROCESSOR

The functions and interrelationships of the data base management processor (DBMP) environment are shown in Fig. 9.6. A basic premise is that the data base machine must be dedicated to the DBMS task. This simple requirement has led some advocates to refer to the DBMP as a *data utility*. From a computer network point of view, the data utility processor (a node in the network) is a DBMP that services the data needs of the other nodes in the network. This is but another example of the similarity between the data base machine and distributed data bases.

A commercial example of a DBMP that uses a record-at-a-time external interface is the ADABAS Database Machine from SOFTWARE AG. For reasons discussed in the performance and usability sections that follow, this machine may offer limited advantages over the completely host-resident version of the ADABAS DBMS.

The commercially available Britton-Lee IDM 500 and the Teradata DBC/1012 are examples of set DBMP. They implement the relational model in a specialized processor optimized for data access and management. Both machines, in addition to being DBMP, also use ADP to improve performance further. These two products will be examined in detail in later sections.

It has been noted that a DBMP may be a collection of *general-purpose* software and hardware. An example of this implementation in limited use today is IMS executing in a dedicated large mainframe. If DB2 should become a standard in many large corporations, it too may be used in a dedicated mainframe as a data base machine. These cases are studied in later sections.

In theory, there are two fundamental goals in offloading many of the DBMS functions from the host to a DBMP: *performance* and *availability*. In practice, *usability* is also considered a prima facie justification for such a move. These claims will now be investigated in light of the architecture of a DBMP.

Performance

The most-often-stated reason for using a DBM is performance. The actual performance improvements that can be realized are, at present, uncertain. Insufficient

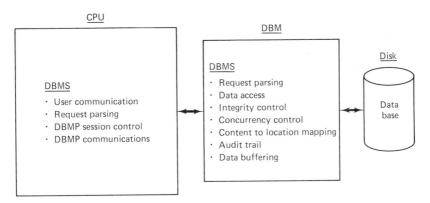

Figure 9.6 DBMP environment: functions and interrelationships.

benchmarks are available, in part due to the limited number of models commercially available and the novelty of the technology.

Performance improvements can be divided into two categories: response time and throughput. **Response time,** in a DBMS environment, refers to the time it takes the system to respond to a user request (a transaction) and is usually measured in seconds (e.g., transaction response time is 2 seconds). **Throughput** is the number of transactions, per unit time, the system can process. Throughput is usually measured in transactions per second at a specified CPU percent busy (e.g., 20 transactions per second at 50% CPU).

A common misrepresentation of DBM performance is the comparison of the performance of an existing host-resident DBMS with that of a data base machine without regard for the DML or data model. A host DBMS using a record DML and the hierarchical model cannot be compared to a DBMP DBMS using a set DML and the relational model, and vice versa.

Response Time. Consider the influence that a data base machine has on response time. A significant component of response time is the servicing of the data base calls issued by the application program. Therefore, improvements can be expected. DBMS servicing of data base requests consists of CPU time and I/O time. Algebraically, for a host resident DBMS, we have:

$$RT = a + b + c + def + dgh + di$$

where RT is the response time for a transaction in seconds
      a is the network time in seconds
      b is the transaction management time in seconds
      c is the application time in seconds
      d is the number of data base requests to the DBMS
      e is the average number of I/O per DBMS request
      f is the average I/O service time in seconds
      g is the number of record waits per DBMS request
      h is the average record wait time in seconds
      i is the DBMS CPU time per DBMS request in seconds

See Fig. 9.7. Assuming no change in the network, transaction management, the application itself, and the data base model in use, variables a, b, c, and d will not be affected by a change from a host-resident DBMS to a data base machine. Furthermore, the record wait time, due to concurrent requests for the same record (product of d, g, and h), will not change. However, the average number of I/O, e, the average I/O service time, f, and the DBMS CPU time, i, may increase or decrease depending upon the DBMP. In addition, the extra time that will be needed to send the request to the DBMP and receive the response must be accounted for; a new link has been added to the chain and so it grows longer.

What will be the total I/O time (product of d, e, and f) and total DBMS CPU time (product of d and i) of the data base machine? How will it compare to the host-resident DBMS? What will be the host-DBMP communications time? It is important to note that, from the perspective of the host, the I/O time and DBMP

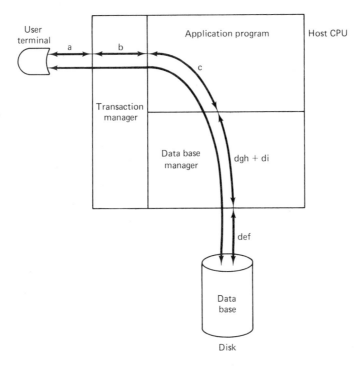

Figure 9.7 Host-resident–DBMS response time: $RT = a + b + c + def + dgh + di$.

processor time are second-order factors. Three new variables are now introduced into the response-time equation when a DBMP is handling the bulk of the DBMS task:

$$RT = a + b + c + dj + d(k + l)$$

where RT, a, b, c, and d are as previously defined

      j is the average DBMP service time per host request
      k is the average host-DBMP transmission time
      l is the average DBMP-host transmission time

as shown in Fig. 9.8. The new host-visible response time characteristics are dj, the DBMP service time, and dkl, the host-DBMP-host communications time. The DBMP service time is:

$$dj = dmn + dop + dq$$

where d and j are as previously defined

      m is the average number of I/O per DBMS request
      n is the average I/O service time in seconds
      o is the number of record waits per DBMS request
      p is the average record wait time in seconds
      q is the DBMS CPU time per DBMS request in seconds

Several comparative conclusions may be drawn:

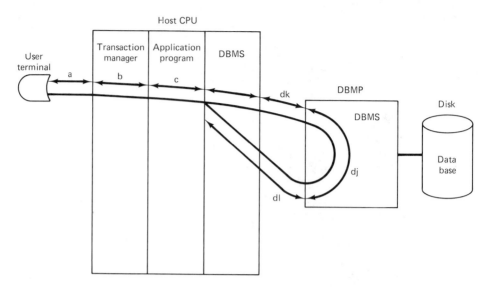

Figure 9.8 DBM response time: $RT = a + b + c + dj + d + (k + 1)$.

$$dmn = def \text{ (I/O service times are equal)}$$

$$dop = dgh \text{ (record wait times are equal)}$$

provided that the I/O time, *ef,* and the record wait time, *gh,* are the same whether the DBMS executes in the host or the DBMP. This equality assumption is reasonable when considering the following:

1. The data model used in both cases is the same.

2. The I/O time in a host-resident DBMS has been optimized. Very fast disk devices are used. Multiple I/O to different disk drives are performed simultaneously thereby increasing parallelism. Disk accesses are heavily buffered. Efficient CPU-to-disk protocols are used. If the DBMP were to use faster disks or buffer the data more efficiently, the host DBMS could have too. The I/O time, then, is heavily dependent upon the data model used and anything that could be done outboard in the DBMP to improve the I/O situation could also be done in the host. The exception here would be some sort of device that could significantly reduce I/O time but could be used only by a DBMP and not a host CPU. Incompatibility between a host CPU and a new storage technology would be transitory.

   If the DBMP were to incorporate multiple parallel I/O servers, the I/O may be overlapped to an extent and consequently reduce the end-to-end I/O time; the same approach could be used in a general-purpose host.

3. Record wait time is dependent on the workload mix and independent of the point of concurrency control. The length of time an application program holds a record and prevents others from accessing it depends on the design of the application program. The application program is not sensitive to which im-

plementation of the DBMS is in use, and record locks will therefore be held for the same length of time. Consequently, other application programs will wait for the locked record for the same amount of time regardless of the DBMS implementation in use. It must be assumed that the granularity of locking (record group, record, segment, or field) would be the same in both implementations; otherwise the same functional capabilities are not being compared.

This is, at last, the point at which the algebraic performance advantage of the DBMP can be determined. There are two factors remaining from the preceding equations:

1. What is the difference between *di* and *dq,* the times for the host CPU and the DBMP CPU?
2. What is the value of *d(k* + 1), the host-DBMP communication time?

These two factors define the performance improvement (PI) of a DBMP:

$$PI = di - dq - d(k + 1)$$

A verbal translation of this equation is:
The improvement in the response-time performance of a transaction when a data base machine is used is equal to the reduction in CPU time for the data base calls less the cost of the additional communications involved.

If the data base request of CPU time of a host-resident DBMS is equal to the DBMP CPU time in a data base machine, the introduction of the DBMP has *increased* the response time of the transaction by an amount equal to *d(k* + 1), the **communications cost** of adding the DBMP. Therefore, as an absolute minimum,

$$di = dq + d(k + 1)$$

is required to achieve a break-even proposition. From a performance point of view, the DBMP only complicated the system with no performance payback.
Optimally, then,

$$di > dq + d(k + 1)$$

is needed. The CPU savings must be significantly more than the communications cost if the data base machine is to be worthwhile.

If multiple parallel processors are used in the DBMP, it may be possible to reduce the end-to-end CPU time of a data request. A similar result could be effected by using parallel host processors.

If specialized hardware and microprogramming are used in the DBMP, it is conceivable that the DBMP CPU time would be much less than the host CPU time. However, the percentage of the response time that is due to CPU utilization by the DBMS must be considered. Since CPU time typically is an incidental part of a transaction's response time, any improvement realized by the use of a DBMP will have an inconsequential effect on response time. This doesn't contradict the notion that a DBMS is CPU-bound. A DBMS can indeed drive the CPU load to very high levels for the total work performed, but the I/O service times are, by far, the most quantitative contributors to a given transaction's response time.

An important relationship exists between the performance improvement offered by a DBMP and the DML used. It has already been seen that the communications component introduced by the use of a DBMP is a significant performance factor. A record DML will necessarily generate more messages between the host and the DBMP than would a set DML. Because of the significant reduction in communications from host CPU to DBMP that can be realized, it is generally agreed that a set DML is absolutely necessary to realize performance gains from a DBMP.

In conclusion, *the DBMP will not improve response time to any worthwhile extent but may increase it. A set DML is mandatory to achieve any response-time reductions.*

Throughput. It may be disapppointing to realize that the DBMP does *not* offer significant response-time improvements and may, in fact, increase response time. However, the throughput side of performance is quite a different story.

Introduction of a DBMP into a DBMS environment will result in an increase in the total processor power (MIPS, or million instructions per second) of the system. Now $n + 1$ processors are doing the work of n processors. If the DBMP itself is a multiprocessor, the ratio is even higher. The increase in parallel execution of the workload will result in greater throughput as long as the interprocessor communications cost between the host and DBMP does not become significant.

Whether the throughput would increase more by the addition of host processors or the addition of DBMP processors depends on the ratios - i/q and i/RT. If the component of response time due to host-resident DBMS CPU (i/RT) is low, the system throughput benefits more from the addition of host processors. If i/RT is high, adding a DBMP improves throughput. If $i > q$, then DBMP processors are the answer to greater throughput given that i could not be increased just by using a faster host CPU. If $q > i$, then the DBMP would never be the correct throughput solution.

There is an important throughput consideration when assessing the possibilities of a DBMP: *cost*. If a host-resident DBMS on a specific CPU is capable of handling 30 data base requests per second at 90% CPU busy, the DBMP is advantageous from a performance standpoint only if it can handle the same load for a lower cost. Otherwise, increased throughput could be achieved on a more financially sound basis by the addition of a second host processor and no DBMP. There are too few large-scale DBMP systems in use today to state a conclusion, but it is likely that general-purpose mainframes will remain the cost-effective solution to throughput growth.

Usability

Data base machines are often credited with improved usability when compared with their host DBMS counterparts. By usability we refer to the *ease of use* of the DBMP once the end user is connected to the machine directly or indirectly. Usability does not include the flexibility of the DBMS to accept requests from many different user types (that is, different CPU from different vendors). This characteristic is included in the next section.

To measure the usability of a DBMS, questions related to the DBMS interface language are considered:

- How much training is required to access the data?
- What data processing skill level and background is needed?
- Is the syntax of the requests natural and consistent?
- Are the semantics (command meanings) of the language easily recognizable?
- Is the system user-friendly?
- Can simple requests be entered simply?

The usability improvement claims of data base machines are impressive but, when closely studied, are often unrelated to the data base machine itself. Typically, the ease of use of a DBMP-based DBMS relative to a host DBMS is not at all due to the DBMP itself but rather the data model used.

DBM theory and technology have progressed in parallel with relational data model theory and technology. Products became available in both areas at roughly the same time. In fact, several product introductions included a relational DBMS executing within a DBMP. This led to confusion concerning which improvements were a result of the machine and which were to the relational DBMS itself.

Hierarchic and network DBMS are intricate and require specialized knowledge to use. The notions of segments and navigation are not natural in many applications. Relational DBMS are much more natural, as testified by the terms *table* and *row*.

After investigating the usability assertions of many commercially available DBMP, it can be concluded that there is nothing intrinsically more usable about a DBM than a conventional DBMS. Comparing a conventional relational DBMS such as DB2 or SQL/DS to a relational DBM shows little difference in usability.

Availability

The DBMP is a self-contained, autonomous DBMS. Consequently, it is not dependent on any supporting mainframe, minicomputer or microcomputer. The DBMP defines the interface to be used by the outside world to access the data it manages. As long as the users of the DBMP follow the interface rules, the users are allowed to access the data managed by the machine, subject to security considerations. This characteristic of a DBMP makes it an ideal candidate to serve as a *data utility* or *data server* in a computer network.

Today, most large data bases are managed by conventional DBMS executing on large mainframes. This configuration tends to lock the data base into that environment and make the data inaccessible to all others. As an example, the corporate data base may be managed by a DBMS executing on multiple large mainframes. Operational jobs and online systems perform high-volume updates and inquiries against the data base on a daily basis. On the other hand, the corporate decision makers use microcomputers with highly refined decision support software.

The DBMP provides the data access needed by both these user types. Funneling this diverse range of user access and performance requirements through a single DBMP is, however, an untenable proposition as neither user group is serviced adequately. Operational users are restricted in their abilities to take the data base off-line for maintenance and routine high-volume processing because the data would be needed by the ad hoc requests of the decision support systems. Decision makers are subjected to erratic performance due to heavy operational loads on the data base, and statistical data change from iteration to iteration as the data base is updated.

While it is true that the DBMP offers new levels of data availability to a broader range of users, capitalization on this feature may be a long time in coming for existing large corporate data bases. It simply is not practical for companies to move their huge data bases to a DBMP environment until the viability of the DBM concept is proven and the cost effectiveness dwarfs the migration cost.

The new levels of data availability offered by DBM will make them attractive for use in new data base environments, but—for the time being—the largest percentage of data in data bases will remain in host-resident, conventional DBMS systems.

Britton-Lee IDM 500

The IDM 500, from Britton-Lee, Inc., was one of the first commercially available DBMP. Since its introduction in the early 1980s, several models have been added that more or less use the same architecture as the IDM 500. The focus is on the 500.

The IDM implements the relational data model. Its syntax and semantics are quite similar to QUEL, the language used by INGRES. As noted, there exists no defined subset of the conventional DBMS function that must be assumed by a machine before it is a DBMP. In the Britton-Lee case, IDM stands for intelligent database machine, and most of the DBMS function set has been moved outboard to the machine. The IDM 500 is, indeed, a stand-alone, self-contained DBMS. The user's system, attached to the IDM, is responsible for the following:

1. Accepting input from the terminal (TPM and TM functions).
2. Scheduling the host application program.
3. Parsing the application requests to the data base. Parsing involves breaking down the request into its verb (command) and parameters associated with the request.
4. Sending the parsed string to the IDM.
5. Receiving the response from the IDM.
6. Formatting the returned data into the application program receiving area.
7. Defining the start and end of atomic units of work. An atomic unit of work (AUW) is the smallest recoverable transaction in the system. All data base changes made by the AUW transaction are applied together or none of them are. The DBMS ensures this consistency.

From this list it can be seen that the traditional DBMS functions are no longer executed on the host. The IDM performs the following:

1. Data access
2. Data buffering
3. Concurrency control
4. Transaction management
5. Data security
6. Data base backup
7. Failure recovery
8. Integrated data dictionary
9. Audit trail creation

The IDM 500 internal architecture is shown in Fig. 9.9. The external interface is through a serial interface, typically used by stand-alone programmable terminals, or a parallel interface, which is used by mainframes and minicomputers. The parallel interface is limited to a maximum data rate of 250 kilobytes/second, which is considerably slower than the 3 megabytes/second used by many large mainframes for disk communications. This is certainly a transitory limitation but does prevent the use of the machine in multiprocessor mainframe environments, where many large data bases exist today. Minicomputer, microcomputer, and programmable terminal users will certainly find this transfer rate sufficient.

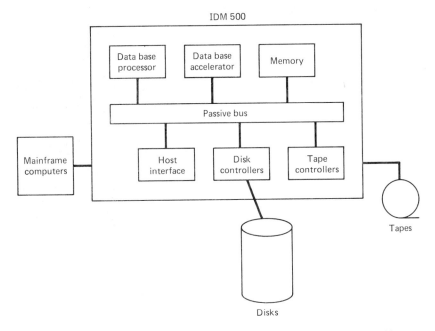

Figure 9.9   Britton-Lee IDM 500 Architecture: Components and interrelationships.

The individual components of the machine are interconnected using a common control and data passive bus. A **passive bus** is an electrical circuit that interconnects other electronic components, providing communications facilities among the components but without modifying the traffic on the bus. The IDM 500 bus allows a large number of levels of parallelism within the IDM.

The data base processor is the "CPU" of the IDM. It is a specialized, high-performance processor connected to the bus. The DBMS function set is implemented within the processor by a combination of microcode and software.

Main memory, which can be expanded to 5.5 megabytes, is used to hold software and to buffer the data moving to and from the disk drives and external interfaces. This memory size provides ample buffering for small to intermediate data base environments, but large mainframe users will need to use multiple IDM to achieve acceptable performance. The IDM has been designed to allow support parallel configurations.

Industry-standard disk drives are used. Up to 16 SMD (standard modular disk) drives are supported per IDM with a maximum data storage capability of 32 billion bytes. The 16 drives can be distributed over 4 independent disk control units. Each control unit interfaces to the bus. The data dictionary, audit trails, and recovery files share the disk storage with the data bases themselves. A mirrored disk option is available that provides high data availability by automatically maintaining multiple copies of the same data.

A tape drive controller and up to 8 tape drives can be attached to the bus. These drives can be used for data base backup and recovery.

An optional specialized processor can be connected to the bus. Britton-Lee refers to it as the *data base accelerator.* The accelerator uses a pipeline design to improve the performance of the search logic implemented in the data base processor. The pipeline approach allows the processor to process effectively more instructions per unit time by processing parts of multiple instructions simultaneously. As data is read from the disk, the accelerator compares the data against the original search criteria. If there is a match, the data is stored in memory. Otherwise the data is discarded. The accelerator then redrives the I/O to the disk to continue the search. Rated throughput increases from 10 transactions per second to 30 per second when the accelerator is used. The IDM 500 has been classified as a DBMP. With the accelerator, the IDM has characteristics of an ADP as well. This kind of data base machine is described in a later section.

Teradata DBC/1012

In 1984, the Teradata Corporation introduced the DBC/1012 data base machine. It is a DBMP intended for use in the IBM large mainframe environment. As such, it offers limited data *availability* to heterogeneous users (users on different CPU from different vendors), but on the other hand, its *performance* characteristics are exceptional. The relational model is used throughout, and the data manipulation language, called TEQUEL (Teradata QUEL), is similar to the SQL syntax and semantics of System R, SQL/DS, and DB2. Figure 9.10 shows the architecture of the Teradata machine.

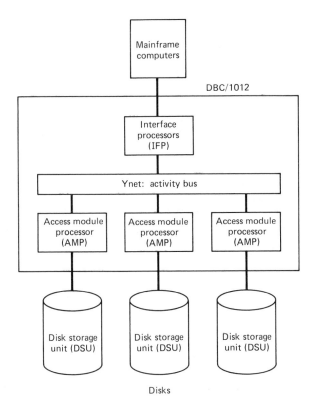

Figure 9.10 Teradata DBC/1012 architecture: Components and interrelationships.

Host System Interface (HSI). The **host system interface (HSI)** is an interface program that routes application data requests from the host to the DBC machine and returns the data sent from the DBC to the requesting application. The hub of the host-resident interface is the Teradata Director Program (TDP). The TDP establishes, maintains, and terminates the communications channel between the host and the DBC/1012 as well as transmits and receives all data.

End users access the DBC/1012 indirectly through the host CPU. A facility called interactive TEQUEL (ITEQ) is provided that accepts TEQUEL statements directly from the user's terminal and routes them to the TDP for processing by the DBC without the need of any application program.

COBOL programs can contain embedded TEQUEL statements. A preprocessor is supplied that converts the TEQUEL statements to corresponding calls to host interface execution-time subroutines contained in the **call-level interface** (CLI) library. Alternately, other languages may use the CLI routines by calling them directly without the need of a preprocessor.

The HSI contains a set of utilities that are used to load, back up, and restore the data bases on the DBC. This reduces the autonomy of the DBC, since it requires a host processor to perform routine data base maintenance jobs. For very large data bases, the host to DBC interface may be quite busy for extended periods while data bases are backed up, and this may affect the performance of the transaction processing also sharing the interface.

From a description of the host system interface, it can be seen that the majority of the DBMS CPU cycles have been offloaded from the host CPU. This is certainly one of the strengths of the DBC/1012 as DBMP.

Interface Processor (IFP). The **interface processor (IFP)** manages the interface between the host computer and the DBC/1012. There can be one or more IFP per DBC/1012 for redundancy and performance. Host computer channels are connected directly to the IFP.

When the IFP receives a TEQUEL request from the host, the request is parsed, and the data dictionary (system data base that contains information about all the user data bases) is consulted to resolve variable names and perform integrity checks. Once the request is determined to be syntactically and semantically correct, the request is reduced to a series of primitives for execution. The primitives are sent to the appropriate access module processor using the Ynet bus for disk access.

Ynet. The **Ynet** is an interprocessor active bus that routes data and control information between the IFP and the AMP. The Ynet is duplexed for redundancy and performance.

The IFP pass AMP requests to the Ynet for forwarding to the appropriate AMP. The Ynet provides the routing control function. When the data requested by the IFP is ready at the AMP, the AMP passes it to the Ynet for transfer back to the requesting IFP. The Ynet sorts and merges the data automatically as part of its AMP-to-IFP routing.

Access Module Processor (AMP). The **access module processor (AMP)** determines the disk location of the requested data and interfaces with the disk drives to access it. It receives the requests from the Ynet.

The AMP contains the data base manager of the DBC. Data base retrieve, insert, delete, and update operations are performed as well as rollback, recovery, reorganization, and logging.

Disk Storage Unit (DSU). The **disk storage unit (DSU)** is the actual disk storage medium used to store the data. The disks are conventional random access devices that use fixed, sealed modules as the storage medium. The disk capacity, access time, and transfer rate are of the same order of magnitude as DASD found on mainframe systems. Consequently, any exceptional performance of the DBC/1012 cannot be due to the use of DASD, with exceptional performance compared to host-based systems.

IMS As A Data Base Machine

A data base machine can be comprised of a general-purpose DBMS executing in a general-purpose processor. As long as it is dedicated to the DBMS task, it is a data base machine. Therefore, the use of IMS in a mainframe might be considered as a dedicated DBMP.

ASSOCIATIVE DATA PROCESSOR

The DBMP is a complex machine with capabilities of the order found in general-purpose mainframes and minicomputers. There is a second kind of data base machine that has a single specific task. The **associative data processor (ADP)** replaces location addressable secondary storage control with content addressable control. The ADP is sometimes referred to as a *content addressable processor.*

Most secondary storage systems (disk, tape, etc.) use an addressing scheme wherein the computer accessing the device must provide the physical address of the data to be read or written to the storage medium. Physical addresses usually contain embedded device-dependent information such as cylinder, track or sector. Two limitations exist with this approach:

1. *Unnatural access.* The accessing computer has, as its first order of business, the knowledge of what data is needed, not where it resides in secondary storage. When an application program asks for a record from a file, it refers to the record number or the key of the record desired, not the physical location of the record. The operating system or DBMS must perform the translation.
2. *Device dependence.* The accessing computer must "know" about the specific device type involved and cater to its physical characteristics. When a file is moved from one storage device type to another, the addressing transformation changes.

An ADP accepts data content information and associates it with the physical location of the data on the storage medium. The accessing computer passes the key of the record desired to the ADP with no knowledge at all of the physical location of the data.

The primary advantage of an ADP lies in its ability to relieve the host computer of physical device dependencies and thereby naturalize the protocols used. In addition, since the ADP is not given any physical location information, it is free to optimize the placement and access of the data. Parallel search and access paths can be implemented in the ADP to improve performance without any assistance or knowledge of the host. Often DBMP are endowed with an ADP capability. The reader is referred to Chapter 4 for additional information on the subject of content addressable storage.

QUESTIONS

1. What are the perceived advantages of a data base machine?
2. List the basic data base functions of a DBMS.
3. List the transaction functions of a DBMS.

4. What is a DDL and what purpose does it serve?
5. What is a DML and what purpose does it serve?
6. What are the components of a DBMS and what are the interrelationships?
7. Identify the three types of users of the DBM.
8. How do DBM share data bases and maintain integrity?
9. What is the difference between a record DML and a set DML? What are the advantages and disadvantages of both?
10. What is meant by the statement that a DBMS is theoretically a CPU-bound process?
11. What constitutes a data base machine?
12. List the functions offloaded from the host by a communications processor and the corresponding functions offloaded by a DBMP.
13. What are the two categories of data base machines, and what are their characteristics?
14. State algebraically the response time of a system that includes a DBMP, and identify the ways in which a DBMP may outperform a host DBMS.
15. Are DBMP more cost-effective than host DBMS systems and why?
16. What DBMS functions are not handled by the IDM 500 and Teradata DBC/1012? Where are they performed?
17. How are data bases in an IDM 500 or a Teradata DBC/1012 backed up?

CHAPTER 10

Distributed
Data Bases

Distributed data processing (DDP) is a major classification of data processing methods. Within DDP, two types of distribution are possible:

- *Distributed processing.* Execution of an application program results in the program using CPU (central processing unit) cycles on more than one CPU in a network of processors. Program A on CPU 1 may call subroutine B but request that it execute on CPU 2 and within the same recovery scope as A; the processing performed has been *distributed.* The single recovery scope means that the resource changes performed by program A and subroutine B must be fully executed or neither set can be executed. In this way, integrity is maintained across the network.
- *Distributed data.* A single file or data base is partitioned and the data partitions reside on different nodes (processors) in a network of processors. A bank may have a single checking account data base with part of it in San Francisco and part in Los Angeles. Both sites can access the entire data base regardless of the location of the data in the network.

It is quite possible and highly likely that both distributed data and distributed processing are used in a DDP environment. In this book, only distributed data is discussed and then only as it applies to data bases.

The concept of a data base and a DBMS (data base management system) has been, to this point, confined to a single physical system. The data base totally resides at one site and is managed by a single copy of the DBMS. These concepts can be extended to the distributed data base environment. Distributed data base theory and technology are in their youthful stages, at least when compared to other data base concepts. For this reason, most of the notions involved have not as yet been demonstrated in production computer networks.

A fundamental issue in this new field is the question, What is a distributed data base? There are many diverse answers, depending on one's perspective. In this book, a distributed data base is defined in quite a different way than is generally found in most texts on the subject. The distribution attribute is assigned to the data base manager, as shown in Fig. 10.1, instead of to the data base itself. Although this approach is novel in several ways, more importantly it allows for a precise definition of a distributed data base, which is often difficult to achieve when assigning the distribution characteristic to the data itself.

The current trend in DBMS implementations is toward the distribution of the workload and data. Prior to this trend, DBMS usage was based on single centralized systems for the following reasons:

1. *Economies of scale.* Shared, multiuser DBMS systems could capitalize on the power of large centralized systems. Very large scale integrated (VLSI) electronics and its attendent improvements in price and performance were not available, thereby raising the cost of multiple smaller networked machines.

2. *Nature of existing DBMS products.* Distributed capabilities were not incorporated into the products.

3. *Data communications technology.* The state of the art had not matured sufficiently.

4. *Little perceived need.* A definite need for distribution had not been established.

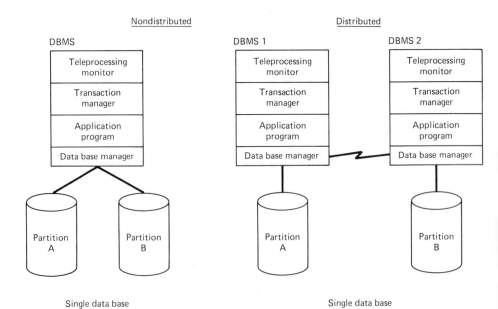

Figure 10.1 Distributed data base: A characteristic of the DBM, not the data base.

5. *Vogue.* Centralized, mainframe environments were in style; decentralized, distributed environments were not.

DISTRIBUTED DATA BASE DEFINED

A distributed data base is a partitioned data base where a network of data base managers is involved in the control of the various partitions and each instance of a data element is controlled by only one data base manager in the network. This definition is depicted in Fig. 10.2.

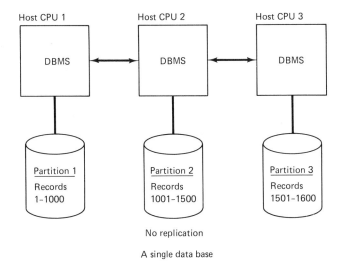

No replication

A single data base

Figure 10.2 Distributed data base: A partitioned data base with a network of DBM.

There are some related definitions:

1. A data base is **partitioned** if the contents of the data base are grouped into separate sets, where each set can be manipulated individually from the others. Vertical partitioning, as shown in Fig. 10.3 for a hierarchical data base, requires that each partition contain complete data base records. Horizontal partitioning, as shown in Fig. 10.4 for a hierarchical data base, allows the data to be split between the partitions along subrecord or segment lines depending on the data base schema. Both vertical and horizontal partitioning may be used together in the same data base.

2. Any given data item may exist in more than one partition, in which case there are multiple copies of the same data. This is referred to as **replicated data.** Data bases may be partitioned and replicated at the same time. Figure 10.5(a) shows a nonpartitioned, nonreplicated data base, (b) shows a partitioned data base without replication, (c) shows a replicated data base without partitioning, and (d) shows a partitioned replicated data base.

3. The individual partitions of the distributed data base may be intersections of or unions with data from other partitions of the data base.

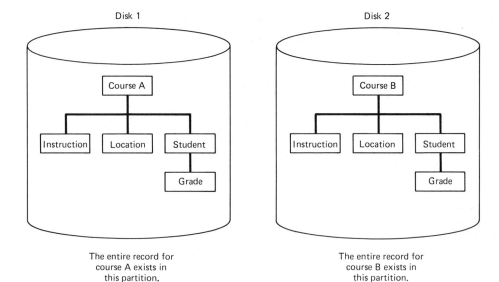

The entire record for course A exists in this partition.

The entire record for course B exists in this partition.

Figure 10.3 Vertical partitioning: The entire record hierarchy exists in each partition.

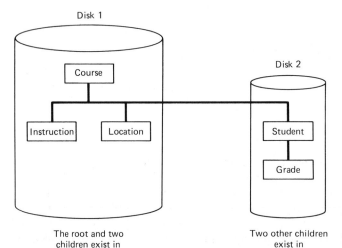

The root and two children exist in this partition.

Two other children exist in this partition.

Figure 10.4 Horizontal partitioning: Only portions of the record hierarchy exist in each partition.

4. More than one DBM (data base manager) is always involved in the control of a distributed data base. If only one DBM is responsible for the control and access to the entire data base, the data base is not distributed. This is illustrated in Fig. 10.6.

5. Only one data base manager controls and has access to a given data item instance. Requests for the data item from other DBM in the network must be routed to the owning DBM. This is illustrated in Fig. 10.6.

Basic Concepts   Section I

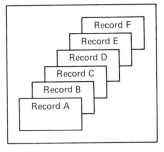

(a) No partitioning, no replication

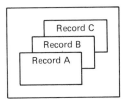 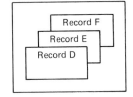

(b) Partitioned, no replication

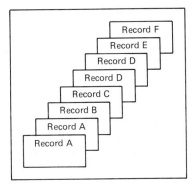

(c) No partitioning, replicated

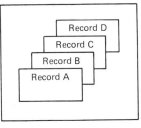 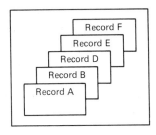

(d) Partitioned, replicated

Figure 10.5 Partitioning and replication.

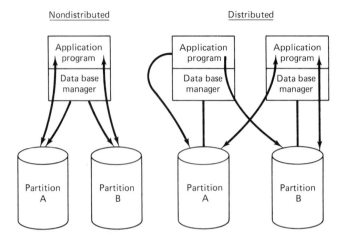

Nondistributed   Distributed

Figure 10.6 Distributed data base defined.

A distributed data base does not require geographic dispersement of the data. However, geographic dispersement of the data is a sufficient condition to state that the data base is distributed, since no one DBM could execute in multiple disjoint processors. However, geographic dispersion is not a necessary condition. It is possible for a data base, existing totally in one site, to be partitioned and managed by multiple DBM at that same site. Many of the benefits and problems with a geographically dispersed data base also apply to the single-site distributed data base. Indeed, most of the distributed data bases in existence today have all data base partitions within the same computer site.

REASONS FOR DISTRIBUTING DATA

Dividing a data base into partitions and then controlling the partitions by the use of independent networked DBM is a complex and resource-intensive function. In many cases this complexity and added cost is offset by the benefits accrued:

1. *Application processing efficiency.* The data can be moved closer to the point where it is to be used most often. This is referred to as taking the data to the work.

2. *Increased data availability.* Failure at any subset of the DBM network nodes still leaves the other nodes and their partitions available for use. If some or all of the data is replicated, then the entire data base can remain available even when some nodes aren't available.

3. *Organizational flexibility.* The data base may be partitioned according to departmental units within the organization (i.e., corporation, university, etc.), and each organizational unit can have complete control over its portion of the data base. The organization is not forced to centralize the data resource due to data processing constraints.

4. *Increased data accuracy.* Moving the partitions closer to the source of entry

and usage of the data may improve the chances of correct, true, and timely data.

5. *Network-wide access.* Any user, with the necessary security clearance, can access any data in the data base regardless of its location in the network subject to performance considerations.

6. *Increased capacity.* Multiple DBM network nodes can handle a higher volume of work than a single DBM on a single processor complex.

7. *Simplified system expansion.* Nodes can be added to a network easier and with less disruption than is the case of a single centralized system.

8. *Improved performance.* Since the data is usually closer to the work and, therefore, to the user, improved response times are likely. If the data is not optimally located for performance, it can be migrated to the node where it is needed. This data migration in the network may be on a temporary or a permanent basis.

Distributed data bases are useful in operational systems and decision support systems. Operational systems benefit from the increased capacity and flexibility. Decision support systems can effectively share the data base with operational systems with less performance impact and by using different hardware than the host. For example, the operational system may be using large mainframes, whereas a manager uses a personal computer to access a subset of the data base that has been distributed to the personal computer itself.

SCOPE OF DISTRIBUTION

An important consequence of the distribution of a data base is the need for awareness of the various nodes in the network to which the data base is distributed and the intrinsic access rights to the partitions. This attribute can be classified as follows:

- *Public data base.* With proper security clearance, any user executing on any node in the network can access any partition of the data base, regardless of the location of the target partition.
- *Private data base.* Only a user program executing on the node where the partition resides is permitted to access the data in the partition. The work must be moved to the data.

TERMINOLOGY

Distributed data base implementations are rare, but papers and theoretical evaluations on the subject are starting to become available. Since the general theory has not been sufficiently developed and the road to practice will indeed be a long one, definitions and understandings have proliferated. It is difficult to find any two researchers or practitioners that agree even on the basics.

Three concepts that require a uniform definition are *shared data base, repli-*

cated data base, and *distributed data base.* The distributed data base discussions found later in this chapter will require a rigorous understanding of these terms.

Shared Data Bases

A data base is **shared** if the data items are not duplicated (i.e., only one copy of each item exists) and more than one data manager can directly access the data concurrently, with full integrity.

IMS data sharing is an example of a shared data base capability. In this example, a single copy of a data base with no required duplication of data items is shared by more than one copy of the IMS data manager, DL/I. The multiple DL/I managers can execute on the same processor (intrasystem), as shown in Fig. 10.7, or on separate disjoint processors (intersystem), as shown in Fig. 10.8. Each DL/I data manager has direct I/O (input/output) hardware access to the data base. None of the data managers must contact the others for data access. To maintain integrity in this concurrent access environment, the DL/I DBM exchange access information among themselves.

Shared data bases have the following advantages:

1. *Improved performance.* Low-priority work can be run separately from high-priority work.
2. *Increased capacity.* More work can be run per unit time with full access to the data base.
3. *Improved data availability.* Data base maintenance work (backups, reorganizations, etc.) can be performed in parallel with productive use of the data. The data base never needs to be taken offline.

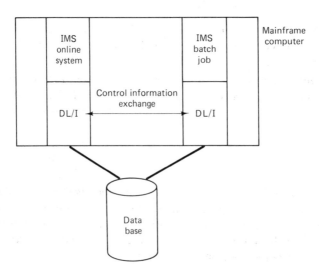

Figure 10.7 Intrasystem shared data base: Direct data access by all DBM with full integrity.

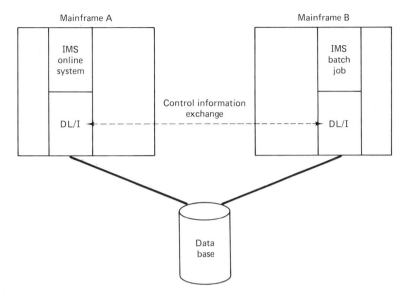

Figure 10.8 Intersystem shared data base: Direct data access by all DBM with full integrity.

Distributed Data Bases

A data base is **distributed** if it is partitioned and a network of data base managers is involved in the control of the various partitions and each instance of a data item is controlled by only one DBM in the network.

There are few commercially available DBMS products that provide a distributed data base capability. Single processor (intrasystem) distributed data is shown in Fig. 10.9 and separate disjoint processors (intersystem) are shown in Fig. 10.10. Each DBM has direct I/O hardware access to their partitions of the data base. Any DBM wishing to access the data residing in a partition owned by another DBM must route the data request to the owning DBM. The multiple DBM must exchange access information among themselves to provide for deadlock detection.

The advantages of a distributed data base are as follows:

1. *Heterogeneous access.* Different types of DBMS systems can access the data that is stored in a form unknown to them. The schema-related dependencies are handled by the owning DBMS. As an example, an application program is executing and issues a data request to DBM A on the same CPU. DBM A, a hierarchic DBMS, determines that the requested data is managed by DBM B on a different CPU. The request is sent to DBM B, where the data base is accessed. The data base is actually a relational data base, but this is masked from DBM A because it is DBM B that accesses the data base. DBM A passes the data back to the application program. In this case, a hierarchic DBM has indirectly accessed a relational data base. The schema-related transformation is handled by DBM B.

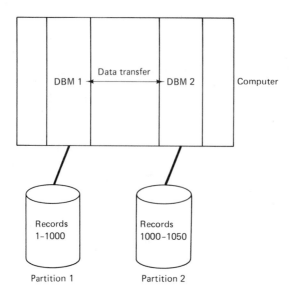

Figure 10.9 Intrasystem distributed data base: Each partition is controlled by one DBM.

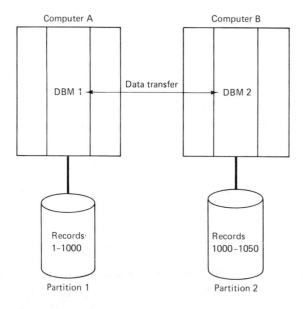

Figure 10.10 Intersystem distributed data base: Each partition is controlled by one DBM.

2. *Reduced redundancy.* Different types of DBMS systems can access data that is stored in a form unknown to them due to schema or hardware incompatibilities but without the need for redundancy of the data base. Assume that a large operational data base exists in an IMS environment. An end user on another CPU is using DB2 to access various relations but needs to access the IMS data as well. If both IMS and DB2 support distributed data bases, DB2 can pass requests to IMS without the need to understand hierarchic schemas.

Basic Concepts   Section I

Since neither product is capable of distributed data base access, the IMS data base must be extracted and a redundant version of the IMS data is placed in a DB2 relational data base.

Replicated Data Bases

A data base is **replicated** if some of the data items are duplicated (i.e., multiple copies of a given item exist), a network of DBM participate in the control of the various copies of the data, and each instance of a data item is controlled by only one DBM in the network.

There are few commercially available DBMS that support a replicated data base capability. An example of a single-system, replicated data base is shown in Fig. 10.11, and separate disjoint processors (intersystem) are shown in Fig. 10.12. Each DBM has direct I/O hardware access to the copies they own. Access to other copies is not available. To maintain integrity in this multiple-copy environment, a subset of the DBM is often nominated to control the copies.

The following are advantages of replicated data bases:

1. *Performance.* A copy of a subset of the data base at a user location gives more direct access and fewer delays.
2. *Data availability.* A replicated copy can be available when other copies are not.

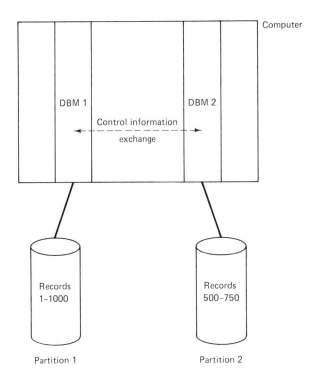

Figure 10.11 Intrasystem replicated data base: Each partition is controlled by one DBM.

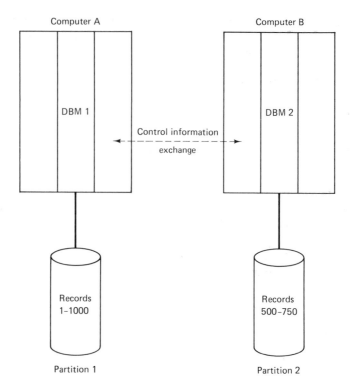

Computer A

Computer B

DBM 1

DBM 2

Control information
exchange

Records
1–1000

Records
500–750

Partition 1

Partition 2

Figure 10.12 Intersystem replicated data base: Each partition is controlled by one DBM.

Partitioning

There are at least two ways to partition a data base:

- *Horizontal.* For the hierarchical model, all occurrences of a specific segment or entity type exist in only one of the partitions. IMS data set grouping is an example of a horizontal partitioning capability. For the relational model, the rows (tuples) are spread across the various partitions.
- *Vertical.* For the hierarchic model, records of the data base are spread across multiple partitions. Each partition contains the full hierarchy or full entity set. IMS DEDB areas are an example of vertical partitioning. For the relational model, the columns (attributes) are spread across the various partitions.

A data base may also be partitioned both ways at once.

INQUIRY PROCESSING

There are several complex issues that must be adequately handled by a full-function, distributed DBMS. Most of the complexities arise out the need for the application to perform updates of several different data bases or partitions that reside in different nodes of the network.

Since inquiry-only processing of distributed data bases is substantially less complicated, this mode is studied first. Subsequently, the complexities involved in update processing are investigated.

When an application program issues a request for data, the DBMS must locate the data, access it, and pass it back to the requesting program. Locating the data in a nondistributed system is straightforward. The target data base is passed to the DBMS by the requesting program, and the DBMS either owns the data base or it doesn't. On the other hand, in the distributed data base environment, the DBMS must first recognize that it does not own the data base and then determine the owning DBMS.

The process of determining which DBMS owns the data is referred to as **site resolution.**

Site Resolution

After a DBMS has received and parsed a data request from an application, the data must then be located. In a nondistributed environment, the location requirement reduces to a question of whether the data is owned by this DBMS or not.

In a distributed environment, the issue is more complex. If the requested data resides in a partition owned by the DBMS, then no special location mechanism is needed. Otherwise a function called *site resolution* is employed to determine the owning DBMS.

Site resolution is the process of determining the node and DBMS in the network that should be contacted to access the data. Note that site resolution does not determine the node-DBMS combination that owns the data, but instead it determines the one that should be contacted. This convention enables the daisy chaining of site resolution processes and can reduce the complexity and size of the site resolution process in any given DBMS. A simple example of the need for passing the final site resolution to another node is demonstrated by a personal computer node. The personal computer may not contain the entire network data catalog because of the size of the catalog or because of the loss of catalog control at the main site. The personal computer would know where some data base records reside in the network, but the site resolution process for other records would be limited to a here or not here decision. If the decision is not here, then send the site resolution request to a catalog network node, who would then determine the actual node-DBMS information and route the request.

In general, networkwide site resolution can be simplified by not requiring that each node know of all other nodes and the data owned by the nodes. Temporary and permanant movement of partitions from one node to another can be more easily accommodated as well.

Site resolution can be accomplished using a combination of techniques most suited to the data and application requirements:

1. *Table lookup.* The target data base and partition names are used as operands of a node-DBMS table lookup. The key of the requested record may also be used. The table is kept current with the network configuration.
2. *Catalog.* An advanced and sophisticated version of the table lookup.
3. *Hashing.* The target node-DBMS is determined mathematically by using a hashing or randomizing technique that produces consistent results across the network.
4. *Dictionary node.* A node or group of nodes in the network are defined as dictionary nodes. As such, they will provide any other node with site resolution answers, partial or complete.
5. *API specification.* The application program interface (API) to the DBMS provides an application specification capability wherein the program can assist with or totally determine the node-DBMS to be communicated with.

Site resolution requires network definition information, DBMS system information, and application-dependent information. This diverse set of requirements can make this task a most burdensome part of the design and implementation of a distributed data base system.

DML Performance Dependencies

The choice of a data management language (DML) for a distributed DBMS (i.e., a DBMS that will participate in a distributed data base environment) can have significant impact on the performance of the internodal data requests.

DML can be divided into two groups: DML that handle records and DML that handle sets. A record DML makes available only one record per data request. DL/I, used with IMS, is an example. The application program issues a single DL/I request and receives back at most a single data base record. For instance: Retrieve the record with a specific key value; that record alone is returned. If the program wishes to see all the records with keys in a given range, multiple serial DL/I calls must be made.

A set DML may return one or more records to the requester. SQL, used with DB2, is a set DML. The example of retrieving a specific record is also supported by a set DML. However, the program may request all the records within a key range in one request and receive all of them back as a single response—hence the name *set* DML.

In a distributed data base environment, the choice of either DML for a single record request has little effect on performance. Both will perform site resolution for the single record and both will access the network *once* for the record.

For an application that requires a range of records and the range is known, set DML outperform record DML considerably. The record DML in general performs site resolution and goes into the network once for each record. Optimization techniques may be used to reduce the number of times that site resolution and network access is performed by a record DML at the expense of flexibility in the site resolution process.

The set DML performs site resolution once for the entire set of records and goes into the network once for each node that is the product of the site resolution process. If the entire set of records requested resides at one node, the set DML has, in the best case, eliminated $n - 1$ site resolution requests and $n - 1$ network accesses, where n is the number of records in the resultant set.

This discussion has centered around the external schema DML, that is, the application to DBMS interface. If the internal DML is considered, a set DML may perform identically to a record DML, depending upon the design of the DBMS. If the set DML reduces the application request to a series of individual record requests before accessing the network, the performance savings has been lost as each record is requested uniquely. This problem usually does not occur because the set nature of the external DML is also implemented in the internal DML.

UPDATE PROCESSING

The concepts of site resolution and DML performance dependencies, described for inquiry-only processing, also apply to a lesser degree to update processing.

For a DML that requires an application-generated retrieval request before an update, site resolution is required for the update request. A DML that accepts stand-alone update requests requires site resolution after the parsing and validation of the update call.

Record versus set DML performance differences apply to updates in the same way as inquiries. However, the frequency of nonsingular set updates is less than for inquiries, and so the performance impact is not so acute. In other words, while it is common for an application program to request a set of records in one call to the DBM, seldom is more than one record updated by the application program in one DML call. Retrieval of a set of records is more prevalent than updating a set of records. Consequently, set DML performance approaches record DML performance for update activity in a distributed data base.

When a distributed data base has some of its partitions replicated, update processing requires that the participating DBMS be able to control the **versions** of the same data items. Networkwide integrity and synchronization must be maintained in a distributed data base with distributed update capabilities. These concepts are considered in the next sections.

Synchronization

A DBMS maintains complete data integrity of the data bases within its control. When a transaction program updates several data base records as part of the processing of a single input transaction, the program expects that all the updates will be made by the DBMS or that none of them will. For the DBMS to do otherwise would leave the set of data bases corrupted, at least from a logical data point of view.

This all-or-none DBMS process is referred to as **data base synchronization.** In a nondistributed environment, the DBMS owns all the data bases accessed by the application program. Therefore, the synchronization process is totally within its control. In a distributed data base environment, the application program may have updated data bases owned by several different DBMS. A single DBMS no longer can control the entire synchronization process.

Typically, the DBMS directly associated with the program acts as a synchronization controller in a distributed environment. It undertakes its normal data base synchronization process for data bases it owns as well as requesting that the other DBMS do the same.

Consider an example where an application program has updated data bases owned by three different DBMS. The DBMS local to the application program will update its data bases and instruct the other two DBMSs to do the same. Suppose that one of those two DBMS is incapable of performing all its updates and therefore must back out any updates already done to enforce the all-or-none rule. It may be too late to tell the coordinating DBMS so that a networkwide backout can be performed. The result is that networkwide data base integrity is lost.

To implement distributed data base systems requires that this integrity problem not exist. A technique referred to as **two-phase synchronization** has been developed to ensure networkwide integrity and effectively provide protocols that will allow the multiple DBMSs to work in concert during the synchronization process. Since the word *commit* is often used in place of synchronization, *two-phase commit* is sometimes used as well.

Essentially, two-phase synchronization requires that each DBMS participating in the distributed data base network perform its data base updates in two steps. In the first step, the coordinating DBMS asks all DBMSs involved in a given transaction to *prepare* to perform all its data base updates. The prepare phase requires that each DBMS determine whether or not all its updates can be performed. The coordinating DBMS demands a phase 1 response from each DBMS either indicating it can or it can't perform its updates. The coordinator waits until a yes or no is received from all DBMS.

At the point when the answers have all been received, no updates have been performed anywhere in the network. If any DBMS says no, the coordinating DBMS tells all the DBMS to discard their data base updates. This is called an *abort*. If all DBMS answer yes to the prepare, then the coordinator instructs each of them to proceed with phase 2, which is called *commit*. The coordinator is not able to accept the inability of any DBMS to perform its updates after it has said yes to the prepare.

The two-phase commit then consists of a *prepare-commit* or a *prepare-abort* sequence. In both cases, networkwide integrity is ensured.

From a performance point of view, there are several opportunities for improvement in the basic two-phase commit:

- If one of the DBMS does not respond to a phase 1 (prepare) request in a timely way, all the other DBMS involved in the transaction synchronization are suspended. The coordinator can be programmed to a timeout after a predefined time interval and presume an abort direction for phase 2. This has been called *presumed abort* and can improve performance when one or more nodes in the network fail.

- A prepare phase is needed for only $n - 1$ of the DBMS involved. This reduces the overall time for the synchronization process.

- As soon as the coordinator receives a no response from any of the DBMS involved, an abort decision can be made immediately and sent to all the other DBMS that are still working on the prepare request.

The synchronization process and, therefore, the two-phase commit process apply to inquiry transactions as well but are not as important as in distributed update transaction systems. The functions performed during the synchronization process of an inquiry transaction involve the releasing of data base resources and not the updating of the data. The only inconsistency that can occur for inquiry transactions is that some DBMS may free their data base locks on records, whereas others don't. Records may be left unavailable to other transactions in the network, but data base corruption will never occur.

Replication Control

When replicating some subset of a data base, the copies may be arranged in a hierarchy wherein there are one or more **primary** copies and one or more **secondary** copies. The primary copies are considered the masters. They contain the data that is considered accurate. The secondary copies may, as time goes on, become less accurate than the primary copy from which they were made. Periodic refreshment of the secondary copies from the primary may be required. The users of secondary copies do not have a need for current-to-the-minute data, or such timely and dynamic change may conflict with the need, such as in decision support systems.

Alternatively, the copies may be viewed as peers. The true and accurate state of the data can be determined only by pooling the most current data from each copy. This synchronization process must be performed by the participating DBMS, but its invocation may be automatic or operator requested.

Sometimes it is useful to combine the hierarchic approach with the peer approach, as shown in Fig. 10.13. This combination is used where multiple operational DBMS systems need to access their own current copy of the data base and decision support DBMS systems need access to a not-so-current copy of the data base simultaneously.

Concurrency

The replication of some or all partitions of a data base requires the study of concurrency levels. When a data base partition is not replicated, all accesses are funneled to the single disk drive where the partition resides. Even in a shared data base environment, the multiple DBMS still ultimately meet at the disk drive level. This has both availability and performance implications.

By replicating some of the data, higher levels of data base availability and performance can be achieved. With replication, multiple DBMS access different copies of the same data items with the possibility of little or no common hardware and software.

With this greater concurrency capability comes the need to maintain consistency of data. The DBMS must know which are primary copies and which are secondary copies. If an update is attempted against a secondary copy, the update must

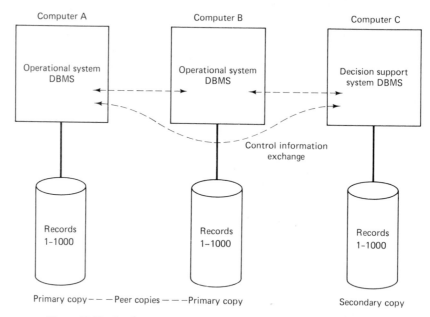

Figure 10.13 Replicated data base: Both hierarchic and peer copies exist.

be forwarded to a primary copy site. An update to a primary copy must be immediately and uniformly applied to all primary copies or to none. Some replicated data base DBMS systems enforce a rule that says that no application program that accesses a secondary copy of a data base can update it; it can only read it. This simplifies the concurrency-control issue at the expense of reduced function to the end user.

QUESTIONS

1. What can be distributed in a data processing system?
2. Does the distributed data base issue share similarities with the data base machine issue? If so, what are they?
3. What is a distributed data base? a replicated data base?
4. What are the reasons that traditional DBMS systems were centralized and not distributed?
5. What is data base partitioning? What is horizontal and vertical partitioning as it relates to hierarchic and relational data bases?
6. What are the reasons for distributing a data base?
7. What is a shared data base? How does sharing relate to distributing?
8. What are the advantages of distributing a data base?

9. What is site resolution? What are the techniques that can be used to perform site resolution?

10. What dependencies exist between the DML type (set or record) and distribution?

11. In what ways is query processing in a distributed data base environment a more intense process than update processing?

12. What is two-phase commit, and what are its strengths and weaknesses?

SECTION II

SPECIFIC DBMS EXAMPLES

"This extraordinary monument of theoretical genius
accordingly remains, and doubtless will forever
remain, a theoretical possibility."

A biographer of Charles Babbage,
inventor of the computer (1883)

CHAPTER 11

Production Systems: IMS

IBM's Information Management System (IMS) is a full-function data base management system. IMS is widely used in banking, manufacturing, insurance, government, and in many other environments. IMS supports a very broad range of functions, the most prominent of which are discussed in this chapter. IMS is divided into two major products, full function and Fast Path. Fast Path is briefly described in a box in this chapter.

HIERARCHICAL STRUCTURES

The basic mode of organizing data in IMS is through a hierarchical structure. Fig. 11.1 illustrates a simple hierarchical structure. The structure is made up of segments. Within each segment exist data elements. The data elements may be keyed or nonkeyed, although there can be at most one keyed element per segment. The segments are arranged by levels. At the top of the hierarchy is the employee segment, which is at level 1. The segment at level 1 is referred to as the root segment.

At the next hierarchical level—level 2—are pay, reviews, and deductions. The employee segment is a *parent* to each of these segments. In turn, they are the *children,* or dependents, of the employee. There can exist zero or more children per parent. A child segment cannot exist without a parent, although a parent can exist without children.

The multiple occurrences of a dependent segment are called *twins.* An example of twin segments (or physical twins) are the multiple pay segments that exist for an employee. Different segment types at the same level are called *siblings.* The figure

264

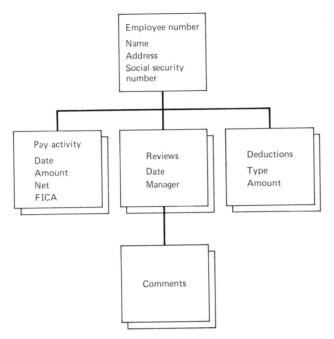

Figure 11.1 A simple hierarchical data base, with five segment types. The data base is defined over three hierarchical levels. The key of the root is employee number. The key of the pay data and review data is date. The key of the deduction data is type. Comments has no key.

shows a third-level segment, *comments,* which is dependent on reviews. IMS segments may be fixed length or variable length.

DATA BASE RECORDS

The most important unit of data in structuring IMS data bases is the data base record. A **data base record** is defined as a root and all its dependents, as shown in Fig. 11.2. A data base record is the unit in which IMS stores and transports data. There is one and only one root per data base record. The key of the root serves as the primary key for the data base record. It is useful to envision how a data base record is actually laid out on DASD (direct access storage device). Figure 11.3 shows a typical layout. In this figure the root is first inserted on DASD. Then the first occurrence of a segment going down and to the left of the hierarchical structure is inserted, in this case segment B_1. If this segment has any dependents, they are inserted. Next the second occurrence of the segment type (B_2) is inserted, followed by its dependents. Once all segments of this type have been inserted, the segment to the right is inserted, followed by its dependents. In the example shown, this is the first occurrence of segment type C; C_1 is inserted. Next the dependents of C_1 are inserted. Then C_2 is inserted, and so forth.

The order IMS follows in inserting segments into data base records onto DASD is top to bottom, left to right. If the structure can be traversed downward, then it is traversed. If there are more occurrences of the segment, they are processed. If there are no more occurrences, the structure is traversed and loaded from left to

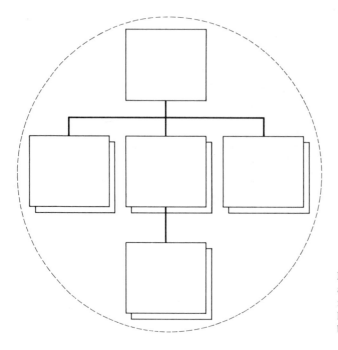

Figure 11.2 A data base record—a root and all of its dependents. A data base record has one and only one root. The key of the root is the key of the data base record.

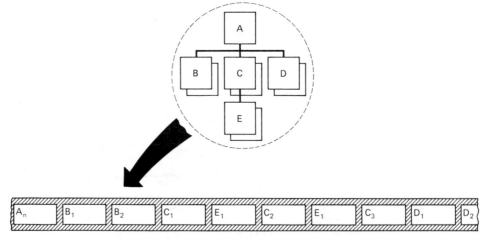

Figure 11.3 The physical layout of a data base record. The record for key A_n is first laid into the DASD space. Next, the first occurrence of B, B_1, is inserted after A. The next occurrence of B is inserted, until all B's have been inserted. Next, the first occurrence of C, C_1, is inserted. The next insertion is the first record that belongs to C_1, which is E_1. All the E's that belong to C_1 are inserted. Next, C_2 is inserted, followed by the E's that belong to it. Note that the E_1 that follows C_2 is not the same E_1 that follows C_1. After all the C's and E's are inserted, then the D's are inserted.

Specific DBMS Examples   Section II

right. The result is a physical layout of the data into a data base record corresponding to the top-to-bottom, left-to-right traversal of the structure, starting from the root. This is sometimes referred to as the *hierarchical* order of segments. The data base records are laid into physical blocks, as shown in Fig. 11.4.

Hierarchical insertion in IMS is done on a segment-by-segment basis. A segment can be inserted if its parent exists or if it is a root and no other root segment exists with the same key. The full path of insertion (i.e., the segment identification and key of each segment hierarchically above the segment to be inserted) is normally supplied. Deletion is done hierarchically, so when a parent is deleted, all children are automatically deleted. For example if a root is deleted, then the entire data base record is deleted.

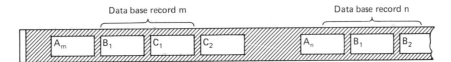

Figure 11.4 Block layout of data base records.

SEGMENTS

Each segment contains two types of data—user data and system data. The user data in the segment is masked by a PL-1 or COBOL data layout (i.e., the user data is presented to the programmer in a work area, and a COBOL or PL-1 layout is used to format the data into individual fields). The nonuser data in the segment is system data and is called a *prefix*. The prefix contains such information as segment identification, delete information, and pointers. The user data is accessible to the programmer, whereas the prefix data is available to the system, as shown by Fig. 11.5.

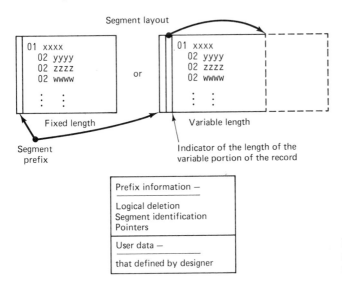

Figure 11.5 Prefix information is accessible to IMS. User data is accessible to programmer.

IMS supports several types of pointers, the most popular forms of which are shown here. They are physical twin, physical child, and physical parent pointers. For the data base structure developed in Fig. 11.1, pointers are defined and are illustrated by Fig. 11.6.

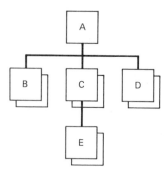

A: Physical twin to next root,
  physical child to B, C, and D

B: Physical twin to other B's,
  physical parent to A

C: Physical twin to other C's,
  physical child to E,
  physical parent to A

D: Physical twin to D's,
  physical parent to A

E: Physical twin to E's,
  physical parent to C

Figure 11.6   Typical IMS pointers.

Using the pointers shown, the structure can be traversed from the root to any dependent and back to the parent. Figure 11.7 shows the usage of the physical twin pointer that exists from one root to the next. This is a very important pointer as it serves to identify and locate each data base record. The usage of the physical twin pointers inside the data base record is shown by Fig. 11.8. In this case the first occurrence of the dependent segment is accessed, i.e., the A_1 to B_1, the A_1 to C_1, and the A_1 to D_1 connections are made. Figure 11.9 shows the usage of the physical twin pointers below the root segment and the physical twin pointers for segment C.

The connections between twins B_1, B_2, . . . B_n, C_1, C_2, . . . C_n, and so forth are made through these pointers, as is the connection from C to E (which is a physical child pointer).

The final pointers depicted are the physical parent pointers. These pointers allow a direct path to be followed to the parent of any given segment. Thus the paths between E_1 and C_2, D_2 and A_1, B_2 and A_1, and C_1 and A_1 can be quickly traced. These pointers are illustrated by Fig. 11.10.

A more realistic view of data (after data has been inserted, updated, deleted, and so forth) as it might reside on DASD is shown by Fig. 11.11. In this case it is seen that there is some free space separating segments and that segments are not in the perfectly loaded order shown in prior figures. Also shown in the figure is a **free**

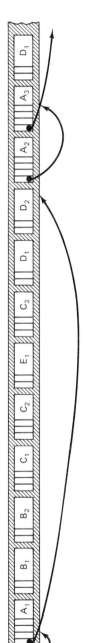

Figure 11.7 Block to root, root to physical twin pointer, connecting data base records.

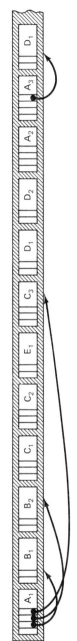

Figure 11.8 Root to physical twin pointers: segment A to B_1, C_1, and D_1.

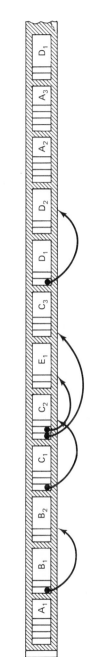

Figure 11.9 Physical twin pointers: segments B, C, D, and E; physical child pointer: segment C.

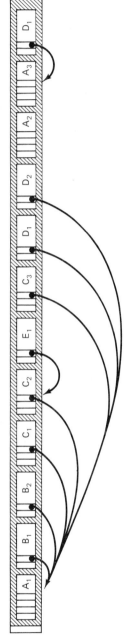

Figure 11.10 Physical parent pointers: all segments.

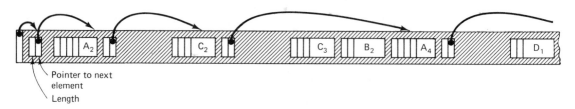

Pointer to next
element

Length

Figure 11.11 A more realistic view of data: segments out of sequence, free space in selected places.

space element, which is nothing more than a chain of pointers marking free space. A pointer in the block prefix points to the first free space element. The free space element being pointed to contains two pieces of information: the total amount of free space for which the element exists and the pointer to the next free space element.

POINTERS

The usage of pointers is illustrated by a simple request to find segment E_1, as shown in Fig. 11.7. First the block in which E_1 exists is located by means of a randomizer or an index. Next, the physical twin pointer for the root segment is searched until the appropriate root is located. In this case the root, A_1, is the appropriate root and is the first root encountered. Next, the physical child pointer from A_1 to C_1 is searched to locate the proper twin chain. Since E_1 exists beneath C_2, the physical twin pointer from C_1 to C_2 is used. Finally, the physical child pointer from C_2 to E_1 is used to locate E_1. Note that the programmer only specifies *what* segment is desired—that is, the programmer specifies segment E_1 that belongs to C_2 that belongs to A_1. The programmer does not specify *how* the search is to proceed or what pointers are to be used. IMS makes that determination.

FAST PATH

An increasingly popular option of IMS is the **Fast Path option** (FP). Prior to release 1.3 of IMS, FP was generally run by large banks to achieve a high degree of response time over a large amount of transactions. Fast Path is now used by many different businesses other than large banks. In general, FP allows the user to run many more transactions and still achieve very quick response time. In addition, FP is able to handle very large volumes of data with a high availability profile. FP achieves its high throughput by means of shortening the path length of transactions (i.e., lessening the average number of machine cycles used for a transaction).

Some of the salient features of FP are two unique types of data bases, DEDB and MSDB (main storage data bases). DEDB are randomized and are stored on DASD. They are divided into areas. An **area** is a physical subdivision of the DEDB that can be handled independently for many activities, such as reorganization, and recovery. DEDB can be physically divided and processed

---

because of areas, unlike other IMS data bases such as HDAM or HIDAM. One of the features of DEDB is a different overflow philosophy that is specified by a unit of work (UOW). Another feature is the ability to replicate data bases, enhancing the retrieval and availability capabilities (at the expense of DASD and multiple writes upon update). No secondary indexes or logical relationships are allowed in Fast Path, although the programmer can construct a logical relationship if desired.

MSDB reside in main storage and as such do not require I/O (unless of course they are paged out of main memory). This enhances the throughput that is possible. MSDB are typically used for small, critical amounts of data, such as security tables, operational control, and so forth.

MSDB can be processed using normal IMS calls or by using field/verify calls for update processing. Field/verify calls are able to achieve a significant throughput advantage over traditional Get/Repl logic because of the internal integrity processing. Other FP features include improved search algorithms, a special utility region, and WFI (wait for input) mode processing for normal FP transactions.

OVERFLOW

When a record goes into overflow, as illustrated by Fig. 11.12, too many records are being placed into too small a space. The result is that the data base record is extended over more than one block. The overflow condition also occurs when there is adequate total space in a block to insert a segment, but when no single free space element exists that is large enough to fit the segment being inserted. When the data goes into overflow, the order of the segments is maintained.

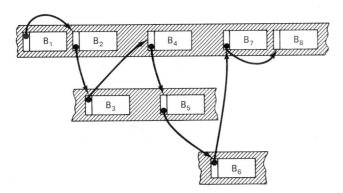

Figure 11.12 When a data base record doesn't fit into a single physical block, the record is moved to overflow but still remains a data base record. However, it requires more I/O to process the record. The logical sequence of the data is maintained despite its physical sequence.

BLOCK LOCATION

Data base records are located by either a randomizer or an index. The IMS access method for randomization is either HDAM (hierarchical direct access method) or DEDB (data entry data base, a Fast Path access method). The IMS randomizer operates in the standard fashion, with a key being given as input and an address being generated as the output of the randomizer. No I/O (input/output) is required to pass through the randomizer. The address that is generated in the HDAM environment is a block/root anchor point, or RAP. A RAP is the equivalent of an offset, as discussed earlier. Each block is defined to have a fixed number of RAP. One result of randomization is that records are stored in an order that makes sense only to the randomizer, as shown in Fig. 11.13. The result of the randomizer directing two or more roots to the same block/root anchor point is shown by Fig. 11.14.

The second mode of locating blocks is through an index. There are two common indexed access methods in IMS, hierarchical indexed sequential access method (HISAM) and hierarchical indexed direct access method (HIDAM). Of the two, HIDAM is much more popular because HISAM uses physical juxtaposition of data to maintain segment ordering. HIDAM, on the other hand, uses pointers in the same way that HDAM does to manage data within the data base record. The result of using physical juxtaposition of data is that when insertion or deletion occurs space is wasted and the algorithms of data management become difficult. However, when pointer options are used by HIDAM, normal IMS space management occurs.

One option available in IMS is the placement of an index in main memory. Electing this option speeds up data access but at the same time adds more requirements on main memory, which is normally a precious resource. As a rule, small indexes that are very critical are the best candidates for loading into main storage. The monitoring of hierarchical direct (HD) data bases (HDAM, HIDAM) is normally done by a utility called space management utility (SMU). SMU monitors many useful things such as the statistical analysis of the spread of data, the integrity of index/data relationships, free space, overflow, and so forth.

EXPLICIT RELATIONSHIPS

IMS allows data to be related by other than the physical definition of the data base. There are at least three types of IMS data relationships possible other than the basic physical relationship: secondary indexes, IMS supported logical relationships, and application program supported relationships. IMS full function allows all three types of relationships, whereas IMS Fast Path allows only application supported logical relationships. As an example of IMS supported logical relationships, consider Fig. 11.15. In this figure are two relationships, a unidirectional relationship from part to supplier and a bidirectional relationship from part to supplier and from supplier to part. IMS allows either symbolic or direct (or symbolic *and* direct) pointers to implement the relationship.

This same relationship can be implemented by application support rather than IMS support. All that is entailed is that the programmer ensure the integrity of the relationship rather than IMS. Application supported relationships are nearly always implemented by means of a symbolic pointer, since an application supported direct pointer normally involves a lower level of detail than is desirable at the application level.

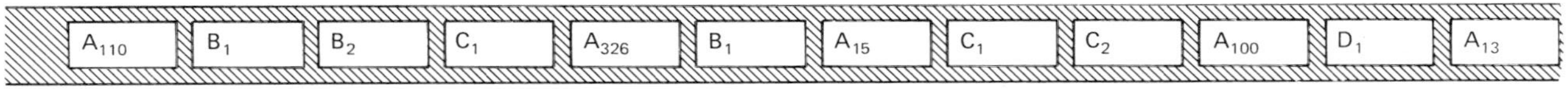

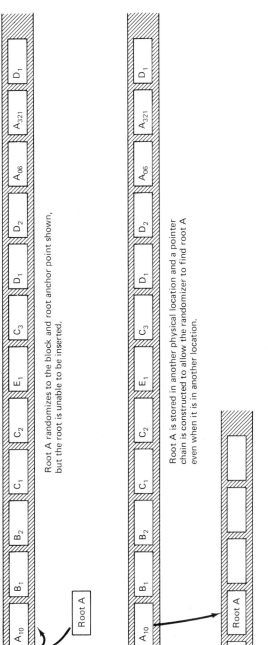

Figure 11.13 Physical layout of randomized data. Access from one root to the next must not depend on the sequencing of the roots.

Root A randomizes to the block and root anchor point shown, but the root is unable to be inserted.

Root A is stored in another physical location and a pointer chain is constructed to allow the randomizer to find root A even when it is in another location.

Figure 11.14

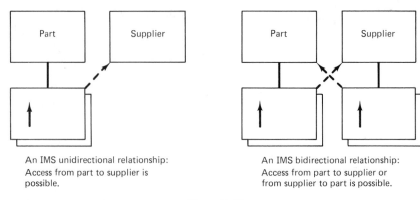

An IMS unidirectional relationship: Access from part to supplier is possible.

An IMS bidirectional relationship: Access from part to supplier or from supplier to part is possible.

Figure 11.15

Since application symbolic pointers use a randomizer when pointing into a randomized data base, there is no performance difference. Only when application supported symbolic pointers are directed into an indexed data base is there a potential performance difference.

An option that is available with logical relationships is intersection data. **Intersection data** is that data that is dependent on both sides of the logical relationship. It exists in the same segment as the symbolic or direct pointer.

DBDGEN

A data base is defined to IMS by means of a DBDGEN (a dee-bee-dee-jin), which stands for a data base definition *gen*eration. A DBDGEN is the basic definition of the physical components of the system, describing segments, access methods, keys, randomizer or index, physical data set reference, and so forth. Figure 11.16 illustrates a DBDGEN for the data base depicted in Fig. 11.1. Underlying IMS at the physical level closer to the system is either virtual storage access method or overflow sequential access method (VSAM or OSAM). Much of the physical block movement, basic data management, and cataloging is done at this level.

A program accesses data through a program control block (PCB). A PCB describes a portion of all or part of a data base as defined by a DBDGEN and limits what a program can do with that part of the data. More than one PCB can exist

```
DBD     NAME=EMPLOYDB,ACCESS=HDAM
SEGM    NAME=EMPL,BYTES=46
FIELD   NAME=(SSNO,SEQ),BYTES=9,START=26
FIELD   NAME=NAME,BYTES=25,START=1
SEGM    NAME=PAYDATA,PARENT=EMPL,BYTES=36
FIELD   NAME=(PAYDATE,SEQ),BYTES=6,START=1
FIELD   NAME=PAYAMT,BYTES=9,START=7
SEGM    NAME=REVIEW,PARENT=EMPL,BYTES=10
FIELD   NAME=(RVDATE,SEQ),BYTES=6,START=1
SEGM    NAME=COMMENTS,PARENT=REVIEW,BYTES=72
SEGM    NAME=DEDUCT,PARENT=EMPL,BYTES=36
FIELD   NAME=DDTYPE,BYTES=1,START=1
```

Figure 11.16 An IMS DBDGEN for the data base shown in Figure 11.1.

Specific DBMS Examples   Section II

for a program, and is defined by a Program Specification Block (PSB), which is nothing more than a collection of PCBs. Figure 11.17 shows a PCB for a program that can access the employee segment and can update the pay data and review segment. The PCB is specified by the calling program to determine the data and the program's view of the data. Parameters that are associated with the PCB are also accessed by the program. The format of a set of typical parameters is shown by Fig. 11.18.

The parameters associated with a PCB supply information to the programmer as to the success of the data base call and the specifics of exactly what has happened. The parameter of most interest is the *status* field. Status tells the programmer of the activity taken by the system as a result of a call issued to IMS by the programmer. If the call is successfully completed, a status of bb (or blanks) is returned. This indicates that no mishap has occurred. The result of the call, if it is a retrieval, is

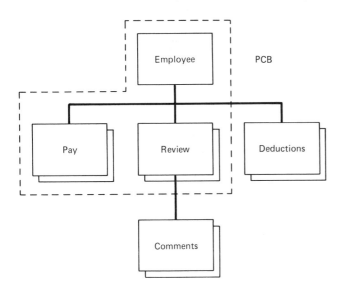

```
PCB        TYPE=DB,DBDNAME=EMPLOYDB,KEYLEN=9
SENSEG     NAME=EMPL,PROCOPT=G
SENSEG     NAME=PAYDATA,PARENT=EMPL,PROCOPT=A
SENSEG     NAME=REVIEW,PARENT=EMPL,PROCOPT=A
```

Figure 11.17 The PCB describes a subset of the DBDGEN that can be viewed by a program. The PCB also describes what can be done to the data.

```
DLITPLI: PROC(EMPL_PCB) OPTIONS(MAIN);
          :              :
          :              :
                         :
DCL 01 EMPLO1PCB              BASED(EMPL_PCB),
       02 DBDNAME             CHAR(8),
       02 SEGLVL              CHAR(2),
       02 STATUS              CHAR(2),
       02 PROCOPT             CHAR(4),
       02 RSRVD               BIN FIXED(31),
       02 SEGNAME             CHAR(8),
       02 FBACKLN             BIN FIXED(31),
       02 NOSEGS              BIN FIXED(31),
       02 FBACKAREA           CHAR(19);
```

Figure 11.18 PCB parameters in a PL-1 program.

placed in the I/O area. If the call is an insert, the contents of the I/O area are inserted into the data base. If the call is made to retrieve data and no data is found, the status of GE is returned. If a call is made to insert data and the data already exists, a status of II is returned. The programmer checks the value of the status field as a matter of course after every call.

Other fields of interest in the PCB parameter area are the FBACKAREA and the FBACKLN. The FBACKAREA contains the value of the concatenated key that was successfully retrieved. The FBACKLN indicates the length of the concatenated key that has been retrieved. For example suppose that a call is issued for SSNO = 363-18-2173 and pay data date 830724. A status of GE is returned, indicating that the call could not be satisfied. But the key feedback area contains a value of 363182173bbbbbb and the key feedback length equals 9. This indicates that the segment for SSNO = 363-18-2173 was found, but the pay segment for 830724 was not found. Had the root segment not been found, the key feedback area would contain nonsensical data and the key feedback length would contain a value of zero. The status would have been the same, GE. Had the root and pay data segments been found, the status would have been bb and the key feedback area would have contained 363182173830724. The key feedback length would have been 15.

ANATOMY OF A DATA BASE CALL

It is best to illustrate the actual dynamics of a data base call. Figure 11.19 shows the relationship between a program, main storage, data, and the PCB parameters

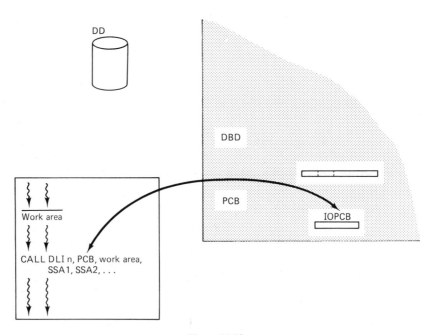

Figure 11.19

Specific DBMS Examples   Section II

of IMS. The PCB parameters in the program refer to the IOPCB area in main storage. (IOPCB, the Input/Output Program Control Block, is the area where control information is passed to the programmer from the online controller.) The physical data set (DD) is referenced by the DBD, as depicted by Fig. 11.19. The call issued by the program is shown in step 1 of Fig. 11.20. The PCB is first referenced to determine what data definition and what processing options are available to the program as shown by step 2. Next the DBD is referenced, as shown by step 3, to determine the actual data base characteristics. The DBD directs the call to the proper physical data set. The data is located and sent into the buffer area in main storage, as shown by step 4. Step 5 shows that the actual segment being called for by the program is selected from the buffer area and is shipped to the programmer's work area (or I/O area).

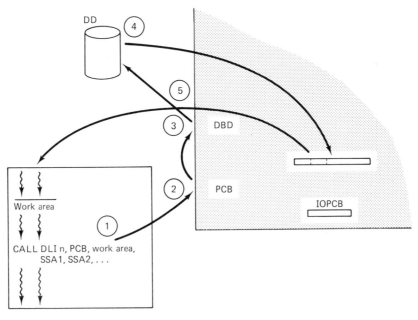

Figure 11.20

CALL SYNTAX

There are four basic types of data base calls in IMS, the get (or G) call, the replace (or REPL) call, the delete (or DLET) call, and the insert (or ISRT) call, as seen in Fig. 11.21. Get calls are used for retrieval of data or positioning within the data base. Replace calls are used to update nonkey data (keyed data cannot be altered by a replace call). Delete calls are used to delete data. Both replace and delete calls must be immediately preceded by some valid call of the hold type, either a GHU, a GHN, or a GHNP. Insert calls are used to load data into the data base.

The PCB is *always* located at some segment in the data base, either by default or as a conscious decision. Before the PCB is used the first time, it is located at the beginning of the data base to which it points by default. Thereafter, it is located at

GU	Get unique	
GN	Get next	
GNP	Get next within parent	
GHU	Get hold unique	
GHN	Get hold next	
GHNP	Get hold next within parent	
REPL	Replace	
DLET	Delete	**Figure 11.21** Common types of IMS
ISRT	Insert	calls.

the last location that has been accessed. Some calls—such as GU—do not depend on data base positioning; they reset the data base position to the first of the data base every time they are used. Other calls, GN, REPL, and DLET, depend very much on data base positioning. A GN call retrieves the next segment to which it is directed from the location where it currently is at.

A GU call is a call to locate a specific segment. A GN call is a call to retrieve the next segment encountered from the current position. A GHU is the same as a GU, except that it allows a delete or replace call immediately following it. A GHN call is the same as a GN call, except that it allows data to be held for update or deletion.

The get calls that end in P hold constant the *parentage* of the segment retrieved. The parentage of a segment refers to the physical parent of the segment last retrieved. In the case of the first retrieval using a PCB or a retrieval of a root segment, no parentage is set (although in any case there is a positioning in the data base that is set, either consciously or by default). But in other cases of data base traversal, parentage is established each time a data base access is made. When a hold is issued, parentage is not affected. As an example, consider Fig. 11.22. A GU is issued for employee with SSNO=481181109 and the root is found. Now a GNP is issued for the pay segment, yielding the segment with key 830630. The next GNP yields the segment 830615, and the third GNP yields the pay segment for 830531. The fourth GNP receives a status of GE because there are no more segments beneath the root.

Now consider a call pattern of GU to root SSNO=910174617. The root is

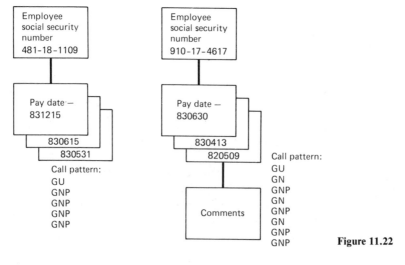

Figure 11.22

Specific DBMS Examples   Section II

retrieved. A GN is issued for the pay segment type, and the pay data for 831215 is located. Unlike the GNP of the previous call pattern discussed, parentage is moved to the pay level. A GNP is now issued for comments, but no such comment segment exists beneath the pay for 831215. Next a GN is issued for a pay segment and the 830413 segment is retrieved. Parentage and data base position are moved with it. A GNP call is issued, and no pay segment is found. Next a GN call is issued, and parentage is now placed at the pay segment for 820509. Now a GNP call is issued, and a comments segment is found. The next GNP call finds no more comment statements and a 'GE' status code is issued. At this point parentage remains at the pay level for the segment with key 820509.

SEGMENT SEARCH ARGUMENTS

Navigation through an IMS data base is achieved by calls to IMS and by the use of segment search arguments, or SSAs. One or more SSAs can be added to a data base call to qualify or direct the search of IMS through the data base. An SSA operates on fields of data that have been previously defined. An IMS call may have no SSA or may have several. As an example of how an SSA might be used, consider the following simple (pseudo) calls:

— GN, SSA=EMPL
(This SSA specifies that the next employee segment is to be retrieved. If there are no more employee segments, the GB status, or end of data base condition, is raised. The search starts from wherever the PCB is positioned. If the call is the first to be issued by the program against the PCB, the search starts at the beginning of the data base. No other segment type than EMPL can satisfy this call.)

— GU, SSA=EMPLbbbb(SSNO=459701872)
(Search the data base for the employee whose root key is 459701872.)

— GU, SSA=EMPLbbbb(SSNO=459701872), SSA=REVIEWbb(RVDATE =830607)
(Search the data base for the review of 830607 for the employee whose social security number is 459-70-1872.)

— GU, SSA
=EMPLbbbb   (SSNOgt907611124&NAMEneJONESbbbbbbbbbbbbbbbbbbb-bbb)
(Search the data base for the first employee with social security number greater than 907-61-1124 and whose name is not equal to Jones.)

DATA BASE CALLS

Data base calls to IMS are issued in a format illustrated by the following example. Figure 11.23 shows a skeleton PL-1 program in which two calls are issued, one to the key of a particular employee and another to the pay data for a particular date. Note that the outputs of the call are placed in the EMPLDATA or the PAYDATA

```
DLITPLI: PROC(EMPL_PCB) OPTIONS(MAIN):
DCL 01 EMPLO1PCB                        BASED(EMPL_PCB),
        02 DBDNAME                      CHAR(8),
        02 SEGLVL                       CHAR(2),
        02 STATUS                       CHAR(2),
        02 PROCOPT                      CHAR(4),
        02 RSRVD                        BIN FIXED(31),
        02 SEGNAME                      CHAR(8),
        02 FBACKLN                      BIN FIXED(31),
        02 NOSEGS                       BIN FIXED(31),
        02 FBACKAREA                    CHAR(19);
DCL 01 EMPLDATA,
        02 NAME                         CHAR(25),
        02 SSNO                         CHAR(9),
        02 SEX                          CHAR(1),
        02 BIRTHDATE                    CHAR(6),
        02 EYES                         CHAR(1),
        02 HAIR                         CHAR(1),
        02 WEIGHT                       DEC FIXED(3,0),
        02 FILLER                       CHAR(1);
DCL 01 PAYDATA,
        02 PAYDATE                      CHAR(6),
        02 PAYAMOUNT                    DEC FIXED(7,2),
        02 PAYFICA                      DEC FIXED(7,2),
        02 PAYSTATE                     DEC FIXED(7,2),
        02 PAYFEDERAL                   DEC FIXED(9,2),
        02 PAYINSURANCE                 DEC FIXED(7,2),
            .    .                          .    .
            .    .                          .    .
            .    .                          .    .
DCL P4                                  Bin Fixed(31) INITIAL(4);
DCL P5                                  BIN FIXED(31) INITIAL(5);
DCL GU                                  CHAR(4) INITIAL('GU  ');
DCL GN                                  CHAR(4) INITIAL('GN  ');
DCL EMPSSA                              CHAR(24) INITIAL ('EMPL    (SSNO=xxxxxxxxx)';
DCL PAYSSA                              CHAR(24) INITIAL ('PAYDATA (PAYDATE=xxxxxx)';
        .    .                              .    .
        .    .                              .    .
        .    .                              .    .
SUBSTR(EMPSSA,15,9)=SSNOVALUE;
SUBSTR(PAYSSA,18,6)=PAYDATESEARCH;
CALL PLITDLI (P4, GU, EMPL_PCB, EMPLDATA, EMPSSA);
        IF STATUS='  ' THEN  ......        /* process record */
        IF STATUS='GE' THEN  ......        /* record not found */
        IF STATUS='GB' THEN  ......        /* end of data base */
        ELSE  ......                       /* abnormal condition */
        .                    .
        .                    .
        .                    .
CALL PLITDLI (P5, GN, EMPL_PCB, PAYDATA, EMPSSA, PAYSSA);
        IF STATUS='  ' THEN  ......        /* process record */
        IF STATUS='GE' THEN  ......        /* record not found */
        ELSE  ......                       /* abnormal condition */
        .                    .
        .                    .
        .                    .
END DLITPLI;
```

Figure 11.23 Sample PL-1/DL I program.

I/O area, respectively. These areas are the recipient of the I/O activity needed to service the calls. Also, the GB status code is checked after the GU call but not after the GN call. The end of data base condition cannot occur after data base position has been established and the SSA specify the segment that has already been retrieved.

To better understand exactly how IMS calls and IMS call patterns work, consider the small (for pedagogic purposes) data base, as shown in the box IMS Calls.

IMS CALLS USING SSA

RETRIEVAL AND POSITIONING CALLS USING SSA
(Assuming data base repositioning for the start of each call)

Call	SSA	Segment Retrieved	Number	
1. GU	—	Acct 156	1	
2. GU	ACT	Act 830101	2	
3. GU	ACCT(ACCTNO=974)	Acct 974	9	
4. GU	ACCT(ACCTNO=699)	————	—	(GE status, segment not found)
5. GU	ACCT(ACCTNO=974), ACT(ACTDATE=830806)	Act 830806	11	
6. GU	ACCT(ACCTNO=103), PAY	————	—	(GE status, segment not found)
7. GU	ACCT(ACCTNO=72), PAY(PAYDATEgt820709)	Pay 830609	24	
8. GU	ACT(ACTDATEgt830606)	Act 830806	11	

CALL COMBINATIONS
(Assume data base repositioning at the start of each sequence)

Call	SSA	Segment Retrieved	Number	
1. GU	ACCT(ACCTNO=974), ACT	Acct 974	9	
GNP	—	Act 830606	10	
GNP	—	Act 830806	11	
GNP	—	Act 830809	12	
GNP	—	Act 830812	13	
GNP	—	Act 831126	14	
GNP	—	Act 831227	15	
GNP	—	————	—	(GE status, segment not found)
2. GU	ACCT(ACCTNO=103)	Acct 103	6	
GN	—	Act 820607	7	
GN	—	Act 820607	8	
GN	—	Acct 974	9	(Hierarchical boundary crossed)
3. GN	PAY	Pay 830422	5	
GN	PAY	Pay 820429	16	
GN	PAY	Pay 820527	17	
GN	PAY	Pay 820930	18	
GN	PAY	Pay 830609	24	
GN	PAY	Pay 830609	25	
GN	PAY	————	—	(GB status, end of data base)

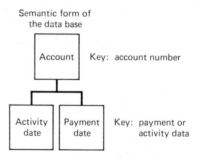

Semantic form of
the data base

| Account | Key: account number |

| Activity date | Payment date | Key: payment or activity data |

The layout of the data. Note that the actual physical order of
the data is of no consequence as far as this example is concerned

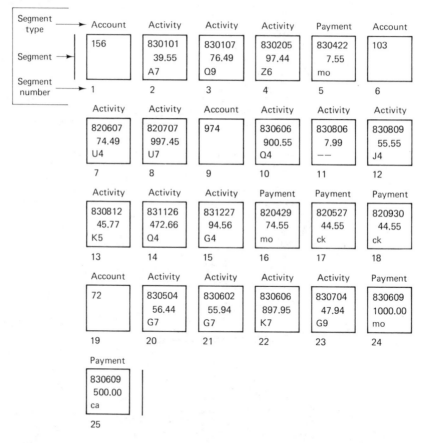

Segment type →	Account	Activity	Activity	Activity	Payment	Account
Segment →	156	830101 39.55 A7	830107 76.49 Q9	830205 97.44 Z6	830422 7.55 mo	103
Segment number →	1	2	3	4	5	6

	Activity	Activity	Account	Activity	Activity	Activity
	820607 74.49 U4	820707 997.45 U7	974	830606 900.55 Q4	830806 7.99 ——	830809 55.55 J4
	7	8	9	10	11	12

	Activity	Activity	Activity	Payment	Payment	Payment
	830812 45.77 K5	831126 472.66 Q4	831227 94.56 G4	820429 74.55 mo	820527 44.55 ck	820930 44.55 ck
	13	14	15	16	17	18

	Account	Activity	Activity	Activity	Activity	Payment
	72	830504 56.44 G7	830602 55.94 G7	830606 897.95 K7	830704 47.94 G9	830609 1000.00 mo
	19	20	21	22	23	24

	Payment
	830609 500.00 ca
	25

Figure IMS Calls.1 This data base will be acted against by a series of calls. The result of the call is shown. For the purposes of this illustration, the data base is assumed to be returned to the condition shown before the next set of calls is issued, something that does not happen in practice.

Call	SSA	Segment Retrieved	Number	
4. GU	ACCT(ACCTNO=72), PAY(PAYDATE=830609)	Pay 830609	24	
5. GU	ACCT	Acct 156	1	
GN	ACCT	Acct 103	6	
GN	ACCT	Acct 974	9	
GN	ACCT	Acct 72	19	
GN	ACCT	————	—	(GB status, segment not found)
6. GN	—	Acct 156	1	
GN	—	Acct 830101	2	
GN	—	Act 830107	3	
GN	—	Act 830205	4	
GN	—	Pay 830422	5	(Hierarchical type crossed)
GN	—	Acct 103	6	(Hierarchical boundary crossed)

INSERTION CALLS USING SSA
(Assume initial positioning in data base)

Call	SSA	Activity
1. ISRT	ACCT(ACCTNO=72)	'II' status code returned, segment already exists, insertion occurs between segments 8 and 9 assuming the randomizer places acct 166 between acct 156 and acct 974.
2. ISRT	ACCT(ACCTNO=166)	
3. ISRT	ACCT(ACCTNO=156), PAY(PAYDATE=830602)	Segment is inserted between segments 5 and 6.
4. GU	ACCT(ACCTNO=72)	Position is established at segment 19.
ISRT	ACT(ACTDATE=830509)	Activity segment is inserted between segments 20 and 21.

DELETION CALLS AND SSA
(Assume initial positioning in data base)

Call	SSA	Activity
1. GHU	ACCT(ACCTNO=72)	Position is established at segment 19.
DLET	————	Segments 19, 20, 21, 22, 23, 24, 25 are deleted.
2. GHU	ACCT(ACCTNO=72), ACT	Segment 20 is established.
DLET	————	Segment 20 is deleted.
3. GHU	ACCT(ACCTNO=72), ACT(ACTDATE=830704)	Segment 23 is established.
DLET	————	Segment 23 is deleted.
4. GHU	ACCT(ACCTNO=974), ACT(ACTDATEgt820105)	Segment 10 is established.
DLET	————	Segment 10 is deleted.

REPLACE CALLS
(Assume initial positioning in data base)

Call	SSA	Activity
1. GHU	ACCT(ACCTNO=156), ACT(ACTDATE=830107)	Segment 3 is retrieved and is available for update. The activity balance is changed to 79.36.
REPL	————	Segment is replaced with 79.36 as activity balance.

EXAMPLES OF INCOMPLETE OR ILLEGAL CALLS
(Assume initial positioning in date base)

Call	SSA	Activity
1. GHU	ACT(ACTDATE=830107), ACCT(ACCTNO=156)	SSA are not in hierarchical sequence.
2. GU	ACT(ACTDATE=830205), PAY(PAYDATE=830422)	Two segments cannot normally be retrieved at once, unless a special type of call, a pathcall, is specified.
3. REPL	—	No preceding GHxx call.
4. DLET	—	No preceding GHxx call.
5. ISRT	ACCT(ACCTNO=72)	Segment already exists.

(*Note:* For the purposes of this illustration, the *exact* format of an SSA has not been followed. In practice, the format of the SSA must be precisely followed.)

MODES OF OPERATION

There are two basic modes of operation in IMS, batch and online. Within the online mode there are two ways to process data, by a message processing program (MPP, or the online portion of IMS) or by means of a batch message processor (BMP, or the batch portion of IMS that is controlled by the online controller). MPP and BMP run in a region of main storage that is defined to and controlled by the online controller. Within the batch mode of processing, a data base can be held exclusively (for update) or, if not being updated, can be shared by more than one batch program, as shown by Fig. 11.24. The online mode of processing is depicted by Fig. 11.25, while the mixed BMP and MPP online mode of processing is shown by Fig. 11.26.

The online IMS environment is established by means of an IMS gen, which is broken into two phases, stage I and stage II. (Note: An IMS gen is the process by which the online controller is initialized and prepared for execution.) The IMS gen is usually controlled by the data base administrator. It contains control definitions (which are necessary to the execution of online IMS) for the following:

- Transactions
- Security
- Data bases
- The network

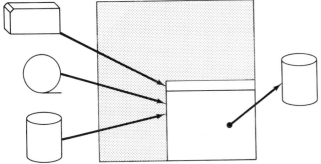

The batch data base environment, where a single
program has exclusive control of a data base.

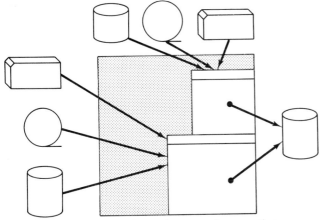

The batch data base environment, where more than
one program is accessing a data base at the same time.

Figure 11.24

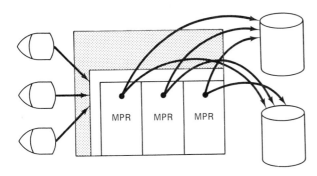

MPR   MPR   MPR

Figure 11.25 The online environment,
with the control region and online
message processing regions (MPR).

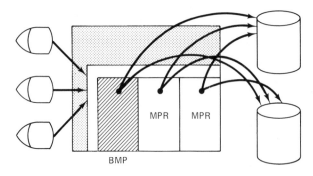

Figure 11.26 The online environment with batch processing, with a control region, online message processing regions (MPR), and a batch message processing region (BMP).

- Buffer pools
- Region definition (MPP, BMP regions)
- Main storage allocation and usage
- SCP interface

On an operational level IMS is controlled by a master terminal operator (MTO). The MTO has minute-by-minute responsibility for the control of the online region. When a line is down, when a data base is to be started, when a program abends—all these conditions fall under the control of the MTO.

ONLINE CONCEPTS

IMS operates online by means of sync point processing. A **sync point** is that amount in the life of an online transaction after the moment when online updates are automatically backed out by the system if an abnormal condition occurs and prior to when updates are committed to the system. A sync point is a commitment point. Prior to a sync point, updates are made to the buffer area in main storage. After a sync point, updated buffers are written to the data base. Upon writing to the buffer, a log record is written as well. The log record contains copies of the activities of the online controller in time sequence. In the eventuality that a data base must be restored, an image copy of the data base is used to reconstruct the original form of the data base. Next, log records are run against the image copy to restore the data in its updated form. The general recovery strategy thus depends on sync point processing, log tapes, image copies, and restoration utilities.

CHAPTER 12

Inverted File System: Model 204

Model 204, by Computer Corporation of America, is an inverted file data base management system. Model 204 is capable of handling very large data bases, is quite flexible, and can be used in batch and online. Model 204 is distinguished from other DBMS (data base management systems) in that it does much processing in indexes and uses sophisticated data compression and search techniques to the extent that Model 204 is CPU (central processing unit) bound, rather than I/O (input/output) bound. Model 204 employs a very intricate structuring of data, much more so than most DBMS, to achieve high throughput and flexibility at the same time.

There are several levels at which Model 204's data structures must be understood to appreciate fully the sophistication of Model 204. The levels are the table level, the record/page level, and the index level. Each of these levels will be explored in depth.

TABLE LEVEL

Model 204 is composed of five **tables,** a file control table, a dictionary table (Table A), a data table (Table B), a primary index table (Table C), and a secondary index table (Table D). The relationship of these tables is shown by Fig. 12.1.

The file control table is static in size and contains basic control information such as the physical identification of the dataset(s) associated with the data base. All other tables have a variable size. Table A contains dictionary information and is divided into three sections, a field name section, a few-valued field section, and

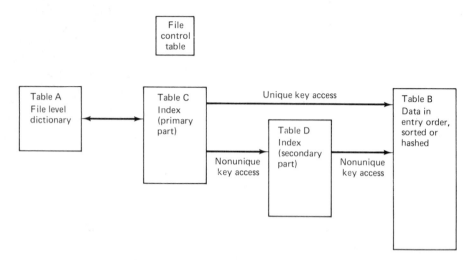

Figure 12.1 The internal data structure of Model 204.

a many-valued field section. Field names, codes, and other types of data are stored in Table A. Figure 12.2 illustrates the file control table and Table A.

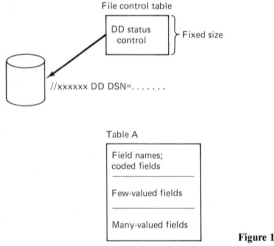

Figure 12.2

Table B contains the data in a Model 204 data base. The basic unit of storage is a page (as it is for all tables). A page as it exists on DASD is shown by Fig. 12.3. In Model 204 there is one and only one page size per installation. Page size is determined by the device on which data is stored. Tables C and D contain Model 204's indexes. Keys or other data directly pointed to that occur only once are found in Table C; if there are multiple records in Table B that are being pointed to, then the

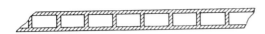

Figure 12.3 In Model 204 the data resides in Table B. It is divided into physical units called *pages*. Pages are all the same length.

keys (or encoded values of the keys) are stored in index D. Tables A and C are hashed, whereas Table D is sequential. In addition to the duplicate keys stored in Table D, user procedures are stored there as well. For the purposes of this chapter, a pointer is a page/offset pointer. Model 204 documentation refers only to a record number when identifying the location of a record.

RECORD/PAGE LEVEL

The **record/page level** of Model 204 goes down to the very detailed physical level. The most basic unit of Model 204 is the field. A field can be in string or binary format. In Model 204, all fields are variable length.

Fields are grouped into records. A record may be composed of at most one primary (or physical) key for hashed or sequentially organized data. However, data in Model 204 is usually defined as entry sequenced. Any number of fields can be placed into a Model 204 record. Also, a key structure can be built for any field (although there is at most one physical key sequence). Fields can be preallocated or can be inserted dynamically. If preallocation is specified, then space is reserved whether or not the field is inserted. Also, if field space is preallocated, then there can never be more fields than have been allocated. Because fields are variable in length and because there are a variable number of fields in a record, records are necessarily variable length.

Fields may be coded. Encoding applies especially to fields that are physically long and that are repetitiously scattered throughout the data base (see Fig. 12.4).

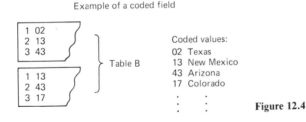

Example of a coded field

Table B

Coded values:
02 Texas
13 New Mexico
43 Arizona
17 Colorado

Figure 12.4

Through encoding, Model 204 is able to compact data very tightly, thus making the most of an I/O when an access to Table B must be done. However the process of encoding and decoding requires resources as data is accessed or stored. Figure 12.5 illustrates a page in Table B. When a record is too large for a page, the record can span pages, as shown by Fig. 12.6.

Fields:
01 fname
02 lname
03 address
04 dependent
05 age
06 sex

Record 1	01 Bill 02 Inmon 03 949 Wyatt 04 Melba 04 Sarah 05 38 06 M
Record 2	02 Mohr 04 Kay 04 John 04 David 06 M
Record 3	01 Maryce 02 Jacobs 05 39 06 F
Record 4	01 Kathy 02 Allan 03 Detroit 05 36 06 F

Figure 12.5 A page in Model 204.

01 little old woman who lived in the shoe 04 Sam 04 Mary 04 Todd

04 Jane 04 Sue 04 Dick 04 Bart 04 John 04 Ted 04 Elizabeth 04 William

04 Bob 04 Kathy 04 Jim 04 Sarah . . . .

Figure 12.6 Records can span a page.

INDEX LEVEL

The index level of Model 204 data structuring is best understood in terms of how it relates to the different Table B data organizations. In Table C, the unique index is hashed. Table D is organized sequentially. Consider a simple data base, as shown in Fig. 12.7.

The data base, Table B, is sequenced by entry. In this organization there are five pages with two records per page. Of course, this is an artificial structure for the purposes of the book. A real Model 204 data base would have much more data,

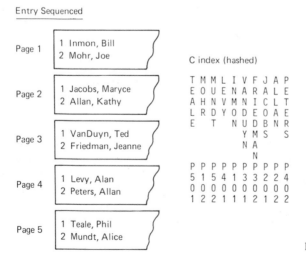

Figure 12.7

Specific DBMS Examples   Section II

a diversity of data, and a different distribution of data over the physical pages. Table C is built. It is hashed, so there is no apparent order to the keys as they reside in the index. Each key is unique and has a record number (or page/offset) associated with it. The notation PnOn indicates page *n*, offset *n*. In practice, the record number is formatted strictly according to CCA's internal specifications. However the PnOn format serves as a reminder of what is being specified. Had there been duplicate keyed records, an entry into the D index would have been created, as shown in Fig. 12.8. In index C, note that when duplicate keys exist, there is a simple indication that index D points to the data. In practice, the index in C points to a location in index D.

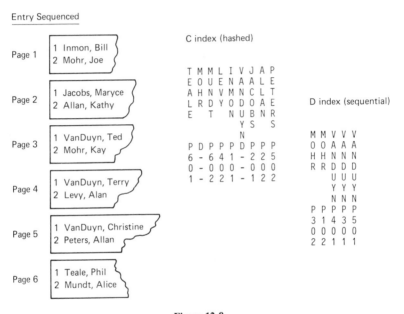

Figure 12.8

When the sequence of Table B is sorted, an index is created (Fig. 12.9). When there are duplicate entries, the D index is used as shown by Fig. 12.10.

The final option is to create Table B in a hashed organization for which there are no pointers in Tables C or D, as shown by Fig. 12.11.

The different organizations of Table B have advantages and disadvantages. Table B is quickest to access when it is hashed, as there is no I/O (or index) to search to get to the data. However, collisions are a problem, and Table B cannot be easily expanded when it is hashed.

Table B is in a natural order when it is physically sequenced on a key. The physical ordering can be very useful if there will be many requests to retrieve or otherwise use the data in the physical order in which it is stored. But the physical ordering of data is best maintained when there is a small number of inserts and deletes because data management becomes an issue when data is volatile. When data

Sorted on a single key; lname

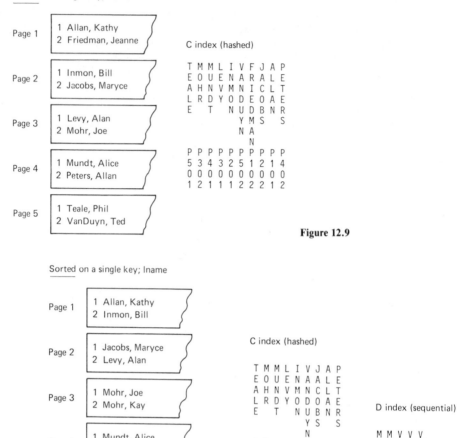

Page 1
1 Allan, Kathy
2 Friedman, Jeanne

Page 2
1 Inmon, Bill
2 Jacobs, Maryce

Page 3
1 Levy, Alan
2 Mohr, Joe

Page 4
1 Mundt, Alice
2 Peters, Allan

Page 5
1 Teale, Phil
2 VanDuyn, Ted

C index (hashed)

```
T  M  M  L  I  V  F  J  A  P
E  O  U  E  N  A  R  A  L  E
A  H  N  V  M  N  I  C  L  T
L  R  D  Y  O  D  E  O  A  E
E     T     N  U  D  B  N  R
                Y  M  S     S
                N  A
                N
P  P  P  P  P  P  P  P  P  P
5  3  4  3  2  5  1  2  1  4
0  0  0  0  0  0  0  0  0  0
1  2  1  1  1  2  2  2  1  2
```

Figure 12.9

Sorted on a single key; lname

Page 1
1 Allan, Kathy
2 Inmon, Bill

Page 2
1 Jacobs, Maryce
2 Levy, Alan

Page 3
1 Mohr, Joe
2 Mohr, Kay

Page 4
1 Mundt, Alice
2 Peters, Allan

Page 5
1 Teale, Phil
2 VanDuyn, Terry

Page 6
1 VanDuyn, Ted
2 VanDuyn, Christine

C index (hashed)

```
T  M  M  L  I  V  J  A  P
E  O  U  E  N  A  A  L  E
A  H  N  V  M  N  C  L  T
L  R  D  Y  O  D  O  A  E
E     T     N  U  B  N  R
                Y  S     S
                N
P  D  P  P  P  D  P  P  P
6  -  6  4  1  -  2  2  5
0  -  0  0  0  -  0  0  0
1  -  2  2  1  -  1  2  2
```

D index (sequential)

```
M  M  V  V  V
O  O  A  A  A
H  H  N  N  N
R  R  D  D  D
      U  U  U
      Y  Y  Y
      N  N  N
P  P  P  P  P
3  1  4  3  5
0  0  0  0  0
2  2  1  1  1
```

Figure 12.10

is loaded once and there is a very low percentage of updates and deletes, the physically sequential ordering of Table B is optimal. Entry sequencing of Table B avoids many of the problems of data management and is the normal ordering of Model 204 data. However, entry-sequenced data must be sorted if an ordering of the data is desired. However, since much of the processing in Model 204 is done in the indexes, the actual physical order is not of major consequence.

Hashed

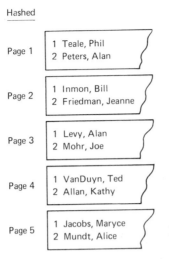

| Page 1 | 1 Teale, Phil |
| | 2 Peters, Alan |

| Page 2 | 1 Inmon, Bill |
| | 2 Friedman, Jeanne |

| Page 3 | 1 Levy, Alan |
| | 2 Mohr, Joe |

| Page 4 | 1 VanDuyn, Ted |
| | 2 Allan, Kathy |

| Page 5 | 1 Jacobs, Maryce |
| | 2 Mundt, Alice |

Figure 12.11 Hashed on a single key: lname.

MODEL 204 DESIGN OPTIONS

After the specification of fields, the simplest design option is that of whether a field should be keyed or nonkeyed. For a sequenced or hashed file, there must be one and only one primary key. But any field can be keyed in Model 204. If a field is keyed, an index is built on the field, as shown in Fig. 12.12. In this figure it is seen that the field sex (either F or M) is keyed. Entries appear in both the C and D index. In the C index, there is merely a reference to D. In the D index, the key and the appropriate record number (PnOn) are stored. If there were many B records being

Sorted

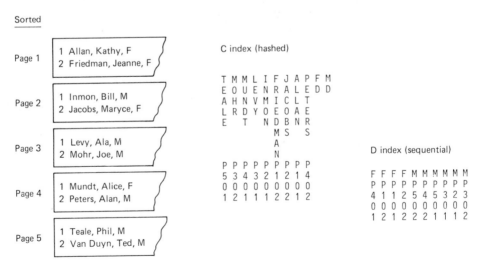

| Page 1 | 1 Allan, Kathy, F |
| | 2 Friedman, Jeanne, F |

| Page 2 | 1 Inmon, Bill, M |
| | 2 Jacobs, Maryce, F |

| Page 3 | 1 Levy, Ala, M |
| | 2 Mohr, Joe, M |

| Page 4 | 1 Mundt, Alice, F |
| | 2 Peters, Alan, M |

| Page 5 | 1 Teale, Phil, M |
| | 2 Van Duyn, Ted, M |

C index (hashed)

```
T M M L I F J A P F M
E O U E N R A L E D D
A H N V M I C L T
L R D Y O E O A E
E   T   N D B N R
        M S     S
        A
        N
P P P P P P P P P
5 3 4 3 2 1 2 1 4
0 0 0 0 0 0 0 0 0
1 2 1 1 1 2 2 1 2
```

D index (sequential)

```
F F F F M M M M M M
P P P P P P P P P P
4 1 1 2 5 4 5 3 2 3
0 0 0 0 0 0 0 0 0 0
1 2 1 2 2 2 1 1 1 2
```

Figure 12.12

pointed to (over 1500), Model 204 would automatically convert the index into a bit map.

Even if a field is not keyed, it can be accessed, as shown in Fig. 12.13. However, when a field is searched for which there is no index, Model 204 cannot do any processing in the index and must physically search each record in Table B. This is much less efficient than searching in the index because when an index search is done, an access to Table B will be done only on those records that are hits (i.e., satisfy the search criteria).

Accessing a Nonkeyed Field

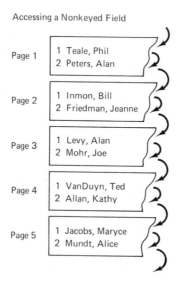

Figure 12.13 How many Alan's are there in the data base? Alan is an fname and is not keyed. A search must be done sequentially, one page at a time.

Multiple search criteria can exist for both key and nonkey fields. When such a search is specified, Model 204 qualifies the data first on the indexed field and then on the nonindexed fields, thus minimizing the amount of B records that must be directly searched.

A second basic design option is whether to specify numeric fields as *numeric range* or not. When data is specified as numeric range, entries are built in the C and D index. However, there are more entries inserted into the indexes than if the fields were keys. This facilitates key range searches, which are done in the indexes. Figure 12.14 shows a numeric range option as it exists in the indexes.

The criteria for whether a field should be keyed or numeric range depend on these factors:

— Is selection processing to be done in the index?
— Is the ordering of records a frequently useful feature?
— Is the data almost always accessed as a part of the record through some other field sequence?

If the first two criteria are met, then the field is probably a candidate for key or numeric range. If the third criterion is met, then the field is best nonkeyed or non-numeric range.

Numeric Range Data

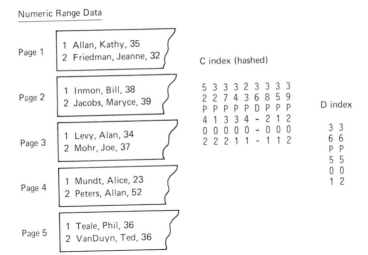

Figure 12.14

Another interesting design option is the invisible key. An invisible key is one that exists only in the index, not in the record in Table B, as shown by Fig. 12.15. When invisible keys are specified, there is a saving of space, but the saving is balanced by the fact that if the record is entered on something other than the invisible key, then the invisible key value cannot be obtained.

Sorted Invisible Key

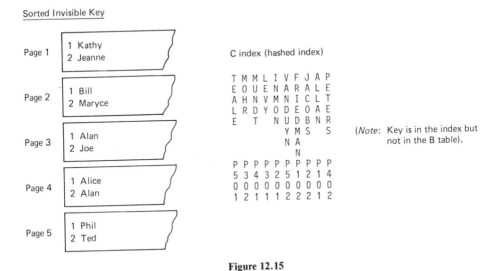

Figure 12.15

Another important design option is the linkage of files or data bases that is possible. Model 204 does not use pointers to link data bases together. Instead, files are linked by means of a common field, as shown by Fig. 12.16. In this figure the

Connecting two record types:

Record type A: name, address, social security number, dependents

Record type B: social security number, pay period date, net, gross, FICA, fed tax, insurance

Record type A occurrences

Bill Inmon, 5856 So Robb, 459701872, Melba
Kathy Allan, 1196 E Outer, 635210012
Jeanne Friedman, Village Hill Lane, 366291811, Sam
Phil Teale, 639 Court, 481109116, Suzanne

Record type B occurrences

459701872, 831115, 2000, 1796, ...
635210012, 831115, 2500, 2216, ...
391481160, 831115, 1500, 1395, ...
366291811, 831115, 3050, 2765, ...
481109116, 831115, 3750, 3666, ...
459701872, 831230, 2000, 1796, ...
635210012, 831230, 2500, 2266, ...
391481160, 831230, 1500, 1456, ...
366291811, 831230, 3050, 2956, ...
481109116, 831230, 3750, 3695, ...
459701872, 840115, 2000, 1895, ...

Figure 12.16 Record types A and B are related by a common key value, social security number.

values in record type A are linked with associated values in record type B based on social security number. For example, the social security number of Kathy Allan is found in record type A and is used to locate Kathy's pay information in record type B. The ability to relate data by means of key values is the basis for Model 204's statement that it is a relational-like DBMS.

Another design feature is the ability to defer updates. On occasion it is desirable to defer the updating of an index after Table B has been updated because the system is busy. (There are some cases where the integrity of the data will not allow this feature to be used, but there are other cases where the integrity of the data is not hindered.) The updated data is inserted into Table B, but the index is not up-

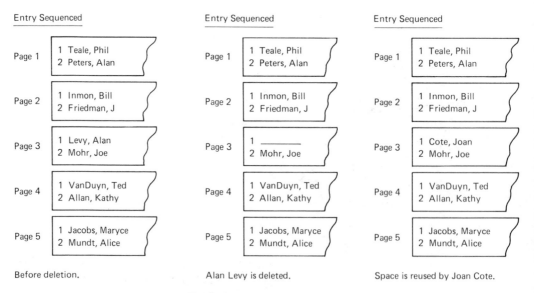

Figure 12.17 Reuse of space in Model 204.

dated until later, when the system is less busy. This allows the workload of the system to be spread over a large amount of time at the expense of some loss of data integrity.

Another option concerns the reuse of space after deletion. In one case (entry sequencing), the next sequentially available space is used, even when there are available spaces that have been made available by deletion. In this case the designer can opt to use the space made available by deletion, as shown in Fig. 12.17.

A unique feature of Model 204 is the dynamic redefinition of fields that is possible without doing an entire data base reorganization. Figure 12.18 illustrates

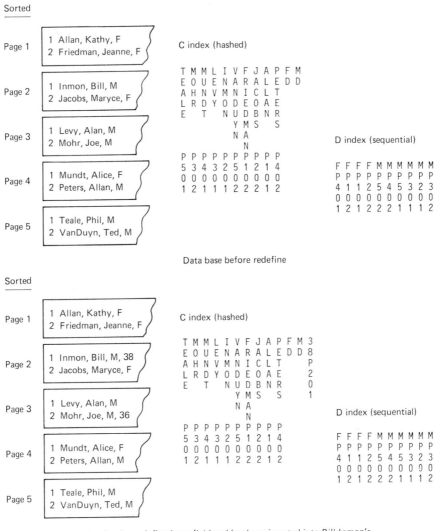

Age has been defined as a field and has been inserted into Bill Inmon's record. The data base looks like this after the redefine and insert.

Figure 12.18

a data base where age is added to a personnel file after redefinition. After redefinition, Bill Inmon's age is added to Table B, producing an index entry in Table C. Note that no massive unload/reload of data was done, as is common in other DBMS.

UPDATING IN MODEL 204

Model 204 is best understood as a dynamic tool for managing data. Two examples illustrate the workings of Model 204. The first example is simple and involves the update of a keyed field, salary, as shown in Fig. 12.19. Prior to update Jeanne Friedman's salary is 4000. It is keyed and exists as a pointer to Table D from Table C, since Bill Inmon's salary is also 4000. Jeanne's salary is to be changed to 5000.

The first action that occurs is that Jeanne Friedman's data in Table B is changed. Then 4000 is deleted from the Table D index because it is no longer multivalued. The 4000 entry in Table C is then pointed to Bill Inmon's record. Next the entry for 5000 is randomized. Since it does not currently exist in the table, it is inserted. Then the record number for Jeanne Friedman is added. If the field had not been keyed, the index activity would not have been necessary. Now consider a more complex case of update, as depicted by Fig. 12.20. In this case Jeanne Friedman marries John Williams. Jeanne chooses to change her name to Jeanne Williams. Since last name is the primary key on which Table B is sequenced, more than a simple change is required.

The first step to making the change is to locate Jeanne Friedman's record in Table B. Once located, it is stored in main memory and the record in Table B is deleted. Now Jeanne Williams' record is stored in Table B using the data stored in main memory. Only the last name changes. Next, Friedman is deleted from the D index because there no longer are multiple occurrences. Finally, the value for Friedman is set to P201 in the C index and an entry is made there for Williams.

The amount of work required for the second update is much more than was required for the simple update because the key field on which the data is sequenced is changed. Figure 12.21 shows an example of deferred updating based on the previous example. In this case Jeanne Friedman is deleted from Table B and Jeanne Williams is added. The indexes are updated only after deferred processing is done.

BUILDING A MODEL 204 DATA BASE

The different aspects of Model 204 are best displayed by a sample of creation and usage of a data base. For the purposes of this book, the data base described are necessarily small; in a real data base design, the data base would probably be much larger. However, the basic design steps and considerations are essentially the same.

The data base that is to be built is for the personnel of a small company. The fields will be as follows:

— Name (first and last)
— Address
— Dependents

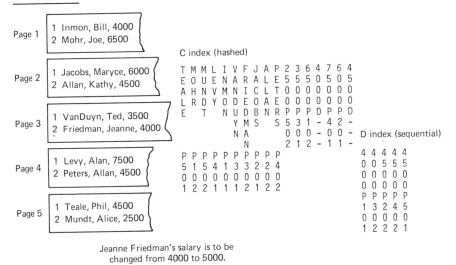

Jeanne Friedman's salary is to be
changed from 4000 to 5000.

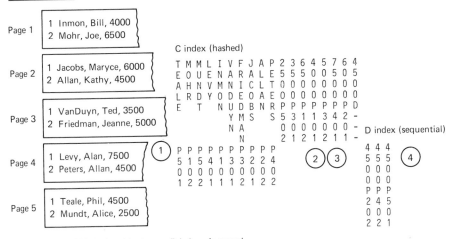

1. 5000 is placed in Jeanne Friedman's record.
2. 4000 is deleted from D index.
3. 4000 is shown pointing to P101 in C index.
4. 5000 is randomized and inserted into C index and
   then is pointed to the proper location.

Figure 12.19

— Sex
— Company
— Salary
— Start date
— College

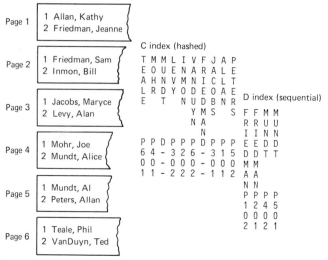

Table B is sorted on lname.

Jeanne Friedman marries John Williams and decides
to change her name to Jeanne Williams.

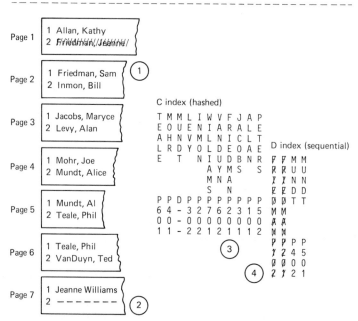

1. Jeanne Friedman is located. Her data is stored in memory, and the entry is deleted.
2. Jeanne Williams' data is stored in Table B from the data stored in memory.
3. The C index entry for Friedman is adjusted to point to Sam Friedman; the entry for Williams is randomized and placed in the C index with the proper pointer.
4. The D index is adjusted by deleting references to Friedman.

Figure 12.20

Deferred Updating

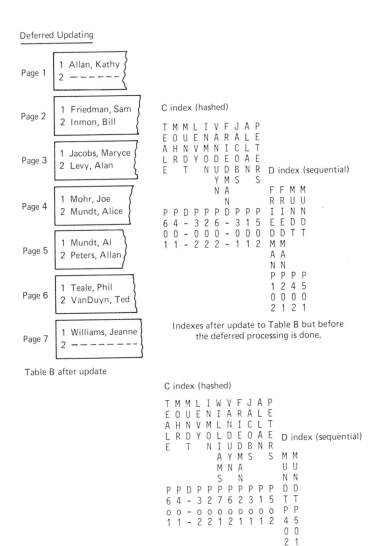

Table B after update

Indexes after update to Table B but before the deferred processing is done.

Indexes after deferred updating has been executed.

Figure 12.21

The company is small and currently has 17 employees, but growth is expected. The data base designer decides to encode the previous company at which each person has worked. Another option the data base designer chooses is the FOR-EACH-VALUE for both company and education (college) fields. The sequential key of the data base will be last name. Other key fields will be sex and company. Numeric range is specified for salary. The invisible key option is specified for start date.

The file is created by the execution of the procedure found in Fig. 12.22. The parameters found in Fig. 12.22 are calculated from the expected configuration of the data base. Next, the fields are specified. This is done by execution of the state-

File Control Table

DDNAME=//PERSONL
status=active

File Creation Jc1 and Parameters

```
//       EXEC
//PERSONL      DD DSNAME=M204,FILE,PERSONL,DISP=SHR
//CCAIN        DD *
PAGESZ=6184
CREATE FILE PERSONL
PARAMETER ASTRPPG=20,ATRPG=1,FVFPG=2
PARAMETER MVFPG=1,BRECPPG=60
PARAMETER BSIZE=1,BRESERVE=113
PARAMETER CSIZE=1,DSIZE=1
END
OPEN PERSONL
INITIALIZE
EOJ
//
```

Figure 12.22

Field Creation

```
OPEN PERSONL
INITIALIZE
SORT LNAME(KEY OCCURS 1)
DEFINE FNAME
DEFINE ADDRESS
DEFINE DEPENDENT
DEFINE BIRTHDATE
DEFINE SEX (KEY)
DEFINE COMPANY (KEY CODED FRV FEW-VALUED)
DEFINE STARTDATE (INVISIBLE KEY)
DEFINE COLLEGE (FRV)
DEFINE SALARY (NUMERIC RANGE BINARY)
```
Figure 12.23

ments by the data base administrator, as seen in Fig. 12.23. Now that the file has been created, initialized, and defined, data is loaded into the file. The results of the load are shown by Fig. 12.24, where Table B has been loaded with data.

Other tables (C and D) are shown after the load by Figs. 12.25 and 12.26. The contents of Table A are shown by Fig. 12.27.

MODEL 204 LANGUAGE FACILITIES

Model 204 is composed of a full range of language facilities for the use and manipulation of Model 204 data bases. The user may select as simple or as complex a subset of Model 204 language facilities as is suitable. This section focuses on Model 204 in its most basic form. Reference to Model 204 manuals can be made for more advanced forms of the manipulation language.

Every Model 204 request has certain control words:

— LOGIN. The command that starts a user terminal session.

— OPEN. The opening of a file or a group. This is required as at least one file must be opened for the request to be executed.

— BEGIN. The starting of the user language request.

Table B after being loaded with the
personnel data fields:

01 fname	06 sex
02 lname	07 company
03 address	08 salary
04 dependent	09 start date
05 birthdate	10 college

Page 1

```
1 01 Tom 02 Bird 03 569 Keelson 06 M 07 01 08 6000 10 WSU
2 01 Jan 02 Bird 06 F 10 WSU
3 01 Donna 02 Collins 03 LaHonda 06 F 07 02 08 2500 10 U Ga
4
5
```

Page 2

```
1 01 Sam 02 Friedman 03 West Orange 04 Jeanne 04 Linda 06 M 07 03
2 01 Sylvia 02 Friedman 04 Jeanne 04 Linda 06 F 10 Princeton
3 01 Jeanne 02 Friedman 03 Natick 06 F 07 04 08 5000 10 Harvard
4 02 Inmon 05 450720 03 Denver 04 Sarah 04 Melba 06 M 07 04 08 5500 10 Yale
5
```

Page 3

```
1 01 Maryce 02 Jacobs 06 F 08 7000 10 NMSU 10 U Den 10 U Tx
2 01 Joe 02 Mohr 03 Denver 06 M 07 05 08 4500 10 Puget Sound
3 01 Kay 02 Mohr 03 Denver 06 F
4 01 Alice 02 Mundt 03 Concord 06 F 07 06 08 1750
5
```

Page 4

```
1 01 Melba 02 Nowak 03 Denver 04 Sarah 05 440716 06 F 07 06 10 U Leeds
2 01 Alan 02 Peters 06 M 07 06 08 4000
3
4
5
```

Page 5

```
1 01 Phil 02 Teale 03 Concord 06 M 07 06 08 4000 10 St Andrews
2
3
4
5
```

Page 6

```
1 01 Peter 02 Van Andel 03 Holland 06 M 07 01 08 5000 10 Eindhoven
2 02 Van Duyn 03 San Jose 04 Christine 06 M 07 04 08 5500 10 TCU 10 SMU 10 Yale
3 02 Van Duyn 03 San Jose 04 Christine 06 F 07 04 08 4500 10 Harvard 10 Yale
4
5
```

Figure 12.24

— CLOSE. The closing of a file or a group that has been previously opened.
— LOGOUT. The termination of a user's terminal session.

The general format of these control commands is:

    LOGIN......
    OPEN.......

    BEGIN......

Table C: the contents after loading the personnel data

LNAME	SEX	COMPANY	STARTDATE	SALARY
Van Andel – P601	M – Table D	0 – Table D	791223 – P304	6000 – P101
Jacobs – P301	F – Table D	5 – Table D	740301 – P203	2500 – P103
Nowak – P401		3 – Table D	810107 – P501	5000 – Table D
Friedman – Table D		1 – P103	830613 – P603	5500 – Table D
Mundt – P304		4 – P302	810728 – P103	7000 – P301
Van Duyn – Table D		2 – P201	790613 – P402	4500 – Table D
Bird – Table D				1750 – P304
Mohr – Table D				4000 – Table D
Teale – P501				
Collins – P103				
Peters – P402				
Inmon – P204				

Figure 12.25

Table D: the contents after loading the personnel data

LNAME	SEX	COMPANY	SALARY
Bird – P101	F – P102	0 – P101	4000 – P402
Bird – P102	F – P103	0 – P601	4000 – P501
Friedman – P201	F – P202	3 – P203	4500 – P302
Friedman – P202	F – P203	3 – P204	4500 – P602
Friedman – P203	F – P301	3 – P205	5000 – P203
Mohr – P302	F – P303	3 – P602	5000 – P601
Mohr – P303	F – P304	3 – P603	5500 – P204
Van Duyn – P602	F – P401	5 – P304	5500 – P602
Van Duyn – P603	F – P603	5 – P402	
	M – P101	5 – P501	
	M – P201		
	M – P204		
	M – P302		
	M – P402		
	M – P501		
	M – P601		
	M – P602		

Figure 12.26

Table A: the contents after loading

(Note: Assume a 3380 disk device; page size = 6184)
FRV: IBM, ADR, Ret, Amdahl, C & L, B of A
FRV: WSU, U Ga, Princeton, Havard, Yale, U Tx, U Denver, NMSU, Puget Sound, U Leeds, St Andrews, Eindhoven, TCU, SMU

Few-valued (Coded)
(0) IBM, (1) ADR, (2) Ret, (3) Amdahl, (4) C & L, (5) B of A

Field Names:

01	fname	06	sex
02	lname	07	company
03	address	08	salary
04	dependent	09	start date
05	birthdate	10	college

Figure 12.27

Specific DBMS Examples   Section II

```
CLOSE......
OPEN.......


BEGIN......


CLOSE......
LOGOUT.....
```

The syntax of Model 204 can be illustrated by examples. The following examples will be executed against the PERSONL data base as shown in Fig. 12.24. A simple request is illustrated by Fig. 12.28. In this case the PERSONL data base is searched for any record whose first name is SAM. Since SAM is not keyed, the search is done entirely in Table B. Once the record or records are found, the first name, last name, and address are printed. There is only one person in the data base with the first name Sam, the record located at P201. The results of the query are:

Sam Friedman West Orange

1. FIND ALL RECORDS FOR WHICH
   FNAME=SAM
2. FOR EACH RECORD IN 1
   PRINT FNAME AND LNAME AT 20 AND ADDRESS AT 40   **Figure 12.28**

The request shown in Fig. 12.29 is to find all records where last name is Friedman with a dependent named Jeanne. This search is a combination of a search for a keyed field and a nonkeyed field. The lname is searched first, finding three Friedmans. Then the specific records are searched, two of which have dependents named Jeanne. The output of the query is:

Sam Friedman
Sylvia Friedman

1. FIND ALL RECORDS FOR WHICH
   LNAME=FRIEDMAN
   DEPENDENT=JEANNE
2. FOR EACH RECORD IN 1
   PRINT FNAME AND LNAME   **Figure 12.29**

The request in Fig. 12.30 shows multiple conditions for a query, looking for all records where the address is Denver and with dependents named Sarah. This search must be done entirely in Table B and all records must be searched. There are two records that satisfy the query, records P204 and P401. The output of the query is:

```
"Inmon 450720 Denver Sarah Melba M Amdahl 5500
Yale"
"Melba Nowak Denver Sarah 440716 F BofA U
Leeds"
```

```
1. FIND ALL RECORDS FOR WHICH
   ADDRESS=DENVER AND DEPENDENT=SARAH
2. FOR EACH RECORD IN 1
   2.1 PRINT ALL INFORMATION
   2.2 SKIP 2 LINES                           Figure 12.30
```

The request shown in Fig. 12.31 shows a deletion of college where last name is Bird and first name is Jan. There is one record that qualifies, P102. The field, WSU, is deleted. Had there been more records that satisfied the criteria, the deletion of college would have occurred in multiple places.

```
1. FIND ALL RECORDS FOR WHICH
   LNAME=BIRD AND FNAME=JAN
2. FOR EACH RECORD IN 1
   DELETE COLLEGE                             Figure 12.31
```

The company Amdahl is added to the record for Kay Mohr by the request in Fig. 12.32. Had there been more Kay Mohrs in Table B, Amdahl would also have been added to their records. Prior to the addition, the record for Kay Mohr did not have a company associated with it. Had she had a field associated and Amdahl had been added, then she would have had two companies in her record. Also, note that in Table B only the code for Amdahl is added, not the actual value, since company is encoded.

```
1. FIND ALL RECORDS FOR WHICH
   LNAME=MOHR AND FNAME=KAY
2. FOR EACH RECORD IN 1
   ADD COMPANY=AMDAHL                         Figure 12.32
```

A change of values is indicated by the request shown in Fig. 12.33. All salaries of 4000 are to be raised to 4500. Note that this request is satisfied in the index. Only those records that have value = 4000 will be accessed because numeric range has been specified for the salary field. The changes will be made to records P402 and P501.

```
1. FIND ALL RECORDS FOR WHICH
   SALARY=4000
2. FOR EACH RECORD IN 1
   CHANGE SALARY TO 4500                      Figure 12.33
```

The creation of a record is illustrated by Fig. 12.34. In this case the record for T. F. Chang is created. The fields of IBM and salary are stored with this record. Note that index maintenance must be done for lname and company. Numeric range activity will occur for the addition of salary.

```
1. STORE RECORD
   FNAME=TF
   LNAME=CHANG
   COMPANY=IBM
   SALARY=5500      Figure 12.34
```

OTHER LANGUAGE FEATURES

In addition to the simple activities of retrieval, update, deletion, and creation, Model 204 has a diverse set of capabilities:

— Optional processing termination facilities based on the amount of work done (STOP IF COUNT IN n EXCEEDS m). This facility prevents unwanted output from being processed or massive displays of output when wrong keys have been inadvertently entered.

— Request stop and continuation features (MORE .....). This facility allows logical checkpoints to be taken by the user. In the eventuality that some malfunction occurs, the entire process need not be executed.

— Report generation facilities, including sorting, headers, formatting, page breaks, and so forth.

— Loop capabilities and multiply occurring fields. These features allow subscripted data to be handled with ease.

— Procedures. Input lines saved for future use.

— Mathematical functions.

— Full-screen formatting.

A final language capability of Model 204 is the capability to group files. In Model 204 different files can be grouped logically into a single entity and processed as such. The use of this facility is that different files can be logically related (such as 1983 data, 1982 data, 1981 data, etc.). The grouping feature allows the data to be treated as a single file.

MODEL 204 SYSTEMS CONSIDERATIONS

Model 204 runs in a batch mode, on online mode, and a mixed online and batch mode. Data integrity is at the record level. A point of special interest is that the language processing facilities of Model 204 reside in the nucleus. Each online user has 4k bytes for usage. The single occurrence of the language processor means that there is absolutely a minimum of overhead required (in terms of main storage) and that there is no need for cross region communications, as would be the case if every user operated from a separate region. Some of the system facilities of Model 204 include journaling and an audit trail, debugging, monitoring, and security facilities. Model 204 offers extensive recovery facilities, including checkpointing, roll forward, and roll back.

CHAPTER 13

Decision Support Systems: SQL

Structured query language (SQL, pronounced see-kwell) is a relational data base management system and is a major component of IBM's DB2 (Data Base 2) software. In many ways SQL is the prototype for relational systems. The strength of SQL (and other relational systems) is its flexibility. It is very easy to use and to change, something that occurs only in degrees with other DBMS (data base management systems). The basic structure of data in SQL is the table. Data is organized, stored, and accessed by tables. The great flexibility of SQL lies in the way data is interrelated between tables. Tables are connected by common data values, and the user can dynamically connect tables. This means that the user has great freedom while actually using the system. The user is not dependent on the data processing department for definition of data or processes that use the data.

As in all DBMS, the in-depth understanding of the DBMS must occur in at least two levels, the physical level and the syntax level. The first discussion is at the physical level. The physical level discussed is based on DB2, but it is worthwhile to note that there are other implementations of SQL.

PHYSICAL IMPLEMENTATION

The lowest unit of information in SQL is the field. Fields can be in four formats:

— Fixed length, no null values allowed
— Fixed length, null values allowed

— Variable length, no null values allowed
— Variable length, null values allowed

If a field can have null values there is a prefix for the field. In the notation shown, the prefix has a value of P or N, for present or null. If a field cannot have null values, there is no field prefix for it. If a field is variable in length, it has a prefix indicating the length of the field. Note that a variable length field that is nonnull may have a length of zero, which is the equivalent of being null. The possibilities are shown by Fig. 13.1.

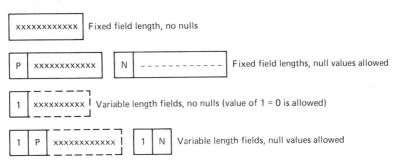

Figure 13.1 The types of fields supported by SQL.

Fields are defined into rows or records. A row is commonly called a *tuple*. Rows can be fixed length or variable length. If a row contains only fixed fields, it is fixed in length. But if a row contains one or more variable length fields, then it is variable in length. Fields fitting in a row are shown by Fig. 13.2. Rows are fitted into pages. A page is either 4k or 32k in length. If a page is 32k, it is made up of eight 4k Virtual Sequential Access Method (VSAM) **control intervals,** or ci. (A control interval is the basic unit of physical organization in VSAM. It is roughly equivalent to a block of data. An I/O (input/output) must be done to go from one ci to another.) Rows fit entirely within a page, i.e., rows do not span a page. Otherwise, it is made up of one 4k ci. SQL is defined to VSAM exclusively. The arrangement of pages is shown by Fig. 13.3.

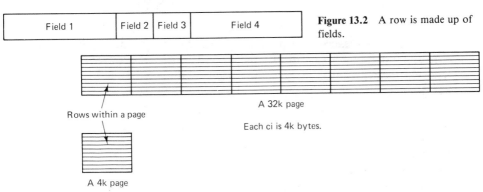

Figure 13.2 A row is made up of fields.

Figure 13.3

Rows can be added or deleted one at a time, or they can be loaded and deleted en masse. Columns can be added to a row once defined, but even if the column is for a fixed length field, the row is then defined as variable in length. When a row is deleted the space is marked reusable. The space can be used for the occurrence of another row or the extension of an existing variable length row, as shown by Fig. 13.4.

Row that has been deleted

Figure 13.4

Pages are arranged into table spaces. Table spaces come in two forms, simple table spaces or partitioned table spaces. A simple table space can hold several types of tables together or a single table. A partitioned table space holds only one type of table, but the table is divided into 64 units called **partitions,** as seen in Fig. 13.5. Simple table spaces are good for small, interrelated tables, while partitioned tables are good for large tables.

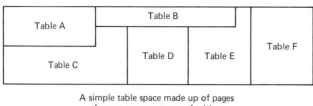

A simple table space made up of pages
for one or more types of tables

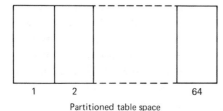

Partitioned table space

Figure 13.5

Data is sequenced into pages either randomly or sequentially. If the data is entered randomly it is said to be **nonclustered.** If it is entered sequentially, it is said to be **clustered.** In any case there is an index pointing to designated fields. The index has three levels, the **root page** level, the **intermediate page** level, and the **leaf page** level. The two top levels are used to point to the leaf pages in much the same way as master indexes are used in other systems. The leaf pages actually point to the pages where the rows reside. A direct access into the data base uses three levels of indexing, while sequential accesses use only the leaf pages. If the data is clustered, the leaf pages point to rows within one page and to rows in another page when the sequential order is interrupted by the physical boundaries of a page. But when the data is not clustered, the leaf pages point to data in a random fashion. Figure 13.6 illustrates some index arrangements.

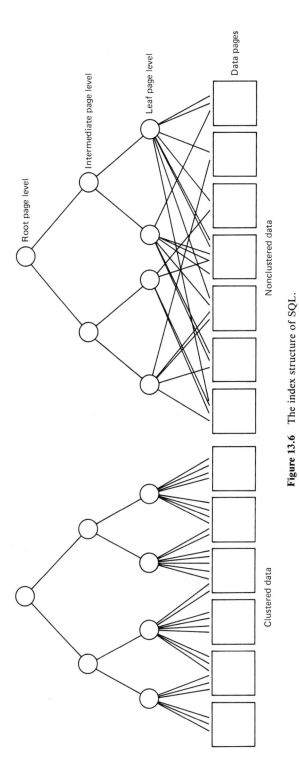

Figure 13.6 The index structure of SQL.

Root page level

Intermediate page level

Leaf page level

Data pages

Nonclustered data

Clustered data

The pointer from the leaf page to the data page is in the form of page/offset, as has been seen in other DBMS. The first part of the pointer indicates in which page the data is located, while the second part of the pointer indicates an offset within the page. The offset is accessed to find the actual location of the row within the page. This facility allows data management to occur within the page without affecting the index. For example a row can be moved from one location to another within the page, and all that must be changed is the value of the location within that page. No index manipulation is necessary. Figure 13.7 shows the pointer from the leaf page to the data.

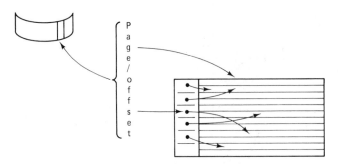

Figure 13.7

RELATIONAL OPERATORS

The format of the syntax of SQL is simple and easy to use. In its simplest form SQL looks like this:

```
SELECT field1, field2, ....
FROM table
WHERE field=argument
```

The syntax is such that users can begin to use SQL a very short time after being exposed to it. Consider the table in Fig. 13.8. Now the request SELECT NAME1, NAME2, SSNO FROM EMPLTABL WHERE EMPNO='006' is entered. The result of the request is:

```
Name1 Name2 SSNO
Pete Zoll 021-22-5651
```

To satisfy the request, the three levels of indexes are searched, then the page is located. Once within the page, the proper offset is located, and the value stored in the offset is used to locate the row. Once the row is located, the fields being sought are located and the values of the fields are determined. Then the field values are returned.

Suppose the request SELECT NAME1, NAME2, SSNO FROM EMPLTABL WHERE EMPNO='005' is entered. The result is a return of null values since there is no row with an EMPNO='005'.

Suppose a user wishes to select all information from a table and wishes to

EMPLTABL data base

EMPLNO	NAME1	NAME2	DEPT	SSNO	BLDG	INS	JOBCLASS
001	Bill	Inmon	002	145-67-1872	010	01	001
002	Melba	Carte	006	401-84-1975	062	01	695
006	Pete	Zoll	001	021-22-5651	911	02	011
007	John	Kam	002	391-01-4211	924	01	510
008	Keni	Patton	006	002-63-0112	409	03	311
009	Joan	Cote	001	403-44-6311	624	01	651

Figure 13.8

qualify the information so that only keys greater than a certain value are selected. Such a request might look like this:

```
SELECT*
FROM EMPLTABL
WHERE EMPNO>'004'
```

If the request is run against the table in Fig. 13.8, then the results are as shown in Fig. 13.9. The operator * indicates all fields are to be selected. Boolean operators are used as part of the selection criteria.

EMPLTABL data base

EMPLNO	NAME1	NAME2	DEPT	SSNO	BLDG	INS	JOBCLASS
006	Pete	Zoll	001	021-22-5651	911	02	011
007	John	Kam	002	391-01-4211	924	01	510
008	Keni	Patton	006	002-63-0112	409	03	311
009	Joan	Cote	001	403-44-6311	624	01	651

Figure 13.9

Now suppose a row is to be deleted. The syntax of the request would look like this:

```
DELETE EMPLTABL
WHERE EMPNO='006'
```

The results of the delete are shown by Fig. 13.10. In this case, the row for Pete Zoll is deleted. The space is available for reuse.

EMPLTABL data base

EMPLNO	NAME1	NAME2	DEPT	SSNO	BLDG	INS	JOBCLASS
001	Bill	Inmon	002	145-67-1872	010	01	001
002	Melba	Carte	006	401-84-1975	062	01	695
007	John	Kam	002	391-01-4211	924	01	510
008	Keni	Patton	006	002-63-0112	409	03	311
009	Joan	Cote	001	403-44-6311	624	01	651

Figure 13.10

But suppose the entire table is to be deleted. A command like

```
DELETE EMPLTABL
```

is entered, and the entire table is deleted.

Inserts are done in a like manner. The command to insert is given and is followed by the fields to be inserted. The fields that are inserted correspond to the order of the fields as they exist in the row. For example, the following request is entered:

```
INSERT INTO EMPLTABL:
<'005','ALICE','MUNDT','006','362-73-
7000','911','01','696'>
```

The results of this command are shown by the data base in Fig. 13.11.

EMPLTABL data base

EMPLNO	NAME1	NAME2	DEPT	SSNO	BLDG	INS	JOBCLASS
001	Bill	Inmon	002	145-67-1872	010	01	001
002	Melba	Carte	006	401-84-1975	062	01	695
005	Alice	Mundt	006	362-73-7000	911	01	696
006	Pete	Zoll	001	021-22-5651	911	02.	011
007	John	Kam	002	391-01-4211	924	01	510
008	Keni	Patton	006	002-63-0112	409	03	311
009	Joan	Cote	001	403-44-6311	624	01	651

Figure 13.11

Suppose that not all fields are to be inserted. The user can specify which fields are to be inserted by the following format:

```
INSERT INTO EMPLTABL (EMPNO, NAME1, NAME2,
SSNO):
<'010','BILL','BIDDLE','456-11-9711'>
```

SQL then matches the field name with the field value and inserts into the data base. Null values are placed in the data base where fields have not been entered. The results of the insert are shown by Fig. 13.12.

EMPLTABL data base

EMPLNO	NAME1	NAME2	DEPT	SSNO	BLDG	INS	JOBCLASS
001	Bill	Inmon	002	145-67-1872	010	01	001
002	Melba	Carte	006	401-84-1975	062	01	695
006	Pete	Zoll	001	021-22-5651	911	02	011
007	John	Kam	002	391-01-4211	924	01	510
008	Keni	Patton	006	002-63-0112	409	03	311
009	Joan	Cote	001	403-44-6311	624	01	651
010	Bill	Biddle	---	456-11-9711	---	--	---

Figure 13.12

Rows do not have to be entered one at a time manually. They can also be entered from other tables if the other tables exist. Figure 13.13 shows a table called NEWEMP. A command is entered that looks like this:

```
INSERT INTO EMPLTABL:
SELECT EMPNO NAME1, NAME2
FROM NEWEMP
WHERE DATE>830630
```

The results of the request are shown in Fig. 13.13.

Updates are performed much like inserts. Field name and field values are specified. Suppose that Joan Cote has married Greg Estep and wishes to change her name. The following command will effect the change:

```
UPDATE EMPLTABL
SET NAME2='ESTEP'
WHERE EMPNO='009'
```

The results of the update look like the data base shown in Fig. 13.14.

But update does not have to occur on an individual row basis. All rows (or all qualifying rows) can be updated by a single command. For example, Fig. 13.15 shows an employee's salary history data base. The following command is issued to calculate net pay:

```
UPDATE EMPLPAY
SET FICA=FICA*.1
NET=GROSS-(FICA+STATE+FEDERAL+CONTRIB+INSUR)
```

Figure 13.16 shows the data base after execution of the command.

Entire tables can be created from existing tables. Suppose that a new table, EMPNAMBL, is to be created from EMPLTABL. The following command is used to create the table:

```
SELECT NAME1 NAME2 EMPNO BLDG
FROM EMPLTABL
GIVING EMPNAMBL
```

The results of the execution of the command are shown by Fig. 13.17.

Figure 13.18 shows a building location and address table. It is possible to join the BLDGTABL and the EMPNAMBL tables by the following command:

```
JOIN BLDGTABL AND EMPNAMBL OVER BLDG GIVING
EMPBLDG
```

This command is possible because there is a common field value, BLDG, between the two tables. The resulting data base looks like that shown in Fig. 13.18. Other relational operators are COUNT, SUM, and AVERAGE. Using the EMPLPAY data base, the following commands are executed:

```
SELECT COUNT(*)
FROM EMPLPAY
```

NEWEMP data base

EMPNO	NAME1	NAME2	DATE
016	Tom	Hawkes	830601
021	Jim	Sievers	830622
022	Chris	Witzel	830714
031	Ann	Maeda	830715

EMPLTABL data base

EMPLNO	NAME1	NAME2	DEPT	SSNO	BLDG	INS	JOBCLASS
001	Bill	Inmon	002	145-67-1872	010	01	001
002	Melba	Carte	006	401-84-1975	062	01	695
006	Pete	Zoll	001	021-22-5651	911	02	011
007	John	Kam	002	391-01-4211	924	01	510
008	Keni	Patton	006	002-63-0112	409	03	311
009	Joan	Cote	001	403-44-6311	624	01	651
002	Chris	Witzel	- - -	- - - - - - -	- - -	- -	- - -
031	Ann	Maeda	- - -	- - - - - - -	- - -	- -	- - -

Figure 13.13

EMPLTABL data base

EMPLNO	NAME1	NAME2	DEPT	SSNO	BLDG	INS	JOBCLASS
001	Bill	Inmon	002	145-67-1872	010	01	001
002	Melba	Carte	006	401-84-1975	062	01	695
006	Pete	Zoll	001	021-22-5651	911	02	011
007	John	Kam	002	391-01-4211	924	01	510
008	Keni	Patton	006	002-63-0112	409	03	311
009	Joan	Estep	001	403-44-6311	624	01	651

Figure 13.14

EMPLPAY data base

EMPLO/DATE	GROSS	FICA	STATE	FEDERAL	CONTRIB	INSUR	NET
001/830115	2000	135	89	195	50	62	1469
001/830130	2000	135	89	195	0	0	1581
001/830215	2000	135	89	195	50	62	1469
002/830115	1666	128	76	225	10	37	1190
002/830130	1666	128	76	225	0	0	1237
002/830215	1666	128	76	225	10	37	1190
007/830115	2500	160	115	230	15	95	1885
007/830130	2500	160	115	230	0	0	1995
007/830215	2500	160	115	230	15	95	1885

Figure 13.15

EMPLPAY data base

EMPLO/DATE	GROSS	FICA	STATE	FEDERAL	CONTRIB	INSUR	NET
001/830115	2000	135	89	195	50	62	1455
001/830130	2000	135	89	195	0	0	1567
001/830215	2000	135	89	195	50	62	1455
002/830115	1666	128	76	225	10	37	1177
002/830130	1666	128	76	225	0	0	1224
002/830215	1666	128	76	225	10	37	1177
007/830115	2500	160	115	230	15	95	1869
007/830130	2500	160	115	230	0	0	1979
007/830215	2500	160	115	230	15	95	1869

Figure 13.16

EMPNO	NAME1	NAME2	BLDG
001	Bill	Inmon	010
002	Melba	Carte	062
006	Pete	Zoll	911
007	John	Kam	924
008	Keni	Patton	409
009	Joan	Cote	624

Figure 13.17

BLDGTABL data base

BLDG	NAME	LOCATION	ZIP	SEC
010	Admin	222 Jackson, Littleton, Co	80127	011
062	Hdqtrs	45 Main, Denver, Co	80202	012
409	Pump Sta 1	Rte 15, Ft Greeley, Co	80225	011
624	Pump Sta 4	West and 4th, Vail, Co	80130	002
911	Monitor 76	4th and Main, Aspen, Co	80176	011

EMPLNO	NAME1	NAME2	BLDG	BLDGNAME	LOCATION	ZIP	SEC
001	Bill	Inmon	010	Admin	222 Jackson, Littleton, Co	80127	011
002	Melba	Carte	062	Hdqtrs	45 Main, Denver, Co	80202	012
006	Pete	Zoll	911	Monitor 76	4th and Main, Aspen, Co	80176	011
007	John	Kam	924				
008	Keni	Patton	409	Pump Sta 1	Rte 15, Ft Greeley, Co	80225	002
009	Joan	Cote	624	Pump Sta 4	West and 4th, Vail, Co	80130	002

Figure 13.18

Result: 9 (There are 9 rows of employee pay activity.)

```
SELECT COUNT(*)
FROM EMPLPAY
WHERE GROSS>1975
```

Result: 6 (There are 6 rows of employee pay activities where gross pay is more than 1975.)

```
SELECT SUM(GROSS)
FROM EMPLPAY
WHERE EMPLNO='007'
```

Result: 7500

```
SELECT EMPLNO SUM(GROSS)
FROM EMPLPAY
GROUP BY EMPLNO
```

Result:

```
EMPLNO SUM
001 6000
002 4998
007 7500
```

```
SELECT EMPLNO AVERAGE(CONTRIB)
FROM EMPLPAY
GROUP BY EMPLNO
```

Result:

```
EMPLNO AVG
001 33
002 7
007 10
```

USER VIEWS

SQL supports user views that are a logically defined view of data. A user view can portray a table, a subset of a table, or a conglomeration of several tables. A view of data exists logically, not physically, even though it must be supported at the physical level by the existence of the data in some table. A physical support of a view that is constructed from multiple physical tables is shown by Fig. 13.19.

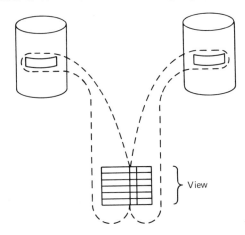

Figure 13.19 A view that is supported by multiple physical data bases.

The user has no idea what the data looks like physically. The following syntax supports a simple view of data:

```
DEFINE VIEW EMPLOYNET (EMPLNO, DATE, NET)
AS SELECT EMPLNO, DATE, NET
FROM EMPLPAY
```

The command causes the following view to be created:

```
EMPLOYNET
EMPLNO DATE NET
001 830115 1469
001 830130 1581
001 830215 1469
002 830115 1190
002 830130 1237
002 830215 1190
007 830115 1885
007 830130 1995
007 830215 1885
```

PHYSICAL UNDERPINNINGS OF RELATIONAL OPERATORS

Despite the simplicity of operation at the syntax level, SQL often undertakes much activity to accomplish the job being requested. As a simple example suppose a data

EMPLTABL data base

	EMPLNO	NAME1	NAME2	DEPT	SSNO	BLDG	INS	JOBCLASS
ci	001	Bill	Inmon	002	145–67–1872	010	01	001
	002	Melba	Carte	006	401–84–1975	062	01	695
	006	Pete	Zoll	001	021–22–5651	911	02	011
ci	007	John	Kam	002	391–01–4211	924	01	510
	008	Keni	Patton	006	002–63–0112	409	03	311
	009	Joan	Cote	001	403–44–6311	624	01	651

Figure 13.20

base exists as in Fig. 13.20. In this simple case, each page is full. A request is entered to add a new row that looks like this:

```
INSERT INTO EMPLTABL:
<'004','Ted','VanDuyn','003','046-39-
0011','113','02','414'>
```

Since the table is physically sequenced on EMPLNO, the result of the insertion looks like Fig. 13.21. The data has been physically split over three pages and the indexes have been adjusted. All this work that occurs "under the covers" requires I/O and machine resources despite the simplicity at the syntax level.

EMPTABL data base

	EMPLNO	NAME1	NAME2	DEPT	SSNO	BLDG	INS	JOBCLASS
ci	001	Bill	Inmon	002	145–67–1872	010	01	001
	002	Melba	Carte	006	401–84–1975	062	01	695
ci	004	Ted	VanDuyn	003	045–39–0011	113	02	414
	006	Pete	Zoll	001	021–22–5651	911	02	011
ci	007	John	Kam	002	391–01–4211	924	01	510
	008	Keni	Patton	006	002–63–0112	409	03	311
	009	Joan	Cote	001	403–44–6311	624	01	651

Figure 13.21

A more complex example of the physical underpinnings of a SQL request is shown by:

```
SELECT NAME1 NAME2 SSNO
FROM EMPLTABL
WHERE NAME2='NOWAK'
```

Since the table is not physically keyed on NAME2 (and it is assumed that there is no index on the field), then the entire data base must be scanned. The ability of SQL to do entire data base scans easily allows the user much flexibility coupled with the capability of using many machine resources.

Another perspective of the physical environment of SQL is illustrated by the

Specific DBMS Examples   Section II

EMPLTABL data base

EMPLNO	NAME1	NAME2	DEPT	SSNO	BLDG	INS	JOBCLASS
001	Bill	Inmon	002	145-67-1872	010	01	001
002	Melba	Carte	006	401-84-1975	062	01	695
006	Pete	Zoll	001	021-22-5651	911	02	011
007	John	Kam	002	391-01-4211	924	01	510
008	Keni	Patton	006	002-63-0112	409	03	311
009	Joan	Cote	001	403-44-6311	624	01	651

BLDGTABL data base

BLDG	NAME	LOCATION	ZIP	SEC
010	Admin	222 Jackson, Littleton, Co	80127	011
062	Hdqtrs	45 Main, Denver, Co	80202	012
409	Pump Sta 1	Rte 15, Ft Greeley, Co	80225	011
624	Pump Sta 4	West and 4th, Vail, Co	80130	002
911	Monitor 76	4th and Main, Aspen, Co	80176	011

Figure 13.22

following example. Two tables, EMPLTABL and BLDGTABL, are shown in Fig. 13.22. This question is asked: In what building does Melba Carte work? Melba is employee 002 and is quickly located through the EMPLTABL index. Now her building number, which happens to be 062, is located. The building index is now used, and the address of the building is determined to be Headquarters, 45 Main, Denver, CO. The servicing of the request was done in an efficient manner.

But suppose the reverse question is asked: What employees are there that work in pumping station 4, Vail, CO? The question can be answered but not efficiently. The key of the pumping station is located. Then using that key, EMPLTABL is searched. This requires one I/O for each c_i in the EMPLTABL, since every row must be searched. (*Note:* It is assumed that there is no index on building number for EMPLTABL.) This is obviously inefficient. If it is necessary to go from building to employee on a frequent basis, then a cross reference should be created.

If there is only one employee per building, then the employee can be included in the building table. But that distribution of employees is very unlikely. So a table must be created to cross reference multiple employees per building. Such a table looks like the XREF table shown in Fig. 13.23.

Building/Employee

Cross Reference Table

010/001
010/003
010/864
010/971
010/983
062/002
062/011
409/008
409/771
409/836
⋮   ⋮

Figure 13.23

SQL AT THE SYSTEM LEVEL

The level of integrity of SQL is either at the table space or page level, depending on the type of activity that is occurring. In addition, when data definition activity is occurring, SQL may opt to lock out other activity until the definition processing is completed.

Deadlocks are resolved at the system level. The system determines which transaction has been in the system the longest and uses that information to resolve the deadlock. SQL runs under three online pieces of software, IMS/VS, CICS/VS, and TSO. The teleprocessing facilities are dependent on these pieces of software because SQL does not have independent processing capabilities. A unique feature of SQL is the BIND facility, which automatically chooses the optimal path for data access. Indexes may be created or deleted optionally for a field and may be created or deleted online, unlike many other DBMS that require the data base to be stopped, unloaded, redefined, and then reloaded. Other system definition activity, such as column creation, may be executed online as well. SQL contains the normal utilities such as image copy, recovery, reorganization, loading, and so on. These utilities support (among other things) full backup and recovery as well as monitoring facilities.

CHAPTER 14

Fourth-Generation Systems: FOCUS

Fourth-generation DBMS (data base management systems) are characterized by their integrated approach to end user requirements and the nonprocedural nature of the language used. Integration of end user requirements consists of providing a complete set of functions using a common and consistent command syntax. Nonprocedural languages allow the user to describe the desired result from the data base access and eliminates describing how to access the data. COBOL, FORTRAN and PL-1 are examples of procedural languages. The programmer usually spends considerable time programming the *procedure* the machine is to follow to achieve the desired result. Nonprocedural languages, on the other hand, simply describe the desired result and the software in the DBMS determines the procedure to be used to achieve that result.

A simple example involves a personnel data base inquiry. The end user wants a list of all employees with a yearly salary over $25,000. In COBOL, the programmer would code the procedure of iteratively reading all data base records in the personnel data base and comparing the salary value with the constant of $25,000. In a fourth-generation language, the programmer would code a simple request: LIST ALL EMPLOYEES WITH GREATER THAN $25,000. The query processor in the DBMS would itself access the data base records and produce the same list as the COBOL program without the need of writing and compiling a program.

The advantage of fourth-generation languages lies in the ability to produce new application systems faster than third-generation systems such as COBOL, etc. Often the end user can program the application directly without assistance from data processing personnel. This increased application system development can effectively reduce the application backlog by getting the new system up and running faster with fewer highly trained staff. Applications that were due to be automated years in the future because of a shortage of programmers can now be considered for immediate implementation by the end user using a fourth-generation language and DBMS.

Often the performance of fourth-generation languages is considerably poorer than the performance of a procedural-based version of the same application because the computers in use today are procedural by nature. It appears to the fourth-generation system user that no procedure is needed to guide the machine. However, under the covers of the fourth-generation system is a procedure, since the machine requires one to operate. The fourth-generation system has, in fact, brought together a series of general procedures, written by the product vendor, to accomplish the end result desired by the end user. These general procedures cannot usually perform as well as a procedure customized to the specific problem at hand by a COBOL programmer. It has been found, though, that these general procedures can often outperform the programs written by mediocre third-generation language programmers, and so this performance disadvantage of fourth-generation systems is less important.

FOCUS, a product of Information Builders, Inc., is a fourth-generation system and will be used here to illustrate the concepts. FOCUS is an integrated DBMS product because it includes all the basic functions of an end user DBMS:

- DBM (data base manager)
- Query/update language
- Report writer
- Graphics
- Decision support functions

In addition, the end user language of FOCUS is of the nonprocedural type and therefore greatly simplifies the application development process.

DATA BASE MANAGER

As shown in Fig. 14.1, the FOCUS data base manager is capable of reading a wide variety of existing data sources including the following data base types:

IMS
TOTAL
IDMS
ADABAS

Also included are the following flat-file types:

QSAM: sequential
ISAM: indexed
VSAM: indexed, sequential, direct

but updating is not supported for any of these.

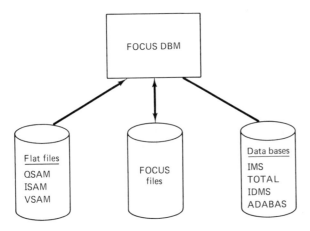

Figure 14.1 FOCUS DBM: A wide variety of data bases is supported.

Flat files
QSAM
ISAM
VSAM

FOCUS files

Data bases
IMS
TOTAL
IDMS
ADABAS

FOCUS includes its own data base model, called the **shared-relational** structure. The shared-relational model bears broad resemblance to a combination of the four industry models—hierarchical, inverted, network, and relational—with the following salient characteristics:

- *Multipath data bases.* Hierarchies among data groupings may be defined with one-to-one, one-to-many, and many-to-one relationships allowed as shown in Fig. 14.2. Hierarchical siblings at each level are not required.

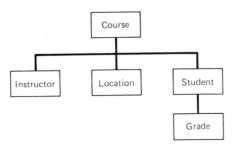

Course

Instructor   Location   Student

Grade

Figure 14.2 FOCUS shared-relational data base: A single structure is composed of one or more related segments.

- *Data base cross reference.* Separate data bases can be logically linked together much in the same way as logical data bases in IMS but without the need to embed pointers and link information in the participating data bases. Index fields are used for the purpose of creating the associations, which gives good flexibility to change the associations at will but creates the attendant slower performance that comes with such techniques. The granularity of the linkages is at the data subgrouping level, which is called a *segment* in FOCUS terminology. An example of a data base cross reference is illustrated in Fig. 14.3.
- *Data base inversion.* All segments are associated by bidirectional pointers permitting dynamic inversion of the data base at any point with reasonable I/O

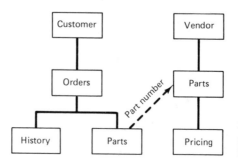

Figure 14.3 FOCUS data base cross reference: The customer order data base is related to the vendor data base.

performance. This produces alternate views of the same data base as shown in Fig. 14.4.

- *Relational constructs.* FOCUS data bases can be created as tables consisting of only one segment type. These tables can then be logically linked using the relational join operator to produce composite tables. Files and data bases other than FOCUS shared-relational data bases may participate in the relational operations.

When structural changes are to be made to a FOCUS shared-relational data base, the entry in the master dictionary is first modified, and then a rebuild utility, supplied with FOCUS, is executed to effect the change in the data base itself.

Any field in a FOCUS shared-relational file can be indexed. These indexes can be established after the original data base is loaded, without the need for data base rebuilding. Segments in the data base can be maintained in ascending or descending order based on one or more key fields in the segment.

End users may access FOCUS data bases exclusively, wherein no other users share the data base or the data bases are shared. The concurrent sharing is referred to as **simultaneous user processing.** In this concurrent mode, multiple end user requests are sent to a central FOCUS long-running job that processes the requests

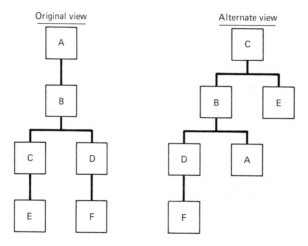

Figure 14.4 FOCUS alternate data base view: The original (physical) view of the data is inverted at segment C.

Specific DBMS Examples   Section II

and returns the responses to the end user's copy of FOCUS. The end user can be made unaware of the fact that a specific fourth-generation data request is being routed to a centralized FOCUS controller. This transparency eliminates the need for the nonprogramming end user to understand the complexities of data sharing and control.

Regardless of which data base or file type is used, all the FOCUS fourth-generation query, report writing, and decision support functions are available. Further, data from some or all of these source types may be intermixed within a single FOCUS request or program.

Each file and data base that FOCUS accesses must be defined to FOCUS in the FOCUS master dictionary. The FOCUS master dictionary is a separate file that only contains these definitions. An example of a definition for an IMS data base is:

```
SEGNAME=STUDENT
   FIELD=NAME,NM,A20,A20,$
   FIELD=ADDRESS,ADDR,A20,A20,$
SEGNAME=COURSE
   FIELD=CODE,CD,A4,A4,$
   FIELD=GRADE,GR,I2,I2,$
SEGNAME=HISTORY
   FIELD=YEAR,YR,I2,I2,$
   FIELD=AVERAGE,AVG,F2.1,F2.1,$
```

The finest-granularity element in the FOCUS file definition is the field. Each field must be given a name and—optionally—an alias, each of which may be up to 12 characters long. Later, when the user is accessing the data base or file using FOCUS, the field can be referred to by its name, its alias, or a unique abbreviation of either.

Related fields can be grouped into segments and segments into files. Sequential files may have only one segment, whereas complex data bases, such as an IMS data base, may have many segments.

In addition to a field's name and alias, its data format and editing options are specified. The format specifications tell FOCUS the length and data type that it will find when accessing the actual file (internal format), whereas the editing options define the format in which the data is to be displayed to the user (external format). Basic editing features, such as leading zero suppression, are provided as well as more sophisticated functions, such as date conversion. Since the FOCUS master dictionary file is physically separate from the data files and data bases, fields and their characteristics can be changed independently. Any new specifications are automatically incorporated in the next execution of FOCUS against the subject file or data base.

Data access security levels can also be defined in the FOCUS master dictionary, as shown in the previous example. Read, write, read/write and update security can be assigned to FOCUS relational data bases, whereas the other supported file types are limited to read level security definition. An interesting and useful extension to the access definition specifications is the possibility of limiting the number of records that can be accessed by a FOCUS user in a single data base request. While technically this capability is not a security definition, it does provide the administrator of the master dictionary with the ability to limit the amount of I/O performed by FOCUS for a single request from a single user, thereby controlling overall system performance to a certain degree.

Data access security granularity in FOCUS is the file, segment, field, or field value. This flexibility provides security schemes not possible in many operational-type DBMS systems. The following example demonstrates the point:

User 1 may access the salary field of the personnel data base only if the employee is in department 556 and only if the salary amount is less than $19,000.

QUERY/UPDATE LANGUAGE

The capability that distinguishes FOCUS from the more traditional DBMS products is its nonprocedural language. With this fourth-generation language, considerably less data processing knowledge is required to use a computer for decision support applications. Consider the FOCUS language statements:

```
TABLE FILE PERSONNEL
SUM SALARY
BY DEPARTMENT
ACROSS DIVISION
IF YEAR FROM 80 to 84
END
```

This program will produce a list of the salary budgets by department for each company division for the years 1980 through 1984. The program size can be sharply contrasted to the number of lines of code that would be required using COBOL, for instance. The desired result is specified in the FOCUS program, and the sort and selection criteria are determined by FOCUS using the master dictionary.

While the strength of the FOCUS language lies in its data base query capability, the language can also be used to update a data base. The FOCUS statements

```
MODIFY FILE PERSONNEL
PROMPT EMPLNAME EMPL# DEPARTMENT# DIVISION SALARY
MATCH EMPL#
ON MATCH TYPE ''EMPLOYEE ALREADY ON FILE.''
ON MATCH REJECT
ON NOMATCH INCLUDE
DATA
```

constitute a function for adding new employees to the personnel data base. Notice how simple the error-checking statements are to code for duplicate employees.

FOCUS provides a data base editor to simplify the process of updating the fields in a data base without writing a detailed FOCUS program. FOCUS query, update, and data base editing statements can be combined and saved as a single command for later execution by command name only. Transaction-processing constructs are provided to allow the creation of sophisticated FOCUS programs using the simple fourth-generation language.

FIDEL (FOCUS interactive data entry language) is a simple 3270-based screen builder. FIDEL provides the nonprogrammer with a straightforward means of building layouts or masks for CRT-type terminals without the need of detailed data processing knowledge concerning the device itself. The layouts can be changed by editing the mask descriptions.

FOCUS provides a *host language interface* (HLI) to allow third-generation programs written in COBOL, FORTRAN, PL/I, and assembler to access FOCUS data bases. Most of the fourth-generation language constructs available to the end user of FOCUS are available to the programmer. HLI is suitable for implementation of new application transactions which have performance requirements outside the range of FOCUS fourth-generation programs or for transaction programs that need to access and update both FOCUS and non-FOCUS data bases.

REPORT WRITING AND GRAPHICS

Second to the powerful nonprocedural language of FOCUS, the report-writing capability significantly reduces the time it takes to produce a formatted report. In its most primitive form, FOCUS will automatically format any data request according to a set of defaults that place sort fields on the left and other data fields on the right in the order they were found on the original user request. The field names from the master dictionary are used as the column headings with automatic spacing and page numbering.

Customized reports can be produced with full control of

- Page headings and footings
- Page subheadings and subfootings
- Grand totals
- Page numbering control
- Column positioning
- Vertical spacing
- Underlining

An end user often directs FOCUS through commands entered in a display terminal. Consequently, the reports produced by FOCUS are displayed at the same terminal. When it is time to produce a printed copy of the report, the following two commands are entered:

```
OFFLINE
RETYPE
```

Recall the FOCUS program to produce a salary budget history report by department for each division during the last 5 years:

```
TABLE FILE PERSONNEL
SUM SALARY
BY DEPARTMENT
ACROSS DIVISION
IF YEAR FROM 80 to 84
END
```

The word *table* in the first statement tells FOCUS that the results of the query are to be generated in tabular format.

```
TABLE FILE PERSONNEL
```

is changed to

```
GRAPH FILE PERSONNEL
```

FOCUS produces a histogram (the default graph form) instead of a table. If the statement

```
SET PIE=ON
```

is added at the beginning of the program, FOCUS produces a pie chart instead of a histogram. If the FOCUS user requests the pie chart from a color graphics terminal, then FOCUS uses default colors to improve the readability of the chart. Graph details such as colors, scaling, and labeling can be refined by the user after the original default graph has been produced.

The FOCUS graphics set includes bar charts, histograms, connected point plots, pie charts, and scatter diagrams. Multiple variables can be placed on the same graph. These flexibilities in control are made available with extensions to the fourth-generation language.

DECISION SUPPORT FUNCTIONS

A common function performed by decision makers is statistical analysis. FOCUS provides a set of formal statistical functions that are integrated within the fourth-generation language itself:

- Regression analysis
- Analysis of variance
- Correlations
- Exponential smoothing
- Discriminant analysis
- Factor analysis
- Descriptive statistics
- Time series
- Crosstabs

The example presented earlier showed the method of computing salary budgets by department for each division over the last 5 years:

```
TABLE FILE PERSONNEL
SUM SALARY
BY DEPARTMENT
ACROSS DIVISION
IF YEAR FROM 80 to 84
END
```

The FOCUS user now wishes to extrapolate the departmental budgets for next year based on the previous 4 years. To do so, a statement is first added at the end of the FOCUS program to save the table produced from the last 5 years. The saved table will be used as input to the statistical analysis.

```
TABLE FILE PERSONNEL
SUM SALARY
BY DEPARTMENT
ACROSS DIVISION
IF YEAR FROM 80 to 84
ON TABLE HOLD
END
```

Next the analyze command is entered and the TIMESER function is requested for time series analysis. The parameters for the analysis are requested interactively by FOCUS:

```
TABLE FILE PERSONNEL
SUM SALARY
BY DEPARTMENT
ACROSS DIVISION
IF YEAR FROM 80 to 84
ON TABLE HOLD
END
ANALYZE FILE HOLD
ENTER STATISTICAL OPERATION DESIRED-
TIMESER
NUMBER OF OBSERVATIONS = 5
ENTER NAME OF TIME VARIABLE-
YEAR
ENTER TIME FOR 1 VARIABLE-
1 YEAR
ENTER COMMAND-
FIT
ENTER NAME OF VARIABLE-
SALARY
DO YOU WISH TO KEEP PREDICTED VALUES-
KEEP
HOW MANY PERIODS DO YOU WISH TO EXTRAPOLATE-
1
DO YOU WISH TO KEEP RESIDUALS-
```

```
NORESIDUALS
ENTER THE TYPE OF EQUATION YOU WISH TO FIT-
LIN
ENTER COMMAND
DISP
ENTER UP TO 4 VARIABLES TO DISPLAY
YEAR DIVISION DEPARTMENT SALARY
ENTER FIRST TIME PERIOD TO DISPLAY
80
ENTER LAST TIME PERIOD TO DISPLAY
85
```

These FOCUS statements will perform a linear time-series analysis on the salary data and display the results.

FOCUS also includes a set of additional language statement key words that, together with the basic FOCUS language, can be used to address the needs of financial planners who are working with balance sheets, budgets, spread sheets, etc. The extensions provided constitute the financial modeling language of FOCUS. Comparisons of financial data can be performed easily. In addition, "what-if" questions can be answered using the standard language primitives with the extensions for financial analysis.

CHAPTER 15

Distributed Data Base Systems: CICS/ISC, R*

There are few DBMS (data base management system) products that have implemented most distributed data base (DDB) capabilities. Some high-availability systems, such as the Tandem XMP distributed transaction processing system, have implemented some distributed functions but fall short of a complete DDB. An example of a DDB function that has not been implemented in many products is the networkwide data base synchronization process. This process maintains consistency of all the fragments of the distributed data base.

The Inter-System Communications (ISC) component of the IBM Customer Information Control System (CICS) is one of the few products that has implemented a DDB synchronization process, at least to a limited extent. The capabilities included in CICS/ISC are described in this chapter.

A more complete example of a distributed DBMS is System R* (R Star), which is a prototype system developed by IBM to study DDB concepts. R* is based on the IBM System R prototypical relational DBMS. CICS/ISC is used to handle the communications between the System R systems that are linked together in a distributed network. Since CICS/ISC is presented first in this chapter, the subsequent study of R* is simplified.

CICS/ISC

The IBM CICS is a teleprocessing monitor (TP monitor). The two basic functions of a TP monitor are terminal network management and transaction management.

When an end user at a terminal enters input to the system, CICS coordinates the communication between the terminal and the host. Once the input has been completely received, CICS schedules the appropriate application program to process the input message. Throughout the execution of the program, CICS maintains resource integrity by acquiring exclusive control of the resources used by the program. Upon successful completion of the transaction, CICS sends the output message to the original inputing terminal.

CICS also includes a potpourri of functions that can be used by a system designer to implement a DDB system. Since CICS is a TP monitor and not a DBMS, some other product is needed to implement the data base capabilities. DL/I, the DBM (data base manager) of IMS, is often used with CICS to form an integrated distributed DBMS. Other DBMS can also be used, such as DB2 from IBM, System/2000 from Intel, or Cullinane's IDMS, but only IMS is used as an example in this chapter.

The term *potpourri* was used to describe the DDB support offered in CICS. From a system designer's point of view, CICS provides a DDB lumber yard, from which can be built a DDB house to one's own liking. There are few intrinsic restrictions in the design possibilities, and CICS totally assumes that the application developer will choose the right lumber for the job. While this provides substantial flexibility in the design of distributed systems, it also places the burden for the integrity and concurrency decisions on the designer.

The set of functions in CICS provided to build distributed systems is called ISC. ISC is a product realization of a part of IBM's master communications architecture called SNA (systems network architecture). The portion of the architecture implemented in ISC is intended for general program-to-program communications. As such, heterogenous DDB systems can be built linking diverse hardware and software systems that have all agreed to follow the communications protocol described by SNA.

CICS provides two categories of distributed capabilities:

1. *DBMS function shipping*. IBM calls this capability simply **function shipping**, but DBMS function shipping more accurately relates the concept. A single request from an application program to the DBMS can be routed to another DBMS in the same node or another node in the network. ISC provides the routing and control as well as maintains network integrity of resources.

2. *Application function shipping*. IBM calls this function **distributed transaction processing** and it comes in two flavors, **synchronous** and **asynchronous**. An application program running under CICS A can invoke an application subroutine under CICS B on the same or another CPU. The subroutine may run within the same recovery scope as the mainline, in which case it is synchronous application function shipping, or the subroutine may run in its own recovery sphere independent of the mainline, in which case it is asynchronous application function shipping. The synchronous-asynchronous decision can be made by the application program or defined to CICS by the system programmer.

Function Shipping

DBMS function shipping in CICS is illustrated in Fig. 15.1. The processing proceeds as follows:

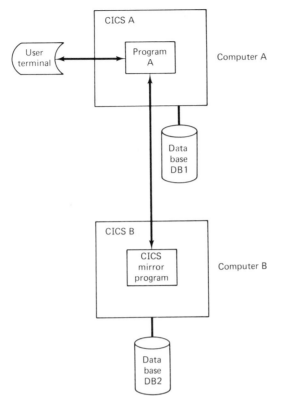

CICS A

User terminal

Program A

Computer A

Data base DB1

CICS B

CICS mirror program

Computer B

Data base DB2

Figure 15.1 CICS/ISC function shipping: Program A requests data from both CICS A and CICS B.

1. Program A (the program) is scheduled for execution by CICS A due to the transaction received from the terminal.

2. The program issues a call to DL/I (the IMS DBM) to access data located in data base 1 (DB1). Since DB1 is owned by CICS A, CICS A passes the call directly to DL/I. The call is handled locally.

3. The program then issues a call to DL/I for data located in data base 2 (DB2). Since DB2 is owned by CICS B, CICS A passes the call to CICS B for processing. If both CICS A and B reside on the same CPU, then a memory-to-memory communications path may be used. Otherwise, for the cases where the two CICS systems are on different CPU in the same location or geographically separated, a communications link of some sort is used by CICS/ISC to send the request.

4. CICS B receives the request and passes it to DL/I.

5. The response from DL/I is returned to the program via CICS B and CICS A.

6. When the program completes the processing of the transaction input, CICS A attempts to commit the data base and other changes made by the program. In doing so, if changes were made in the DL/I calls sent to CICS B, CICS B is contacted to commit its resource changes in unison with CICS A. Both CICS

systems must agree to commit or not commit; otherwise data base integrity may be lost. The two-phase commit process, described in Chapter 10, is used for synchronization in CICS/ISC.

7. CICS A sends the output message to the originating terminal.

Notice that the application program was unaware of the location and ownership of any given data base that it wished to access. CICS was the point at which the site resolution question was answered using tables built and maintained by the CICS system programmer. **Site transparency** is the term used to describe a DDB where the transaction manager (CICS) or the data base manager (DL/I) solely makes the site resolution determination. Because the application program never knows where a data base resides in the network, site transparency offers the advantage of simplified application development and elimination of the need to change the application program when distribution characteristics change. Distribution characteristics are actually data base characteristics, and therefore DL/I (the data base manager) and not CICS (the transaction manager) should perform site resolution. This anomaly is due primarily to organizational issues within the IBM company as opposed to technical design decisions.

A potential performance slowdown in the execution of the application program may occur each time a data base call is issued that requires network access to another CICS system. The elapsed-time cost of the transmission of the request and reception of the response may easily be an order of magnitude or more than the cost of the I/O (input/output) to the data base itself. If several *remote* data base calls are issued by the application program, the performance issue becomes more acute. This concern is usually alleviated by limiting the number of transaction occurrences that perform remote data base access or by sending an intermediate response to the original terminal user indicating that the final response may be delayed.

A basic requirement of a DDB system and certainly a strength of the CICS/ISC design is the use of a single recovery scope. All data bases updated, both local and remote, by a single transaction are all in the same recovery scope. In other words, CICS ensures that the other CICS systems involved in the processing of the program's data base calls coordinate their updates to the data base in concert and that if one or more CICS systems are unable to coordinate their calls, then none of the others will either.

Distributed Transaction Processing

A serious limitation of DBMS function shipping occurs when many data base calls are sent to another site for processing (remote calls). CICS/ISC offers a solution to this limitation if large subsets of the remote calls will all be processed on the same remote CICS system. This CICS/ISC capability is called **user function shipping** or, in CICS terms, **distributed transaction processing** and is illustrated in Fig. 15.2.

When the application program calls the subroutine, CICS needs to know if the subroutine will be considered part of the originating program or not. If both the originating application program and the subroutine are considered to be in the

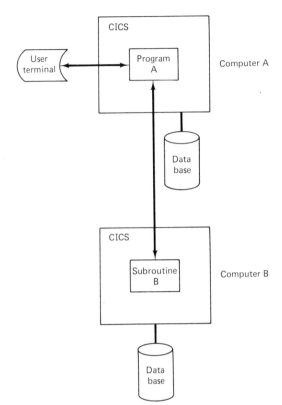

CICS

User
terminal

Program
A

Computer A

Data
base

CICS

Subroutine
B

Computer B

Data
base

Figure 15.2   CICS/ISC distributed
transaction processing: Essentially, this
is user function shipping.

same recovery scope, then this scenario is called **synchronous** transaction processing; both the program and the subroutine are in the same time domain. Otherwise,
if the subroutine and the program proceed on their own without regard for the other
data base updates, the scenario is called **asynchronous** transaction processing; the
time domains exist with no intersection between them.

R*

In the 1970s, IBM developed a prototype DBMS, called **System R,** based on the
relational model of data. Subsequently, IBM productized the System R software,
creating SQL/DS and DB2. Research continued at IBM on the possibility of ex-
panding the System R DBMS to give it distributed data base capabilities. The prototype resulting from the distributed data base research is R*, which will, quite
likely, form a basis for a distributed relational DBMS.

The architecture of R* is based on bringing together three separate components. A copy of System R resides at each location that is to participate in the
distribution. Communications among the sites is provided by CICS/ISC. A third
component, the transaction manager, coordinates the execution of multisite transactions. This overall design of R* is shown in Fig. 15.3.

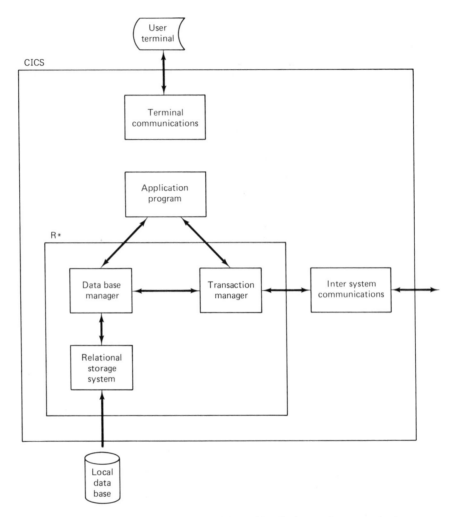

Figure 15.3 R* architecture. CICS/ISC provides the internode communications, a two-phase commit protocol.

R* emphasizes site autonomy wherein full control of extra-site data access is implemented and manipulation of local data does not require interaction with any other site. R* also stresses transparent site resolution, from the programmer's perspective. This requires extensions and restrictions to entity naming. R* does not support replication or data base partitioning.

An application program, executing in an R* environment, issues all requests for data to the local copy of R*. The R* DBM performs the site resolution function and either accesses the local data base or routes the data request to the R* site where the data resides. The transaction manager at the local site coordinates the operation of the other R* sites called upon to satisfy local application program data requests.

R* exemplifies the definition of a distributed data base defined in a previous chapter. Since CICS/ISC is used for intersite communication, no restrictions are placed on the physical location of each copy of R*. Several copies of R* may reside on the same computer, on different computers at the same data center, or on geographically dispersed computers. Two different copies of R* on the same machine are as much a distributed system as two different machines geographically dispersed. Multiple data managers are involved in each case.

Application programs can delineate the bounds of a single recovery scope. The set of data updates, both local and remote, within a single recovery scope is considered atomic. When the application program indicates to R* that the transaction has ended (i.e., the end of the recovery scope), R* performs a networkwide commit of related data updates. Two-phase commit is implemented using the protocols implemented in CICS/ISC. Either all the updates are performed or none of them are, thereby ensuring networkwide data integrity.

CHAPTER 16

dBASE II: A DBMS by Ashton-Tate for Microprocessors

Data base in the microworld shares many similarities with data base on larger processors. More instructive than the similarities, however, are the differences.

DIFFERENCES

Perhaps the most profound difference between the two types of DBMS (data base management systems) is that entire data bases are loaded into the main memory of the microprocessor and are operated on there, as seen in Fig. 16.1. The figure shows that when the user opens a data base, the data base is loaded into main memory. When the user closes the data base, the data base is rewritten to disk storage. Changes made to the data base are reflected in the rewrite.

Such a one-time transfer of data base to and from the main memory of the microprocessor (a load to/load from process) greatly simplifies many common data base activities, such as recovery procedures, back-out, sync point processing, and so forth. At the same time, the simplification causes some concomitant limitations, the most obvious of which is a limitation of the size of the data base. The following are some of the limitations of a simple load to/load from approach:

- *Data base size.* Main memory is only finitely large. Any data space requirements beyond what can be placed in available storage must be placed in another data base. When placed in another data base, there is a problem with concurrent access.
- *Auxiliary main memory usages.* These usages are indexes, working areas, pro-

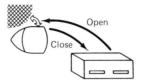

Open

Close

Figure 16.1

gram load space, and so forth. Main memory limitations can become a great constraint.

- *Back-up, recovery limitations.* While micro-DBMS offer some facilities for back-up and recovery, the facilities are crude compared to large-scale DBMS.
- *Shareability of data.* Once data is in main memory, it is under the control of the main user. While this control is very pleasing to the main user, it means that data cannot be shared with other users at the same time. If there is no desire to update the data base, then multiple copies of the data can be proliferated with impunity.

In addition to simplicity (which in a complex environment is its own virtue), there are some major advantages to the single load to/load from approach:

- *No contention for system resources from other users.* It goes without saying that if there is only one user, then there is no interference from other users. If there is a performance problem, it stems directly from the person using the microprocessor.
- *Limited need for DBMS overhead.* Given the limitation on the amount and type of data found in a microdata base, one offsetting advantage is the minimal need for standard DBMS structural overhead, as is typical with large-scale DBMS. For example if there is prefix data associated with a record, there is minimal information in the prefix.
- *Quick access.* Having the data base in main storage allows the end user as quick access as is possible.

There is no need to worry about some of the typical I/O concerns found in large-scale DBMS. By the same token, there is no need for the buffering of data going to and from main storage and DASD.

So the simplicity of a load to/load from approach results in a relatively clean approach to data base. Other differences in micro-DBMS are at a higher level. In general, micro-DBMS have a greater emphasis on the usability of systems rather than the infrastructure required by large-scale DBMS for such functions as online data integrity, data base recovery, etc. The emphasis on micro-DBMS usability can be referred to as an emphasis on the "front end," because the usability features are very apparent to the end user. The emphasis on a supporting infrastructure typical of large-scale DBMS is an emphasis on the "back end," since the end user is usually unaware of the background activity that is occurring.

Some typical front-end functions of micro DBMS that are not particularly popular or apparent with large-scale DBMS are report writers, screen control, browse facilities, and powerful data manipulation commands. Some of the back-end capabilities that are typical of large-scale DBMS are online sharing of data, a low level of data integrity, and the ability to handle large amounts of data.

Another basic difference between the two types of DBMS lies in the data definition language and its control. In a large-scale DBMS, the end user probably never sees the data definition language, whereas in the micro-DBMS environment, the data definition is available to all who use it.

SIMILARITIES

While there are unquestionably many differences between the two types of DBMS, there are even more similarities. Some of the similarities will be illustrated in terms of dBASE II, a software product by Ashton-Tate.

dBASE II has two file organizations, sequential and random. Sequential files contain either fixed-length or variable-length records. Records are divided into fields. dBASE II does not support variable fields. Random files must be specified with fixed record lengths. There are two types of keys in a dBASE II data base, **primary** and **secondary.** The primary key is unique, while the secondary key may be unique or nonunique. There is only one primary key. There may be zero or more secondary keys.

Field names can be up to 10 characters. There are three types of fields, **character, numeric,** or **logical.** Logical fields contain an indicator of either yes or no. Interestingly, data management in dBASE II, at the simplest level, is on a par with large-scale DBMS both in terms of function done and in terms of the way the function is achieved.

USING dBASE II

As an example of using dBASE II, consider the following simple example involving a personnel file. Five fields make up a record, employee number, name, address, age, and sex. The first step is to define the structure. To do that, enter

CREATE PERSONL

dBASE II will return and prompt with

FIELD NAME,TYPE,WIDTH,DECIMALPLACES

Now enter-

```
001 EMPL    C 007
002 NAME    C 035
003 ADDR    C 035
004 AGE     N 003
005 SEX     C 001
```

This data definition has described five fields, employee number, name, address, age, and sex. All are character fields except age. Age can accommodate people over 100 years old. Thirty-five bytes are provided for name and address. One byte is provided for sex.

After the data base definition has been described to dBASE II, the data base needs to be indexed. To index the data base the following is entered:

```
USE PERSONL
INDEX ON EMPNO TO PERSONL
```

This command provides an indexing capability to the employee number field of the personnel data base. Now enter 50 or so entries in the data base, for the purpose of creating a data base to be used for display and update. The entry can be done by means of the APPEND command. Enter

```
USE PERSONL
APPEND
```

After the records are added, list them. Enter

```
USE PERSONL
LIST ALL
```

Now find the first record for a female (i.e., where SEX=F). Enter

```
ENTER LOCATE FOR SEX=F
```

This simple demonstration has shown several basic uses of dBASE II. In fact, dBASE II has several levels of sophistication—only the most basic has been shown. The most basic level is the one that is the most user-friendly. To use dBASE II at the user-friendly level requires very little training. However, dBASE II has an entirely different level of complexity, where it is possible to program screens and transactions.

SECTION III

DATA BASE TUTORIAL

"The Americans have need of the telephone, but we do not. We have plenty of messenger boys."

Sir William Preece
Chief Engineer of the British Post Office (1876)

CHAPTER 17

Tutorial Description

THE PRODUCTION CONTROL/SHIPPING INTERFACE PROBLEM*

The Terrific Trailer Company manufactures many different kinds of trailers, which require a wide variety of different parts. The different lines of trailers that Terrific carries are designed for small cars, large cars, vans, trucks, jeeps, and campers. Some trailers are single axle and some are double axle. Some are open air and some are closed. Some carry only 500 pounds and some can carry up to a ton.

Terrific sells retail to individuals and wholesale to rental companies. In addition, the Army and Marines have contracts for large numbers of trailers. Although most of the trailers are for the United States and Canada, a growing percentage are for foreign consumption. While there are many similarities between domestic and foreign trailers, there are a few essential differences, such as tail-light coloring, wiring voltage, license plate positioning, and so forth.

The engineering that Terrific requires is complex. The basic trailer design is constantly changing due to marketing pressure, military contract pressure, and so

(*Note: This is a fictional problem. There is no intended attempt to portray a real company, even though the data processing problems portrayed are very realistic.

Chapter 17 is a definition of the problem. The problem is presented so that it can be solved in many different forms—in IMS, Model 204, SQL, and FOCUS in particular. It is intended that in the tutorial following the statement of the problem, the reader refer to both this book and the manuals listed as references for each chapter. There are many details about the languages, which are necessary to complete the tutorial, that are not in this book. The reader needs to become acquainted with the reference manuals as part of the mastery of the subject of data base.)

on. To keep track of these changes, Terrific decides to build an automated bill of material and other related systems. The other systems include engineering changes, purchase orders, and shipments. Because of the size of the job to be done, Terrific undergoes a conceptual design in an effort to produce a blueprint for which a data base architecture can be built. Figure 17.1 shows the ERD (entity relationship diagram) that is a byproduct of the conceptual design effort. In the ERD it is seen that the part number has a recursive relationship with itself to satisfy the needs of the bill-of-materials processing (both up and down the structure and engineering changes). Three recursive relationships are identified, the substitute part relationship, the assembly to subassembly (the "from") relationship, and the subassembly to assembly (the "into") relationship.

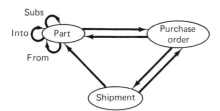

Figure 17.1

There is a dual relationship between purchase order (po) and part. For any part, it is necessary to see what po exists for it. For any po it is necessary to see what parts are ordered. There is a singular relationship between part and shipment. For any shipment it is necessary to see what part it contains.

There is a third relationship—a dual one—between po and shipment. For any po it is necessary to determine what shipments were made to satisfy that order. For any shipment it is necessary to determine what po are being satisfied.

The next phase of conceptual design is the expansion of the ERD into a more detailed data model. Figure 17.2 shows the entities as they have been expanded. The different fields are shown in the figure. The keys of each of the groupings of data are underlined. The attributes that belong to the groupings of data are immediately beneath the keys. Where data is required for the formation of a relationship, a line is drawn from the grouping to the data that will be used to make the connection.

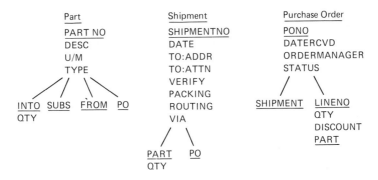

Figure 17.2

For example, there is a line from the grouping of order number data to shipment. That connection is used to connect any given po to a shipment. All that exists in the shipment connection is the key of the shipment to which the po is pointing. Since the connection is made by means of keys, the field shipment is underlined.

Note that the conceptual design at this point (and indeed up to the point of physical design) does not imply any particular DBMS. The design can be implemented by IMS, Model 204, SQL, or FOCUS (or a host of other DBMS not covered in this book).

The third phase of conceptual design now commences, using the structure found in Fig. 17.2. At this point the physical lengths of the fields are determined, the existence criteria are established, the alternate access paths are determined, the frequency of occurrence of the data is outlined, and so forth. One of the most important parts of this phase is the foundation laid for future designs. One of the primary considerations is the key structure. Will the key structure adopted fit all the foreseeable requirements or will there be limitations? The key structure should fit both current and future requirements. Another consideration is the field existence requirement. Do the fields that exist in the design fit only immediate requirements or both immediate and future requirements?

The third major criterion is the satisfaction of access paths. Again the consideration is whether only current or both current and future access paths are satisfied.

In the example shown it is assumed that all of these requirements have been taken into consideration. However in a nontextbook case, it is entirely likely that many relationships and entities are missing, such as supplier, inventory, and so forth.

Figure 17.3 shows the different fields with their physical characteristics. For example PARTNO is 19 bytes long and is not variable in length. It is a key. If the entity exists at all, it is mandatory that the field be present. It is not used as an alternate access path (since, of course it is used for primary access).

The next field, description (DESC), is variable in length, up to 25 bytes in length. It is not a key and may or may not exist if the entity exists. It is not used for alternate access.

The field U/M, or unit of measure, is two bytes in length, is not a key, is optional, and is used for alternate access if it does exist. The field SUBS (or substitute part) is 19 bytes in length, is used to form a recursive relationship, and may or may not exist. The field INTO is like SUBS except that when it exists, it has a field, QTY, which must exist.

The remaining fields are likewise defined. Figure 17.4 shows related data definition information that must be satisfied.

FUNCTIONS

The processes that are accomplished by the system are

- The initial loading of data: part, shipment, po data bases
- Insertion of data by individual transaction: part, shipment, po data bases

	(var) Length	Key	Existence	Alternate Access	Multiple Occurrences
Part					
PARTNO	char(19)	Yes	Mandatory	—	N/A
DESC	max char(25)	—	Optional	—	No
U/M	char(2)	—	Optional	Yes	Yes
TYPE	char(1)	—	Optional	—	Yes
SUBS	char(19)	Yes	Optional	—	N/A
INTO	char(19)	Yes	Optional	—	N/A
QTY	bin fixed(31,0)	—	Mandatory	—	No
FROM	char(19)	Yes	Optional	—	N/A
PO	char(15)	Yes	Optional	—	N/A
Shipment					
SHIPMENTNO	char(25)	Yes	Mandatory	—	N/A
DATE	char(6)	—	Optional	Yes	No
TO:ADDR	max char(75)	—	Optional	—	No
TO:ATTN	max char(25)	—	Optional	—	No
VERIFY	char(3)	—	Optional	—	Yes
PACKING	max char(15)	—	Optional	—	No
ROUTING	max char(80)	—	Optional	—	No
VIA	char(3)	—	Optional	—	Yes
PART	char(19)	Yes	Optional	—	N/A
QTY	bin fixed(31,0)	—	Mandatory	—	No
PO	char(15)	Yes	Optional	—	N/A
Purchase Order					
PONO	char(15)	Yes	Mandatory	—	N/A
DATERCVD	char(6)	—	Optional	Yes	No
ORDERMANAGER	max char(25)	—	Optional	Yes	No
STATUS	char(1)	—	Optional	—	No
SHIPMENT	char(25)	Yes	Optional	—	N/A
LINENO	bin fixed(15,0)	Yes	Mandatory	—	N/A
QTY	bin fixed(15,0)	—	Mandatory	—	No
DISCOUNT	bin fixed(15,2)	—	Optional	—	No
PART	char(19)	Yes	Mandatory	—	No

Figure 17.3 Physical characteristics of the data.

- Deletion of data by individual transaction: part, shipment, po data bases
- Update of data by individual transaction: part, shipment, po data bases
- Archival sweep of data based on dates
- Alternate acces of data: part, shipment, po data bases
- Bill of material explosion of data
- Data base reporting—part, shipment, po data bases

The satisfaction of the function for the Terrific Trailer Company can be classified into six sections:

1. The initial load of data
2. Data insertion by individual transaction

Part
  25,000 occurrences initially
  5000 occurrences: annual growth
  1.5 updates per record per month
  Primary key: partno
  Alternate key: U/M
  Overnight batch processing: 2 hours
  Uptime: 6:00 A.M. to 5:30 P.M.
  Peak period: 10:30 A.M. to 11:30 A.M., 1:30 P.M. to 3:30 P.M.
  Servicing: foreign, retail, military, fleet
  Responsibility: engineering, production control

Purchase Order
  5000 occurrences initially
  500 inserts per month
  475 deletes per month
  10.63 updates per record per month
  Primary key: shipment number
  Alternate key: date received, order manager
  Overnight batch processing: 30 minutes
  End-of-month batch processing: 3 days
  Uptime: 8:00 A.M. to 4:00 P.M.
  Peak period: none
  Responsibility: cost accounting

Shipment
  750 occurrences initially
  25 inserts monthly
  Periodic archiving of data
  2.6 updates per record per month
  Primary key: shipment number
  Alternate key: date
  Overnight batch processing: archival sweep
  Uptime: 8:00 A.M. to 4:00 P.M.
  Peak period: none   **Figure 17.4**   Additional data
  Responsibility: shipping docks, cost accounting   characteristics.

3. Data manipulation (update, deletion) by individual transaction
4. Reports
5. Data integrity verification
6. Archival activity

INITIAL LOAD

The data that is to be loaded into the data base initially is shown in Fig. 17.5. In this figure the data that is to be loaded into the data base is shown. Note that no relationships are built at this point. For an explanation of what data should be loaded, consider the first shipment occurrence, KJY-432-61. The key must be loaded as well as the address, contact, and routing instructions. Note that no data, verification, or via data is loaded.

Now consider shipment key LJF-14VHL. The key is loaded as well as packing and routing instructions. Three occurrences of via data are loaded and all remaining fields are blank.

After the data bases are loaded, a snapshot, or image copy of the data bases, is taken. The name of the snapshot of the data is DBSNAP1. Should it be desired

Shipment No	Date	To:addr	To:attn	Verify	Packing	Routing	Via
KJY-432-61	—	4th and Main, Boulder, CO	Ms. Taylor	—	cbox#4	DVRORDJFK	—
SM-231-58	—	1211 First, Tyler, TX	Mr. Chassing	—	stfoam	DVRELPSFO	—
WHI-5856	831215	4th and Main, Boulder, CO	—	std,frj,tr	cbox#4	DVRELP(wcall)	—
TJB-596-RS	831229	4th and Main, Boulder, CO	Jim Wallace	std,frj	—	DVRORDNWK	—
LJF-14VHL	—	—	—	—	wcare	DVRLAX	wc1,JN,emf
GA1-8913dirk	840311	—	Scott Henderson	std	—	ORD(call-msg3431)	—
JFOS-10425med	840307	1211 First, Tyler, TX	Margot Fulmer	std,tr	cbox#4	DVRLAX	wc1,JN,emf
RSACKS-614mV	—	—	—	—	stfoam	DVRATL	—

Purchase Order	Date Received	Order Manager	Status
000156001	830109	Max Hopper	o
000094311	831215	Lance Myers	c
000156002	831213	Pete Hill	o
000094400			o
000156101		Wino Geleen	o
0156102-1A	840315	Max Hopper	c
000156102-1A-1	840316		c
00111		Max Hopper	o
156-A2	840406	Max Hopper	o
000156101-1A		Max Hopper	o
000156110-2AB		Max Hopper	o
000156110-2AC	840419		o
00011		Dave Vincent	o
00011-1A	840419	Pete Hill	c
00011-1B		Paul Dobbins	o
00011-1C	840419	Max Hopper	o

Part Number	Description	U/M	Type
AK137	Screw	—	r,u,c,s
AZT10	Plate	lb,pp	f,c
JM431	Manifold driver	pp,lb	—
JN431	Manifold frame	pp,lb	r,u
KK003	Nut	—	f,s,t,u,j,l
KK004	Bolt	—	f,s
KR132T	—	pp,fr	f,u
KS1	—	pp	f
LM431	Differential deterrent	lb	r,u
In6316	—	—	—

Figure 17.5 Initially loaded data.

to restore the data base to this initial form, the snapshot can be used to load the data bases.

DATA INSERTION

The next step is to insert data into each of the data bases. Insertion should be done by individual transactions. The data to be inserted is as follows.

Shipment Insertions

```
DATE=840612 for key SM-231-58
TO:ADDR=1 Easy Street, Steamboat Spgs, Co for
key GAI-8913dirk
TO:CONTACT=Cheryl Estep for key JFOS-10425med
VERIFY=tr for key GAI-8913dirk
VERIFY=std for key KJY-432-61
PACKING=wcrate for key GAI-8913dirk
VIA=wcl for key JFOS-10425med
SHIPMENTNO=000156103 for a new record
```

Shipment Insertions (Relationships)

Next the relationships between shipment and parts are to be established. The values to be loaded are shown by the table in Fig. 17.6. After the relationships between shipment and part are established, the relationships between shipment and po are established. The data values are shown by the table in Fig. 17.7.

The transactions that insert part numbers are executed next. The part data to be inserted is as follows.

Part Insertions

```
DESC=tongue plate for key KS1
U/M=lb for key AK137
```

Shipment	Part	Quantity
WHI-5856	AK137	600
WHI-5856	KS1	2
WHI-5856	LM431	4
WHI-5856	KK003	36
WHI-5856	KK004	38
TJB-596-RS	LM431	6
TJB-596-RS	AK137	95
TJB-596-RS	KS1	1
GAI-8913dirk	AK137	10
JFOS-10425med	AK137	10
JFOS-10425med	LN6316	2000
JFOS-10425med	KK003	36
JFOS-10425med	KK004	40

Figure 17.6 Shipment/part data.

Shipment	PO
KJY-432-61	156-A2
SM-231-58	00011
WHI-5856	00011-1A
WHI-5856	00011-1B
LJF-14VHL	000156102-1A
GAI-8913dirk	000156101
GAI-8913dirk	000156102-1A
GAI-8913dirk	000156102-1A-1
GAI-8913dirk	000156101-1A
JFOS-10425med	000094311
RSACKS-614mv	00011-1C

Figure 17.7 Shipment/purchase order data.

```
U/M=fr for key AZT10
TYPE=f for key KR132T
TYPE=f for key LN6316
PARTNO=YAT17nygiant for a new record
```

Part Insertions (Relationships)

Next the part number/substitute part relationship is established. The following shows the values for that relationship:

```
PARTNO=KK003, SUBSTITUTE PART=KK004
```

The bill of materials data is now loaded. The values of the FROM and the INTO relationships are shown in the table in Fig. 17.8. The part/po relationship is next established. The table in Fig. 17.9 is used to build that relationship.

Part	Part	Part	Part	Quantity
KS1	LM431	JM431	LN6316	3
KS1	AK137	JN431	LN6316	15
KS1	KR132T	LN6316	KR132T	3
LM431	KK003	AZT10	KR132T	25
AK137	KK004	KK004	AK137	15
JM431	LN6316	KK003	LM431	10
JM431	AZT10	LM431	KS1	2
LN6316	JM431	AK137	KS1	10
LN6316	JN431	KR132T	KS1	3

FROM data		INTO data	

Figure 17.8

Part	PO
AK137	00011
AK137	000156101
AK137	156-A2
AK137	000156001
KS1	000094400
KS1	000156002
KS1	000094311

Figure 17.9 The part/purchase order data.

The purchase order data is the next to be inserted by individual transactions. The values to be inserted are as follows:

Po Insertions

```
DATERCVD=830720 for key 000156101
ORDERMANAGER=Tom Work for 000094400
PONO=000156118-1A for a new record
```

Po Insertions (Relationships)

The po/shipment relationship is now created by using the data found in the table in Fig. 17.10. The final insertion activity requires that the po/line item relationship be completed. The values in the table found in Fig. 17.11 are used to complete the relationship. Now that the insert transactions have been executed, another snapshot of the data base needs to be taken. The snapshot should be called DBSNAP2.

PO	Shipment
156-A2	KJY-432-61
00011	SM-231-58
00011-1A	WHI-5856
00011-1B	WHI-5856
000156102-1A	LJF-14VHL
000156101	GAI-8913dirk
000156102-1A	GAI-8913dirk
000156102-1A-1	GAI-8913dirk
000156101-1A	GAI-8913dirk
000094311	JFOS-10425med
00011-1C	RSACKS-614mv

Figure 17.10 Purchase order/shipment data.

PO	Line Number	Quantity	Discount	Partno
00011	1	2000	——	AK137
000156101	1	655	10%	AK137
156-A2	1	32	5%	AK137
000156001	1	1	——	AK137
000094400	1	2500	——	KS1
000156002	1	4	2.5%	KS1
000094311	1	250	——	KS1

Figure 17.11 Purchase order/line item data.

DATA MANIPULATION

Other activities than insertion are to be executed next. Individual transactions should be executed for the following.

Part Data Base

Change the DESC of AK137 from screw to baseplate.
Change the U/M of KS1 from pp to pq.
Change the TYPE of LM43 from f to u.

Po Data Base

Change the DATERCVD of 156-A2 from 840406 to 840621.

Change the ORDERMANAGER of 00011 from Max Hopper to Pete Hill.

Change the STATUS of 00011 from 0 to c.

Shipment Data Base

Change the DATE of WHI-5856 from 831215 to 840625.

Change the TO:ADDR of KJY-432-61 from 4th & Main, Boulder, CO, to 1211 First, Tyler, TX.

Change the TO:ATTN of RSACKS-614mv from Margot Fulmer to Rose Scearcy.

Change the VERIFY of WHI-5856 from std to jer.

Change the PACKING of JFOS-10425med from cbox#4 to stfoam.

Change the ROUTING of LJF-14VHL from JN to KF.

Delete Activity

Part Data Base

Delete part number KK004. Ensure that all relationships with which KK004 participates are also deleted.

Delete U/M for AZT10 where U/M = pp.

Delete TYPE = F for AZT10.

Delete all U/M for KS1.

Delete all TYPEs for KK003.

PO Data Base

Delete PO = 000156110-2AC. Ensure that all relationships with which 000156110-2AC participates are also deleted.

Delete LINENO = 1 for PO = 00011. Make sure that all corresponding relationships are deleted.

Delete shipment number KJY-432-61 for po = 156-A2. Make sure that all corresponding relationships are deleted.

Shipment Data Base

Delete shipment LJF-14VHL. Ensure that all relationships in which LJF-14VHL participates are also deleted.

Delete po 00011 from shipment SM-231-58. Ensure that all corresponding relationships are deleted.

Delete PART=KS1 for shipment WHI-5856. Ensure that all corresponding relationships are deleted.

Take a snapshot of the data and call it DBSNAP3.

Reset the data base to the status as of DBSNAP2.

REPORTS

Create a report that builds a bill-of-materials explosion of the structure. Begin the explosion at part KS1.

Create a report that shows into what part each part goes (an implosion of the bill of materials).

Create a report that shows all purchase orders and all po order data.

Create a report that displays all shipments with all shipment data.

Create a report that shows shipments that have parts, and show the part and quantity.

Create a report that shows shipments that have po. Show the po.

Create a report that takes as input a data parameter YYMMDD, and list all po greater than or equal to that date.

Create a report that accepts as input a routing order and then reports which shipments are to be routed that way.

Create a report that lists parts by order of U/M.

Create a report that lists shipments in order of date.

DATA INTEGRITY

Build a program that checks the integrity of the various data relationships. For example, when a po exists beneath part, does a corresponding po exist in the po data base, and, if it does, is there a reverse pointer to the part data base? Verify the following relationships:

Part/po
Part/substitute part
Part/into
Part/from
Shipment/part
Shipment/po
Po/shipment
Shipment/part

Build a program that verifies that all mandatory fields in fact are present. The mandatory fields are

QTY of into of part data base

QTY of part of shipment data base

STATUS of po data base

QTY of line number of po data base

ARCHIVAL DATA

Write a program that accepts a date and deletes all po with a DATERCVD earlier than the date. Store the deleted po on an archival file. Make sure that all relationships remain valid.

Write a similar program for the date of shipments.

CHAPTER 18

IMS Tutorial

The purpose of the tutorial is to give the reader hands-on experience in the design, development, and implementation of a realistic data base system. To this end the tutorial guides the reader, step by step, through the different activities required in the development process. It is necessary to have access to manuals to determine specific formats and parameters. The tutorial leads the reader through the different activities in the proper order; it is up to the reader actually to execute the activities. Ultimately, the real learning process comes through doing activities and experiencing the successes and failures that ensue.

In the case of this chapter it is necessary to have access to the IMS environment to execute the tutorial. There are five general activities that must be executed to translate the tutorial problem from a conceptual design into an actual executing system. The activities are *environmental definition, transaction (or process) definition, data base definition, system coding,* and *system integration and implementation.*

ENVIRONMENTAL DEFINITION

Before any activity can begin in IMS it is necessary to prepare the online environment for the system. This normally includes data base identification, transaction identification, and security identification to what is known as the **IMS gen** (IMS generation, or the direct specification of control blocks to IMS that allow it to run). It may also include network specification if new terminals are to be added or if the existing system is to interact with existing terminals in any way other than normal system operation. (For example if certain terminals are going to be restricted in the usage of the system being defined, this must be specified.) For the purposes of the tutorial, it is assumed that no new terminals are being added or that there is nothing specified other than normal system operation as far as the tutorial is concerned.

The first environmental issue to be decided is whether the tutorial is to be run on the test or production system. The answer here is clear; the test system must be used. IMS online production is a sensitive environment and new systems (especially tutorials!) are not appropriate for the production environment. Only systems that are fully tested are appropriate for production.

The second environmental decision is whether to run the tutorial in IMS full function, IMS Fast Path, or mixed mode. Although either environment (Fast Path or full function) can be chosen, since the tutorial (were it to be a full-fledged production system) is neither for high-volume transaction processing nor for a large amount of data, the choice will be IMS full function.

DATA BASE IDENTIFICATION

The data bases are easy to identify in this case. There will be a parts data base, a shipments data base, and a purchase order data base. At this point, all that is required for the IMS gen is a naming of the data base. The names *parts, shipment,* and *po* are selected. These names will be the names associated with the DBDGEN.

The identification of transactions is not as straightforward as the identification of data bases. A fundamental decision must be made. The individual activities—insertion, deletion, and update—can be accomplished by a single transaction, a transaction that accomplishes all the function for a single data base, or separate transactions for each function for each data base.

If a single transaction is chosen to do all the work, the result is inevitably a very large transaction, not unlike a batch program that sequentially passes tapes. Such a large transaction is a candidate for violation of the standard work unit, so that approach is discarded.

The approach of defining a single separate transaction for each function to be done to each data base certainly does not violate the standard work unit, but it requires many transactions to be defined to the IMS gen and requires much programmer activity. A happy middle ground is the approach of a single transaction for all the function that will be required for a data base. (As an example, the parts data base has a single online transaction that inserts new records and fields, deletes records and fields, and modifies fields within a record.) The data base modification transactions will be PARTTX, SHIPTX, POTX.

Next the batch work must be defined. There are several types of batch work, reports, archival activity, and system integrity. The major question here is whether the batch activity will be in pure batch or BMP (batch message processing). When a job is run in pure batch, the data base must be removed from the online environment (and hence is unavailable for online access); it is then available for IMS batch processing. This removal may be done directly by the master terminal operator (MTO) or may come as a by product of the online system shutting down overnight. If the activity is to be run as a BMP, it can run while the online environment is up and active but under a few restrictions. The first restriction is that many BMP are not normally run at the same time and that each BMP is check-pointed to make optimal use of online resources. For the sake of the tutorial, the reports that must be run are run as BMP, and the archival and integrity activity are run in pure batch. For this purpose, then, 15 BMP are defined to the IMS gen. The BMP are named RPT1, RPT2, . . . RPT15. They will be used, as needed, for the different reports to be run.

Now the environmental decisions have been made. The IMS gen is ready to be prepared for the tutorial. To summarize, the components defined to the IMS gen are

Data bases: PARTS, SHIPMENT, PO
Transactions: PARTX, SHIPTX, POTX
BMP: RPT1, RPT2, . . . , RPT15

DATA BASE DEFINITION

After the environment is prepared, the data bases must be prepared. (*Note:* This activity may be done concurrently with transaction definition.) Although it is clear that there need to be three data bases, the exact formatting of the data bases is not clear. The data base design decisions are best determined by referring to Fig. 17.3.

From the conceptual design, the contents of the segments are laid out, as shown in Fig. 18.1. This layout makes several assumptions—that the largest value possible will be taken for certain fields, such as DESC (belonging to part), TO:ADDR and TO:ATTN (belonging to shipment), and so forth. Another assumption is that variably occurring fields will be stored as arrays internal to the segment. For example, U/M (belonging to part) can have up to 10 occurrences. (The design will have difficulties if ever there are more than the maximum number of occurrences allowed for by the design.) The result of these design decisions is that the segments defined to IMS are fixed length. IMS data management in full function usually performs better with fixed-length segments.

Another design decision that has been made is in the determination of the relationships between data bases (e.g., the part/po relationship). There are three basic choices: to build an IMS logical relationship with direct pointers, to build an IMS logical relationship with symbolic pointers, or to let the application programmer build and maintain the relationships using data contained within the data bases to make the connection. The design option that has been chosen is to let the programmer build the relationship. The next major data base decision to be made is what access method should be chosen. There are two types of choices here, between ISAM-OSAM and VSAM, and between HDAM and HIDAM. The parts data base is selected to be HDAM/OSAM and the other two data bases are HIDAM VSAM.

Finally the alternate access paths need to be satisfied. There are at least two ways to satisfy alternate accessing of data, through a secondary index or through a data base scan, strip, and sort. For the purposes of the tutorial, the part data base

Part Segment

PARTNO*	char(19)
DESC	char(25)
U/M(10)	char(20)
TYPE(20)	char(20)
	84 bytes

Part/Subs Segment

SUBS*	char(19)
	19 bytes

Part/Into Segment

INTO*	char(19)
QTY	bin fixed(31,0)
	23 bytes

Part/From Segment

FROM*	char(19)
	19 bytes

Part/PO Segment

PO*	char(15)
	15 bytes

PO Segment

PONO*	char(15)
DATERCVD	char(6)
ORDERMANAGER	char(25)
STATUS	char(1)
	47 bytes

PO/Shipment Segment

SHIPMENT	char(25)
	25 bytes

PO/Lineno Segment

LINENO	bin fixed(15,0)
QTY	bin fixed(15,0)
DISCOUNT	bin fixed(15,2)
PART	char(19)
	25 bytes

Shipment Segment

SHIPMENTNO*	char(25)
DATE	char(6)
TO:ADDR	char(75)
TO:ATTN	char(25)
VERIFY(10)	char(30)
PACKING	char(15)
ROUTING	char(80)
VIA(20)	char(60)
	316 bytes

Shipment/Part Segment

PART*	char(19)
QTY	bin fixed(31,0)
	23 bytes

Shipment/PO Segment

PO*	char(15)
	15 bytes

Figure 18.1

will have an index on U/M and the shipment data base will have one on DATE. The alternate access requirements for the po data base will be met by strip and sort techniques.

Now the DBDGEN is ready to be executed. The following summarizes what must go into the DBDGEN.

Data base names: PART, SHIPMENT, PO.

Data base layout: See Fig. 18.1.

Access methods: PARTS, HDAM/OSAM; other data bases, HIDAM VSAM.

Secondary indexes: U/M (part), DATE (shipment).

After the DBDGEN are executed, space needs to be allocated for the data bases. Either the standard allocation routines or VSAM's IDCAMS are used to define the data bases. An allocation of two cylinders should be adequate for the data bases and their indexes, since the tutorial is actually a very small amount of data. After space has been allocated and the DBDGEN is successfully executed, the data bases can be loaded, using the initial values found in Fig. 17.5. The initial load can be done using the IMS utility called DLT0 or a specially written application program. In any case, a special program specification block (PSB) must be generated. The special PSB is for loading, with a PROCOPT = L. At this point an image copy of the data base is taken and is named DBSNAP1.

TRANSACTION DEFINITION

Three online transactions must be defined, one for the activity of each data base. The designer begins by creating message format services (MFS) screens for each transaction. In building the MFS screens, the designer ensures that all functions that need to be fulfilled are, in fact, fulfilled, and at the same time makes the screens as user-friendly as possible. MFS is what the user sees when a transaction is called up and, as such, is the direct interface with the user.

After the screens are defined, the PSB for the online transactions are defined. The PSB are the views that a transaction has of the data. PSB are created for each transaction. As soon as the PSB are created, the application control block (ACB) can be genned. The ACB is nothing more than a pairing of the PSB and DBD for each online transaction. The next question facing the designer is whether the transactions will be written in COBOL or PL-1. For the purposes of the tutorial, either language can be used.

Next comes the actual design of the transactions. The designer uses the functional specifications for each data base as a guideline, as outlined in the sections on data insertion and manipulation in Chapter 17. The transaction must be able to insert and delete segments and to insert, delete, alter, and access fields within a segment. The specifications for the transaction are written before the transaction itself is written. The specifications are reviewed prior to coding to ensure that all functions that must be satisfied in fact are satisfied.

Finally, coding begins for the transaction based on the specifications. After the code is compiled, it is tested. The best vehicle for testing is batch terminal simulator (BTS), in which the program is executed in batch against the data base and the call patterns and the results of the calls are output as a result of the test. Once tested thoroughly, the program is put into the online system and is available for operation.

BMP

After the online transactions are written, the reports can be written. The functional specifications for the reports are found in Chapter 17. The designer should create report layouts that fulfill the requirements and display the information in a meaningful fashion.

BATCH PROCESSING

Both the archived and integrity auditing of the system are done in pure batch. The programs are written to meet the specifications found in Chapter 17. The archival data should be collected offline so that it is stored sequentially with data that has been previously stripped off.

IMPLEMENTATION AND INTEGRATION

Once the data bases have been loaded and defined, the transactions have been specified, coded, and tested, and the environment prepared, a full-scale integrated testing is ready to begin. If for any reason the tests prove to be less than valid, the data bases can be restored by means of the image copies that have been periodically taken.

Since the data bases have not been defined to the production system, if failure occurs it will produce a minimum of disruption to the data processing environment.

CHAPTER 19

Model 204 Tutorial

The purpose of the tutorial is to give the reader hands-on experience in the design, development, and implementation of a realistic data base system. To this end the tutorial guides the reader, step by step, through the different activities required in the development process. It is necessary to have access to manuals to determine specific formats and parameters. The tutorial leads the reader through the different activities in the proper order; it is up to the reader actually to execute the activities. Ultimately, the real learning process comes through doing activities and experiencing the successes and failures that ensue.

In this chapter it is necessary to have access to the Model 204 environment to execute the tutorial. There are many differences between IMS and Model 204 development and design. In IMS there are many steps to be accomplished before the system is usable, as is typical of a DBMS (data base management system) that manages operational data. In Model 204 it will be seen that many of the same activities will occur, except that in Model 204 the activities are accomplished very quickly.

The first activity of the designer is to design the data bases. Figure 17.3 is used for the basic data specifications. Whereas in IMS space has to be reserved for data whether the field would exist or not, in Model 204 space is allocated only when the field is present. Also, in IMS space is reserved for the maximum number of occurrences of data whether they occur or not, but in Model 204 space is used only for occurrences that actually exist. Another difference is in the way variable-length data is handled. In Model 204 fields that are variable in nature are allowed to vary, while in the chosen IMS design, variable-length fields are defined to be as long as the maximum value the field can attain. For these reasons Model 204 is able to compact the data it manages very tightly, while the equivalent data in IMS is loosely compacted (i.e., there is much dead space in the IMS data bases as designed). The specifications of Fig. 17.3 make the job of the designer in Model 204 easy. It is clear that at least three files need to be defined—one for parts, one for shipments, and one for po. What is not clear is whether the connecting field data (such as part/into, part/po, po/shipment, etc.) should be included in the primary fields or should be made into separate files. Either choice is a viable design option.

For the purpose of the tutorial, bill of materials relationships (part/into, part/from, and part/subs) are put into a separate file (called BOM, for bill of material). So four separate files will be defined to Model 204.

The next design step is to calculate table space for the four files. Because of the size of the tutorial, not much physical space will actually be needed, making the exercise of space calculation less important than it is in the case of a live data base design.

The next design consideration centers around the exact form that the data base will take. For example, are invisible keys to be used? Are FOR-EACH-VALUE attributes to be assigned? The physical options to be taken by the tutorial are

FOR-EACH-VALUE: type of PART

ENCODING: description of PART

NUMERIC RANGE: quantity of LINE NO of PO

KEYS: PARTNO (PART), U/M (PART), SHIPMENTNO (SHIPMENT), DATE (SHIPMENT), PONO (PO), DATERCVD (PO), ORDERMANAGER (PO), INTO (BOM), FROM (PO), SUBS (BOM), PART (BOM)

The next major consideration is the physical sequencing of the files. The BOM file will be in entry order sequence. The other files will be ordered by their primary keys, PARTNO, SHIPMENTNO, and PONO. Now the files are ready to be created. The creation job is executed creating the files and giving the initial allocation parameters that have been previously created.

After creation, the files are then initialized. Here sort fields are identified, along with other fields and field characteristics. Once initialized the file is ready for loading.

After the files are prepared for usage, activity can now be run against the files. Using values specified in Fig. 17.5, the data is loaded by a transaction in the form of

```
STORE RECORD
PONO=000165001
DATERCVD=830109
ORDERMANAGER=Max Hopper
STATUS=o
```

Then data from Figs. 17.6, 17.7, 17.8, 17.9, 17.10, and 17.11 is used to load data relationships into the appropriate files.

After data is loaded then individual insertion manipulations of data are done, as outlined in the sections on shipment insertions, part insertions, and po insertions in Chapter 17.

After the insertion manipulations come the change and deletion manipulations, as outlined in section III of the tutorial. Finally the reports and data integrity jobs are done, as specified in sections IV and V of the tutorial. The last step is the archival activity of section VI of the tutorial. The activities performed are all done in the Model 204 language freeform at the terminal. There is no programmed processing (unless, of course, it is desired). The user builds the activities as needed.

CHAPTER 20

SQL Tutorial

The purpose of this tutorial is to give the reader hands-on experience in the design, development, and implementation of a realistic data base system. To this end the tutorial guides the reader, step by step, through the different activities required in the development process. It is necessary to have access to manuals to determine specific formats and parameters. The tutorial leads the reader through the different activities in the proper order; it is up to the reader actually to execute the activities. Ultimately, the real learning process comes through doing activities and experiencing the successes and failures that ensue.

In this chapter it is necessary to have access to the SQL environment to execute the tutorial. The usage of SQL is contrasted to IMS in the ease of use and development. In general, SQL systems require less activities and effort than does IMS (as was the case with Model 204). The data requirements that are defined in Fig. 17.3 serve as the basis for data specifications in SQL. There will be three primary tables, one for parts, one for shipment, and one for po. In addition, separate tables are required for each relationship, part/subs, part/into, part/from, part/po, ship-ment/part, shipment/po, po/shipment, and po/lineno.

Another design consideration arises in the handling of the fields that can occur multiple times. There are at least two options. One option is to name the fields separately, such as U/MFIRST, U/MSECOND, U/MTHIRD, and so forth. This option allows all U/M to be placed in the primary data table (at the expense of "unnormalizing" the data).

The second option is to create separate tables for multiply-occurring fields. The second option is the one that will be taken. There will be a part/U/M table, a shipment/verify table, and a shipment/via table. Variable length fields will cause

```
CREATE TABLE PART
    (PARTNO            CHAR(19) NOT NULL,
     DESC         VARCHAR(25))

CREATE TABLE PARTUM
    (PARTUM            CHAR(19) NOT NULL,
     UM                CHAR(2)  NOT NULL)

CREATE TABLE PARTTYPE
    (PARTTYPE          CHAR(19) NOT NULL,
     TYPE              CHAR(1)  NOT NULL)

CREATE TABLE PARTSUBS
    (PARTSUBS          CHAR(19) NOT NULL,
     SUBS              CHAR(19) NOT NULL)

CREATE TABLE PARTINTO
    (PARTINTO          CHAR(19) NOT NULL,
     INTO              CHAR(19) NOT NULL,
     INTOQTY       BIN FIXED(31,0) NOT NULL)

CREATE TABLE PARTFROM
    (PARTFROM          CHAR(19) NOT NULL,
     FROM              CHAR(19) NOT NULL)

CREATE TABLE PARTPO
    (PARTPO            CHAR(19) NOT NULL,
     POPART            CHAR(15) NOT NULL)

CREATE TABLE SHIPMENT
    (SHIPNO            CHAR(25) NOT NULL,
     SHIPDATE          CHAR(6)  NOT NULL,
     TO:ADDR       VARCHAR(75),
     TO:ATTN       VARCHAR(25),
     PACKING       VARCHAR(15),
     ROUTING       VARCHAR(80))

CREATE TABLE SHIPVERIFY
    (SHIPNO            CHAR(25) NOT NULL,
     VERIFY            CHAR(3)  NOT NULL)

CREATE TABLE SHIPVIA
    (SHIPNO            CHAR(25) NOT NULL,
     VIA               CHAR(3)  NOT NULL)

CREATE TA3LE SHIPPART
    (SHIPNOPART        CHAR(25) NOT NULL,
     SHIPPART          CHAR(19) NOT NULL,
     SHIPPARTQTY   BIN FIXED(31,0) NOT NULL)

CREATE TABLE SHIPPO
    (SHIPPO            CHAR(25) NOT NULL,
     POSHIP            CHAR(15) NOT NULL)

CREATE TABLE PO
    (PONO              CHAR(15) NOT NULL,
     DATERECVD         CHAR(6),
     ORDERMGR      VARCHAR(25),
     STATUS            CHAR(1))

CREATE TABLE POSHIP
    (POSHIPNO          CHAR(15) NOT NULL,
     SHIPPO            CHAR(25) NOT NULL)

CREATE TABLE POLINENO
    (POLINENO      BIN FIXED(15,0) NOT NULL,
     LINEQTY       BIN FIXED(15,0) NOT NULL,
     DISCOUNT      BIN FIXED)15,2),
     LINEPART          CHAR(19) NOT NULL)
```

Figure 20.1

Data Base Tutorial   Section III

no problem. Indexed fields (on other than the primary index) likewise are easily handled. Fields that are optional are designed with the NULL attribute. In all there are three primary tables, eight relationship tables, and four multiple-data occurrence tables that will be built.

Once it is decided what the format of the data is to be, the next step is to prepare the SQL environment for the definition of the tables. The designer has the option of allocating space directly or letting SQL manage the space allocation. Since the tables in the tutorial are small, it is more convenient to let SQL do the allocation.

A storage group is defined first. The basic activities such as VSAM definition are automatically handled. After the space is allocated, the format of the data is actually defined to SQL, as shown in Fig. 20.1. After the data has been prepared, the data bases are ready to be loaded. The transactions that will do the loading are built using the standard insert format of SQL. There is not the distinction between loading and normal manipulation that there is in IMS.

If the tutorial has been done in IMS, it is instructive to load SQL data from IMS using the extract facilities. The copy of the data base—DBSNAP2—should be used for loading. If not, the data needs to be loaded by individual transaction.

All the data manipulation activities prescribed in section III of the tutorial should be executed. This serves to exercise each type of activity that would normally be done on a data base. Of special interest is the building of the report of the bill of materials explosion and implosion. The reader may wish to use SQL exits into other languages to keep track of the explosion and implosion relationships.

CHAPTER 21

FOCUS Tutorial

This tutorial is intended to give the reader experience in the use of FOCUS by designing and implementing the production control/shipping interface problem described earlier in the tutorial.

To implement the system, FOCUS on a mainframe computer or FOCUS/PC on a personal computer is required. FOCUS is a fourth-generation language and as such there is a sharp contrast to IMS in terms of in ease of use and implementation steps. FOCUS implementation complexity and ease of use is on the order discovered with SQL.

The data characteristics shown in Fig. 17.3 will be used to define three FOCUS files; the parts file, the shipment file and the po file. In addition, cross references can be used to define the relationships that exist between the data bases. The definition of the segments in the files is shown in Fig. 21.1. FOCUS files are quite similar to IMS data bases, as can be seen by comparing Fig. 21.1 with Fig. 18.1.

Using the file layouts, create the FOCUS file descriptions. Then allocate the disk space needed for the FOCUS files before loading them by using the FOCUS USE command.

As with SQL, transactions that are used to load a FOCUS file are defined to the system in the same way as transactions that manipulate the data. FOCUS requires seven attributes to be defined for each transaction. With the use of the MODIFY FILE CAR command, define the load transactions.

Perform all the data manipulations shown in section III of the tutorial. All activities can be performed directly from the terminal, but use of the transaction processing language simplifies some of the interactions.

File Name	Segment Name	Field Name	Usage
PARTS	PART	PARTNO	A19
		DESC	A25
		UM (10)	A20
		TYPE (20)	A20
	PARTSUBS	SUBS	A19
	PARTINTO	INTO	A19
		QTY	I9
	PARTFROM	FROM	A19
	PARTPO	PO	A15
SHIPMENT	SHIPMENT	SHIPNO	A25
		DATE	A6
		TOADDR	A75
		TOATTN	A25
		VERIFY (10)	A30
		PACKING	A15
		ROUTING	A80
		VIA (20)	A60
	SHIPPART	PART	A19
		QTY	I9
	SHIPPO	PO	A15
PURCHASE	PO	PONO	A15
		DATERCD	A6
		ORDERMGR	A25
		STATUS	A1
	POSHIP	SHIPMENT	A25
	POLINE	LINENO	I5
		QTY	I5
		DISCOUNT	I5
		PART	A19

Figure 21.1 FOCUS segment definition.

Since FOCUS is capable of accessing IMS data bases directly, it would be instructive to define the IMS data bases created in a previous part of this section, to FOCUS and access them directly.

Bibliography

A GENERAL DATA BASE BIBLIOGRAPHY

CERI, S., and G. PELAGATTI. *Distributed Databases—Principals and Systems.* New York: McGraw-Hill, 1984.

CICS/VS Version 1 Release 6 Intercommunication Facilities Guide, IBM Technical Manual, SC33-0133, 2nd ed. IBM Corporation (June 1983).

DATE, C. J. *An Introduction to Database Systems Volume II.* Reading, MA: Addison-Wesley, 1983.

DAVIES, C. T. "Data Processing Spheres of Control." *IBM Systems Journal* 17, No. 2 (1978).

DBC/1012 Data Base Computer Concepts And Facilities. Release 1.0, Inglewood, CA: Teradata Corp. 1983.

DRAFFAN, I. W., and POOLE, F. *Distributed Data Bases.* Cambridge: Cambridge University Press, 1980.

INMON, W. H. *Effective Data Base Decision.* Englewood Cliffs, NJ: Prentice-Hall, 1981.

———. *Information Systems Architecture: A System Developer's Primer,* Englewood Cliffs, NJ: Prentice-Hall, 1986.

JOHNSON, L. R. *System Structure in Data, Programs, and Computers.* Englewood Cliffs, NJ: Prentice-Hall, 1970.

KROENKE, D. M. *Database Processing: Fundamentals, Design, Implementation.* 2nd ed. Palo Alto, CA: Science Research Associates, 1983.

LAMPSON, B. W. et al. *Distributed Systems—Architecture and Implementation.* International Workshop, Munich, September 1983, Springer-Verlag, Berlin (1981).

LEILICH, H. O., and M. MISSIKOFF. *Database Machines.* International Workshop, Munich, September 1983, Springer-Verlag, Berlin (1983).

PAKER, Y., and J. P. VERJUS. *Distributed Computing Systems—Synchronization, Control and Communication*. New York: Academic Press, 1983.

ROTHNIE, J. B., JR., et al. *Introduction to a System for Distributed Databases (SDO-1), ACM Transactions on Database Systems,* vol. 5, no. 1 (March 1980).

YELAVICH, B. M. *An Overview of CICS/VS and IMS/VS ISC.* IBM Technical Bulletin, G320-5856, IBM Corporation (July 1980).

DATA BASE MACHINES

BRIDGES, TERRY. "Database Machines—What and Why." *Data Management* (November 1982).

EPSTEIN, ROBERT. "Why Database Machines." *Datamation* (July 1983).

RAUZINO, VINCENT. "The Present and Possible Future—Database Machines." *Computerworld, In Depth* (May 13, 1983).

ROSS, RON. "Database Machines: Still a Question Mark." *Computerworld, In-Depth* (July 7, 1983).

SMITH, RANDY. "Smart Memory, Part I." *BYTE* (April 1979).

———. "Smart Memory, Part II." *BYTE* (May 1979).

RELATIONAL SYSTEMS

BLASGEN, M. W. et al. "SYSTEM R: An Architectural Overview." *IBM Systems Journal* 20, no. 1 (1981).

DATE, C. J. *An Introduction to Database Systems,* Reading, MA: Addison-Wesley, 1975.

"Fishing for Trout." *Datamation* (June 1983).

IBM Database 2 Programming Announcement 5740-XYR.

INMON, W. H. "What Price Relational?" *Computerworld* (November 28, 1983).

"MIPS, MIPS, MIPS." *Datamation* (July 1983).

SANDBERG, G. "A Primer on Relational Database Concepts," *IBM Systems Journal* 20, no. 1 (1981).

MODEL 204

Command Reference Manual, CCA.

File Manager's Technical Reference Manual, CCA.

Model 204, Product Overview, CCA.

System Manager's Technical Reference Manual, CCA.

Terminal User's Guide, CCA.

User Language Manual, CCA.

IMS Database/Application Design Review, G320-6009.

IMS/VS Application Programming: Designing & Coding, IBM Manual SH20-9026.

IMS/VS Database Administration Guide, IBM Manual SH20-9025.

IMS/VS Fast Path Feature—Description and Design Guide, IBM Manual G320-5775.

IMS/VS Primer, IBM Manual SH20-9145.

IMS/VS System Administration Guide, IBM Manual SH20-9178.

IMS/VS Utilities Reference Manual, IBM Manual SH20-9029.

INMON, W. H., and FRIEDMAN, L. J. *Design Review Methodology for a Database Environment,* Englewood Cliffs, NJ: Prentice-Hall, 1981.

KAPP, D., and LEBEN, J. F. *IMS Programming Techniques: A Guide to Using DL1,* New York: Van Nostrand Reinhold, 1983.

Data Base Glossary

access pattern   The general sequence in which the data structure is accessed—i.e., from tuple to tuple, from segment to segment, etc.

active data dictionary   A repository of data that is used centrally, actively, and on a mandatory basis in the development, maintenance, and system generation phases of data base.

ADABAS   An inverted file DBMS by Software, AG.

address   The location at which an occurrence of data resides. On DASD, addresses are generally located by spindle, cylinder, track, and offset.

ADR   The software company that markets the DBMS, DATACOM/DB and Ideal.

application blocking of data   The grouping of different occurrences of the same type of data by the application programmer. The application programmer takes care of data placement, location, deletion, overflow, etc.

archival data bases   Repositories of data that have aged but that might have historical value or other analytical uses.

ATM (Automated Teller Machine)   A mechanical device employed by banks and financial institutions used in the handling of customer transactions.

attribute   Data element belonging to an entity; attributes are nonkeyed.

audit trail   Data that is available to trace activity; typically used for data base transactions or for terminal activity.

availability   The percentage of time the online system is up and running versus the amount of time the system ought to be up and running.

back-end processor   A data base machine.

batch environment   A sequentially dominated mode of processing; in batch, input is collected and batched for future processing throughout the day. Once collected, the batch input is transacted sequentially against one or more data bases.

batch window   The time when the online system is available for batch or sequential processing. The batch window occurs during nonpeak processing hours.

bill of materials   A listing of the materials used in a manufacturing process. The structure of how the materials are used in the manufacturing process is able to be derived from the bill of materials.

block   A basic unit of data structuring; the physical unit of transport and storage. A block contains one or more records. Sometimes called a page.

block splitting   A data management activity that allows a fully packed block to be split into two or more blocks, where each new block contains some free space.

Britton-Lee IDM 500   a back-end processor; a data base machine.

buffer   A work space, usually in memory, where blocks or other types of data are stored. Buffers have many other uses outside data management than for block storage. For example, in teleprocessing messages are stored in terminal buffers prior to transmission.

bus   The hardware connection that allows data to flow from one component to another, such as from the CPU to the line printer.

checkpoint   A time during program execution where processing has been committed. Processing may be restored up to the moment in time when a valid checkpoint has occurred. When a checkpoint occurs, many data base management resources are freed so that other activities may use those resources.

CICS/DL/I (Customer Information Control System/Data Language 1)   A common teleprocessing monitor (CICS) that is coupled with a popular data base manipulation language DL/I).

COBOL (COmmon Business-Oriented Language)   A popular procedural language used primarily for business processing. The language was founded by Grace Murray Hopper, among others.

collision   The event that occurs when two or more records of data have been randomized to the same location.

commonality of data   Similar or identical data that occurs in different systems. The recognition of commonality of data is one of the major issues of conceptual data design.

compaction   The compression of data into a smaller space than the data naturally occupies. For example the word *possesses* can be compacted into pos2ses.

compilation   The transformation of source code, usually procedural, into machine usable code. The transformation is done by means of a compiler. COBOL, FORTRAN, and PL-1 are all common compilers.

connector   A symbol used to indicate that one occurrence of data has a relationship with another occurrence of data. Connectors are used in conceptual data base design. Connectors can be implemented hierarchically, relationally, in an inverted fashion, or by a network.

content addressable memory   Main storage that is able to be addressed by the contents of the data in the memory, as opposed to conventional location addressable memory.

control data base   A data base containing data other than that that directly related to the function of the application; typical control data bases are terminal data bases, security data bases, audit data bases, tables data bases, etc.; although control data bases are necessary, it is mandatory that they be implemented properly.

CPU (Central Processing Unit)   The "engine" of the computer.

CPU-bound   A workload executing in a computer with much more logic and arithmetic activity than I/O activity. In such a case the total work done by the computer is limited by the speed of the CPU. DBMS are notorious for becoming I/O-bound, rather than CPU-bound. Scientific processing machines are typically CPU-bound.

CRT (Cathode Ray Tube)   A terminal, a video display unit, etc.

cylinder   A set of tracks on a spindle; a major measurement of space on a DASD unit.

DASD (Direct Access Storage Device)   A storage medium commonly called a *disk;* the normal medium for storage for data base, which may be hard or soft.

data abstraction   The process of defining larger classes of data for which two or more data elements belong; the process is commonly used in conceptual data base design. For example, parent and child can both be abstracted as human being.

data base   A collection of useful data.

data base administrator   The person or organizational unit responsible for many aspects of data base, such as data base design, recovery, or reorganization.

data characteristics   Aspects relating to data other than keys, elements, attributes, etc; typical characteristics include number of occurrences, volatility, relative frequency of occurrence, and physical size.

data dictionary   An inventory of data; the formal collection of information about information.

data base machine   A hardware device dedicated to performing data manipulation activities, freeing up other processors for other types of work.

data base restructuring   The act of changing the form of the data, as defined to the DBMS. For example, prior to restructuring there are three relational tables; after restructuring there are five relational tables.

data definition syntax   The language used to describe the structure of the data base to the DBMS.

data driven process   An activity whose resource consumption is dependent on the amount or configuration of the data on which the activity operates.

data element   The most basic unit of data definition. A data element represents a single unit of information. For example, sex, age, height, name are all data elements that relate to a person.

data integrity   The insurance of the timeliness and accuracy of the data in a data base; usually applies to the online system.

data layout   The structure of data as viewed by a programmer, usually defined by COBOL or PL-1 layouts of data.

data manipulation syntax   Language that is used to communicate to the DBMS for the actual changing of data; typical syntax operates on data insertion, deletion, access, and update. Syntax may be record at a time or set at a time.

data structure   The implied arrangement of data; the data structure may be physical or logical. There are many ways to implement data structure.

data view (dv)   One-half of a user view, the other half being a process view; a dv is how a user perceives the data used in doing his or her job.

DBM (Data Base Manager)   The part of the DBMS that is charged with the placement and location of data.

DBMS (Data Base Management System)   The software that provides data management facilities as well as program, user, and teleprocessing interfaces.

DBMS exits   Standard DBMS software entries for individual customization of the DBMS. Typically such exits will not impair a shop from going from one release of the software to another.

DB2 (Data Base 2)   A relational software product from IBM.

deadly embrace   The event that occurs when transaction A desires to get at data protected by transaction B when at the same time transaction B desires to get at data protected by transaction A. Processing comes to a halt until either A or B is given access to data.

decision support systems (dss systems)   Nonoperational systems that allow management to have access to information useful for the management of the business. Typical dss include forecasting, demographic analysis and trend analysis.

decompaction   The opposite of compaction; data is stored in a compacted form but must be decompacted upon use to make sense to the user.

decryption   The opposite of encryption; data is stored in an encrypted form and must be decrypted upon use to make sense to the user.

dependent segment   From the hierarchical data model, a segment whose existence depends upon another. The parent/child relationship is a form of dependency—the child depends upon the parent for existence.

development mode   The mode of operation in which systems are being developed.

dimension   A collection of user views (from conceptual design). A dimension is a major way of looking at data. Each scope of integration has at least one dimension; the primary business-based dimension.

dis (data item set)   From conceptual data base design, the midlevel of design. The dis is created from an entity. Whereas an entity is devoid of detail, the dis represents a fleshing out of detail, in preparation for the physical model of the data base.

disk   The medium of storage most common for data bases; DASD.

distributive data base   A data base controlled by more than a single processor; each processor has control over its portion of the data base, together all processors combine to control the entire data base.

download   The stripping off of data from one data base (usually an operational data base) for the usage in another environment (usually decision support).

dual data base approach   The philosophy involving physically separate dss and operational data bases, as opposed to the truth data base approach.

encryption   The transformation of data by means of an algorithm from one form to another so that the data is unrecognizable in its transformed representation; encryption is done for security reasons. Should an unauthorized person stumble on the transformed data, the data would be useless without the transformation algorithm.

entity   Something about which information needs to be stored; from conceptual data base design.

ERD (Entity Relationship Diagram)   The highest form of data modeling in conceptual data base design; comprised of entities and relationships.

Fast Path   An option commonly available with release 1.3 of IMS; used for moving many transactions and for managing large amounts of data.

FIFO/FILO   The designation of the order of storing and retrieving data. FIFO = First In/First Out; FILO = First In/Last Out.

file   A precursor to data base; a collection of related data sometimes called a *master file.*

flat file   A sequential file; a file whose records have no structure other than the appearance of one after the other.

FOCUS   A fourth-generation software package from Information Builders, Inc.

front-end processor   A teleprocessing concentrator and router, as opposed to a back-end processor, or a data base machine.

hashing   The activity of transforming a key into an address; a hasher is merely a piece of code that accepts a key value as input and produces an address in a data base as output.

hierarchical   The structuring of data into a series of parent/child relationships; each hierarchical structure begins with one occurrence of data at the lowest level (the *root*) and then continues with zero or more occurrences and types of data beneath the root. Each occurrence beneath the root may then have zero or more occurrences and types of data, and so forth.

hit   An occurrence of data that satisfies one or more search criteria.

host   The processor receiving and processing a transaction.

IDMS   An operational network DBMS offered by Cullinet.

IDMS/R   A relational DBMS offered by Cullinet.

IMS   Information Management System, an operational DBMS offered by IBM.

index   A collection of keys and addresses. Usually the index is organized sequentially according to the order of the keys; the index is used to locate the address of any given record.

integrity   For data or transactions, the insurance that once an activity is committed, it does not get erased.

interactive   A mode of processing combining some aspects of online processing and some aspects of batch processing; in interactive processing, the user can directly interact with data over which the user has exclusive control. In addition, the user can cause sequential activity to occur on the data.

interpretive   A mode of data manipulation in which the commands to the DBMS are translated as the user enters them, as opposed to the programmed mode of data manipulation.

inverted list   A data structure in which a flat file is indexed.

I/O (Input/Output)   The activity done by the computer for the transferring of data to or from the processor to DASD. An I/O involves a shift from electronic speeds of data transfer to mechanical speeds that are far slower.

is a type of   An analytical tool used in abstracting data in conceptual data base design. For example, a cocker spaniel and an English setter are types of dogs.

join   The relational operation where two tables are connected by means of commonly held data. For example, the bill of materials table and the shop floor table could be joined on part number.

junction   From the network environment, an occurrence of data that has two or more parent segments. For example, an order for supplies has to have a supplier parent and a part parent.

key   A data element used to identify data. Keys may be unique or nonunique: For example, social security number may be unique for a personnel data base and sex may be a nonunique key for the same personnel data base.

level of abstraction   The level of abstraction appropriate to a dimension. The appropriateness of the level of abstraction depends entirely on the user that is most appropriate to the dimension.

level of integrity   The physical unit of storage at which online integrity is kept. The level of integrity typically is at the data base level, the block level, or the record level.

line   The hardware by which data flows to or from the processor; typically lines go to terminals, printers, other processors, etc.

line polling   The activity of the teleprocessing monitor in which different lines are queried to see whether they have data that needs to be transmitted.

line time   The amount of time required for a transaction to go either from the terminal to the processor or from the processor to the terminal; typically line time is the single largest component of online response time.

living sample   A representative data base, typically used for analytical work in the face of a very large data base. Periodically, the very large data base is stripped of data so that the living sample represents a cross section of the large data base. Then statistical activity can be done against the living sample data base without disturbing the large data base.

lockup   The event that occurs when a data base is being used exclusively and other programs desire to access the data base but cannot.

logical deletion   Logical deletion occurs when a data base record is deleted from the data base but is physically left on the data base. Even though the record is physically present, it is not accessible by the user.

Log on/log off   The activity typically used to initiate an interactive session.

magnetic tape   The medium most closely associated with sequential processing; a large ribbon on which magnetic images are stored and retrieved.

mainframe   A large processor, usually serving the needs of many users.

master file   A concept from sequential processing where a given file holds the definitive data for a given system.

maximum transaction throughput   An important measurement that describes the maximum arrival rate of transactions that can be handled by a processor given

Data Base Glossary

a powerful machine that is well tuned and that is running a well-designed application.

MCAUTO (McDonnell Douglas AUTOmation)   A leading data processing and software company.

message   The data input by the user in the online environment that is used to drive a transaction or the data that is output to the user as a result of the execution of a transaction.

mips (million instructions per second)   The standard measurement for processor size and speed for mini- and mainframe computers.

microprocessor   A small processor serving the needs of a single user.

mode of operation   A related body of systems that execute in a similar fashion and have distinctive operational characteristics from other modes of operations; typical modes of operations are the operational, the dss, the archival, and the development.

MODEL 204   An inverted list DBMS by Computer Corporation of America.

modulo   An arithmetic term describing the remainder that is derived as part of the division process: 10 modulo 7 is 3. Modulo is usually associated with the randomization process.

monitor   Software that periodically checks status, such as a teleprocessing monitor, or a data base monitor that analyzes the makeup of a data base.

msdb (main storage data base)   A data base that exists entirely in main storage; a very fast access data base that is always a small data base.

msm (minimum structure model)   From conceptual data base design; a midlevel model of data.

MTO (Master Terminal Operator)   The computer operator in charge of the running of the online system.

MTTRc (Mean Time To Recovery)   The average amount of time required to bring an online data base back up after a crash has occurred.

MTTRo (Mean Time To Reorganize)   The average amount of time required to reorganize a data base.

network   The configuration of terminals, communications lines, and processors.

NOMAD   A fourth-generation language from Dun and Bradstreet.

nonprocedural   Syntax that directs the computer about *what* to do, not how to do it; typical nonprocedural languages include RAMIS, FOCUS, NOMAD, and SQL.

normalization   The act of producing a stable data structure. Data in third normal form relates to the whole key. Normalization is a part of conceptual data base design and normalization can be done top-down or bottom-up.

null values   Values indicating that a field has not been assigned with any values. For example, if age=0, then the indication is that an employee has not indicated his or her true age.

offset pointer   An indirect pointer. An offset pointer exists inside a block, the index points to the offset. If data must be moved, only the offset pointer in the block must be altered. The index remains untouched.

online   The mode where users access data directly and quickly; many users can access and change data without outside interference from other users. Response time is measured in seconds in the online environment.

operations   The organizational unit responsible for making the computer environment operable.

optic disc   A storage media dependent on lasers, as opposed to magneticism. Optical disk is normally write only, usually much cheaper than DASD, and is highly reliable.

overflow   The area of DASD where data is sent when collisions occur or records go when they need to be written and there is no space in primary DASD.

page fixed   In a virtual environment when programs or data are defined so that they cannot be removed from main storage, they are said to be page fixed. Only a limited amount of storage can be page fixed.

parallel I/O   In a nonmainframe environment, when more than one processor does I/O it is called parallel **I/O** (see **distributed data base**).

parsing   The algorithm that translates syntax into meaningful machine instructions; parsing determines the meaning of the statements issued in the data manipulation language.

passive data dictionary   A repository of data that optionally can be used in the definition, development, and maintenance process.

partitioning   The division of data along some lines (functional, random, organization, etc.); particularly applicable to the distributed data base environment.

peak period processing   The time of day when the most activity regularly hits the online system; for most online systems this is Monday through Friday, from 10:00 A.M. until 3:30 P.M.

peer level DBM   A data base manager that manages an equivalent amount or type of data.

performance   Online response time; the amount of time from the depressing of the entry key until the first of the reply returns. There is internal response time and external response time; internal response time measures the time from the beginning execution of the transaction until the transaction leaves the output buffer and external response time measures the response time visible to the user.

physical model   The conceptual model of the data from which a physical data base design can be done; this is sometimes called the detailed level of data base design.

physical pairing   An arrangement of hierarchical segments where relationship information is stored in both sides of a relationship (as opposed to a unidirectional relationship or a virtual pairing, where data relationships are stored entirely on one side of the model).

PL-1 (Programming Language 1)   An all-purpose programming language originally developed by IBM.

pools   The buffers made available to the online control region.

prefix space   The overhead space that every occurrence of data has that allows the systems to form a structure of the data.

primary business-based dimension   In conceptual data base design, the basic view of the data and processes that apply to the general business of the enterprise.

Every conceptual data model has at least one dimension, the primary business-based dimension.

procedural A type of language where the programmer tells the program *how* to proceed; typical procedural languages include COBOL, PL-1, and Fortran.

processor The hardware at the center of processing; processors are divided into three categories, mainframes, minicomputers, and microcomputers.

processor cycles The hardware internal cycles that do many functions that drive the computer, such as initiate I/O, perform logic, move data, and perform arithmetic functions.

program area The portion of main memory where applicatoin programs are executed.

protocol The call format used by teleprocessing.

protection bit in msdb, a bit that determines whether data is available for general public access.

punched cards 80-column punched cards were an early medium on which data and input were stored; they are fairly rare today.

QBE (Query By Example) A query language offered by IBM; originally founded by Dr. Moshem Zloof et al.

Quel The data management language offered by Ingres.

queue time The amount of time a transaction spends after being transmitted to the processor and before going into execution; queue time is dependent on many factors: the system load, the level of integrity, the priority of the transaction, etc. Queue time can become the largest factor in poor online response time.

RAMIS The fourth-generation language offered by Martin Marietta.

random access The ability to access data on its values rather than sequentially; in random access records 1, 2, 3, . . . , n do not have to be accessed to arrive at record $n + 1$.

randomizer A hashing algorithm.

records One of the basic units of data storage; equivalent to a tuple, segment, etc. One or more records are found in a block.

recovery The act of restoring a data base (usually online) to a prior point in time; recovery is used when a data base has experienced some difficulty that makes its further operation difficult or impossible.

recursion The definition of something in terms of itself. For example, a bill of materials is usually defined in terms of itself.

redundancy Multiple occurrence of the same thing. Redundancy may involve programs or, more commonly, data.

relational An organization of data where the user views the data in terms of tables.

relationship (1 : 1, 1 : n, m : n, or nonexistent) The status of occurrences of data where the existence of one occurrence of data implies something about the existence of another occurrence of data.

reorganization The activity of taking data stored in one location and removing it to another location, usually for the benefit of performance. Reorganization is done for three reasons, to rectify the internal cleanliness of data, to restructure the data, or to recover the data (in rare cases).

response time   see **performance**.

roll in/roll out   The rapid restoration of a main storage data base from DASD or the rapid transferral of a main storage data base from memory to DASD.

schema   A view of data (see **data view**).

scope of integration   The formal English language definition of what the boundaries of the system are and are not.

SCP (System Control Program)   The operating system; typical SCP are MVS, OS, and MS/DOS.

secondary indexes   Indexes to data based on other than the primary key. For example, suppose a personnel data base's primary index is on employee number; then secondary indexes may exist for sex, department and age. A secondary index is also called an *alternate index*.

segment   In a hierarchical environment, the basic unit of data transportation and storage.

semantics   The definition of data; its form and structure.

sequential processing   Programs and activities that access and manipulate data in a sequential fashion; dominated by magnetic tapes and DASD that is used in a sequential manner.

serial processing   Programs that must be run synchronously, i.e., one after the other; processing that depends on one part finishing before the other part begins.

session   The term for the work accomplished in one sitting in an interactive environment.

set at a time   The method of accessing data by entire groups of data at once; typical of nonprocedural languages.

sibling segments   From the hierarchical environment, different segment types that exist beneath the same parent segment.

single record access (record at a time)   The method of accessing data a record at a time, as typified by the procedural environment.

skip sequential   The mode of accessing data where data is accessed directly, followed by long periods of sequential accesses, and then followed by another set of direct and sequential accesses.

smart terminal   A terminal capable of performing basic edits on data without returning to the host.

snapshot   Data that has been "frozen" as of some moment in time; snapshots are associated with downloads and transferring data from the operational to dss environment.

sparse index   An index that contains only selected entries to the primary data base. For example, a personnel index may contain index entries only to employees who have been promoted a full grade in the last year.

spindle   The common term for a disk; disks rotate on a spindle.

SQL   A fourth-generation language offered by the IBM Corporation.

storage   The place where data is held for processing; typically on tape, DASD, main storage, cards, etc.

structural integrity Insurance that the simple data base structures will be protected by the DBMS.

subject data base A collection of like data relevant to the enterprise.

super index A higher order index; an index of an index.

SWU (Standard Work Unit) A measurement of the processing that any given on-line transaction can do; one of the foundations of consistent online performance.

symbolic addressing The reference to another location by means of a key or concatenated key; a symbolic address must be translated into a direct address by means of an index or randomizer before the linkage between pointer and pointee can be made.

syntax Language.

system log An audit trail of relevant system happenings, such as transaction entries, data base changes, etc.

system of record The final authority as to the accuracy of data; by definition, the system of record is correct. There can be only one system of record.

tables The basic unit of storage of data in the relational environment.

teleprocessing The transmittal of data to and from the processor to the terminal.

TERADATA DBC/1012 A back-end processor; a database machine.

terminal CRT.

throughput The amount of data and programs a processor is capable of handling in a given period of time; a term associated with the batch environment.

time sharing The IBM term for interactive processing; sometimes called TSO (Time Sharing Option).

TIS A fourth-generation language offered by Cincom systems.

TPM (Teleprocessing Manager) Similar to the DBM.

track One of the basic units of data location on DASD.

transaction A unit of work accomplished online.

truth data base approach The approach to data base that declares that a single data base will serve all purposes; operational and dss data bases are merged into a single data base.

tuning The act of optimizing the buffer pools and the basic configuration of an online system for online processing response time.

tuple One of the basic units of data in the relational model; equivalent to a record.

unload/reload The reorganization utility so named for its basic acts of unloading and reloading data.

user The ultimate operator of the system; the person(s) for whom the system is built.

user view Made up of data views and process views (see **data views**).

variable fields Fields that may or may not occur in a given record.

variable-length fields Fields that may vary in length when they occur.

VDU (Video Display Unit) A terminal.

VM/CMS (Virtual Memory/Conversational Monitoring System) An IBM interactive operating system.

VSAM (Virtual Sequential Access Method) A basic IBM access method.

BMP (Batch Message Processor)   An online region where sequential processing is done.

data base record   a root and all its physical dependents.

DBDGEN (Data Base Definition GENeration)   The definition of the data base to IMS.

DEDB (Data Entry Data Base)   The primary Fast Path access method.

DLET   The command to delete a segment.

free space element   The pointer in a block indicating how much free space there is and where the next free space is.

GHN (Get Hold Next)   A call reserving the next segment encountered for update processing.

GHNP   Similar to GHN, except that the rules of parentage are followed.

GN   A call requiring IMS to retrieve the next segment.

GU   A call to IMS requiring IMS to retrieve a specific segment.

HDAM   (Hierarchical Direct Access Method).

HIDAM   (Hierarchical Indexed Direct Access Method).

HISAM   (Hierarchical Indexed Sequential Access Method).

image copy   The snapshot of the data base taken so that the data base is recoverable to some point in time.

IMS gen   The description of the IMS system to the SCP.

ISRT   The command to insert a segment.

MPP (Message Processing Program; also called the MPR, or Message Processing Region)   The transaction processing portion of IMS as opposed to BMP.

OSAM (Overflow Sequential Access Method)   A standard access method.

PCB (Program Control Block)   The definition to the program of the data that can be accessed.

physical twin   An occurrence of more than one segment beneath the same parent.

pointers   Addresses; may be direct or symbolic.

PSB (Program Specification Block)   A collection of PCB.

prefix   The area where IMS stores pointers, logical deletes, etc.

REPL   The command to replace data after it has been altered.

SSA (Segment Search Argument)   Data to direct IMS to the proper segment.

sync point   The moment in time when an IMS update has been committed; prior to a sync point the activity of a transaction can be backed out.

UOW (Unit of Work)   One of the basic measurements of data in Fast Path DEDB data bases.

WFI (Wait For Input mode)   Occurs when transaction load modules have been preloaded into the processing region.

MODEL 204 TERMS

few valued, many valued   Attributes describing the values an data can assume.

file control table   The table describing whether a file is open or not.

invisible keys   Keys that exist only in the index, not in the primary data area.

Log in/log out   Commands to initiate or terminate a Model 204 session.

Open   Command to open a file.

Table A   The data dictionary table.

Table B   The primary data table.

Table C   The primary index table.

Table D   The secondary index table.

Index

I/O (*continued*)
83, 84, 87, 89, 90, 91, 92,
96, 97, 100, 109, 127, 129,
130, 139, 144, 148, 150,
187, 188, 190, 191, 192,
200, 201, 204, 205, 207,
220, 221, 224, 226, 227,
231, 232, 234, 238, 250,
251, 253, 272, 276, 287,
291, 320, 325, 328, 330,
336, 341
IOAREA, 280
I/O bound, 97
IOPCB area, 277
Irlm, 222
"Iron", 23
ISA (Information Systems
Architecture), 183, 211
ISAM, 324

Join, 19, 82, 87, 89
Journaling, 307
Junction, 77, 153

Key, 27, 28, 34, 43, 45, 46,
50, 58, 60, 64, 66, 67, 69,
75, 82, 83, 84, 85, 90, 125,
127, 137, 140, 143, 175,
180, 181, 183, 184, 204,
256, 264, 265, 272, 274,
288, 289, 291, 293, 294, 342

LAN (Local Area Network),
120
Language translator, 126
Leaf page, 310
Level of abstraction, 167, 172
Level of conceptual modeling,
168
Level of integrity, 153
Line (communication), 23, 40,
107
Line polling, 227
Line time, 97, 104
Line traffic, 137
Living sample, 158
Load module, 190
Load to/load from, 340, 341
Local perspective, 164
Location, 86
Location addressible memory,
85
Lockup, 115
Log, 107, 111, 138, 145, 240

Logical deletion, 27
Logical relationship, 191, 192,
271, 274
Logical view of data, 56, 57
Log record, 286

Machine, 97, 104, 125, 270
Magnetic tape, 2, 6, 138, 164,
180
Mainframe, 6, 7, 8, 10, 13,
17, 118, 138, 155, 156, 219,
234, 235, 237, 214, 245
Mainframe-micro link, 156
Main memory, 4, 5, 6, 23,
24, 25, 26, 28, 66, 82, 85,
97, 111, 117, 127, 148, 227,
238, 272, 276, 277, 286,
298, 307, 340, 341
Market projection, 211
Master file, 2, 3, 14, 97
MCAUTO, 189
Menu, 114, 157
Message, 107, 127
Message queue, 107, 109
Microprocessor, 6, 8, 17, 23,
40, 106, 117, 118, 119, 120,
131, 155, 156, 219, 235, 237
Microprogramming, 226, 233
Millisecond, 100
Minicomputer, 23, 219, 235,
237, 241
MIPS (million instructions
per second), 234
MODEL204, 20, 125, 131,
287, 288, 289, 290, 294,
295, 297, 298, 302, 305, 307
Mode of operation, 36, 38,
39, 41, 284
Modulo, 48, 50
Monitoring, 136, 145, 160
MPP, 284, 286
MSDB (main storage data
base), 270, 271
Msm (minimum structure
model), 175
MTAR (maximum transaction
arrival rate), 156
MTO (master terminal opera-
tor), 144, 148, 149, 150,
152, 160, 286
MTTRc, 208
MTTRo, 208
Multiple user concurrency,
221

Naming convention, 209
Nanosecond, 100
Navigation, 235
Network, 10, 13, 42, 56, 57,
77, 78, 87, 91, 94, 111, 121,
122, 153, 227, 228, 230,
235, 243, 244, 246, 249,
251, 253, 255, 256, 325, 339
Network access, 220
Network junction record, 143
Network management func-
tions, 226
NOMAD2, 19, 38
Nonclustered, 310
Nonprocedural language, 97,
114, 124, 125, 129, 328
Nonvariable field, 141
Normalization, 180, 182
Normalized structure, 181
Null values, 309
Numeric, 342
Numeric range, 294

Offset, 48, 49, 53, 59, 60, 82,
140
Offset pointer, 289
Online, 6, 10, 12, 13, 15, 16,
17, 38, 57, 96, 97, 102, 104,
106, 108, 109, 111, 112,
114, 115, 116, 117, 118,
123, 131, 137, 138, 140,
143, 144, 145, 149, 150,
152, 155, 156, 157, 158,
159, 160, 186, 188, 189,
190, 192, 195, 197, 199,
208, 209, 221, 235, 284,
286, 287, 307, 342
Online application program,
220
Online architecture, 109
Online controller, 102, 104,
284
Online transaction, 116
Operating system, 153, 220,
221
Operational, 9, 12, 16, 18, 19,
20, 36, 37, 38, 39, 40, 41,
125, 152, 154, 155, 156,
157, 186, 209, 211
Optical disk storage, 8, 9
ORACLE, 124
OSAM, 274
Output buffer, 107, 108, 112
Output message, 108

Overflow, 53, 55, 82, 126, 137, 140, 141, 143, 204, 205, 271, 272
Overflow blocks, 125
Overflow chain, 126
Overhead, 49, 59, 92, 186, 201, 204, 205, 208
Oversegmentation, 204

Package (software), 155, 159
Page, 288, 309, 320, 322
Page fix, 160
Page/offset, 312
Parallel processors, 233, 250
Parallel search, 241
Parent, 44, 77, 92, 151, 264, 267, 268, 278, 279
Parse, 126, 129, 240, 255
Partial reorganization, 140
Partitioned, 245, 248, 251, 254, 255, 256, 310
Password, 111
Path length, 270
Pattern of growth, 51
PCB, 274, 276, 277
Peak processing period, 97
Performance, 13, 18, 19, 38, 39, 70, 120, 141, 145, 153, 156, 159, 160, 187, 188, 195, 197, 198, 218, 228, 229, 230, 233, 234, 236, 238, 240, 249, 250, 253, 257, 258, 336
Performance (secondary indices), 68
Personal computer, 213, 255
Photo optical storage, 185
Physical address, 58, 224, 241
Physical attribute, 131
Physical block, 54, 55, 56, 70, 82, 140
Physical characteristics, 178
Physical child, 268
Physical child pointer, 270
Physical form of data, 57
Physical juxtaposition, 91, 92
Physically bound data, 190, 191
Physically separate data, 190
Physical model, 168, 176, 183, 184, 199, 213
Physical occurrence, 91
Physical pairing, 74
Physical separation of data, 208

Physical storage level, 4
Physical view of data, 56
Pipeline, 238
PL-I, 14, 161, 267, 279, 329, 335
Pointer, 62, 63, 69, 77, 82, 84, 86, 92, 140, 204, 267, 268, 270, 272, 312
Pointer chain, 127
Prefix, 50, 5l, 59, 201, 267, 309
Prepare-abort, 258
Prepare-commit, 258
Presumed abort, 258, 259
Primary business based dimension, 170, 171, 172
Primary copy, 259, 260
Primary data base, 130
Primary index, 67, 75
Primary key, 34, 68
Prioritization, 107, 160
Private data base, 249
Procedural language, 124
Procedural syntax, 125
Process design, 164
Processing workload, 197
Processor, 23, 40, 85, 104
Processor cycles, 225
Production, 17
Program execution, 100, 131
Program specifications, 199
Programmer, 72, 91, 101, 124, 127, 165
Programmer productivity, 15
Programmer work area, 29, 30, 32, 102, 107, 112, 113, 115, 118, 143, 150
Projections, 36
Protection bit, 150
Protocol, 152, 221, 241, 339
Protocol conversion, 226
PSB, 275
Public data base, 249
Punched cards, 2, 4, 5, 13

QBE, 19
QSAM, 324
Quality of definition, 174, 175
QUEL, 236
Query, 17, 19, 192, 201, 204
Query language, 161

Queuing, 38, 97
Queue time, 104

R*, 333, 337, 338, 339
RAMIS, 38
Random access, 90
Randomize, 45, 46, 48, 53, 56, 69, 82, 83, 84, 90, 91, 94, 97, 102, 127, 137, 139, 187, 200, 204, 270, 271, 272, 274, 342
Read/write head, 7
Record, 24, 26, 27, 29, 30, 32, 33, 34, 40, 42, 45, 48, 49, 50, 51, 53, 54, 58, 59, 60, 63, 66, 67, 68, 82, 83, 87, 90, 92, 93, 94, 100, 102, 104, 116, 125, 126, 129, 138, 140, 141, 143, 144, 152, 153, 155, 157, 165, 190, 221, 222, 223, 271, 289, 298, 305, 306, 309
Record-at-a-time, 19, 124, 224, 229
Record distribution, 54
Record length, 50
Record lock, 233
Record prefix space, 59
Record size, 70
Record wait time, 230, 232
Recovery, 57, 136, 137, 138, 139, 141, 144, 145, 150, 156, 159, 187, 213, 221, 223, 224, 227, 240, 307, 322, 339, 340, 341
Recursive, 154, 173, 175
Redundancy, 15, 34, 37, 38, 39, 41, 165, 197, 198
Regions, 160
Relational, 17, 19, 20, 42, 78, 87, 94, 179, 186, 190, 191, 229, 235, 251, 253, 254, 308, 315, 319, 324, 326
Relationship, 92
Reliability, 13, 37, 188, 221, 225
Reordering of data, 63
Reorganization, 136, 138, 139, 140, 143, 144, 145, 153, 159, 213, 221, 240, 297, 322
Replicated data, 245, 249, 253
Reports, 14, 105, 106, 165
Report writer, 324, 329